Knut Tveitereid—the author

Born in Norway in 1973, Knut is a theology graduate and author, who has also written the Norwegian best-seller 'i'. He is currently the youth worker at Storsalen, a large church in Oslo, Norway.

www.storsalen.no

Alie Stibbe—the translator

Born in England in 1960, Alie is a freelance writer and translator, and contributes to BRF's Bible reading notes for women, *Day by Day with God*. Alie is married to Mark Stibbe, vicar of St Andrew's Chorleywood. They have four children, three of whom are teenagers.

www.st-andrews.org.uk

word bytes

The Completely Manageable Bible
in 365 readings

KNUT TVEITEREID

Translated and adapted by Alie Stibbe

Published by
The Bible Reading Fellowship
First Floor, Elsfield Hall
15–17 Elsfield Way, Oxford OX2 8FG
ISBN 1 84101 337 4

Original edition published in Norwegian under the title *En helt overkommelig Bibel*
by The Norwegian Bible Society, Oslo, Norway © Det Norske Bibelselskap 2001

UK edition first published 2003
10 9 8 7 6 5 4 3 2 1 0

Acknowledgments
Unless otherwise stated, scripture quotations are taken from the *Contemporary English Version* © American Bible Society 1991, 1992, 1995. Used by permission/Anglicizations © British & Foreign Bible Society 1997.

Scripture quotations taken from the *Holy Bible, New International Version*, copyright © 1973, 1978, 1984 by International Bible Society. Used by permission of Hodder & Stoughton Limited. All rights reserved. 'NIV' is a registered trademark of International Bible Society. UK trademark number 1448790.

Time-line of the Bible is copyright © British & Foreign Bible Society.

A Mini Dictionary for the Bible is taken from the Contemporary English Version © 1995 – American Bible Society. Used by permission.

Maps on pages 412, 413 and 415 are copyright © British & Foreign Bible Society. Maps on pages 410, 411 and 414 are copyright © BRF.

'Now to live the life' by Matt Redman, © 1997 Thankyou Music. Adm. by worshiptogether.com songs, excl. UK and Europe, adm. by Kingsway Music. tym@kingsway.co.uk. Used by permission.

A catalogue record for this book is available from the British Library

Printed and bound in Finland

Contents

A word from the author

Word Bytes: The Completely Manageable Bible—
the whole Bible in minute-long bites!

In one sense, the Bible is a completely manageable book. The Bible's main point, the clue to its meaning, is so easy to understand that anyone at all can grasp it. It's all about Jesus. It's all about you. It's all about living the life and walking the talk—yes, about experiencing fullness of life here and now as we prepare for eternity.

In another way, the Bible is a rather unmanageable book. It talks about immense, difficult things, said in ways which, at best, were normal several thousand years ago in cultures very different from our own.

The size of the Bible alone can be off-putting. We're not talking about one book—we are talking about 66. We're talking about amazing stories and beautiful poems, sure—but we're also talking about long lists of laws and details of who was related to whom. All said and done, the Bible consists of 1,500 pages of hard-packed info.

Word Bytes was written so that it'd be easier for you to cope with reading the Bible. So that you'd get away without a forty-year hike through the wilderness in Leviticus and wouldn't get lost in lists of relatives and incomprehensible words of judgment spoken over Edom. So that you'd get over the difficult bits. I hope you'll find that *Word Bytes* helps you discover God's amazing word!

A day consists of 1,440 minutes. In one minute you can't access the whole world, but with *Word Bytes* you can access more than you think. Among other things, you can access...

... all the best bits in the Bible.
... all the greatest personalities.
... all the most intense stories.

Yes, you actually access most of the books in the whole Bible!

You can even manage to read the short commentary—in all of a minute. You don't believe it? Then try me!

Knut

PS: Siri, Ellen and Geir—many thanks for your editing input. Very many thanks to the Norwegian Bible Society—and especially to Hans-Olav, for kick-starting the idea. Also to Ståle—the PC whizz kid. Very many thanks to Merete, Kristian, Christoffer and Kirsti—and all the others—who have given me masses of brilliant feedback. I am learning something new every week!

Let God have all the glory!

A word from the translator

This book was originally written in Norwegian for Christian young people in Norway. BRF in England was so impressed with the response to the book there that they asked me to translate it into English, so that you can benefit from Knut's wisdom and sense of humour.

It's been an amazing privilege and an incredible journey preparing this book for you. My intention has been that this book should be fun for you to read and relevant to your experience. Although our Norwegian cousins only live a hop across the North Sea, there are many things they experience that are not usual in England. Where I've come across such things, I've adapted Knut's text to suit English culture. Where I have made changes, I have tried to copy Knut's style and keep to the thought he originally had in mind.

We have used text from the *Contemporary English Version* of the Bible. The full CEV is published by HarperCollins Publishers and Bible Society. For more information, visit Bible Society's website at www.biblesociety.org.uk.

The Norwegian Bible that Knut used was more traditional than the CEV. Sometimes this has made it difficult for me to translate what Knut has written without some extra explanation. I do hope I've made things clear enough for you. When all is said and done, the main thing is that you learn more about Jesus and keep following him!

Alie Stibbe

Comments that follow each daily reading

Good news
A message from God that will make everyday life easier.

Head, shoulders, knees and toes
Something which means a bit of physical activity, for example, kneeling.

Check it out
Reference to what other Bible passages say about the same theme.

Weird and wonderful
There are actually loads of extraordinary things in the Bible.

Download
A verse that's so good it's worth taking a few seconds to memorize.

Di:SaipL
How to live as a disciple of Jesus every day.

Listen to your heart and fill in
Grab a pencil and say what you think.

Hmm... just a thought
A quick, meditative thought or quote.

Big word
The explanation of a difficult word or phrase.

Refresh
A word of encouragement or warning from the Bible.

Did you know that...
Draws out some facts that make the text easier to understand.

Bible personality
An important person in the Bible.

#öfi#%/$&!!?!
Inexplicable things which there isn't any sense in trying to explain.

Story
A quick story or illustration that explains the Bible passage.

Answers to questions you might have about this book

How do I use *Word Bytes*?

There are at least three ways to read this book.

1. Follow the dates on the top of each page.
2. Surf through the links at the bottom of each page.
3. Just flip through it at random.

You are completely free to use the book as you like, but I recommend the first option—follow the dates—because each page of *Word Bytes* builds on what has been said before.

How is *Word Bytes* organized?

We have tried to make the organization as logical as possible and have followed the story of the Bible from the creation (1 January) to Jesus' return (31 December). The whole story is divided into convenient sections according to when the events actually happened—for example, 'Exiled in Babylon', 'The life of Jesus', 'The Church kicks off'.

Between these sections are some Bible passages arranged in themes—for example, 'The Ten Commandments', 'Easter', and 'Parables Jesus told'. These have been inserted into the overall story of the Bible in the place where they make the most logical sense. It would be good if you took a minute or two to study the 'Contents' page at the front of the book so that you get an idea of what topics are covered.

What do I do if I haven't read *Word Bytes* for a few days?

Whatever you do, don't panic! You are bound to miss a few days now and then. Jump ahead to the right date and read from there. And don't ever, ever get a bad conscience about missing a few days—rather, be happy when you do read!

If, at some stage, you feel you want to catch up on what you have missed, it takes only seven minutes to catch up on a whole week and half an hour to catch up on a whole month.

What do I read first in *Word Bytes*—the Bible passage or the commentary?

You read the Bible first! Let's be clear that the Bible is the important thing here, not the commentary. God's word is about 459 million times more important than Knut's words. A general rule of thumb might be:

1. Read the Bible passage.
2. Read the Bible passage.
3. Read the Bible passage.
4. Read the Bible passage.
5. Read the Bible passage.
6. Read the Bible passage.
7. Think for yourself.
8. Read the commentary.
9. Read the Bible passage.

What is '5 minutes more?' doing at the bottom of the page in *Word Bytes*?

'5 minutes more?' isn't meant to give you the feeling that you'll never get to the end of the page. But you might suddenly want to read more than you can in only one minute. '5 minutes more?' contains, in our opinion, the 365 most important chapters in the Bible. These are arranged in order from Genesis to Revelation.

What do I do if I want to find a particular verse in *Word Bytes*?

Turn to the back of the book, where you will find a list all the Bible verses that have been used and the date of the page where you will find each of them.

What do I do if there is something that I don't understand in *Word Bytes*?

If it is a word, you can look it up in the 'mini dictionary' at the back of the book. This contains explanations of important words and expressions. You may have a similar list at the back of your Bible. We have taken the Bible passages and the mini dictionary in this book from the Contemporary English Version.

If there are things you still don't understand, don't give up. Ask someone you know who is a more experienced Christian—your youth leader, perhaps. It's a good idea to think about things and ask questions.

How much of the Bible is found in *Word Bytes*?

There are about 600 Bible passages or verses in *Word Bytes*, beginning with the first verse of Genesis and ending with the last verse of Revelation. The quotes come from 65 of the 66 books in the Bible. Which book has been left out? I will leave that up to you to find out...

1 January

In the beginning

Day 1: I command light to shine!

In the beginning God created the heavens and the earth. The earth was barren, with no form of life; it was under a roaring ocean covered with darkness. But the Spirit of God was moving over the water. God said, 'I command light to shine!' And light started shining. God looked at the light and saw that it was good. He separated light from darkness and named the light 'Day' and the darkness 'Night'. Evening came and then morning—that was the first day.
GENESIS 1:1–5

In the beginning was the one who is called the Word. The Word was with God and was truly God. From the very beginning the Word was with God. And with this Word, God created all things. Nothing was made without the Word. Everything that was created received its life from him, and his life gave light to everyone. The light keeps shining in the dark, and darkness has never put it out.
JOHN 1:1–5

Never again will night appear, and no one who lives there will ever need a lamp or the sun. The Lord God will be their light.
REVELATION 22:5a

Weird and wonderful

When the sun was created, it had already been light for four days!

If you flip forward a few pages to 4 January, you can read how God creates the moon and the sun. But today, four days earlier, God creates light! Hmm. So when the sun was created, it had already been light for four days. Hmm.

If you have time, you ought to get out your Bible and turn to the last-but-one chapter, which talks about heaven. Read all the way through to Revelation 22:5. In heaven the sun and the moon won't shine any longer, only God. It says that 'No one who lives there will ever need a lamp or the sun. The Lord God will be their light.'

Nothing can live without light from the sun—say your science lessons.
Nothing can live without light from God—says the Bible.

Have a brilliant day—in the light of God.

Links: 18 February, 7 March, 23 November, 25 December

5 minutes more? Genesis 1

2 January

In the beginning

Day 2: Sea and sky

God said, 'I command a dome to separate the water above it from the water below it.' And that's what happened. God made the dome and called it 'Sky'. Evening came and then morning—that was the second day.

GENESIS 1:6–8

The heavens keep telling the wonders of God, and the skies declare what he has done.

PSALM 19:1

With your wisdom and power you created the earth and spread out the heavens. The waters in the heavens roar at your command. You make clouds appear—you send the winds from your storehouse and make lightning flash in the rain.

JEREMIAH 10:12–13

Refresh

Can you prove that God created the world?

People often ask me, 'Do you really believe God created the world?' They think it sounds strange. And if I am honest, the same sort of thoughts creep into my head now and then.

When I'm bothered by such thoughts, I normally say to myself: 'Knut, don't you think it's strange that God created the world?'

'Yes, I do,' I reply to myself.

'But wouldn't it have been even stranger if God hadn't created the world?'

'Yes, I guess it would,' I reply.

'If, for example, it had all started with a random cosmic explosion?'

'Yes, it would be stranger if it had all started with an random cosmic explosion.'

That tends to help.

Links: 4 January, 6 January, 7 March, 25 December

5 minutes more? Genesis 2

3 January

In the beginning

Day 3: Sprouting and growing

God said, 'I command the water under the sky to come together in one place, so there will be dry ground.' And that's what happened. God named the dry ground 'Land', and he named the water 'Sea'. God looked at what he had done and saw that it was good. God said, 'I command the earth to produce all kinds of plants, including fruit trees and grain.' And that's what happened. The earth produced all kinds of vegetation. God looked at what he had done, and it was good. Evening came and then morning—that was the third day.

GENESIS 1:9–13

But when you turn away, they are terrified; when you end their life, they die and rot. You created all of them by your Spirit, and you give new life to the earth.

PSALM 104:29–30

Good news

I will thank God for life

God hasn't finished his creative work. No, right now he's thinking about the crocuses that will sprout in a month or so. He thinks about the grass, the farmers, the football fields. He thinks about all the new children that will be born. He thinks about you.

He knows that if he withdraws his Spirit everything will collapse. But he won't do that. He sends his Spirit and life is created. He wakes you up in the morning and in the evening he lets you get some sleep.

The Lord is our shepherd; we will never be in need. He lets us rest in fields of green grass. He leads us to streams of peaceful water, and refreshes our lives (Psalm 23:1–3).

I will thank God! I will thank God for life!

Links: 1 January, 5 January, 6 January, 7 March

5 minutes more? Genesis 3

4 January

In the beginning

Day 4: Moon and sun, clouds and wind

God said, 'I command lights to appear in the sky and to separate day from night and to show the time for seasons, special days, and years. I command them to shine on the earth.' And that's what happened. God made two powerful lights, the brighter one to rule the day and the other to rule the night. He also made the stars. Then God put these lights in the sky to shine on the earth, to rule day and night, and to separate light from darkness. God looked at what he had done, and it was good. Evening came and then morning—that was the fourth day.
GENESIS 1:14–19

About heaven:
And the city did not need the sun or the moon. The glory of God was shining on it, and the Lamb was its light. Nations will walk by the light of that city, and kings will bring their riches there. Its gates are always open during the day, and night never comes.
REVELATION 21:23–25

Weird and wonderful

The theory of relativity

Here's something for all those who like physics!

Time magazine voted Albert Einstein the most important man in the last century because he developed the theory of relativity. This theory says something to the effect that a metre isn't always a metre!

A metre rule at rest is 1 metre long, but if it begins to move, it becomes longer than a metre (just a tiny bit). But the faster it goes, the longer it gets. The faster, the longer. Faster, longer. Faster, longer.

Einstein's point is that a metre rule that travels at the speed of light is—wait for it—infinitely long. That's right—infinite, eternal. That is relativity theory in a nutshell.

And a clock, says Einstein, runs later and later, the greater the speed it travels at. If the clock reaches the speed of light, it stops ticking altogether—time stands still. Then you have eternity.

Links: 1 January, 3 January, 28 August, 27 December

5 minutes more? Genesis 4

5 January

In the beginning

Day 5: The animals

So God made the giant sea monsters and all the living creatures that swim in the sea. He also made every kind of bird. God looked at what he had done, and it was good. Then he gave the living creatures his blessing—he told the sea creatures to live everywhere in the sea and the birds to live everywhere on earth. Evening came and then morning—that was the fifth day.

GENESIS 1:21–23

Look at the crows! They don't plant or harvest, and they don't have storehouses or barns. But God takes care of them. You are much more important than any birds… Look how the wild flowers grow! They don't work hard to make their clothes. But I tell you that Solomon with all his wealth wasn't as well clothed as one of these flowers… But put God's work first, and these things will be yours as well.

LUKE 12:24, 27, 31

Check it out

The Bible is interested in animals

Jesus gives us a message to take a look at animals—so that we can understand how much God loves us.

Crows, for example:

'Look at the crows! They don't plant or harvest, and they don't have storehouses or barns. But God takes care of them. You are much more important than any birds' (Luke 12:24).

And, for example, sheep:

'Jesus answered, "If you had a sheep that fell into a ditch on the Sabbath, wouldn't you lift it out? People are worth much more than sheep, and so it is right to do good on the Sabbath"' (Matthew 12:11).

And a final example—sparrows:

'Aren't two sparrows sold for only a penny? But your Father knows when any one of them falls to the ground. Even the hairs on your head are counted. So don't be afraid! You are worth much more than many sparrows' (Matthew 10:29).

Links: 6 January, 14 September, 15 September, 16 September

5 minutes more? Genesis 6

6 January

In the beginning

Day 6: Humans

God said, 'Now we will make humans, and they will be like us. We will let them rule the fish, the birds, and all other living creatures.' So God created humans to be like himself; he made men and women. God gave them this blessing and said:

Have a lot of children! Fill the earth with people and bring it under your control. Rule over the fish in the sea, the birds in the sky, and every animal on the earth. I have provided all kinds of fruit and grain for you to eat. And I have given the green plants as food for everything else that breathes. These will be food for animals, both wild and tame, and for birds.

God looked at what he had done. All of it was very good! Evening came and then morning—that was the sixth day.

GENESIS 1:26–31

Then I ask, 'Why do you care about us humans? Why are you concerned for us weaklings?' You made us a little lower than you yourself, and you have crowned us with glory and honour.

PSALM 8:4–5

Head, shoulders, knees and toes

Pinch yourself!

'Pinching yourself' is what some people do if they experience something so wonderful, they think they must be dreaming. They pinch themselves to check they're really awake. Today there is good reason to pinch yourself, because next time you look at yourself in the mirror, you have something to match up with: a word—the word of the day. And the word of the day is: *very*.

No one is 100 per cent satisfied with themselves, but God thinks you are 100 per cent perfect, that you are *very* perfect. When he had finished creating the world, God looked at everything he had done and saw that it was *very* good. There's that word again: *very*!

Pinch yourself and say '*very*' next time you look in the mirror.

Links: 1 January, 17 January, 3 August, 5 December

5 minutes more? Genesis 7

7 January

In the beginning

Day 7: The day of rest

So the heavens and the earth and everything else were created. By the seventh day God had finished his work, and so he rested. God blessed the seventh day and made it special because on that day he rested from his work.

GENESIS 2:1–3

One Sabbath Jesus and his disciples were walking through some wheat fields. His disciples were picking grains of wheat as they went along. Some Pharisees asked Jesus, 'Why are your disciples picking grain on the Sabbath? They are not supposed to do that!' Jesus answered, 'Haven't you read what David did when he and his followers were hungry and in need? It was during the time of Abiathar the high priest. David went into the house of God and ate the sacred loaves of bread that only the priests are allowed to eat. He also gave some to his followers.' Jesus finished by saying, 'People were not made for the good of the Sabbath. The Sabbath was made for the good of people. So the Son of Man is Lord over the Sabbath.'

MARK 2:23–28

Hmm... just a thought

Chill out

Since God had time to relax and enjoy the work of his hands—creation—we really ought to be able to do the same.

Links: 15 February, 26 February, 11 April, 30 July

5 minutes more? Genesis 8

8 January

In the beginning

Naked in the garden

The Lord God put the man in the Garden of Eden to take care of it and to look after it. But the Lord told him, 'You may eat fruit from any tree in the garden, except the one that has the power to let you know the difference between right and wrong. If you eat any fruit from that tree, you will die before the day is over!' The Lord God said, 'It isn't good for the man to live alone. I need to make a suitable partner for him.' ... So the Lord God made him fall into a deep sleep, and he took out one of the man's ribs. Then after closing the man's side, the Lord made a woman out of the rib. The Lord brought her to the man... Although the man and his wife were both naked, they were not ashamed.

GENESIS 2:15–18, 21–22, 25

You belong to the light and live in the day. We don't live in the night or belong to the dark.

1 THESSALONIANS 5:5

Di:SaipL

Light-sensitivity

Many church services and meetings begin with the confession of sins. The point of the confession of sins is not to put people in the worst possible mood, but precisely the opposite.

The point of a time for confession is that it should be useful for us to search through our life and bring things out into the light. Those of us who are Christians shouldn't need to have a light-phobia, but experience shows that Christians, like everyone else, do all sorts of things which they hide from other people's eyes.

This is why confessing your sins is absolutely brilliant. It helps us to get hidden things out into the light, and if we confess our sins we become free people. We no longer have anything to hide. We can live an open life—without shame.

'Keep your eyes on the Lord! You will shine like the sun and never blush with shame' (Psalm 34:5).

Take some time out and think if there is anything you ought to get sorted out with anyone. Ask God to help you do something about it.

Links: 9 January, 10 January, 5 December, 30 December

5 minutes more? Genesis 9

9 January

In the beginning

The tempter

The snake was more cunning than any of the other wild animals that the Lord God had made. One day it came to the woman and asked, 'Did God tell you not to eat fruit from any tree in the garden?' The woman answered, 'God said we could eat fruit from any tree in the garden, except the one in the middle. He told us not to eat fruit from that tree or even to touch it. If we do, we will die.' 'No, you won't!' the snake replied. 'God understands what will happen on the day you eat fruit from that tree. You will see what you have done, and you will know the difference between right and wrong, just as God does.' The woman stared at the fruit. It looked beautiful and tasty. She wanted the wisdom that it would give her, and she ate some of the fruit. Her husband was there with her, so she gave some to him, and he ate it too. Straight away they saw what they had done, and they realized they were naked. Then they sewed fig leaves together to make something to cover themselves.

GENESIS 3:1–7

Hmm... just a thought

Did God really tell you...?

That's strange. The first time the tempter was out and about, he asked the question, 'Did God really tell you...?'

Strange, because it reminds me of a voice I have heard quite a few times.

'Does it really matter, Knut, if you watch that TV programme or not?'

'Knut, do you really believe that God is bothered about you? You're not worth that much, you know.'

'Does the Bible really say anything about waiting till you're married, Knut?'

'If God is good, Knut, then he can't possibly think that...?'

'No, you really don't need to pray for forgiveness, Knut. Not for something so small. You don't believe you have to do that, do you?'

Somehow, I have never doubted that the devil exists.

PS: God has said a lot of things and they are worth listening to.

Links: 10 January, 11 January, 12 January, 31 August

5 minutes more? Genesis 11

10 January

In the beginning

The denial

Late in the afternoon a breeze began to blow, and the man and woman heard the Lord God walking in the garden. They were frightened and hid behind some trees. The Lord called out to the man and asked, 'Where are you?' The man answered, 'I was naked, and when I heard you walking through the garden, I was frightened and hid!' 'How did you know you were naked?' God asked. 'Did you eat any fruit from that tree in the middle of the garden?' 'It was the woman you put here with me,' the man said. 'She gave me some of the fruit and I ate it.' The Lord God then asked the woman, 'What have you done?' 'The snake tricked me,' she answered. 'And I ate some of that fruit.' So the Lord God said to the snake: 'Because of what you have done, you will be the only animal to suffer this curse—for as long as you live, you will crawl on your stomach and eat dust.'

GENESIS 3:8–14

Check it out

What the first sin led to...

Adam blames the woman and the woman blames the snake. No one will take the blame. For the first time there is a bad feeling in the air. Sin doesn't only destroy the relationship between God and people; it also destroys relationships between people, our relationship with the environment and with ourselves.

Check out Genesis 3:16–19. Here you will find a list of some of the concrete consequences of Adam and Eve being so brain-dead that they couldn't keep their fingers out of the proverbial biscuit tin. These are some of the consequences of the first sin:

- women suffering when they give birth
- male chauvinism
- over-cultivation of the natural environment
- weeds (yes, that's what it says!)
- sweat
- stress
- death

Links: 11 January, 12 January, 13 January, 25 September

5 minutes more? Genesis 12

The flight

Then the Lord God made clothes out of animal skins for the man and his wife. The Lord said, 'These people now know the difference between right and wrong, just as we do. But they must not be allowed to eat fruit from the tree that lets them live for ever.' So the Lord God sent them out of the Garden of Eden, where they would have to work the ground from which the man had been made. Then God put winged creatures at the entrance to the garden and a flaming, flashing sword to guard the way to the life-giving tree.
GENESIS 3:21–24

No one in this world always does right... I did learn one thing: we were completely honest when God created us, but now we have twisted minds.
ECCLESIASTES 7:20, 29

Check it out

What the Bible says about clothing yourself...

Since young people are often so obsessed with fashion—here are some of the things it says about clothes in the Bible.

- Clothes were invented because people needed to hide their bodies (Genesis 3:7, 21).
- When people in Bible times got really cross or sad, they used to tear their clothes (Ezra 9:3; Job 1:20).
- Jesus' outer garment was the best of its kind. It was woven as a single piece of cloth and did not have any seams (John 19:23).
- God says that we shouldn't worry about clothes so much, because he will clothe us... (Matthew 6:27–30)
- ... and because, first and foremost, Jesus should be as close to us as the clothes we wear! (Romans 13:14).
- In addition, we must 'wear' compassion, kindness and humility like we wear our clothes (Colossians 3:12, NIV).
- But most of all, love must be our favourite 'piece of clothing' (Colossians 3:14, NIV).

Links: 12 January, 13 January, 14 January, 25 September

5 minutes more? Genesis 16

Death because of Adam, life because of Christ

Adam sinned, and that sin brought death into the world. Now everyone has sinned, and so everyone must die... But the gift that God was kind enough to give was very different from Adam's sin. That one sin brought death to many others. Yet in an even greater way, Jesus Christ alone brought God's gift of kindness to many people. There is a lot of difference between Adam's sin and God's gift. That one sin led to punishment. But God's gift made it possible for us to be acceptable to him, even though we have sinned many times. Death ruled like a king because Adam had sinned. But that cannot compare with what Jesus Christ has done. God has been so kind to us, and he has accepted us because of Jesus. And so we will live and rule like kings.
ROMANS 5:12, 15–17

Just as we will die because of Adam, we will be raised to life because of Christ. Adam brought death to all of us, and Christ will bring life to all of us.
1 CORINTHIANS 15:21–22

Hmm... just a thought

There is a reason why we have hope. Only one. He's called Jesus.

The next few days will be about our new life in Christ.

Links: 13 January, 14 January, 15 January, 16 January

5 minutes more? Genesis 18

Grace in Christ (1)

All of us have sinned and fallen short of God's glory. But God treats us much better than we deserve, and because of Christ Jesus, he freely accepts us and sets us free from our sins.
ROMANS 3:23–24

But God was merciful! We were dead because of our sins, but God loved us so much that he made us alive with Christ, and God's wonderful kindness is what saves you. God raised us from death to life with Christ Jesus, and he has given us a place beside Christ in heaven. God did this so that in the future world he could show how truly good and kind he is to us because of what Christ Jesus has done. You were saved by faith in God, who treats us much better than we deserve. This is God's gift to you, and not anything you have done on your own. It isn't something you have earned, so there is nothing you can boast about. God planned for us to do good things and to live as he has always wanted us to live. That's why he sent Christ to make us what we are.
EPHESIANS 2:4–10

Download...

...about God's kindness and grace

This is one of the verses most central to the Christian faith—well worth learning off by heart.

'You were saved by faith in God, who treats us much better than we deserve. This is God's gift to you, and not anything you have done on your own' (Ephesians 2:8).

PS: Grace is a gift. It costs everything for the one who gives it. The one who receives it gets it completely free. Grace actually means 'free'.

Links: 14 January, 15 January, 29 March, 12 September

5 minutes more? Genesis 22

Grace in Christ (2)

God saved us and chose us to be his holy people. We did nothing to deserve this, but God planned it because he is so kind. Even before time began God planned for Christ Jesus to show kindness to us. Now Christ Jesus has come to show us the kindness of God.
2 TIMOTHY 1:9–10a

Praise the God and Father of our Lord Jesus Christ for the spiritual blessings that Christ has brought us from heaven! Before the world was created, God had Christ choose us to live with him and to be his holy and innocent and loving people. God was kind and decided that Christ would choose us to be God's own adopted children. God was very kind to us because of the Son he dearly loves, and so we should praise God. Christ sacrificed his life's blood to set us free, which means that our sins are now forgiven. Christ did this because God was so kind to us.
EPHESIANS 1:3–7

Story
Paco's story

In one of his books, Ernest Hemingway (an American author) wrote about a Spanish father who tried to re-establish contact with his son. The son had gone off to Madrid and the father didn't have any other way of finding him than by putting an advert in the paper:

'PACO. Come home!
Meet me at such and such hotel,
Such and such time, such and such day.
All is forgiven.
PAPA'

Paco is a very common boy's name in Spain and when the nervous father went to the hotel at the designated time, 800 boys were waiting there for their fathers. They were all called Paco.

There are hundreds of people who need God's kindness and grace.

Links: 15 January, 16 January, 29 March, 12 September

5 minutes more? Genesis 27

15 January

In Christ

Grace in Christ (3)

At that time you did not know about Christ... You were living in this world without hope and without God, and you were far from God. But Christ offered his life's blood as a sacrifice and brought you near God.

EPHESIANS 2:12–13

If you belong to Christ Jesus, you won't be punished. The Holy Spirit will give you life that comes from Christ Jesus and will set you free from sin and death.

ROMANS 8:1–2

If we shared in Jesus' death by being baptized, we will be raised to life with him... He died and was raised to life, never again to die. When Christ died, he died for sin once and for all. But now he is alive, and he lives only for God. In the same way, you must think of yourselves as dead to the power of sin. But Christ Jesus has given life to you, and you live for God.

ROMANS 6:5–11

Download...

...about punishment

'If you belong to Christ Jesus, you won't be punished' (Romans 8:1).

Here is a beautiful prayer written by Edin Løvås:

Lord Jesus Christ
you stand here in front of me,
you are also behind me,
you are by my right side,
you are by my left side,
you are above me,
you are under me,
you surround me on all sides,
you live in my heart,
you know me through and through,
and you love me, Lord Jesus!

FROM *MINUTTER MED JESUS* (*MINUTES WITH JESUS*), EDIN LØVÅS, VERBUM FORLAG (1986)

Links: 16 January, 17 January, 29 March, 12 September

5 minutes more? Genesis 28

16 January

In Christ

New life in Christ (1)

You have accepted Christ Jesus as your Lord. Now keep on following him. Plant your roots in Christ and let him be the foundation for your life. Be strong in your faith, just as you were taught. And be grateful. Don't let anyone fool you by using senseless arguments. These arguments may sound wise, but they are only human teachings. They come from the powers of this world and not from Christ. God lives fully in Christ. And you are fully grown because you belong to Christ, who is over every power and authority.
COLOSSIANS 2:6–10

God has done all this, so that we will look for him and reach out and find him. He isn't far from any of us, and he gives us the power to live, to move, and to be who we are.
ACTS 17:27–28a

Good news

Jesus is with you every day

Let's take, for example, 11 a.m. Sunday morning. Thousands of Christian meetings and church services are being held at this time every Sunday. Think what it would be like if Jesus could only be in one place at a time—if he had to choose which meeting or service he would go to.

Fortunately it's not like that. The Bible says that Jesus is omnipresent—that he is in all places all the time.

This is great, because if Jesus is always everywhere, he is also very close to every person all the time. And if he is close to every person all the time, he is very close to you. Right at this moment. Jesus is on every side of you.

'He gives us the power to live, to move, and to be who we are' (Acts 27:28).

Always!

Links: 17 January, 18 January, 29 March, 12 September

5 minutes more? Genesis 37

17 January
In Christ

New life in Christ (2)

Can anything separate us from the love of Christ? Can trouble, suffering, and hard times, or hunger and nakedness, or danger and death? ... In everything we have won more than a victory because of Christ who loves us. I am sure that nothing can separate us from God's love—not life or death, not angels or spirits, not the present or the future, and not powers above or powers below. Nothing in creation can separate us from God's love for us in Christ Jesus our Lord!
ROMANS 8:35, 37–39

Christ gives me the strength to face anything.
PHILIPPIANS 4:13

Story
Sarah's journey

1.
Sarah likes driving her little blue car.
2.
One day, when she was out driving, it got very foggy.
3.
Sarah stopped the car because she was frightened.
4.
She got her mobile out of her bag and rang Lisa.
5.
Lisa reminded Sarah that we don't need to be afraid because Jesus is always near us.
6.
Sarah and Lisa prayed that Jesus would give Sarah courage to drive home.
7.
Sarah began to drive home slowly.
8.
She was still scared, but trusted Jesus' promise.
9.
She got home safely and thanked Jesus for being with her and helping her.

ADAPTED FROM A STRIP CARTOON BY ELLEN LANDE GOSSNER

Links: 15 November, 1 December, 2 December, 3 December

5 minutes more? Genesis 39

18 January

In Christ

New life in Christ (3)

Anyone who belongs to Christ is a new person. The past is forgotten, and everything is new. God has done it all! He sent Christ to make peace between himself and us, and he has given us the work of making peace between himself and others. What we mean is that God was in Christ, offering peace and forgiveness to the people of this world. And he has given us the work of sharing his message about peace. We were sent to speak for Christ, and God is begging you to listen to our message. We speak for Christ and sincerely ask you to make peace with God. Christ never sinned! But God treated him as a sinner, so that Christ could make us acceptable to God.

2 CORINTHIANS 5:17–21

God rescued us from the dark power of Satan and brought us into the kingdom of his dear Son, who forgives our sins and sets us free.

COLOSSIANS 1:13–14

Did you know that...

...the expression 'in Christ' is used as many as 164 times in the Bible?

The point of the expression 'in Christ' is to bring out who we are. We are ordinary people, but because we believe in Jesus we have got a new identity. (OK—identity can be a difficult word, but you understand what it is, don't you?)

- We have got new identity, new life, in Christ.
- We have re-established contact with our heavenly Father, in Christ.
- We have got thousands of new brothers and sisters, in Christ.
- We have got new direction in life, in Christ.
- We have got eternal life, in Christ.
- We have got new purpose in life, in Christ.

'I have died, but Christ lives in me. And I now live by faith in the Son of God, who loved me and gave his life for me' (Galatians 2:20).

Thank God for your new identity! Your new life!

Links: 6 January, 19 January, 20 January, 21 January

5 minutes more? Genesis 41

19 January

In Christ

New life in Christ (4): Show unity!

All of you are God's children because of your faith in Christ Jesus. And when you were baptized, it was as though you had put on Christ in the same way you put on new clothes. Faith in Christ Jesus is what makes each of you equal with each other, whether you are a Jew or a Greek, a slave or a free person, a man or a woman.

GALATIANS 3:26–28

I want all of them to be one with each other, just as I am one with you and you are one with me. I also want them to be one with us. Then the people of this world will believe that you sent me. I have honoured my followers in the same way that you honoured me, in order that they may be one with each other, just as we are one. I am one with them, and you are one with me, so that they may become completely one. Then this world's people will know that you sent me. They will know that you love my followers as much as you love me.

JOHN 17:21–23

Instead, be kind and merciful, and forgive others, just as God forgave you because of Christ.

EPHESIANS 4:32

Hmm... just a thought...

...about agreement

Christians argue a lot—on TV, in the newspapers, in the classroom—everywhere. It shouldn't be like that.

It says in the Bible that we must be one and show agreement, even about the things we argue about and discuss—all of us!

The Bible says we are all one, in Christ Jesus!

So let's be that, right?

Links: 28 May, 30 May, 1 June, 5 June

5 minutes more? Genesis 42

20 January

In Christ

New life in Christ (5): Joy and peace

Always be glad because of the Lord! I will say it again: be glad. Always be gentle with others. The Lord will soon be here. Don't worry about anything, but pray about everything. With thankful hearts offer up your prayers and requests to God. Then, because you belong to Christ Jesus, God will bless you with peace that no one can completely understand. And this peace will control the way you think and feel. Finally, my friends, keep your minds on whatever is true, pure, right, holy, friendly, and proper. Don't ever stop thinking about what is truly worthwhile and worthy of praise. You know the teachings I gave you, and you know what you heard me say and saw me do. So follow my example. And God, who gives peace, will be with you.

PHILIPPIANS 4:4–9

Always be joyful and never stop praying. Whatever happens, keep thanking God because of Jesus Christ. This is what God wants you to do.

1 THESSALONIANS 5:16–18

Did you know that...

...you have just read the shortest verse in the Bible?

Lots of people think that John 11:35 is the shortest verse in the Bible—where it says that 'Jesus wept'. That's wrong. It might be the shortest in English, but not in Greek—the language the New Testament was written in.

The shortest verse is 1 Thessalonians 5:16. See for yourself:

John 11:35: *edakrusen ho iesous*
1 Thessalonians 5:16: *pantote chairete*

1 Thessalonians 5:16 says, 'Always be joyful'. The Bible's shortest verse is a happy verse—not a sad one.

Links: 23 May, 24 May, 25 May, 26 May

5 minutes more? Genesis 43

21 January

In Christ

New life in Christ (6): Maturity in Christ

We announce the message about Christ, and we use all our wisdom to warn and teach everyone, so that all Christ's followers will grow and become mature.
COLOSSIANS 1:28

I kneel in prayer to the Father. All beings in heaven and on earth receive their life from him. God is wonderful and glorious. I pray that his Spirit will make you become strong followers and that Christ will live in your hearts because of your faith. Stand firm and be deeply rooted in his love. I pray that you and all God's people will understand what is called wide or long or high or deep. I want you to know all about Christ's love, although it is too wonderful to be measured. Then your lives will be filled with all that God is. I pray that Christ Jesus and the church will for ever bring praise to God. His power at work in us can do far more than we dare ask or imagine. Amen.
EPHESIANS 3:14–21

Di:SaipL

Growing in the Christian life

We must become like little children to get into God's kingdom. But, as we all know, all babies grow!

I think you would really be quite surprised if you had a baby that never grew—if you gave it food and did everything you could to help it grow, but the baby never got more than 50cm long or heavier than 4kg, whatever you did. I think you would get a bit wound up...

It's the same with our life in Christ. Even if we must be like little children to get into God's kingdom, it's completely natural to grow as a Christian.

If there are any areas of your life that you know you need to sort out, then get on with it!

Links: 3 February, 19 May, 20 May, 22 October

5 minutes more? Genesis 45

The Lord chooses Abraham

The Lord said to Abram:

Leave your country, your family, and your relatives and go to the land that I will show you. I will bless you and make your descendants into a great nation. You will become famous and be a blessing to others. I will bless anyone who blesses you, but I will put a curse on anyone who puts a curse on you. Everyone on earth will be blessed because of you.

Abram was seventy-five years old when the Lord told him to leave the city of Haran. He obeyed and left with his wife Sarai, his nephew Lot, and all the possessions and slaves they had got while in Haran.
GENESIS 12:1–5a

Bible personality
Abraham—the father of a nation

'Ab' means 'father'
'rah' means 'big'
'am' means 'nation'

Ab-rah-am means 'father of a big nation'. God sought out Abraham and told him he would have an uncountable number of descendants, that through him all the nations of the earth would be blessed. With Abraham we have the beginning of the Bible's 'big story'—the story of how God seeks to bring people back to him after the first sin.

We join the story in the city of Ur (which was situated at the head of the Persian Gulf) when God visits Abraham for the first time. It is a completely normal day 4,000 years ago…

PS: Notice over the next few days how faithful Abraham is to God. Abraham is probably the most faithful person in the whole Bible.

PPS: God needs faithful followers today too.

Links: 23 January, 24 January, 25 January, 26 January

5 minutes more? Exodus 1

23 January

The Fathers: Abraham, Isaac and Jacob (c.2000BC)

God's plan for Abraham

Later the Lord spoke to Abram in a vision, 'Abram, don't be afraid! I will protect you and reward you greatly.' But Abram answered, 'Lord All-Powerful, you have given me everything I could ask for, except children. And when I die, Eliezer of Damascus will get all I own. You have not given me any children, and this servant of mine will inherit everything.' The Lord replied, 'No, he won't! You will have a son of your own, and everything you have will be his.' Then the Lord took Abram outside and said, 'Look at the sky and see if you can count the stars. That's how many descendants you will have.' Abram believed the Lord, and the Lord was pleased with him.

GENESIS 15:1–6

Listen to your heart and fill in

Your heart's desire

Abraham was very old and couldn't have children any more, but God promised him a son anyway. Not only one, but as many as the stars in the sky. Even though it seemed physically impossible, Abraham believed God's promise. He believed that everything is possible with God.

What do you want to pray about? What do you want to pray about most of all?

1. ______________________________

2. ______________________________

3. ______________________________

Jesus once said: 'There are some things that people cannot do, but God can do anything' (Matthew 19:26).

Links: 24 January, 25 January, 26 January, 27 January

5 minutes more? Exodus 2

24 January

The Fathers: Abraham, Isaac and Jacob (c.2000BC)

Abraham laughs very loudly

Abram was ninety-nine years old when the Lord appeared to him again and said, 'I am God All-Powerful. If you obey me and always do right, I will keep my solemn promise to you and give you more descendants than can be counted.' Abram bowed with his face to the ground, and God said:

I promise that you will be the father of many nations. That's why I now change your name from Abram to Abraham… Abraham, your wife's name will now be Sarah instead of Sarai. I will bless her, and you will have a son by her. She will become the mother of nations, and some of her descendants will even be kings. Abraham bowed with his face to the ground and thought, 'I am almost a hundred years old. How can I become a father? And Sarah is ninety. How can she have a child?' So he started laughing.

GENESIS 17:1–5, 15–17

Good news

No to body fixations

Abraham was 99 years old when God promised him a son! Even though Abraham usually believed God, this time he looked at his body and laughed in despair. Not so strange, perhaps. I mean, 99 years old. Hello?

It is easy to get discouraged if we focus on our bodies too much. Today, try to keep God in focus instead—God who says you are *perfect*!

Links: 6 January, 1 March, 14 June, 3 August

5 minutes more? Exodus 3

Abraham is willing to sacrifice Isaac (1)

The Lord was good to Sarah and kept his promise. Although Abraham was very old, Sarah had a son exactly at the time God had said. Abraham named his son Isaac... Some years later God decided to test Abraham, so he spoke to him. Abraham answered, 'Here I am, Lord.' The Lord said, 'Go and get Isaac, your only son, the one you dearly love! Take him to the land of Moriah, and I will show you a mountain where you must sacrifice him to me on the fires of an altar.'
GENESIS 21:1–3; 22:1–2

Abraham had been promised that Isaac, his only son, would continue his family. But when Abraham was tested, he had faith and was willing to sacrifice Isaac, because he was sure that God could raise people to life. This was just like getting Isaac back from death.
HEBREWS 11:17–19

Listen to your heart and fill in

Find five mistakes

Imagine how unbelievably fond Abraham was of his son. At last, having hoped for so many years, he had finally got a son. Now suddenly God wanted him to sacrifice Isaac! Sounds incredibly cruel, if you ask me. Surely no one would do that? Well, in the end he didn't need to. God provided a ram for Abraham to sacrifice instead of Isaac—when he knew that Abraham had been willing to obey him (see Genesis 22:13).

But this story has more to it than meets the eye. In the letter to the Hebrews there is a hint that this story points to something else. To what? To Jesus' sacrifice for us that saves us from certain death.

Find five mistakes: 'God didn't love the people of this world so much that he didn't give his only Son, so that everyone who doesn't have faith in him will not have eternal life and will really die.'

(Clue: look up John 3:16.)

Links: 26 January, 29 March, 12 September

5 minutes more? Exodus 7

Abraham is willing to sacrifice Isaac (2)

Abraham put the wood on Isaac's shoulder, but he carrried the hot coals and the knife. As the two of them walked along, Isaac said, 'Father, we have the coals and the wood, but where is the lamb for the sacrifice?' 'My son,' Abraham answered, 'God will provide the lamb.' The two of them walked on, and when they reached the place that God had told him about, Abraham built an altar and placed the wood on it. Next, he tied up his son and put him on the wood. He then took the knife and got ready to kill his son. But the Lord's angel shouted from heaven, 'Abraham! Abraham!' 'Here I am!' he answered. 'Don't hurt the boy or harm him in any way!' the angel said. 'Now I know that you truly obey God, because you were willing to offer him your only son.'
GENESIS 22:6–12

Refresh

Trials great and small

As Christians we are confronted with trials in all shapes and sizes every day—situations where our faithfulness to God is tested:

- You don't believe all that stuff, do you?
- Oh come on… don't be such a geek!
- Nah, no point you hanging around. Bet you're off to church!
- You're one of those dumb Christians, aren't you?
- Yes, you are, aren't you?
- Look out! Here comes Super Christian!
- Thicko!

Incredibly difficult situations. I know. But it is in situations like these that faith is tested. That's when you grow, when you get stronger and more secure.

The Bible says we should be glad when we go through hard trials (1 Peter 1:6), that we must be happy because what is in store for us in heaven is well worth all the bother.

Go out into your day with your head held high—and keep close to Jesus.

Links: 12 July, 13 July, 17 July, 18 July

5 minutes more? Exodus 12

27 January

The Fathers: Abraham, Isaac and Jacob (c.2000BC)

Isaac's sons: Esau and Jacob

Rebekah still had no children. So Isaac asked the Lord to let her have a child, and the Lord answered his prayer... When Rebekah gave birth, the first baby was covered with red hair, so he was named Esau. The second baby grabbed his brother's heel, so they named him Jacob. Isaac was sixty years old when they were born. As Jacob and Esau grew older, Esau liked the outdoors and became a good hunter, while Jacob settled down and became a shepherd... One day, Jacob was cooking some stew, when Esau came home hungry and said, 'I'm starving to death! Give me some of that red stew at once!' ... Jacob replied, 'Sell me your rights as the firstborn son.' 'I'm about to die,' Esau answered. 'What good will those rights do me?' But Jacob said, 'Promise me your birthrights, here and now!' And that's what Esau did.

GENESIS 25:21, 24–27, 29–30a, 31–33

Good news

You have received the rights of a firstborn 'son'

The rights of the firstborn son were important to Jacob; they made the future secure. His father's money was not the most important thing—the rights of the firstborn son meant that Jacob would also have a special blessing from the Lord.

We also have the rights of the firstborn. Follow the logic:

1. Jesus is God's son.
2. He is God's first and only son.
3. Only he has claim to the rights of the firstborn son of God.
4. If we believe in Jesus, we become his sisters and brothers...
5. ...and God's children.
6. Then we get to share the rights of the firstborn that we have no natural claim to...
7. ...the rights that only Jesus deserves.

See Romans 8:29.

The Bible calls this being adopted as a child of God. And it's FRE-E-E-E-E! You also have a special blessing from the Lord waiting for you—eternal life!

Links: 28 January, 29 January, 30 January, 31 January

5 minutes more? Exodus 14

Joseph, Jacob's son

This is the story of Jacob's family. When Jacob's son Joseph was seventeen years old, he took care of the sheep with his brothers, the sons of Bilhah and Zilpah. But he was always telling his father all sorts of bad things about his brothers. Jacob loved Joseph more than he did any of his other sons, because Joseph was born after Jacob was very old. Jacob had given Joseph a fine coat to show that he was his favourite son, and so Joseph's brothers hated him and would not be friendly to him.

GENESIS 37:2–4

Bible personality

Joseph

Abraham was Isaac's father. Isaac was Jacob's father. Jacob was the father to twelve sons in all. The most well-known of them is our man—Joseph. The story of Joseph is a fantastic tale of God's grace. Many people think that Joseph is an image of Jesus. But listen to this.

Joseph had eleven brothers. They were envious of him because their father liked Joseph better than them, so they sold him as a slave. After a lot of different mishaps, Joseph ended up in the household of the king of Egypt—Pharaoh himself! Joseph was an interpreter of dreams. God helped Joseph to interpret Pharaoh's dreams correctly, which meant that Egypt survived seven years of bad harvests and famine. Meanwhile, people in neighbouring countries starved.

Joseph's eleven brothers came to Egypt as refugees. There they met... guess who... Joseph, who was second in command only to Pharaoh himself. It would have been a fitting punishment for his brothers if Joseph had refused to give them food and permission to stay, but he helped them. He said, 'You tried to harm me, but God made it turn out for the best' (Genesis 50:20).

Links: 29 January, 30 January, 31 January, 1 February

5 minutes more? Exodus 15

Joseph is sold as a slave

But before Joseph got there, [his brothers] saw him coming and made plans to kill him. They said to one another, 'Look, here comes the hero of those dreams! Let's kill him and throw him into a pit and say that some wild animal ate him. Then we'll see what happens to those dreams.' ... They threw him into a dry well... When the Midianite merchants came by, Joseph's brothers took him out of the well, and for twenty pieces of silver they sold him to the Ishmaelites who took him to Egypt... The Midianites sold Joseph in Egypt to a man named Potiphar, who was the king's official in charge of the palace guard.

GENESIS 37:18–20, 24, 28, 36

Listen to your heart and fill in

How much is a man worth?

The brothers sold Joseph as a slave for twenty silver shekels. Twenty shekels is about the same as £4. Joseph was only worth £4 to his brothers!

A brain-teaser:

A boat is sinking. It is taking on water. There are seven people on board. Every minute that the boat stays in the icy water means that the chance of survival gets less. A helicopter is coming, but it can only carry one person at a time to land. You are the captain and must decide in what order the people will be rescued.

They are:

- a multi-millionaire No. ______
- an 80-year-old woman with no family No. ______
- a glamour model No. ______
- a father of two young children No. ______
- a lively teenager No. ______
- a prime minister No. ______
- yourself, the captain No. ______

Hope it's difficult!

Links: 30 January, 31 January, 1 February, 2 February

5 minutes more? Exodus 16

30 January

The Fathers: Abraham, Isaac and Jacob (c.2000BC)

Joseph survives and succeeds

The Ishmaelites took Joseph to Egypt and sold him to Potiphar, the king's official in charge of the palace guard. So Joseph lived in the home of Potiphar, his Egyptian owner. Soon Potiphar realized that the Lord was helping Joseph to be successful in whatever he did. Potiphar liked Joseph and made him his personal assistant, putting him in charge of his house and all his property. Because of Joseph, the Lord began to bless Potiphar's family and fields. Potiphar left everything up to Joseph, and with Joseph there, the only decision he had to make was what he wanted to eat.

GENESIS 39:1–6a

Share your plans with the Lord, and you will succeed.

PROVERBS 16:3

Download...

...about entrusting your plans to the Lord

Take half a minute's time-out and learn this verse by heart.

'Share your plans with the Lord, and you will succeed' (Proverbs 3:16).

Links: 31 January, 1 February, 2 February, 20 May

5 minutes more? Exodus 20

31 January

The Fathers: Abraham, Isaac and Jacob (c.2000BC)

Joseph interprets Pharaoh's dream

The king said to [Joseph], 'I had a dream, yet no one can explain what it means. I am told that you can interpret dreams.' 'Your Majesty,' Joseph answered, 'I can't do it myself, but God can give a good meaning to your dreams.' The king told Joseph:

I dreamed I was standing on the bank of the River Nile. I saw seven, fat, healthy cows come up out of the river, and they began feeding on the grass. Next, seven skinny, bony cows came up out of the river. I have never seen such terrible looking cows anywhere in Egypt...

Joseph replied:

Your Majesty, both of your dreams mean the same thing, and in them God has shown what he is going to do. The seven good cows stand for seven years, and so do the seven good heads of grain. The seven skinny, ugly cows that came up later also stand for seven years, as do the seven bad heads of grain that were scorched by the east wind. The dreams mean there will be seven years when there won't be enough grain.

GENESIS 41:15–19, 25–27

Check it out

A psalm for sleep problems

There are few things worse than a nightmare, waking up all sweaty and exhausted, having dreamt about something that's utterly terrifying and disturbing. Some people never remember their dreams; other people remember what they dream about every single night. No matter which, it could be a good thing to know about Psalm 4—a psalm for sleep problems. I can't really guarantee that it'll help, but it won't hurt anyway.

Listen to the great way it ends:

'I can lie down and sleep soundly because you, Lord, will keep me safe' (Psalm 4:9).

Good night!

Links: 1 February, 2 February, 8 August, 12 May

5 minutes more? Exodus 25

1 February

The Fathers: Abraham, Isaac and Jacob (c.2000BC)

Joseph becomes governor of Egypt

The king and his officials liked this plan. So the king said to them, 'No one could possibly handle this better than Joseph, since the Spirit of God is with him.' The king told Joseph, 'God is the one who has shown you these things. No one else is as wise as you are or knows as much as you do. I'm putting you in charge of my palace, and everybody will have to obey you. No one will be over you except me. You are now governor of all Egypt!' Then the king took off his royal ring and put it on Joseph's finger. He gave him fine clothes to wear and placed a gold chain around his neck. He also let him ride in the chariot next to his own, and people shouted, 'Make way for Joseph!' So Joseph was governor of Egypt... Joseph was thirty when the king made him governor.

GENESIS 41:37–43, 46a

Head, shoulders, knees and toes

A 'praise prescription'

Joseph got heaps of praise and tons of compliments because he was so smart. Perhaps I'm wrong, but I have a feeling somehow that we don't always find it very easy to receive the compliments that we get. Not so strange, perhaps. It isn't always easy to handle compliments—knowing how to reply, and so on.

I learnt a really good 'thank you' technique once—I guess you could call it a 'praise prescription'—and it's gone miles towards helping me handle compliments:

1. Breathe in as deep as you possibly can.
2. Hold your breath.
3. Feel the warmth the compliment gives you.
4. Let your breath out slowly as you say, 'Thanks very much.'
5. Afterwards—send a little 'thank you' to God

God doesn't want us to go round full of embarrassment and false humility just because we are Christians. If you get a compliment, welcome it. Take it on board. Enjoy the warm feeling it gives you—and share it with God.

Links: 2 February, 7 August, 8 August, 9 August

5 minutes more? Exodus 37

2 February

The Fathers: Abraham, Isaac and Jacob (c.2000BC)

Joseph's brothers come and ask for help

Everywhere in Egypt and Canaan the grain crops failed. There was terrible suffering, and our ancestors could not find enough to eat. But when Jacob heard that there was grain in Egypt, he sent our ancestors there for the first time. It was on their second trip that Joseph told his brothers who he was, and Pharaoh learnt about Joseph's family.

ACTS 7:11–13

At once, Joseph's brothers came and bowed down to the ground in front of him and said, 'We are your slaves.' But Joseph told them, 'Don't be afraid! I have no right to change what God has decided. You tried to harm me, but God made it turn out for the best, so that he could save all these people, as he is now doing. Don't be afraid! I will take care of you and your children.' After Joseph said this, his brothers felt much better.

GENESIS 50:18–21

Did you know that...

...this is how the whole crowd ended up in Egypt?

You probably know that Moses led the people of Israel out of Egypt. But do you know how they ended up there in the first place?

To cut a long story short: Joseph was sold by his brothers and inadvertently ended up in Egypt. Some time after this, there was a famine in the country where the brothers lived—and they sought refuge in Egypt. Joseph welcomed them. He had every reason imaginable to turn them away, but he helped them instead. They settled in Egypt—where they eventually ended up working as Pharaoh's slaves.

Joseph and his brothers are considered to be the people from whom the Israelites are descended. Each of the brothers' families became a tribe—and therefore, from that day to this, these twelve brothers have been called Israel's patriarchs (which means 'father of a tribe or nation').

Links: 12 February, 13 February, 14 February, 15 February

5 minutes more? Leviticus 25

3 February

Jesus meets people

Mary and Martha

The Lord and his disciples were travelling along and came to a village. When they got there, a woman named Martha welcomed him into her home. She had a sister named Mary, who sat down in front of the Lord and was listening to what he said. Martha was worried about all that had to be done. Finally, she went to Jesus and said, 'Lord, doesn't it bother you that my sister has left me to do all the work by myself? Tell her to come and help me!' The Lord answered, 'Martha, Martha! You are worried and upset about so many things, but only one thing is necessary. Mary has chosen what is best, and it will not be taken away from her.'
LUKE 10:38–42

Our God says, 'Calm down, and learn that I am God! All nations on earth will honour me.'
PSALM 46:10

Job, consider carefully the many wonders of God.
JOB 37:14

Good news

The best choice

Congratulations! You and Mary have something in common. You have both made the best choice. Cheers!

You could have watched a bit more TV. You could have sent one more text message. You could have taken a nap. You've probably got a mountain of more important and amusing things you could or should have been doing. But congratulations—you've made the best choice. It couldn't be better.

It is important, now and then, to take time out and chill out with God. Congratulations on your good choice.

Links: 25 April, 26 April, 1 November, 3 November

5 minutes more? Numbers 6

Nicodemus

There was a man called Nicodemus who was a Pharisee and a Jewish leader. One night he went to Jesus and said, 'Sir, we know that God has sent you to teach us. You could not perform these miracles, unless God were with you.' Jesus replied, 'I tell you for certain that you must be born from above before you can see God's kingdom!' Nicodemus asked, 'How can a grown man ever be born a second time?' Jesus answered:

I tell you for certain that before you can get into God's kingdom, you must be born not only by water, but by the Spirit...

'How can this be?' Nicodemus asked. Jesus replied:

...The Son of Man must be lifted up, just as that metal snake was lifted up by Moses in the desert. Then everyone who has faith in the Son of Man will have eternal life. God loved the people of this world so much that he gave his only Son, so that everyone who has faith in him will have eternal life and never really die.

JOHN 3:1–5, 9–10a, 14–16

☆ Bible personality
Nicodemus

It seems to me that everyone in Jesus' time was an 'A-type person'—you know, the sort that often get up unbelie-e-e-e-vably early in the morning. In any case, the sentence 'Early next morning, such and such happened...' crops up over and over again.

If you personally are a 'B-type person', it's quite understandable that these early-bird A-types might really stress you out. If so, then Nicodemus is your sort of person! Nicodemus is one of the very few B-type people we see in the Bible. We only meet him three times (John 3:1; 7:50; 19:39), but every time it's in the evening or at night.

If you are a B-type who often lies awake thinking things over, then do what Nicodemus does: take your thoughts to Jesus...

Links: 18 January, 21 May, 13 September, 26 December

5 minutes more? Numbers 17

5 February

Jesus meets people

The woman they wanted to stone

The Pharisees and the teachers of the Law of Moses brought in a woman who had been caught in bed with a man who wasn't her husband. They made her stand in the middle of the crowd. Then they said, 'Teacher, this woman was caught sleeping with a man who isn't her husband. The Law of Moses teaches that a woman like this should be stoned to death! What do you say?' They asked Jesus this question, because they wanted to test him and bring some charge against him. But Jesus simply bent over and started writing on the ground with his finger. They kept on asking Jesus about the woman. Finally, he stood up and said, 'If any of you have never sinned, then go ahead and throw the first stone at her!' Once again he bent over and began writing on the ground. The people left one by one, beginning with the oldest. Finally, Jesus and the woman were there alone. Jesus stood up and asked her, 'Where is everyone? Isn't there anyone left to accuse you?' 'No sir,' the woman answered. Then Jesus told her, 'I am not going to accuse you either. You may go now, but don't sin any more.'
JOHN 8:3–11

Refresh

Single and double standards

One day Jesus will judge the world. That's wonderful—that it's him, I mean, and not other people, who will do it. If they did, it would only make the whole mess worse.

The point of this story is not to show that Jesus is indifferent to sin. The point is that everyone has a skeleton in the closet. So we must stop judging the people around us.

The biggest mistake the Pharisees made was not that they tried to get the woman stoned—or that they tested Jesus. The biggest mistake was that they went away. It says, 'The people left one by one.' If we make a mistake, we mustn't walk away. We must go to Jesus—the righteous judge.

Christianity mustn't be used against others, but on ourselves. What do you want to take to Jesus today?

Links: 10 February, 11 February, 14 April, 22 April

5 minutes more? Numbers 21

6 February

Jesus meets people

The blind man

As Jesus walked along, he saw a man who had been blind since birth... He made some mud and smeared it on the man's eyes. Then he said, 'Go and wash off the mud in Siloam Pool.' The man went and washed in Siloam, which means 'One who is sent'. When he had washed off the mud, he could see. The man's neighbours and the people who had seen him begging wondered if he really could be the same man. Some of them said he was the same beggar, while others said he only looked like him. But he told them, 'I am that man.' 'Then how can you see?' they asked. He answered, 'Someone named Jesus made some mud and smeared it on my eyes. He told me to go and wash it off in Siloam Pool. When I did, I could see.' ... The leaders called the man back and said, 'Swear by God to tell the truth! We know that Jesus is a sinner.' The man replied, 'I don't know if he is a sinner or not. All I know is that I used to be blind, but now I can see!'

JOHN 9:1, 6b–11, 24–25

Di:SaipL

How to witness to your friends

It's not always easy to know everything. Especially when people go on and on about everything in heaven and earth—who Jesus is and why there is so much suffering in the world and about the virgin birth and gay priests and living together and sex before marriage and why you don't get drunk and weird things in the Bible and one thing or another.

It is often best to answer like the young blind man: 'I don't quite know. But I do know one thing, and that is............' And then you tell them one or two things that Jesus has done for you. Much simpler. Much better.

Links: 18 February, 25 February, 24 May, 27 November

5 minutes more? Numbers 22

7 February

Jesus meets people

Zacchaeus

Jesus was going through Jericho, where a man named Zacchaeus lived. He was in charge of collecting taxes and was very rich. Jesus was heading his way, and Zacchaeus wanted to see what he was like. But Zacchaeus was a short man and could not see over the crowd. So he ran ahead and climbed up into a sycamore tree. When Jesus got there, he looked up and said, 'Zacchaeus, hurry down! I want to stay with you today.' Zacchaeus hurried down and gladly welcomed Jesus. Everyone who saw this started grumbling, 'This man Zacchaeus is a sinner! And Jesus is going home to eat with him.' Later that day Zacchaeus stood up and said to the Lord, 'I will give half of my property to the poor. And I will now pay back four times as much to everyone I have ever cheated.' Jesus said to Zacchaeus, 'Today you and your family have been saved, because you are a true son of Abraham. The Son of Man came to look for and to save people who are lost.'

LUKE 19:1–10

Big word

Tax collector

In Norway during the Second World War, some Norwegians supported the occupying German forces. These people were known as quislings—named after the Norwegian Nazi leader Vikund Quisling—and they were deeply hated. The tax collectors in New Testament times were like quislings. They were despicable traitors. They supported the occupying power, the Romans, and collected taxes and other payments from the ordinary people. They often took a little bit extra for themselves, so they became rich—and hated. Zacchaeus was one such person—a tax collector, a quisling. You could say that Zacchaeus was worse—he was the chief tax collector. And he was very short. A really shifty little character. Just ripe to meet Jesus.

Write down a list of the kids in your class—from the most popular to the least popular. Whereabouts do you fit in? Now tear the list into very small pieces and flush it down the loo, and promise God you will never, never, never put people in order of preference like this again.

Everyone is worth the same in God's eyes—and should be in ours.

Links: 23 January, 23 August, 4 September, 11 September

5 minutes more? Numbers 27

8 February

Jesus meets people

A woman who was bleeding

In the crowd was a woman who had been bleeding for twelve years. She had gone to many doctors, and they had not done anything except cause her a lot of pain. She had paid them all the money she had. But instead of getting better, she only got worse. The woman had heard about Jesus, so she came up behind him in the crowd and barely touched his clothes. She had said to herself, 'If I can just touch his clothes, I will get well.' As soon as she touched them, her bleeding stopped, and she knew she was well. At that moment Jesus felt power go out from him. He turned to the crowd and asked, 'Who touched my clothes?' His disciples said to him, 'Look at all these people crowding around you! How can you ask who touched you?' But Jesus turned to see who had touched him. The woman knew what had happened to her. She came shaking with fear and knelt down in front of Jesus. Then she told him the whole story. Jesus said to the woman, 'You are now well because of your faith. May God give you peace! You are healed, and you will no longer be in pain.'

MARK 5:25–34

Refresh

Faith and belief are 'doing' words!

This is my faith. This is my faith. This is my faith. We hear people talk like this all the time—but does it mean anything in reality? These days we usually use the words 'faith' or 'belief' as nouns—'naming' words: *a* faith / belief; *the* faith /belief; *several* faiths / beliefs; *all the major* faiths / beliefs.

The Bible uses the words 'faith' and 'belief' much more as verbs, as 'doing' words. Having faith or believing is something you do—something that must show itself in action, in the way we behave. The Bible even says that if the people around us don't notice the fact that we have faith / believe in Jesus, our faith / belief can be considered dead (James 2:17).

Faith and belief are not found in the heart or in the head. Faith is found in your arms, legs, hands and feet. The woman in today's story is proof of that.

Links: 27 August, 31 August, 1 September, 3 September

5 minutes more? Deuteronomy 1

9 February

Jesus meets people

The first disciples

[1.] The next day, John was there again, and two of his followers were with him. When he saw Jesus walking by, he said, 'Here is the Lamb of God!' John's two followers heard him, and they went with Jesus. When Jesus turned and saw them, he asked, 'What do you want?' They answered, 'Rabbi, where do you live?' The Hebrew word 'Rabbi' means 'Teacher'. Jesus replied, 'Come and see!' ...

[2.] One of the two men who had heard John and had gone with Jesus was Andrew, the brother of Simon Peter. The first thing Andrew did was to find his brother and tell him, 'We have found the Messiah!' The Hebrew word 'Messiah' means the same as the Greek word 'Christ'. Andrew brought his brother to Jesus...

[3.] The next day, Jesus decided to go to Galilee. There he met Philip, who was from Bethsaida, the home town of Andrew and Peter. Jesus said to Philip, 'Come with me.'

[4.] Philip then found Nathanael and said, 'We have found the one that Moses and the Prophets wrote about. He is Jesus... from Nazareth.' Nathanael asked, 'Can anything good come from Nazareth?' Philip answered, 'Come and see.'

JOHN 1:35–46

Di:SaipL

How one becomes several

1. John the Baptist took two friends to meet Jesus. One of them was Andrew.
2. Andrew took his brother, Peter, to meet Jesus.
3. Peter and Andrew met Philip, a friend from home, and introduced him to Jesus.
4. Philip met his friend Nathanael and took him to meet Jesus.

That's how Jesus got his first five disciples.

And that's how Jesus gets new disciples today.

1. By Tom taking Gareth to meet Jesus.
2. Then Gareth takes John with him to meet Jesus.
3. John takes Jade with him.
4. And Jade brings Rachel.

Think of a friend you can pray for—and perhaps one in your youth group, your worship group, your church or school that you can pray with.

Links: 23 August, 26 August, 2 September, 12 October

5 minutes more? Deuteronomy 2

10 February

Jesus meets people

The Samaritan woman (1)

This time [Jesus] had to go through Samaria, and on his way he came to the town of Sychar. It was near the field that Jacob had long ago given to his son Joseph. The well that Joseph had dug was still there, and Jesus sat down beside it because he was tired from travelling. It was midday, and after Jesus' disciples had gone into town to buy some food, a Samaritan woman came to draw water from the well. Jesus asked her, 'Would you please give me a drink of water?' 'You are a Jew,' she replied, 'and I am a Samaritan woman. How can you ask me for a drink of water when Jews and Samaritans won't have anything to do with each other?' Jesus answered, 'You don't know what God wants to give you, and you don't know who is asking you for a drink. If you did, you would ask me for the water that gives life.' ... The woman replied, 'Sir, please give me a drink of that water! Then I won't get thirsty and have to come to this well again.' ... The disciples returned about this time and were surprised to find Jesus talking with a woman. But none of them asked him what he wanted or why he was talking with her.

JOHN 4:4–10, 15, 27

Did you know that...

...there are at least three 'good reasons' why Jesus really shouldn't have talked to this woman?

1. She was a woman. Men and women were not allowed to talk to each other in an open way in public places.
2. She was a Samaritan. The Jews didn't consider the Samaritans to be religious enough. There was a hate relationship between them.
3. She was unpopular. It was midday when this woman came to the well alone. In those days it was normal for the women to go to the well in a group early in the morning, before the sun came up. But this woman was obviously not part of the 'in' crowd—she was definitely 'out'.

Jesus treated everybody he met with respect. He never looked down on anyone—however many 'good' reasons he could have had to do so.

We ought to do the same.

Links: 5 February, 11 February, 1 March, 17 October

5 minutes more? Deuteronomy 3

11 February

Jesus meets people

The Samaritan woman (2)

Jesus told her, 'Go and bring your husband.' The woman answered, 'I don't have a husband.' 'That's right,' Jesus replied, 'you're telling the truth. You don't have a husband. You have already been married five times, and the man you are now living with isn't your husband.' The woman said, 'Sir, I can see that you are a prophet.' ... The woman left her water jar and ran back into town. She said to the people, 'Come and see a man who told me everything I have ever done! Could he be the Messiah?' Everyone in town went out to see Jesus... A lot of Samaritans in that town put their faith in Jesus because the woman had said, 'This man told me everything I have ever done.' They came and asked him to stay in their town, and he stayed on for two days. Many more Samaritans put their faith in Jesus because of what they heard him say. They told the woman, 'We no longer have faith in Jesus just because of what you told us. We have heard him ourselves, and we are certain that he is the Saviour of the world!'

JOHN 4:16–19, 28–30, 39–42

Refresh

Jesus is 'your man', no matter what

There is a neat little point in this story: it doesn't tell us what had gone on between the woman and the five men in her life.

There are two possibilities:

1. Perhaps the woman had sinned—flirted, seduced, married and divorced, married and divorced five times.
2. Perhaps the five men had sinned against her. Perhaps they all in turn had checked her out, used her, been unfaithful and dumped her.

Whatever had happened, the story doesn't tell us anything about it. The point of the story is that Jesus is the man to go to, no matter what the circumstances.

1. Whether it is to have your own sins forgiven
2. Or whether it is to be put back together again because someone has trampled all over you.

Links: 5 February, 10 February, 1 March, 17 October

5 minutes more? Deuteronomy 4

12 February

Moses part 1 (c.1250BC)

Pharaoh begins to hate the Israelites

Many years later a new king came to power. He did not know what Joseph had done for Egypt, and he told the Egyptians:

There are too many of those Israelites in our country, and they are becoming more powerful than we are. If we don't outsmart them, their families will keep growing larger. And if our country goes to war, they could easily fight on the side of our enemies and escape from Egypt.

The Egyptians put slave bosses in charge of the people of Israel and tried to wear them down with hard work. The bosses forced them to build the cities of Pithom and Rameses, where the king could store his supplies. But even though the Israelites were ill-treated, their families grew larger, and they took over more land. Because of this, the Egyptians hated them more than before and made them work so hard that their lives were miserable. The Egyptians were cruel to the people of Israel and forced them to make bricks and to mix mortar and to work in the fields… Finally, the king gave a command to everyone in the nation, 'As soon as a Hebrew boy is born, throw him into the River Nile! But you can let the girls live.'

EXODUS 1:8–14, 22

Di:SaipL

God is wild!

I bet you know what it is like to get stick from people who want to try to tame you—to keep you in line and get you to stop being a Christian… the sort of people who don't like you mentioning that you believe in Jesus. Know what I mean?

You can keep birds in a cage and fish in an aquarium. You can train a dog to do tricks on command—to obey. Even people can be caught, tamed and subdued. History is full of slavery, exploitation and child labour.

But no one can ever tame God. Never, never, never. He is wild. He is holy. He is high and lifted up over the nations. Therefore God's people can never be tamed either!

Links: 2 February, 13 February, 14 February, 3 April

5 minutes more? Deuteronomy 5

13 February

Moses part 1 (c.1250BC)

Moses is put in the river to die

[The Levite woman] later had a baby boy. He was a beautiful child, and she kept him inside for three months. But when she could no longer keep him hidden, she made a basket out of reeds and covered it with tar. She put him in the basket and placed it in the tall grass along the edge of the River Nile. The baby's elder sister stood at a distance to see what would happen to him. About that time one of the king's daughters came down to take a bath in the river, while her servant women walked along the river bank. She saw the basket in the tall grass and sent one of the young women to pull it out of the water. When the king's daughter opened the basket, she saw the baby and felt sorry for him because he was crying. She said, 'This must be one of the Hebrew babies.' At once the baby's elder sister came up and asked, 'Do you want me to get a Hebrew woman to take care of the baby for you?' 'Yes,' the king's daughter answered. So the girl brought the baby's mother, and the king's daughter told her, 'Take care of this child, and I will pay you.' The baby's mother carried him home and took care of him. And when he was old enough, she took him to the king's daughter, who adopted him. She named him Moses because she said, 'I pulled him out of the water.'

EXODUS 2:2–10

Di:SaipL

Let the Lord lead you and trust him to help

One of the things I like about being a Christian is watching how God arranges, directs and sorts things out so that his plans will be fulfilled. God had plans for Moses. He was going to take a part in carrying out the Lord's work. And God arranged everything—sorted it out so that what was planned to happen actually did happen.

God's got plans for you too. Pray today that you will be able to co-operate with his plan for your life. Be open to God today so that he can lead you to people he wants you to help and be the person he wants you to be

PS: I think the way God leads us is amazing—and even irritating! In my experience I have often found it difficult to see what God's plans for my future are, but when I look back, it's always very easy to see that God has directed me. I bet, if you look back on your life in ten years' time, you will see how God has led you to where you are. Whatever happens, 'let the Lord lead you and trust him to help' (Psalm 37:5).

Links: 12 February, 14 February, 15 February, 16 February

5 minutes more? Deuteronomy 6

14 February

Moses part 1 (c.1250BC)

Moses murders an Egyptian and runs away

After Moses had grown up, he went out to where his own people were hard at work, and he saw an Egyptian beating one of them. Moses looked around to see if anyone was watching, then he killed the Egyptian and hid his body in the sand. When Moses went out the next day, he saw two Hebrews fighting. So he went to the man who had started the fight and asked, 'Why are you beating up one of your own people?' The man answered, 'Who put you in charge of us and made you our judge? Are you planning to kill me, just as you killed that Egyptian?' This frightened Moses because he was sure that people must have found out what had happened. When the king heard what Moses had done, the king wanted to kill him. But Moses escaped and went to the land of Midian. One day, Moses was sitting there by a well.

EXODUS 2:11–15

Good news

There's hope for everyone

There wasn't any other—no one. No one else who could have managed it—could have taken Moses the scumbag, the murderer and the coward and made him into the greatest man of God the world has ever seen.

'There has never again been a prophet in Israel like Moses. The Lord spoke face to face with him' (Deuteronomy 34:10).

There isn't any other—no one. No one else who can manage it—to get you to blossom in such a wonderful and meaningful way as God can. If there was hope for Moses, there is hope for you.

Links: 11 January, 15 February, 16 February, 17 November

5 minutes more? Deuteronomy 18

15 February

Moses part 1 (c.1250BC)

The burning bush

One day, Moses was taking care of the sheep and goats of his father-in-law Jethro, the priest of Midian, and Moses decided to lead them across the desert to Sinai, the holy mountain. There an angel of the Lord appeared to him from a burning bush. Moses saw that the bush was on fire, but it was not burning up. 'This is strange!' he said to himself. 'I'll go over and see why the bush isn't burning up.' When the Lord saw Moses coming near the bush, he called him by name, and Moses answered, 'Here I am!' God replied, 'Don't come any closer. Take off your sandals—the ground where you are standing is holy. I am the God who was worshipped by your ancestors Abraham, Isaac, and Jacob.' Moses was afraid to look at God, and so he hid his face. The Lord said:

I have seen how my people are suffering as slaves in Egypt, and I have heard them beg for my help because of the way they are being ill-treated. I feel sorry for them... Now go to the king! I am sending you to lead my people out of his country.

EXODUS 3:1–7, 10

Head, shoulders, knees and toes

Hats in church?

The point is not that Moses had to take off his shoes—or that you might have to take off your baseball cap in church (!) The point is not shoes and hats. The point is awe.

The living God is so, so, so great. He is holy. In his presence you can't do anything other than bow in awe and reverence.

Everyone will experience this sense of awe and reverence one day: 'So at the name of Jesus everyone will bow down, those in heaven, on earth, and under the earth. And to the glory of God the Father everyone will openly agree, 'Jesus Christ is Lord!' (Philippians 2:10–11).

Perhaps you should take a few minutes and kneel by your bed this evening—in awe and reverence.

PS: Awe and reverence can be demonstrated by the feet—but they start in the heart.

Links: 16 February, 9 March, 14 March, 15 March

5 minutes more? Deuteronomy 27

16 February

Moses part 1 (c.1250BC)

God reveals his name to Moses

But Moses said, 'Who am I to go to the king and lead your people out of Egypt?' God replied, ' I will be with you. And you will know that I am the one who sent you, when you worship me on this mountain after you have led my people out of Egypt.' Moses answered, 'I will tell the people of Israel that the God their ancestors worshipped has sent me to them. But what should I say, if they ask me your name?' God said to Moses:

I am the eternal God. So tell them that the Lord, whose name is 'I Am', has sent you. This is my name for ever, and it is the name that people must use from now on.

EXODUS 3:11–15

Check it out

'I Am'

God doesn't say, 'I am the one who will come some time in the future,' or 'I am the one who was a long time ago.' God says, 'I Am.' He is the one who's always there.

A wise man—a philosopher—once said, 'I think, therefore I am.'

Another said, 'I doubt, therefore I am.'

For God, it's good enough for him to say, 'I Am'.

Jesus could be really quite upfront every now and then. For example—check out what he once said when someone claimed that it was impossible for him to be greater than Abraham (John 8:58).

Links: 17 February, 24 February, 8 April, 9 April

5 minutes more? Deuteronomy 28

17 February

Jesus says, 'I am...'

The bread of life

Jesus replied:

I am the bread that gives life! No one who comes to me will ever be hungry. No one who has faith in me will ever be thirsty. I have told you already that you have seen me and still do not have faith in me. Everything and everyone that the Father has given me will come to me, and I won't turn any of them away. I didn't come from heaven to do what I want! I came to do what the Father wants me to do. He sent me, and he wants to make certain that none of the ones he has given me will be lost. Instead, he wants me to raise them to life on the last day. My Father wants everyone who sees the Son to have faith in him and to have eternal life. Then I will raise them to life on the last day...

I am that bread from heaven! Everyone who eats it will live for ever. My flesh is the life-giving bread that I give to the people of this world.

JOHN 6:35–40, 51

Refresh

Access for unauthorized persons

It doesn't say, 'Those who can manage it...'
It doesn't say, 'Those who are without fault...'
It doesn't say, 'Those who consider they are worthy...'
It doesn't say, 'Those who fit the bill...'
It says, '*Those who come to me...*'

One of the many ways to come to Jesus is to go and take Communion at church. There are people who take Communion but don't think much about what they are doing. Obviously that's no good, but it is a minor problem.

What is much worse—much, much worse—is all the people who believe in Jesus but don't come to Communion. Perhaps they feel unworthy or something...

If you know anyone like that, pray that God will help them to know that we can come to Jesus just as we are.

PS: On seven occasions Jesus says, 'I am...' The people who heard him must have thought he was brash and arrogant. 'I Am' was actually God's name (see yesterday). The point is that Jesus was signalling that he, in fact, was God.

Links: 16 February, 21 February, 22 February, 29 August

5 minutes more? Deuteronomy 30

18 February

Jesus says, 'I am...'

The light of the world

Everything that was created received its life from him, and his life gave light to everyone. The light keeps shining in the dark, and darkness has never put it out. God sent a man named John, who came to tell about the light and to lead all people to have faith. John wasn't that light. He came only to tell about the light. The true light that shines on everyone was coming into the world. The Word was in the world, but no one knew him, though God made the world with his Word. He came into his own world, but his own nation did not welcome him. Yet some people accepted him and put their faith in him. So he gave them the right to be the children of God.

JOHN 1:3b–12

Once again Jesus spoke to the people. This time he said, 'I am the light for the world! Follow me, and you won't be walking in the dark. You will have the light that gives life.'

JOHN 8:12

Did you know that...

...light is invisible?

You can't see a beam of light that's travelling through the universe because light is completely invisible. You can only see light when it bumps into something—for example, a particle of dust or a wall or a star. Light needs something to be reflected from before you can see it.

For example... a person.

That person is you!

Live for all to see. Pray for forgiveness often. Be a good reflection—a person God can shine from so that others can see that the light of the world, Jesus, really exists.

Links: 1 January, 16 February, 23 November, 25 December

5 minutes more? Deuteronomy 32

19 February

Jesus says, 'I am...'

The door

Jesus said:

I tell you for certain that I am the door* for the sheep. Everyone who came before me was a thief or a robber, and the sheep did not listen to any of them. I am the door*. All who come in through me will be saved. Through me they will come and go and find pasture. A thief comes only to rob, kill, and destroy. I came so that everyone would have life, and have it fully.

JOHN 10:7–10

*The CEV uses 'gate', but the meaning is the same as 'door'.

I am the one who is holy and true, and I have the keys that belonged to David. When I open a door, no one can close it. And when I close a door, no one can open it. Listen to what I say. I know everything you have done. And I have placed before you an open door that no one can close. You were not very strong, but you obeyed my message and did not deny that you are my followers... Listen! I am standing and knocking at your door. If you hear my voice and open the door, I will come in and we will eat together.

REVELATION 3:7–8, 20

Download...

...about open doors

'And I have placed before you an open door that no one can close. You were not very strong, but you obeyed my message and did not deny that you are my followers' (Revelation 3:8b).

Some walls are impossible to get through. Jesus is no wall. Jesus is a door—an open door. The way to life goes through him. He even said he had come so that we would have life, and have it fully (John 10:10).

Links: 16 February, 20 February, 8 March, 26 December

5 minutes more? Joshua 1

20 February

Jesus says, 'I am...'

The good shepherd

I am the good shepherd, and the good shepherd gives up his life for his sheep. Hired workers are not like the shepherd. They don't own the sheep, and when they see a wolf coming, they run off and leave the sheep. Then the wolf attacks and scatters the flock. Hired workers run away because they don't care about the sheep. I am the good shepherd. I know my sheep, and they know me. Just as the Father knows me, I know the Father, and I give up my life for my sheep. I have other sheep that are not in this sheep pen. I must bring them together too, when they hear my voice. Then there will be one flock of sheep and one shepherd.

JOHN 10:11–16

Christ carried the burden of our sins. He was nailed to the cross, so that we would stop sinning and start living right. By his cuts and bruises you are healed. You had wandered away like sheep. Now you have returned to the one who is your shepherd and protector.

1 PETER 2:24–25

Di:SaipL

Do you hear his voice?

Some people like one style. Other people like a different style. But one thing disciples have in common is that they think it is more important to hear the Shepherd's voice than to get hung up about style issues.

A disciple ought to aim to be able to sit through...

1. A service in a traditional Anglican church with liturgy and even chanted psalms...
2. A celebration in a charismatic church which has lively worship, use of the spiritual gifts and people 'swinging from the chandeliers'...
3. A 'hymn sandwich' in an old people's home where seven old ladies are singing out of tune...

...and be more concerned about hearing the Shepherd's voice than about criticizing one or another style of worship that isn't really their scene.

Links: 16 February, 8 March, 31 May, 12 September

5 minutes more? Joshua 3

21 February

Jesus says, 'I am...'

The resurrection and the life

A man called Lazarus was sick in the village of Bethany. He had two sisters, Mary and Martha. This was the same Mary who later poured perfume on the Lord's head and wiped his feet with her hair. The sisters sent a message to the Lord and told him that his good friend Lazarus was sick...

When Jesus got to Bethany, he found that Lazarus had already been in the tomb four days... Martha said to Jesus, 'Lord, if you had been here, my brother would not have died. Yet even now I know that God will do anything you ask.' Jesus told her, 'Your brother will live again!' Martha answered, 'I know that he will be raised to life on the last day, when all the dead are raised.' Jesus then said, 'I am the one who raises the dead to life! Everyone who has faith in me will live, even if they die. And everyone who lives because of faith in me will never really die. Do you believe this?' 'Yes, Lord!' she replied. 'I believe that you are Christ, the Son of God. You are the one we hoped would come into the world.' ...

When Jesus had finished praying, he shouted, 'Lazarus, come out!' The man who had been dead came out. His hands and feet were wrapped with strips of burial cloth, and a cloth covered his face. Jesus then told the people, 'Untie him and let him go.'

JOHN 11:1–3, 17, 21–27, 43–44

Story

The doctor and the boy with Down's Syndrome

This story is true—you can be sure about that, because a vicar told me it.

There was once a little boy who was in a doctor's surgery.

'When were you born?' asked the doctor.

'Born?' joked the boy. 'When do you mean, the first time or the second time?'

The doctor didn't understand quite what the boy meant, and a puzzled look appeared on his face.

'OK,' said the boy, and began to explain. 'Either you are born once and then you die twice, or you are born twice and you only die once.'

Chew on that one a bit!

Links: 16 February, 26 December, 27 December, 29 December

5 minutes more? Joshua 6

22 February

Jesus says, 'I am...'

The way, the truth and the life

Jesus said to his disciples, 'Don't be worried! Have faith in God and have faith in me. There are many rooms in my Father's house. I wouldn't tell you this, unless it was true. I am going there to prepare a place for each of you. After I have done this, I will come back and take you with me. Then we will be together. You know the way to where I am going.' Thomas said, 'Lord, we don't even know where you are going! How can we know the way?' 'I am the way, the truth, and the life!' Jesus answered. 'Without me, no one can go to the Father. If you had known me, you would have known the Father. But from now on, you do know him, and you have seen him.' Philip said, 'Lord, show us the Father. That is all we need.' Jesus replied:

Philip, I have been with you for a long time. Don't you know who I am? If you have seen me, you have seen the Father. How can you ask me to show you the Father?

JOHN 14:1–9

Di:SaipL

The two ways

There are two ways you can live—how God says or how the world says, God's way or the world's way.

Everybody, and yes, I mean everybody—from your classmates to people on TV—say again and again that the world's way is fun and exciting, everything's possible and permissible and that the future looks good. Just go ahead, because next weekend there's another party.

It can also seem as if everybody's got the impression that God's way is boring and predictable and miserable and strict and serious and 'all they do is sit and pray'. The Bible says that 'everybody'—from your classmates to the people on TV—is wrong. It says that if it's life you're after, then Jesus is the Way.

Links: 13 January, 14 January, 16 February, 31 December

5 minutes more? Joshua 23

23 February

Jesus says, 'I am...'

The vine

[Jesus said,] 'Stay joined to me, and I will stay joined to you. Just as a branch cannot produce fruit unless it stays joined to the vine, you cannot produce fruit unless you stay joined to me. I am the vine, and you are the branches. If you stay joined to me, and I stay joined to you, then you will produce lots of fruit. But you cannot do anything without me. If you don't stay joined to me, you will be thrown away. You will be like dry branches that are gathered up and burnt in a fire. Stay joined to me and let my teachings become part of you. Then you can pray for whatever you want, and your prayer will be answered. When you become fruitful disciples of mine, my Father will be honoured. I have loved you, just as my Father has loved me. So remain faithful to my love for you. If you obey me, I will keep loving you, just as my Father keeps loving me, because I have obeyed him. I have told you this to make you as completely happy as I am.'

JOHN 15:4–11

Weird and wonderful

Grafting Christmas trees

I have an uncle who grows Christmas trees in Norway. Once, when we were visiting him, he picked up a withered branch that was lying on the ground. 'Watch this,' he said. Then he got out a drill and bored a hole in the trunk of a healthy tree. He filled the hole with a sort of jelly before he pushed the dead branch into it. Last of all, he wrapped up the wound with some special tape.

When we came back a year later, the withered branch had obviously begun to take up nutrients. It was alive!

That's the point. Jesus is the tree. We're the withered branches on the ground that God has picked up and grafted into Jesus. We live because of, and only because of, him.

If we stay in him, then he will stay in us. Then we get to live.

Links: 16 February, 19 May, 20 May, 27 August

5 minutes more? Joshua 24

24 February

Names of God

The Lord (Yahweh)

The Lord God told Moses:

...My name is the Lord. But when I appeared to Abraham, Isaac, and Jacob, I came as God All-Powerful and did not use my name.

EXODUS 6:1a, 2–3

Do not misuse my name.

EXODUS 20:7a

Praise the Lord and pray in his name! Tell everyone what he has done. Sing praises to the Lord! Tell about his miracles. Celebrate and worship his holy name with all your heart. Trust the Lord and his mighty power. Worship him always.

1 CHRONICLES 16:8–11

Our Lord, great and powerful, you alone are God.

JEREMIAH 10:6

Weird and wonderful

YHWH

The Old Testament was written in Hebrew—a strange language. When you write Hebrew, you only write the consonants. (When you read Hebrew, you pronounce both the vowels and the consonants, but you have to remember what the vowels are and put them in the right place.)

For example, 'YHWH' is God's name in Hebrew. The problem was, however, that the Jews had such incredibly great respect for God's name that for hundreds of years they avoided speaking out his name when they read the scriptures to each other. Instead they used a word that was a little less holy and meant 'my Lord'.

Eventually they forgot how God's name was pronounced. And we have struggled with it from that day to this. Jehovah's Witnesses think YHWH should be pronounced YeHoWaH—that is 'Jehovah'. Most Bible scholars think it should be pronounced YaHWeH—that is 'Yahweh'. It doesn't really matter, because, in any case, YHWH in English means 'the Lord'.

PS: 'God Almighty' isn't primarily a swear word. It is a name.

Links: 23 January, 16 February, 8 April, 31 December

5 minutes more? Judges 5

25 February

Names of God

The Almighty God (El Shaddai)

Can you understand the mysteries surrounding God All-Powerful?
JOB 11:7

If any of you are clever, you will listen and learn that God All-Powerful does what is right. God always treats everyone the way they deserve, and he is never unfair. From the very beginning, God has been in control of all the world. If God took back the breath that he breathed into us, we humans would die and return to the soil. So be wise and listen!
JOB 34:10–16

God cannot be seen—but his power is great, and he is always fair. And so we humans fear God, because he shows no respect for those who are proud and think they know so much.
JOB 37:23–24

Listen to your heart and fill in

What do you want Jesus to do for you?

If you've been to Sunday school or Bible class, you'll know that when Jesus met ordinary people he often asked them, 'What is it that you want me to do for you?' God the Almighty, the All-Powerful—has the power to do so much.

What would you like God to do for you in the days ahead?

1. ______________________________

2. ______________________________

3. ______________________________

Links: 26 February, 4 April, 25 April, 19 September

5 minutes more? Judges 6

Lord of Hosts (Sabaoth)

I had a vision of the Lord. He was on his throne high above, and his robe filled the temple. Flaming creatures with six wings each were flying over him. They covered their faces with two of their wings and their bodies with two more. They used the other two wings for flying, as they shouted, 'Holy, holy, holy, Lord All-Powerful! The earth is filled with your glory.' … Then I cried out, 'I'm doomed! Everything I say is sinful, and so are the words of everyone around me. Yet I have seen the King, the Lord All-Powerful.' … After this, I heard the Lord ask, 'Is there anyone I can send? Will someone go for us?' 'I'll go,' I answered. 'Send me!' Then the Lord told me to go and speak this message to the people: 'You will listen and listen, but never understand. You will look and look, but never see.'
ISAIAH 6:1b–3, 5, 8–9

Jesus came to them and said:

I have been given all authority in heaven and on earth! Go to the people of all nations and make them my disciples. Baptize them in the name of the Father, the Son, and the Holy Spirit, and teach them to do everything I have told you. I will be with you always, even until the end of the world.
MATTHEW 28:18–20

Good news

The most phenomenal manager in the world

As Christians we have the world's most phenomenal manager. He not only has all the power in the world, but all the power in heaven too. Do you remember—when Jesus was born, an angel came to the shepherds and said, 'Don't be afraid, I have good news for you, which will make everyone happy' (Luke 2:10).

Later in the story it says, 'Suddenly many other angels came down from heaven and joined in praising God. They said, 'Praise God in heaven!' (Luke 2:13–14). The place was crawling with angels, seething with them. And the manager, the commander of all the armies of angels is—you got it—Almighty God, the Lord of Hosts. And like all good managers, God is busy talent-spotting. He asks, 'Is there anyone I can send? Will someone go for us?'

You must make a choice. I have already made mine. I've signed up—and I've got the most phenomenal manager in the world.

Links: 18 August, 16 November, 24 December, 30 December

5 minutes more? Judges 13

27 February

Names of God

King (1)

Who is this glorious king? He is our Lord, the All-Powerful! ... The Lord rules on his throne, king of the flood for ever... God rules the nations from his sacred throne... The Lord is the greatest God, king over all other gods.
PSALM 24:10; 29:10; 47:8; 95:3

I am the Lord All-Powerful, the first and the last, the one and only God.
ISAIAH 44:6

Then I heard what seemed to be a large crowd that sounded like a roaring flood and loud thunder all mixed together. They were saying, 'Praise the Lord! Our Lord God All-Powerful now rules as king.'
REVELATION 19:6

Hmm... just a thought

To all you girls:

If your Father is a king, doesn't that mean that you're a princess?

Links: 11 March, 24 March, 16 July, 29 December

5 minutes more? Judges 14

28 February

Names of God

The zealous one

I demand your complete loyalty—you must not worship any other god!
EXODUS 34:14

Do not make idols that look like anything in the sky or on earth or in the sea under the earth. Don't bow down and worship idols. I am the Lord your God, and I demand all your love. If you reject me, I will punish your families for three or four generations. But if you love me and obey my laws, I will be kind to your families for thousands of generations.
EXODUS 20:4–6

Worship and obey the Lord your God with fear and trembling, and promise that you will be loyal to him. Don't have anything to do with gods that are worshipped by the nations around you. If you worship other gods, the Lord will be furious and wipe you off the face of the earth.
DEUTERONOMY 6:13–15a

Big word

Zealous

God is zealous. To be zealous is almost the same as being jealous. Let me explain. We are God's children, God's beloved children, and because he loves us so much, he has incredibly strong feelings for us. When we give other people first place in our lives and depend on them more than on him, then his zeal is stirred into life. God hates being pushed aside. He wants to have first place. He wants our love, devotion and attention. God has 'loved us so much that he made us alive with Christ', although 'we were dead because of our sins' (Ephesians 2:4–5). That's why he can't quite see why we don't love him back just as much.

Everyone who has known unrequited love knows a little of what this feeling is like. There aren't many things that cause more pain than knowing that the one you love doesn't love you back, that the one you would most like to go out with doesn't want to go out with you. God knows what unrequited love is like. He is zealous.

PS: If you've been dumped or rejected, it's good to know that no one understands better than God!

Links: 21 May, 13 June, 1 August, 3 December

5 minutes more? Judges 15

1 March

Names of God

The God who sees me

Hagar stopped to rest at a spring in the desert on the road to Shur. While she was there, an angel of the Lord came to her and asked, 'Hagar, where have you come from, and where are you going?' She answered, 'I am running away from Sarai, my owner.' The angel said, 'Go back to Sarai and be her slave. I will give you a son, who will be called Ishmael, because I have heard your cry for help. And later I will give you so many descendants that no one will be able to count them all.' ... Hagar thought, 'Have I really seen God and lived to tell about it?' So from then on she called him, 'The God Who Sees Me'.

GENESIS 16:7–11, 13

You have looked deep into my heart, Lord, and you know all about me. You know when I am resting or when I am working, and from heaven you discover my thoughts. You notice everything I do and everywhere I go. Before I even speak a word, you know what I will say, and with your powerful arm you protect me from every side. I can't understand all this! Such wonderful knowledge is far above me.

PSALM 139:1–6

Good news

See and be seen!

The first name of all the names God was given wasn't 'King' or 'Almighty' or 'Lord' or anything like that. It was 'The God who sees me'.

Hagar was a slave girl. Her owner, Abraham's wife Sarai, got irritated with her and drove her off into the desert. Hagar was frightened and alone. She was pregnant too. God met her when she needed it most. He helped her. It was then that Hagar gave God the name 'The God who sees me'.

I hope you know that God sees you. I hope you feel seen. Check out what it says in 1 Samuel 16:7 about how God looks at us: 'People judge others by what they look like, but I judge people by what is in their hearts.'

Links: 10 February, 11 February, 2 March, 26 May

5 minutes more? Judges 16

2 March

Names of God

The mighty one

Our Lord, great and powerful, you alone are God.
JEREMIAH 10:6

The Lord is the greatest God, king over all other gods. He holds the deepest part of the earth in his hands, and the mountain peaks belong to him. The ocean is the Lord's because he made it, and with his own hands he formed the dry land. Bow down and worship the Lord our creator!
PSALM 95:3–6

Mary said: With all my heart I praise the Lord, and I am glad because of God my Saviour. He cares for me, his humble servant. From now on, all people will say God has blessed me. God All-Powerful has done great things for me, and his name is holy.
LUKE 1:46–49

Listen to your heart and fill in

Time for your testimony

In the pure joy of what God has done for her, Mary exclaims, 'God All-Powerful has done great things for me!' What great things has God done for you?

1. ______________________________

2. ______________________________

3. ______________________________

Use a bit of time to thank God for the small things and the big things that he has done in your life.

Links: 24 February, 25 February, 4 April, 28 August

5 minutes more? Ruth 1

The mighty rock

Join with me in praising the wonderful name of the Lord our God. The Lord is a mighty rock, and he never does wrong. God can always be trusted to bring justice.
DEUTERONOMY 32:3–4

Hannah prayed: You make me strong and happy, Lord. You rescued me. Now I can be glad and laugh at my enemies. No other god is like you. We're safer with you than on a high mountain.
1 SAMUEL 2:1–2

You are my mighty rock, my fortress, my protector, the rock where I am safe, my shield, my powerful weapon, and my place of shelter... You alone are God! Only you are a mighty rock.
PSALM 18:2, 31

Weird and wonderful

Mountains

It might seem like God's got a thing about mountains:

- God is called both a rock and a mountain.
- Moses received the ten commandments on a mountain (Exodus 19:20).
- Jesus is called 'the living stone' (1 Peter 2:4).
- He is also called a stone which people stumble over and a cornerstone (Romans 9:33; 1 Peter 2:6, 8).
- Jesus liked being in the mountains (Matthew 14:23).
- Jesus' only sermon is called the Sermon on the Mount—because he gave it on a mountain (Matthew 5:1).
- One of the things he mentioned in that sermon was about building on rock and not on sand (Matthew 7:24–27).
- Jesus and some of his disciples had a vision on a mountain (Matthew 17:1).
- Jesus ascended into heaven from a mountain (Acts 1:12).
- The leader of the disciples was Peter—his name means 'rock' (Matthew 16:18).
- *You* even are called a 'living stone': 'you are living stones that are being used to build a spiritual house' (1 Peter 2:5).

The last point implies that God must have a thing about *you* too!

Links: 4 March, 5 March, 13 August, 16 September

5 minutes more? Ruth 2

4 March

Names of God

My protector

You are my mighty rock, my fortress, my protector, the rock where I am safe, my shield, my powerful weapon, and my place of shelter... You, Lord, are the light that keeps me safe. I am not afraid of anyone. You protect me, and I have no fears... Protect me from hidden traps and keep me safe... If you honour the Lord, his angel will protect you...

Save me, God! Protect me from enemy attacks! ... Listen to my concerns, God, and protect me from my terrible enemies... You are my place of safety and my shield. Your word is my only hope... Rescue me from cruel and violent enemies, Lord!

PSALM 18:2; 27:1; 31:4; 34:7; 59:1; 64:1; 119:114; 140:1

Good news

God is a protector when things get difficult

If up to now you haven't had a particularly tough time in life, it won't be strange if the idea of God being a protector doesn't mean all that much to you.

But if you run into difficult times of some sort, it is great to have stored up somewhere in the back of your mind (for your own safety and protection) the knowledge that God is a protector. You might also want to store away the fact that God is called 'refuge', 'shield', 'rock', 'rescuer' and 'saviour'.

If you've already run into heavy weather, you'll know what I mean, so I won't bother hassling you further!

Links: 3 March, 5 March, 22 June, 24 June

5 minutes more? Ruth 3

5 March

Names of God

My place of safety (refuge)

Discover for yourself that the Lord is kind. Come to him for protection, and you will be glad.

PSALM 34:8

Live under the protection of God Most High and stay under the shadow of God All-Powerful. Then you will say to the Lord, 'You are my fortress, my place of safety; you are my God, and I trust you.' ...

He will spread his wings over you and keep you secure. His faithfulness is like a shield or a city wall. You won't need to worry about dangers at night or arrows during the day...

The Lord Most High is your fortress. Run to him for safety, and no terrible disasters will strike you or your home. God will command his angels to protect you wherever you go. They will carry you in their arms, and you won't hurt your feet on the stones.

PSALM 91:1–2, 4–5, 9–12

Download

Discover for yourself...

Here is a verse written by someone who has sought safety and taken refuge in the Lord and who recommends that others do the same. Learn the verse and then discover its truth for yourself!

'Discover for yourself that the Lord is kind. Come to him for protection, and you will be glad' (Psalm 34:8).

Links: 20 April, 7 July, 28 August, 30 August

5 minutes more? Ruth 4

6 March

Names of God

The Lord Most High

Make them realize that you are the Lord Most High, the only ruler of earth!
PSALM 83:18

It is wonderful to be grateful and to sing your praises, Lord Most High! It is wonderful each morning to tell about your love and at night to announce how faithful you are. I enjoy praising your name to the music of harps, because everything you do makes me happy, and I sing joyful songs. You do great things, Lord. Your thoughts are too deep for an ignorant fool to know or understand.
PSALM 92:1–6

Our holy God lives for ever in the highest heavens, and this is what he says:

Though I live high above in the holy place, I am here to help those who are humble and depend only on me.
ISAIAH 57:15

Good news

Big and little at the same time

We live on the earth, which travels round the sun along with the handful of other planets that are part of our solar system. There are 100 million solar systems in our galaxy, the Milky Way. The research scientists believe there are at least 100 million galaxies out there, and most believe there are even more than that. Many scientists believe that outer space is unending.

Behind all this, above all this, beyond all this, greater than all this is the Lord Most High.

Read the verse from Isaiah again and check out where the Lord Most High lives. He lives high above in the holy place. But he doesn't only live there—and this is the good news for today. He also lives with those who are humble and depend only on him.

Links: 28 June, 4 November, 5 November, 29 December

5 minutes more? 1 Samuel 1

7 March

Names of God

The Creator

Be cheerful and enjoy life while you are young! Do what you want and find pleasure in what you see. But don't forget that God will judge you for everything that you do. Rid yourself of all worry and pain, because the wonderful moments of youth quickly disappear. Keep your Creator in mind while you are young! In years to come, you will be burdened down with troubles and say, 'I don't enjoy life any more.' …

The silver cord snaps, the golden bowl breaks; the water pitcher is smashed, and the pulley at the well is shattered. So our bodies return to the earth, and the life-giving breath returns to God.

ECCLESIASTES 11:9—12:1, 6–7

Refresh

Time flies

You're bound to have heard the expression, 'Time flies when you're having fun.' But I can promise you that time flies whatever you're doing, even when things are boring. A lesson at school can drag, but life runs away with itself at a maddening pace. Suddenly (whoosh!) we're old and grey at the edges.

Use time wisely. Too many people allow themselves to get bored and couldn't care less, lose all their drive and never make a go of anything.

You've been put here on earth to bring glory to God, live life to the full and to help others. Make sure that the world is in a better state when you leave it than when you arrived. The advice we get from one of the psalm writers in the Bible is, 'Teach us to use wisely all the time we have' (Psalm 90:12).

Remember: a day spent hand-in-hand with God is never wasted.

Links: 1 January, 18 January, 5 November, 25 December

5 minutes more? 1 Samuel 2

8 March

Names of God

The good shepherd

You, Lord, are my shepherd. I will never be in need. You let me rest in fields of green grass. You lead me to streams of peaceful water, and you refresh my life. You are true to your name, and you lead me along the right paths. I may walk through valleys as dark as death, but I won't be afraid. You are with me, and your shepherd's rod makes me feel safe. You treat me to a feast, while my enemies watch. You honour me as your guest, and you fill my cup until it overflows. Your kindness and love will always be with me each day of my life, and I will live for ever in your house, Lord.

PSALM 23

Di:SaipL

You sheep, you!

If the Lord is your shepherd, then you're a sheep!

It's actually mega-important to keep saying to yourself, 'I'm a sheep! I'm a sheep! I'm a sheep!' because if you forget it, then you're in danger of forgetting that you need a shepherd, and then you can also suddenly forget that you need a saviour, and then—then everything goes down the drain.

As long as we remain sheep, we conquer. Even if we are surrounded by a thousand wolves, we conquer. But as soon as we become wolves, we are conquered, because we lose the protection of the Shepherd who only feeds sheep and not wolves.

JOHN CHRYSOSTOM (AD345–407)

Baaaaaaaaaaaa!

Links: 19 February, 20 February, 24 May, 26 May

5 minutes more? 1 Samuel 3

9 March

Names of God

The holy one

Yet you are the holy God, ruling from your throne and praised by Israel.
PSALM 22:3

Respect and obey the Lord! This is the beginning of wisdom. To have understanding, you must know the Holy God.
PROVERBS 9:10

I am the Lord, your holy God, Israel's Creator and King.
ISAIAH 43:15

There in the Jewish meeting place was a man with an evil spirit. He yelled out, 'Hey, Jesus of Nazareth, what do you want with us? Are you here to get rid of us? I know who you are! You are God's Holy One.' Jesus ordered the evil spirit to be quiet and come out. The demon threw the man to the ground in front of everyone and left without harming him. They all were amazed and kept saying to each other, 'What kind of teaching is this? He has power to order evil spirits out of people!' News about Jesus spread all over that part of the country.
LUKE 4:33–37

Did you know that...

...in the beginning Christians weren't called 'Christians'—they were usually called 'the holy ones'?

Holy is not the same as boring.

Holy is not the same as solemn and serious.

Holy means (1) being separated from sin and (2) being committed to God.

Paul begins almost all of his letters with 'Dear holy ones' (literally *hagioi*—'the set-apart ones', that is, 'saints'). He calls the first Christians 'the holy ones'. Paul understood that as Christians we are (1) freed from sin and (2) committed to God.

You won't become boring by being a Christian, or solemn and serious either. But you're bound to become holy!

Links: 8 April, 9 April, 30 July, 31 August

5 minutes more? 1 Samuel 9

10 March

Names of God

The Judge

You see that justice is done, and each day you take revenge.

PSALM 7:11

His greatest joy will be to obey the Lord. This king won't judge by appearances ot listen to rumours. The poor and the needy will be treated with fairness and with justice. His word will be law everywhere in the land, and criminals will be put to death. Honesty and fairness will be his royal robes.

ISAIAH 11:3–5

In the past, God forgave all this because people did not know what they were doing. But now he says that everyone everywhere must turn to him. He has set a day when he will judge the world's people with fairness. And he has chosen the man Jesus to do the judging for him. God has given proof of this to all of us by raising Jesus from death.

ACTS 17:30–31

Refresh

Think big

The oldest Christian sermon of all is quoted in a manuscript which is called the second letter of Clement. This sermon was given around AD100. It begins like this:

Brothers and sisters, we should think of Jesus Christ in the same way as if he was God, the judge of the living and the dead. And we shouldn't think too little of our salvation either.

Jesus has taken over the job of Judge from the Father. He is the one who will one day judge the living and the dead—all bad people, all deceitful people, all unrighteous people. Fortunately it is Jesus who will do the judging, the one who has said he will pardon all those who believe.

This is not a small, trivial matter. Think big!

Links: 5 February, 21 July, 10 September, 30 December

5 minutes more? 1 Samuel 16

11 March

Names of God

King (2)

The Lord rules on his throne, king of the flood for ever.
PSALM 29:10

Pilate asked Jesus, 'Are you the king of the Jews?' 'Those are your words,' Jesus answered.
LUKE 23:3

I looked and saw that heaven was open, and a white horse was there. Its rider was called Faithful and True, and he is always fair when he judges or goes to war. He had eyes like flames of fire, and he was wearing a lot of crowns. His name was written on him, but he was the only one who knew what the name meant. The rider wore a robe that was covered with blood, and he was known as 'The Word of God'. He was followed by armies from heaven that rode on horses and were dressed in pure white linen. From his mouth a sharp sword went out to attack the nations. He will rule them with an iron rod and will show the fierce anger of God All-Powerful by trampling on the grapes in the pit where wine is made. On the part of the robe that covered his thigh was written, 'KING OF KINGS AND LORD OF LORDS'.
REVELATION 19:11–16

Di:SaipL

You will inherit the kingdom

In fairytales there is usually some one or other who wins the hand of the princess in marriage and half of her father's kingdom.

The Christian life is not a fairytale. This is reality. In reality, it isn't some Cinderella or Aladdin type who inherits the kingdom. In reality, it is you!

Galatians 3:29 says, 'So if you belong to Christ, you are now part of Abraham's family, and you will be given (inherit) what God has promised' (translator's parentheses).

Live today as if you belong to Christ—the King of kings.

Links: 27 February, 16 July, 5 November, 31 December

5 minutes more? 1 Samuel 17

12 March

Names of God

Redeemer

I know that my Saviour [Redeemer] lives, and at the end he will stand on this earth. My flesh may be destroyed, yet from this body I will see God. Yes, I will see him for myself, and I long for that moment.

JOB 19:25–27

By your teachings, Lord, I am warned; by obeying them, I am greatly rewarded. None of us know our faults. Forgive me when I sin without knowing it. Don't let me do wrong on purpose, Lord, or let sin have control over my life. Then I will be innocent, and not guilty of some terrible fault. Let my words and my thoughts be pleasing to you, Lord, because you are my mighty rock and my protector (Redeemer).

PSALM 19:11–14

Big word

Redeemer

'Redeemer' is really only an old-fashioned word for someone who sets people free. A redeemer was a relative who bought you back if you'd been made a slave, or someone who took care of you if you'd been so unfortunate as to lose your parents. Check out Boaz as an example of a redeemer (23 September).

God is our Redeemer. He sets people free—mainly from sin.

If you've been a Christian for a while, you've probably noticed that some sins are so downright unbelievably impossible to shake off, put aside and get rid of—no matter how much you try and try and try and try. They're in your face over and over again.

If that's happening to you, then you know for sure that you need a redeemer. We can't set ourselves free—but God, our Redeemer, can.

Links: 4 February, 13 March, 30 August, 1 December

5 minutes more? 2 Samuel 2

13 March

Names of God

Saviour

Why am I discouraged? Why am I restless? I trust you! And I will praise you again because you help me, and you are (my Saviour and) my God.
PSALM 42:5

Why am I discouraged? Why am I restless? I trust you! And I will praise you again because you help me, and you are (my Saviour and) my God.
PSALM 42:11

Why am I discouraged? Why am I restless? I trust you! And I will praise you again because you help me, and you are (my Saviour and) my God.
PSALM 43:5

I alone am the Lord; only I can rescue you.
ISAIAH 43:11

Listen to your heart and fill in

Name above all names

Over the last few days you have read about the many names of God. Put a star next to the three names you like best. Tick the ones that you didn't already know.

I AM
The Lord / Yahweh
The Almighty / El Shaddai
Lord of Hosts / Sabaoth
King
Zealous one
The God who sees me
Mighty one
Mighty rock
My protector
My place of safety (refuge)
Lord Most High
Creator
Good shepherd
Holy one
Judge
Redeemer
Saviour

PS: A beloved God has many names. Use these names when you pray. You don't need to say 'God' all the time, you know.

Links: 28 August, 14 September, 15 September, 16 September

5 minutes more? 2 Samuel 7

14 March

Moses part 2 (c.1250BC)

God sends Moses back to Egypt

God said to Moses:

I am the eternal God. So tell them that the Lord, whose name is 'I Am', has sent you. This is my name for ever, and it is the name that people must use from now on. Call together the leaders of Israel and tell them that the God who was worshipped by Abraham, Isaac, and Jacob has appeared to you. Tell them I have seen how terribly they are being treated in Egypt, and I promise to lead them out of their troubles. I will give them a land rich with milk and honey, where the Canaanites, Hittites, Amorites, Perizzites, Hivites, and Jebusites now live. The leaders of Israel will listen to you. Then you must take them to the king of Egypt and say, 'The Lord God of the Hebrews has appeared to us. Let us walk three days into the desert, where we can offer a sacrifice to him.'

EXODUS 3:15–18

Did you know that...

... the Pope had to endorse The Prince of Egypt?

DreamWorks Pictures thought the story of Moses, the slave who liberated all his people from captivity, was so good that they invested a good deal of resources in making it into an animated feature film. It wouldn't be an over-estimation to say that 350 artists, animators and technicians from 35 different countries spent four years making *The Prince of Egypt*. That's about 1,600 years of work in all!

Before *The Prince of Egypt* was premièred, they were so worried about treading on anyone's toes that they asked several hundred church leaders to endorse the movie—including the Pope.

The original version—uncut and uncensored—is in the Bible!

Links: 16 February, 15 March, 16 March, 17 March

5 minutes more? 2 Samuel 7

15 March

Moses part 2 (c.1250BC)

Moses didn't like speaking

Moses replied, 'I have never been a good speaker. I wasn't one before you spoke to me, and I'm not one now. I am slow at speaking, and I can never think of what to say.' But the Lord answered, 'Who makes people able to speak or makes them deaf or unable to speak? Who gives them sight or makes them blind? Don't you know that I am the one who does these things? Now go! When you speak, I will be with you and give you the words to say.' Moses begged, 'Lord, please send someone else to do it.' The Lord became irritated with Moses and said:

What about your brother Aaron, the Levite? I know he is a good speaker. He is already on his way here to visit you, and he will be happy to see you again. Aaron will speak to the people for you.

EXODUS 4:10–15a

♡ Listen to your heart and fill in...

Excuses

We typically have many excuses up our sleeves—loads of good reasons why God ought to ask someone else to do what we should be doing. We just don't want to be asked!

What are your best excuses for not doing what God wants you to?

1. ______________________________

2. ______________________________

3. ______________________________

Pray that God would sort your excuses out one way or another. If God is calling you to do something special, it's because he believes you can do it—because he knows you are perfect for the job. He'll deal with the rest.

Links: 16 March, 17 March, 18 March, 19 March

5 minutes more? 2 Samuel 11

16 March

Moses part 2 (c.1250BC)

Moses and Aaron go to Pharaoh together

So Moses put his wife and sons on donkeys and headed for Egypt… The Lord said:

I am going to let your brother Aaron speak for you. He will tell your message to the king, just as a prophet speaks my message to the people. Tell Aaron everything I say to you, and he will order the king to let my people leave his country. But I will make the king so stubborn that he won't listen to you. He won't listen even when I do many terrible things to him and his nation. Then I will bring a final punishment on Egypt, and the king will let Israel's families and tribes go. When this happens, the Egyptians will know that I am the Lord.

Moses and Aaron obeyed the Lord and spoke to the king. At the time, Moses was eighty years old, and Aaron was eighty-three.

EXODUS 4:20a; 7:1–7

☆ Bible personality

Aaron

Aaron was Moses' elder brother. Since Moses didn't like talking in front of people in public places, Aaron went with him. Everything that Moses heard from God, Aaron passed on to the people or to Pharaoh. Aaron was the first 'priest'. Among other things, it was Aaron who was given the message to pronounce this blessing for the first time.

The Lord bless you and keep you!
The Lord make his face shine upon you and be gracious to you!
The Lord turn his face towards you and give you peace!

NUMBERS 6:24–26 (NIV)

This is why it is called the 'Aaronic Blessing'.

PS: Moses was 80 and Aaron was 83 when all this happened—in God's kingdom, age is not a hindrance. Young or old, he can use you!

Links: 17 March, 18 March, 19 March, 20 March

5 minutes more? 2 Samuel 12

17 March

Moses part 2 (c.1250BC)

Pharaoh hardens his heart

The Lord said, 'Moses, when the king asks you and Aaron to perform a miracle, command Aaron to throw his walking stick down in front of the king, and it will turn into a snake.' Moses and Aaron went to the king and his officials and did exactly as the Lord had commanded—Aaron threw the stick down, and it turned into a snake. Then the king called in the wise men and the magicians, who used their secret powers to do the same thing—they threw down sticks that turned into snakes. But Aaron's snake swallowed theirs. The king behaved just as the Lord had said and stubbornly refused to listen.

EXODUS 7:8–13

But your ancestors refused to listen. They were stubborn, and whenever I wanted them to go one way, they always went the other.

JEREMIAH 7:24

Big word

Stubborn / hard-hearted

Here comes a question that needs a yes / no answer: 'Are you too stubborn and hard-hearted?'

This is a sort of trick question. If you said 'Yes', then you probably aren't. But if you answered 'No', then it might be that you are. Get it?

If we harden our hearts and become stubborn, we could end up like Pharaoh and not realize that God is trying to say something to us. Pray that God will protect your heart, and keep it big and soft, warm and compassionate.

Links: 18 March, 19 March, 20 March, 30 July

5 minutes more? 2 Samuel 22

18 March

Moses part 2 (c.1250BC)

The plagues

The Lord told Moses to get up early the next morning and say to the king:

The Lord God of the Hebrews commands you to let his people go, so they can worship him! If you don't, he will send his worst plagues to strike you, your officials, and everyone else in your country. Then you will find out that no one can oppose the Lord.

EXODUS 9:13–14

He turned the rivers of Egypt into blood, and no one could drink from the streams. He sent swarms of flies to pester the Egyptians, and he sent frogs to cause them trouble. God let worms and grasshoppers eat their crops. He destroyed their grapevines and their fig trees with hail and floods. Then he killed their cattle with hail and their other animals with lightning. God was so angry and furious that he went into a rage and caused them great trouble by sending swarms of destroying angels. God gave in to his anger and slaughtered them in a terrible way. He killed the firstborn son of each Egyptian family.

PSALM 78:44–51

#öfi#%/$&!!?!

Beyond our understanding

There isn't any point at all in trying to explain all this. Pharaoh refused and refused and refused to let the people go. Moses didn't give in. The Lord sent plagues, lots of plagues, terrible plagues. But Pharaoh kept on refusing...

Links: 19 March, 20 March, 19 September, 20 September

5 minutes more? 2 Samuel 23

19 March

Moses part 2 (c.1250BC)

All the firstborn in Egypt are killed

Moses went to the king and said:

I have come to let you know what the Lord is going to do. About midnight he will go through the land of Egypt, and wherever he goes, the firstborn son in every family will die. Your own son will die, and so will the son of the lowest slave woman. Even the firstborn males of cattle will die. Everywhere in Egypt there will be loud crying. Nothing like this has ever happened before or will ever happen again. But there won't be any need for the Israelites to cry. Things will be so quiet that not even a dog will be heard barking. Then you Egyptians will know that the Lord is good to the Israelites, even while he punishes you. Your leaders will come and bow down, begging me to take my people and leave your country. Then we will leave.

Moses was very angry; he turned and left the king... So the king of Egypt saw Moses and Aaron work miracles, but the Lord made him stubbornly refuse to let the Israelites leave his country.

EXODUS 11:4–8, 10

☆ Bible personality

Pharaoh

Pharaoh isn't the name of a person. It is a title—a royal title—except that a pharaoh was in*cred*ibly mightier than a king is today.

You can imagine how mighty they were, the pharaohs, when you look at the pyramids in Egypt. A pharaoh didn't just get a grey gravestone or a little burial chamber—oh, no, a pharaoh got his own little pyramid to be buried in!

Many people believed that when a pharaoh died he became a god—a sun god ('pharaoh' means 'sun'). This meant that he was almost considered as a god while he was still alive.

But the story of Moses shows that, compared with God, Pharaoh was very insignificant.

Links: 18 March, 20 March, 3 April, 4 April

5 minutes more? 1 Kings 1

Moses part 2 (c.1250BC)

God: 'Brush blood on the doorposts'

Moses called the leaders of Israel together and said:

Each family is to pick out a sheep and kill it for Passover. Make a brush from a few small branches of a hyssop plant and dip the brush in the bowl that has the blood of the animal in it. Then brush some of the blood above the door and on the posts at each side of the door of your house. After this, everyone is to stay inside. During the night the Lord will go through the country of Egypt and kill the firstborn son in every Egyptian family. He will see where you have put the blood, and he will not come into your house. His angel that brings death will pass over and not kill your firstborn sons...

Your children will ask you, 'What are we celebrating?' And you will answer, 'The Passover animal is killed to honour the Lord. We do these things because on that night long ago the Lord passed over the homes of our people in Egypt. He killed the firstborn sons of the Egyptians, but he saved our children from death.'

After Moses finished speaking, the people of Israel knelt down and worshipped the Lord.

EXODUS 12:21–23, 26–27

Check it out

Hyssop

Hyssop is a kind of tree, an unusual kind of tree. One of the few times it is mentioned in the Bible is here.

Another time hyssop is mentioned is when Jesus was crucified. It is quite significant that when Jesus was crucified and a soldier offered him wine vinegar—partly out of concern, partly to tease—he used a hyssop branch (so that the sponge of wine would reach up to Jesus on the cross—see John 19:29). The soldier had no idea that what he was doing was deeply symbolic.

One thousand years before Jesus died, the psalmist wrote: 'Wash me with hyssop until I am clean and whiter than snow' (Psalm 51:7).

Can you figure out the prophetic symbolism? Thinking about it gives me shivers down my spine...

Links: 21 March, 2 April, 13 July, 7 November

5 minutes more? 1 Kings 2

21 March

Easter

Jesus, Lamb of God

The next day, John saw Jesus coming towards him and said:

Here is the Lamb of God who takes away the sin of the world! He is the one I told you about when I said, 'Someone else will come. He is greater than I am, because he was alive before I was born.' … I was there and saw the Spirit come down on him like a dove from heaven. And the Spirit stayed on him… I saw this happen, and I tell you that he is the Son of God.

JOHN 1:29–30, 32, 34

As I looked, I heard the voices of a lot of angels around the throne and the voices of the living creatures and of the elders. There were millions and millions of them, and they were saying in a loud voice, 'The Lamb who was killed is worthy to receive power, riches, wisdom, strength, honour, glory, and praise.'

REVELATION 5:11–12

Check it out

Why lambs aren't sacrificed any longer

1. While the people of Israel were still in Egypt, they were told to sacrifice a lamb—a Passover lamb. (Read yesterday's text again if you have time.)
2. Doing this would save them.
3. Later on in history, they regularly sacrificed a lamb as a sin offering in the temple.
4. One reason they did this was to remind themselves that sin has consequences.
5. Why aren't lambs sacrificed any longer? Because Jesus sacrificed his life once and for all.
6. That's why he's called the Lamb of God.
7. His sacrifice saves us.

Check out these two verses:

'Our Passover lamb is Christ, who has already been sacrificed' (1 Corinthians 5:7b).

'Then Christ went once for all into the most holy place and freed us from sin for ever. He did this by offering his own blood instead of the blood of goats and bulls' (Hebrews 9:12).

Links: 17 July, 18 July, 21 August, 18 November

5 minutes more? 1 Kings 3

22 March

Easter

Prophecy about God's suffering servant

He suffered and endured great pain for us, but we thought his suffering was punishment from God. He was wounded and crushed because of our sins; by taking our punishment, he made us completely well. All of us were like sheep that had wandered off. We had each gone our own way, but the Lord gave him the punishment we deserved. He was painfully abused, but he did not complain... The Lord decided his servant would suffer as a sacrifice to take away the sin and the guilt of others. Now the servant will live to see his own descendants. He did everything the Lord had planned.

ISAIAH 53:4–7a, 10

Did you know that...

...seven-branched candlesticks have a symbolic meaning for Jews and Christians?

Both Jews and Christians believe in the Messiah, but the Jews don't believe that the Messiah has come yet. We Christians believe that Jesus is the Messiah.

Both Jews and Christians use seven-branched candlesticks, but never in your life will you get Jews to light the candles on theirs. They will only do that on the day the Messiah comes.

If you think that today's Bible passage describes Jesus, then you ought to drop everything you're doing, and run as quick as you can and buy a seven-branched candlestick and light the candles...*

....as a symbol that Jesus, the light of the world, is the expected Messiah.

PS: Today's Bible passage is a prophecy about the Messiah and was written 600 years before Jesus was born!

* PPS: Remember that lit candles are a major cause of house fires!

Links: 18 January, 17 July, 18 July, 19 July

5 minutes more? 1 Kings 6

23 March
Easter

Jesus tries to explain three times

From then on, Jesus began telling his disciples what would happen to him. He said, 'I must go to Jerusalem. There the nation's leaders, the chief priests, and the teachers of the Law of Moses will make me suffer terribly. I will be killed, but three days later I will rise to life.' ... While Jesus and his disciples were going from place to place in Galilee, he told them, 'The Son of Man will be handed over to people who will kill him. But three days later he will rise to life.' All this made the disciples very sad...

As Jesus was on his way to Jerusalem, he took his twelve disciples aside and told them in private:

We are now on our way to Jerusalem, where the Son of Man will be handed over to the chief priests and the teachers of the Law of Moses. They will sentence him to death, and then they will hand him over to foreigners who will make fun of him. They will beat him and nail him to a cross. But on the third day he will rise from death.

MATTHEW 16:21; 17:22–23; 20:17–19

Di:SaipL

How to serve in the best way possible

Jesus turned most things upside down. He said that those who wanted to be the greatest must be the least, and those who want to be something in God's eyes must serve others.

Jesus himself is the best example. But every time he tried to tell his disciples that he had to suffer and die, they tried not to hear what he said—they ignored him; they misunderstood him. They didn't want to hear that sort of nonsense.

There are two ways to live—God's way and the world's way. God's way is to humble yourself, bend down and try with the best of your ability to help other people have a better life.

As disciples, we should be concerned about serving as many people as possible. Not money—but people.

Links: 5 September, 8 September, 10 September, 12 September

5 minutes more? 1 Kings 8

24 March

Easter

Palm Sunday: Jesus rides into Jerusalem

When Jesus and his disciples came near Jerusalem, he went to Bethphage on the Mount of Olives and sent two of them on ahead. He told them, 'Go into the next village, where you will at once find a donkey and her colt. Untie the two donkeys and bring them to me. If anyone asks you why you are doing that, just say, "The Lord needs them." Straight away he will let you have the donkeys.' ...

The disciples left and did what Jesus had told them to do. They brought the donkey and its colt and laid some clothes on their backs. Then Jesus got on. Many people spread clothes in the road, while others put down branches which they had cut from trees. Some people walked ahead of Jesus and others followed behind. They were all shouting, 'Hooray for the Son of David! God bless the one who comes in the name of the Lord. Hooray for God in heaven above!' When Jesus came to Jerusalem, everyone in the city was excited and asked, 'Who can this be?' The crowd answered, 'This is Jesus, the prophet from Nazareth in Galilee.'

MATTHEW 21:1–3, 6–11

Good news...

...for most people

He could have chosen a castle, but he chose a stable.
He could have chosen people with high-powered jobs, but he chose ordinary people.
He could have chosen respectable people, but he chose tax collectors and sinners.
He could have chosen a horse, but he chose a boring old donkey.
He could have chosen to live, but he chose to die.
He could have chosen to stay up there in heaven where he'd got it made, but he chose to come to earth as a man.
He knew what was waiting for him when he rode into Jerusalem.
He could have avoided it, but he chose not to.

Jesus had a tendency to choose the imperfect people.
And I am really glad about that...

Links: 10 July, 16 July, 5 September, 22 September

5 minutes more? 1 Kings 10

25 March
Easter

Monday: Jesus gets angry

After Jesus and his disciples reached Jerusalem, he went into the temple and began chasing out everyone who was selling and buying. He turned over the tables of the moneychangers and the benches of those who were selling doves. Jesus would not let anyone carry things through the temple. Then he taught the people and said, 'The Scriptures say, "My house should be called a place of worship for all nations." But you have made it a place where robbers hide!' The chief priests and the teachers of the Law of Moses heard what Jesus said, and they started looking for a way to kill him. They were afraid of him, because the crowds were completely amazed at his teaching. That evening, Jesus and the disciples went outside the city.

MARK 11:15–19

Did you know that...

...Majorca in the summer and Jerusalem at Passover are quite similar?

Every summer the number of inhabitants on Majorca is more than doubled—by tourists, mainly British people and other northern Europeans who go there to relax. They practically take over the island.

In Jerusalem in Jesus' time there was a similar situation. About 50,000 to 100,000 people lived there, but every Passover about 300,000 pilgrims came to make sacrifices in the temple. It's here that the money changers and the dove sellers come into the picture, because the 300,000 pilgrims obviously didn't all bring something with them to sacrifice. The dove sellers took advantage of the money to be made from the people's religious practices. They sold sacrificial animals in the temple from their stalls and booths for extortionate prices!

This is what Jesus got really angry about. Jesus was concerned that worshipping God should be free. The Latin word for 'grace' is *gratis*, which means 'free'.

Links: 26 March, 27 July, 1 August, 18 November

5 minutes more? 1 Kings 11

26 March

Easter

Tuesday: Jesus teaches in the temple court

One of [the Pharisees] was an expert in the Jewish Law. So he tried to test Jesus by asking, 'Teacher, what is the most important commandment in the Law?' Jesus answered:

Love the Lord your God with all your heart, soul, and mind. This is the first and most important comandment. The second most important commandment is like this one. And it is, 'Love others as much as you love yourself.' All the Law of Moses and the Books of the Prophets are based on these two commandments.

MATTHEW 22:35–40

When Jesus had finished teaching, he told his disciples, 'You know that two days from now will be Passover. That is when the Son of man will be handed over to his enemies and nailed to a cross.' At that time the chief priests and the nation's leaders were meeting at the home of Caiaphas the high priest. They secretly planned to have Jesus arrested and put to death. But they said, 'We must not do it during Passover, because the people will riot.'

MATTHEW 26:1–5

Download

The two big commandments

Memorize this concise version of Jesus' teaching:

'Love the Lord your God with all your heart, soul, strength and mind. And love your neighbours as much as you love yourself' (see Luke 10:27).

Links: 19 April, 20 April, 6 May, 16 December

5 minutes more? 1 Kings 17

Wednesday: Jesus is anointed

Six days before Passover Jesus went back to Bethany, where he had raised Lazarus from death. A meal had been prepared for Jesus. Martha was doing the serving, and Lazarus himself was there. Mary took a very expensive bottle of perfume and poured it on Jesus' feet. She wiped them with her hair, and the sweet smell of the perfume filled the house. A disciple named Judas Iscariot was there. He was the one who was going to betray Jesus, and he asked, 'Why wasn't this perfume sold for three hundred silver coins and the money given to the poor?' Judas did not really care about the poor. He asked this because he carried the money bag and sometimes would steal from it.

JOHN 12:1–6

Judas Iscariot was one of the twelve disciples. He went to the chief priests and offered to help them arrest Jesus. They were glad to hear this, and they promised to pay him. So Judas started looking for a good chance to betray Jesus.

MARK 14:10–11

Big word

Christ and Messiah

Jesus, the one who is called Christ and Messiah, has taken a day-trip out away from the multitude of people in Jerusalem to the village of Bethany.

While they were eating, Mary suddenly came into the room with a jar, and before anyone realized what was going on, she poured the contents of the jar—which proved to be a very expensive ointment—over the feet of Jesus, the one who was called Christ and Messiah.

Judas reacted. He thought she should have used her money differently. He criticized her. But Jesus, the one who is called Christ and Messiah, remained seated and let her anoint him.

If you still haven't got the hint, it's probably because you don't know that *Christ* and *Messiah* mean 'anointed one'. Mary knew that Jesus would soon fulfil his messianic calling—and so she anointed him.

Links: 7 July, 6 September, 7 September, 8 September

5 minutes more? 1 Kings 18

28 March

Easter

Thursday: Jesus is taken prisoner

Then they sang a hymn and went out to the Mount of Olives. Jesus said to his disciples, 'During this very night, all of you will reject me...' Peter spoke up, 'Even if all the others reject you, I never will!' Jesus replied, 'I promise you that before a cock crows tonight, you will say three times that you don't know me.' But Peter said, 'Even if I have to die with you, I will never say I don't know you.' All the others said the same thing.

Jesus went with his disciples to a place called Gethsemane... Jesus was still speaking, when Judas the betrayer came up. He was one of the twelve disciples, and a large mob armed with swords and clubs was with him. They had been sent by the chief priests and the nation's leaders. Judas had told them beforehand, 'Arrest the man I greet with a kiss.' Judas walked right up to Jesus and said, 'Hello, teacher.' Then Judas kissed him... The men grabbed Jesus and arrested him... All Jesus' disciples left him and ran away.

Jesus was led off to the high priest. Then the chief priests, the nation's leaders, and the teachers of the Law of Moses all met together. Peter had followed at a distance. And when he reached the courtyard of the high priest's house, he sat down with the guards to warm himself beside a fire...

[Then the servant girl] asked him, 'Aren't you one of that man's followers?' 'No, I am not!' Peter answered... Some one [else] asked him, 'Aren't you one of Jesus' followers?' Again Peter denied it and said, 'No. I am not!' One of the high priest's servants... asked, 'Didn't I see you in the garden with that man?' Once more Peter denied it, and at once a cock crowed.

MATTHEW 26:30–31a, 33–36a, 47–49, 50b, 56b; MARK 14:53–54; JOHN 18:17, 25b–27

Links: 7 September, 8 September, 9 September, 10 September

5 minutes more? 2 Kings 2

29 March
Easter

Jesus is crucified

The soldiers led Jesus inside the courtyard of the fortress and called together the rest of the troops. They put a purple robe on him, and on his head they placed a crown that they had made out of thorn branches. They made fun of Jesus and shouted, 'Hey, you king of the Jews!' Then they beat him on the head with a stick. They spat on him and knelt down and pretended to worship him. When the soldiers had finished making fun of Jesus, they took off the purple robe. They put his own clothes back on him and led him off to be nailed to a cross.
MARK 15:16–20

Jesus was taken away, and he carried his cross to a place known as 'The Skull'. In Aramaic this place is called 'Golgotha'. There Jesus was nailed to the cross, and on each side of him a man was also nailed to a cross. Pilate ordered the charge against Jesus to be written on a board and put above the cross. It read, 'Jesus of Nazareth, King of the Jews.' The words were written in Hebrew, Latin, and Greek.
JOHN 19:16b–20a

Jesus knew that he had now finished his work. And in order to make the Scriptures come true, he said, 'I am thirsty!' A jar of cheap wine was there. Someone then soaked a sponge with the wine and held it up to Jesus' mouth on the stem of a hyssop plant. After Jesus drank the wine, he said, 'Everything is done!' He bowed his head and died.
JOHN 19:28–30

Links: 11 September, 12 September, 13 September, 27 November

5 minutes more? 2 Kings 4

30 March

Easter

Saturday: Jesus is dead

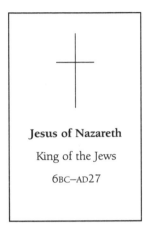

Jesus of Nazareth

King of the Jews

6BC–AD27

Links: 21 October, 4 November, 18 November, 24 November

5 minutes more? 2 Kings 5

31 March
Easter

Sunday: the day death died

On Sunday morning while it was still dark, Mary Magdalene went to the tomb and saw that the stone had been rolled away from the entrance. She ran to Simon Peter and to Jesus' favourite disciple and said, 'They have taken the Lord from the tomb! We don't know where they have put him.' Peter and the other disciple set off for the tomb. They ran side by side, until the other disciple ran faster than Peter and got there first. He bent over and saw the strips of linen cloth lying inside the tomb, but he did not go in. When Simon Peter got there, he went into the tomb and saw the strips of cloth... The disciple who got there first then went into the tomb, and when he saw it, he believed. At that time Peter and the other disciple did not know that the Scriptures said Jesus would rise to life. So the two of them went back to the other disciples.

Mary Magdalene stood crying outside the tomb. She was still weeping, when she stooped down and saw two angels inside. They were dressed in white and were sitting where Jesus' body had been. One was at the head and the other was at the foot. The angels asked Mary, 'Why are you crying?' She answered, 'They have taken away my Lord's body! I don't know where they have put him.' As soon as Mary said this, she turned around and saw Jesus standing there. But she did not know who he was. Jesus asked her, 'Why are you crying? Who are you looking for?' She thought he was the gardener and said, 'Sir, if you have taken his body away, please tell me, so I can go and get him.' Then Jesus said to her, 'Mary!' She turned and said to him, 'Rabboni.' The Aramaic word 'Rabboni' means 'Teacher'.

JOHN 20:1–6, 8–16

Links: 20 July, 27 September, 1 October, 26 December

5 minutes more? 2 Kings 17

1 April

Easter

Death, where is your sting?

I will explain a mystery to you. Not every one of us will die, but we will all be changed. It will happen suddenly, quicker than the blink of an eye. At the sound of the last trumpet the dead will be raised. We will all be changed, so that we will never die again. Our dead and decaying bodies will be changed into bodies that won't die or decay. The bodies we now have are weak and can die. But they will be changed into bodies that are eternal. Then the Scriptures will come true,

'Death has lost the battle! Where is its victory? Where is its sting?'

Sin is what gives death its sting, and the Law is the power behind sin. But thank God for letting our Lord Jesus Christ give us the victory!

1 CORINTHIANS 15:51–57

Head, shoulders, knees and toes

A song on the brain

I'm sure you know what it's like to have a song on the brain. No matter what you do, it goes round and round all day long. Try to get this worship song into your head today:

Thine be the glory, risen, conquering Son,
Endless is the victory Thou o'er death hast won.
Angels in bright raiment rolled the stone away,
Left the folded grave clothes where Thy body lay.
Thine be the glory...

EDMOND LOUIS BUDRY (1854–1932)

Links: 31 March, 27 September, 30 September, 26 December

5 minutes more? 2 Kings 22

2 April

Moses part 3 (c.1250BC)

Exodus: leaving Egypt

At midnight the Lord killed the firstborn son of every Egyptian family, from the son of the king to the son of every prisoner in jail. He also killed the firstborn male of every animal that belonged to the Egyptians... During the night the king sent for Moses and Aaron and told them, 'Get your people out of my country and leave us alone! Go and worship the Lord as you have asked. Take your sheep, goats, and cattle, and get out. But ask your God to be kind to me.' The Egyptians did everything they could to get the Israelites to leave their country fast. They said, 'Please hurry and leave. If you don't, we will all be dead.' ... The Israelites walked from the city of Rameses to the city of Succoth. There were about six hundred thousand of them, not counting women and children. Many other people went with them as well, and there were also a lot of sheep, goats and cattle... The Lord's people left Egypt exactly four hundred and thirty years after they had arrived.

EXODUS 12:29, 31–33, 37–38, 40–41

Did you know that...

...there is a reason why Communion wafers taste strange?

Yeast is quite a modern discovery. The Israelites didn't have yeast. They had something called leaven—a yeasty dough or batter that they mixed with fresh flour to make bread rise. When they had to leave Egypt in a hurry, they had mixed the leaven into the bread dough, but it hadn't had time to begin to ferment and rise. So the Passover festival in memory of the Exodus became known as 'The Feast of the Unleavened* Bread'.

* CEV calls this 'The Feast of the Thin Bread' (see Exodus 14).

And that's why, these days, Communion wafers (used in the more traditional churches) are flat and taste strange—they haven't been allowed to rise. This reminds us that the Communion service has its roots in the Passover and the unleavened bread that the people of Israel took with them out of Egypt.

The symbolic connection between Communion and the Exodus is that just as the people of Israel were saved from slavery, so we have been too. Get it?

Links: 20 March, 3 April, 4 April, 5 April

5 minutes more? 2 Kings 25

3 April

Moses part 3 (c.1250BC)

Pharaoh realizes the situation

When the king of Egypt heard that the Israelites had finally left, he and his officials changed their minds and said, 'Look what we have done! We let them get away, and they will no longer be our slaves.' The king got his war chariot and army ready... When the Israelites saw the king coming with his army, they were frightened and begged the Lord for help. They also complained to Moses, 'Wasn't there enough room in Egypt to bury us? Is that why you brought us out here to die in the desert? Why did you bring us out of Egypt anyway?...' But Moses answered, 'Don't be afraid! Be brave, and you will see the Lord save you today. These Egyptians will never bother you again. The Lord will fight for you, and you won't have to do a thing.'

EXODUS 14:5–6, 10–11, 13–14

Download...

...about a God who acts

You can count on God intervening in your life. Here's a verse that lots of people like. It's not such a bad idea to know this one off by heart.

'The Lord will fight for you, and you won't have to do a thing' (Exodus 14:14).

Links: 2 April, 4 April, 5 April, 6 April

5 minutes more? Ezra 1

4 April

Moses part 3 (c.1250BC)

The Red Sea miracle

The Lord said to Moses, 'Why do you keep calling out to me for help? Tell the Israelites to move forward. Then hold your walking stick over the sea. The water will open up and make a road where they can walk through on dry ground...' Moses stretched his arm over the sea, and the Lord sent a strong east wind that blew all night until there was dry land where the water had been. The sea opened up, and the Israelites walked through on dry land with a wall of water on each side. The Egyptian chariots and cavalry went after them... The Lord told Moses, 'Stretch your arm towards the sea—the water will cover the Egyptians and their cavalry and chariots.' ... The water came and covered the chariots, the cavalry, and the whole Egyptian army that had followed the Israelites into the sea. Not one of them was left alive.

EXODUS 14:15–16, 21–23, 26, 28

Good news...

...for everyone who gets worried easily

If you're the sort of person who gets worried about this and that, and thinks that this or that might be lurking round the next corner...

If you're the sort of person who gets worried about one thing or another and thinks that one thing or another is bound to happen sooner rather than later...

Then say to yourself:

1. God hasn't said that we won't have to face certain challenges...
2. ...but he has promised us, loads of times, that he'll be with us...
3. ...and he has said, loads of times, that we'll come out the other side in one piece.

Nothing is impossible for God.

Links: 5 April, 9 May, 28 August, 27 December

5 minutes more? Nehemiah 3

5 April

Moses part 3 (c.1250BC)

The song of praise afterwards

Because of the mighty power he had used against the Egyptians, the Israelites worshipped [the Lord] and trusted him and his servant Moses. Moses and the Israelites sang this song in praise of the Lord:

I sing praises to the Lord for his great victory! He has thrown the horses and their riders into the sea. The Lord is my strength, the reason for my song, because he has saved me. I praise and honour the Lord—he is my God and the God of my ancestors. The Lord is his name, and he is a warrior! He threw the chariots and army of Egypt's king into the Red Sea, and he drowned the best of the king's officers...

Our Lord, no other gods compare with you—Majestic and holy! Fearsome and glorious! Miracle worker!

The people you rescued were led by your powerful love to your holy place. Our Lord, you will rule for ever!

EXODUS 14:31—5:4, 11, 13, 18

Di:SaipL
Worship

Worship was not discovered in the 1980s in Spirit-filled churches. Worship has been around as long as God has been around, and that is quite a while.

Worship is not a particular style, nor does it mean that the words are up on an OHP screen or come from a video projector, nor does it mean that some lines are sung over and over again. Worship is when people thank God for who he is and the good things he has done, like in today's passage—when he has saved 600,000 men (not including the women and children) from certain death.

If you don't like to sing, it's a good thing to understand that worship comes from the heart—not from the mouth. Sing a song, then—from your heart, and give thanks for everything you think of as it pops into your head.

Links: 6 April, 7 April, 25 April, 15 June

5 minutes more? Nehemiah 8

6 April

Moses part 3 (c.1250BC)

No food and drink

There in the desert they started complaining to Moses and Aaron, 'We wish the Lord had killed us in Egypt. When we lived there, we could at least sit down and eat all the bread and meat we wanted. But you have brought us out here into this desert, where we are going to starve.' The Lord said to Moses, 'I will send bread down from heaven like rain...' ...and the next morning dew covered the ground. After the dew had gone, the desert was covered with thin flakes that looked like frost. The people had never seen anything like this, and they started asking each other, 'What is it?' Moses answered, 'This is the bread that the Lord has given you to eat.' ...

But the people were thirsty and kept on complaining, 'Moses, did you bring us out of Egypt just to let us and our families and our animals die of thirst?' Then Moses prayed to the Lord, 'What am I going to do with these people? They are about to stone me to death!' The Lord answered, 'Take some of the leaders with you and go ahead of the rest of the people. Also take along the walking stick you used to strike the River Nile... Strike the rock with the stick, and water will pour out for the people to drink.' Moses did this while the leaders watched.

EXODUS 16:2–4a, 13b–15; 17:3–5, 6b

Hmm... just a thought...

...about criticism

A critical mind is a good and healthy thing, but there are few things worse than a critical heart.

Links: 10 February, 17 February, 10 June, 29 August

5 minutes more? Job 1

7 April

Moses part 3 (c.1250BC)

Israel and Moses enter into an agreement

The Israelites left Rephidim. Then two months after leaving Egypt, they arrived at the desert near Mount Sinai, where they set up camp at the foot of the mountain. Moses went up the mountain to meet with the Lord God, who told him to say to the people:

You saw what I did in Egypt, and you know how I brought you here to me, just as a mighty eagle carries its young. Now if you will faithfully obey me, you will be my very own people. The whole world is mine, but you will be my holy nation and serve me as priests. Moses, that is what you must tell the Israelites.

After Moses went back, he reported to the leaders what the Lord had said, and they promised, 'We will do everything the Lord has commanded.' So Moses told the Lord about this.

EXODUS 19:1–8

☆ Bible personality

Moses—the greatest prophet in Israel

- Moses is considered to be the greatest prophet of all time in Israel (Deuteronomy 34:10).
- Rather strange, maybe, considering that he actually had a history as a murderer (Exodus 2:12)...
- ...and that he didn't like to speak in public (Exodus 4:10)...
- ...and that he was 80 years old when he started (Exodus 7:7)...
- ...and that he was unbelievably, madly and massively stubborn—so stubborn that at times he stuck to his guns although everybody else thought differently about something.
- Part of the key had to have been that no one else had such frequent and close contact with God as Moses.

'There has never again been a prophet in Israel like Moses. The Lord spoke face to face with him... Moses had seen the invisible God and wasn't afraid of the king's anger' (Deuteronomy 34:10; Hebrews 11:27b).

God can use whoever he wants for whatever he wants, as long as contact between God and that person is as it should be.

Links: 23 January, 8 April, 1 May, 16 September

5 minutes more? Job 2

8 April

The Ten Commandments

No. 1: Other gods

God said to the people of Israel:

I am the Lord your God, the one who brought you out of Egypt where you were slaves. Do not worship any god except me.

EXODUS 20:1–3

The Lord is great and deserves our greatest praise! He is the only God worthy of our worship. Other nations worship idols, but the Lord created the heavens. Give honour and praise to the Lord, whose power and beauty fill his holy temple. Tell everyone of every nation, 'Praise the glorious power of the Lord. He is wonderful! Praise him and bring an offering into his temple. Worship the Lord, majestic and holy.'

1 CHRONICLES 16:25–29

Weird and wonderful

Moses broke the two flat stones that had the commandments on them

I think there is so much aggression in the Old Testament. For example, Moses broke the two flat stones on which God had written the Ten Commandments, because he was so angry.

Not so strange, perhaps, because when Moses came down from the mountain, having got the flat stones, the first thing he saw was a wilful breaking of the first commandment. The people had made themselves a golden calf that they were dancing round and worshipping.

Then he completely lost it: 'As Moses got closer to the camp, he saw the idol, and he also saw the people dancing around. This made him so angry that he threw down the stones and broke them to pieces at the foot of the mountain' (Exodus 32:19).

Thankfully, a little while later he got two more flat stones from God…

Links: 9 April, 24 July, 25 July, 26 July

5 minutes more? Job 3

9 April

The Ten Commandments

No. 1b: Idols and images

Do not make idols that look like anything in the sky or on earth or in the sea under the earth.

EXODUS 20:4

Our God is in the heavens, doing as he chooses. The idols of the nations are made of silver and gold. They have a mouth and eyes, but they can't speak or see. Their ears can't hear, and their noses can't smell. Their hands have no feeling, their legs don't move, and they can't make a sound. Everyone who made the idols and all who trust them are just as helpless as those useless gods.

PSALM 115:3–8

Check it out

Idols

At the time Moses got the Ten Commandments, it was normal for people to make gods for themselves—so-called idols that they worshipped. Strange, but true!

PS: The reason I have called this Commandment No. 1b is because it doesn't actually belong to the Ten Commandments. Martin Luther (the Protestant church reformer of the 1500s), who made the list of the Commandments as we know them, thought that this one was not a commandment in itself, but an explanation of commandment number 1.

PPS: The reason that I have included it anyway is that I think it fits in well in contemporary Western culture. I think we worship so many material things.

PPPS: What do you think?

Links: 30 April, 24 July, 25 July, 26 July

5 minutes more? Job 38

10 April

The Ten Commandments

No. 2: God's name

Do not misuse my name. I am the Lord your God, and I will punish anyone who misuses my name.

EXODUS 20:7

Shelomith, the daughter of Dibri from the tribe of Dan, had married an Egyptian, and they had a son. One day their son got into a fight with an Israelite man in camp and cursed the name of the Lord. So the young man was dragged off to Moses, who had him guarded while everyone waited for the Lord to tell them what to do. Finally, the Lord said to Moses:

This man has cursed me! Take him outside the camp and make the witnesses lay their hands on his head. Then command the whole community of Israel to stone him to death. And warn the others that everyone else who curses me will die in the same way, whether they are Israelites by birth or foreigners living among you.

LEVITICUS 24:10–16

Check it out

The name of the Lord Jesus

This is a list of things that the first Christians did 'in Jesus' name'. They…

…believed and received strength (Acts 3:16)
…had life (John 20:31)
…were made holy and acceptable (1 Corinthians 6:11)
…were healed (Acts 4:10)
…preached and taught (Acts 4:18)
…performed miracles and wonders (Acts 4:30)
…were baptized (Acts 10:48)
…risked their lives (Acts 15:26)
…brought his name honour (Acts 19:17; 2 Thessalonians 1:12)
…exhorted one another (1 Corinthians 1:10)
…met together (1 Corinthians 5:4)
…gave thanks (Ephesians 5:20)

Live your life in Jesus' name.

Links: 15 February, 16 February, 24 February, 25 August

5 minutes more? Job 40

11 April

The Ten Commandments

No. 3: The day of rest

Remember that the Sabbath Day belongs to me. You have six days when you can do your work, but the seventh day of each week belongs to me, your God. No one is to work on that day.

EXODUS 20:8–10a

Jesus left and went into one of the Jewish meeting places, where there was a man whose hand was crippled. Some Pharisees wanted to accuse Jesus of doing something wrong, and they asked him, 'Is it right to heal someone on the Sabbath?' Jesus answered, 'If you had a sheep that fell into a ditch on the Sabbath, wouldn't you lift it out? People are worth much more than sheep, and so it is right to do good on the Sabbath.' Then Jesus told the man, 'Hold out your hand.' The man did, and it became as healthy as the other one.

MATTHEW 12:9–13

Weird and wonderful

A lift on the Sabbath!

Strict Jews are not allowed to work on the day of rest (the Sabbath). And I mean that—not at all. For example, they are forbidden to light a fire on the Sabbath (Exodus 35:3).

Today this law is interpreted as meaning that it is not permitted to turn on a light switch (!) or flick switches that turn on electrical things—for example, lifts. So they have something that is called a 'Sabbath lift' in Israel.

Every Sabbath the lifts go up and down automatically all day from morning to evening. They stop at every floor, and the doors are open all the time so that no one has to push any buttons.

Jesus was critical of the Pharisees having rules just so that people could see how holy they were. Jesus taught that there was no point in keeping religious rules if your motives were wrong—it's what's in your heart that counts.

Check out Matthew 23:27–28 if you want to find out more.

Links: 7 January, 15 February, 26 February, 30 July

5 minutes more? Job 42

12 April

The Ten Commandments

No. 4: Parents

Respect your father and your mother, and you will live a long time in the land I am giving you.

EXODUS 20:12

Children with good sense make their parents happy, but foolish children make them sad… Pay attention to your father, and don't neglect your mother when she grows old. Invest in truth and wisdom, discipline and good sense, and don't part with them. Make your father truly happy by living right and showing sound judgment. Make your parents proud, especially your mother.

PROVERBS 10:1; 23:22–25

Children, you belong to the Lord, and you do the right thing when you obey your parents. The first commandment with a promise says, 'Obey your father and your mother, and you will have a long and happy life.'

EPHESIANS 6:1–3

Refresh

Hassling or honouring

I'm terrible at honouring my parents. I don't believe I'm alone in that. It seems that many young people have swapped one 'h' word for another, so that they think it says they should hassle their father and mother. That's not on!

When my mum last had a birthday, my brothers and I planned a surprise party. We invited some of Mum's friends and provided some simple party food. She was absolutely thrilled. Since then she's talked about almost nothing else. It doesn't take that much to make mums and dads happy—that's the way they are. Think of something about your parents that makes you happy—and tell them! They're bound not to be perfect, but they are the only parents you've got.

There'll be some good advice for parents on another day…

Links: 6 December, 7 December, 9 December, 10 December

5 minutes more? Psalm 1

13 April

The Ten Commandments

No. 5: Murder

Do not murder.
EXODUS 20:13

You know that our ancestors were told, 'Do not murder' and 'A murderer must be brought to trial.' But I promise you that if you are angry with someone, you will have to stand trial. If you call someone a fool, you will be taken to court. And if you say that someone is worthless, you will be in danger of the fires of hell.
MATTHEW 5:21–22

If you hate each other, you are murderers, and we know that murderers do not have eternal life. We know what love is because Jesus gave his life for us. That's why we must give our lives for each other. If we have all we need and see one of our own people in need, we must have pity on that person, or else we cannot say we love God.
1 JOHN 3:15–17

Di:SaipL

Giving your life for someone

Fortunately, most people don't kill other people. Nevertheless, the fifth commandment is relevant to everybody.

This commandment doesn't only mean 'don't take life' from anyone, it also means that we should 'give life' to people. Read that one more time if you didn't quite get the last sentence, and have a good think.

For most of us it sounds gruesome to give your life for someone, in the way that Jesus did. But start small—let's say, five minutes to begin with. Give five minutes every day to someone who needs it. Or two minutes. Or one minute.

And one more thing: start today, otherwise you'll completely forget.

Links: 1 January, 6 January, 20 November, 26 November

5 minutes more? Psalm 8

14 April

The Ten Commandments

No. 6: Marriage

Be faithful in marriage.
EXODUS 20:14

Don't you know that evil people won't have a share in the blessings of God's kingdom? Don't fool yourselves! No one who is immoral or worships idols or is unfaithful in marriage or is a pervert or behaves like a homosexual will share in God's kingdom. Neither will any thief or greedy person or drunkard or anyone who curses and cheats others. Some of you used to be like that. But now the name of our Lord Jesus Christ and the power of God's Spirit have washed you and made you holy and acceptable to God.
1 CORINTHIANS 6:9–11

Have respect for marriage. Always be faithful to your partner, because God will punish anyone who is immoral or unfaithful in marriage.
HEBREWS 13:4

Refresh

It's OK to enjoy sex—but in the right context!

Many people think God is the ultimate kill-joy and that he is against sex. Don't be daft! God is all for sex. Otherwise why do you think he'd have created it? He wants marriage partners to enjoy the sexual side of their relationship—to have lots of sex, intense sex, good sex, long sex, sex over and over again—as much sex as they want.

God is not against sex; he is against pain. And no marriage—no relationship—can tolerate one of the partners mucking around with anyone else. It just brings pain and heartbreak.

Sex is a good thing, but it is a fragile thing. We need to take care of it, and look after it with love.

Love is a good thing, but it is a fragile thing. We need to take care of it, and look after it with marriage.

Marriage is a good but fragile thing. We especially need to look after that.

Links: 22 April, 14 November, 15 November, 14 December

5 minutes more? Psalm 22

15 April

The Ten Commandments

No. 7: Stealing

Do not steal.

EXODUS 20:15

My disciples, I tell you to use wicked wealth to make friends for yourselves. Then when it is gone, you will be welcomed into an eternal home. Anyone who can be trusted in little matters can also be trusted in important matters. But anyone who is dishonest in little matters will be dishonest in important matters. If you cannot be trusted with this wicked wealth, who will trust you with true wealth? And if you cannot be trusted with what belongs to someone else, who will give you something that will be your own? You cannot be the slave of two masters. You will like one more than the other or be more loyal to one than to the other. You cannot serve God and money.

LUKE 16:9–13

Listen to your heart and fill in

What would you have said?

Let's say, completely hypothetically, that you discovered by accident that a good friend of yours had stolen something from a shop.

1. Would you say anything about it to him / her?

2. What would you say?

3. What would you say if he or she suggested doing it again?

Links: 19 April, 6 September, 6 October, 4 December

5 minutes more? Psalm 23

16 April

The Ten Commandments

No. 8: Lying

Do not tell lies about others.
EXODUS 20:16

Who may stay in God's temple or live on the holy mountain of the Lord? Only those who obey God and do as they should. They speak the truth and don't spread gossip; they treat others fairly and don't say cruel things. They hate worthless people, but show respect for all who worship the Lord. And they keep their promises, no matter what the cost. They lend their money without charging interest, and they don't take bribes to hurt the innocent. Those who do these things will always stand firm.
PSALM 15:1–5

You will know the truth, and the truth will set you free.
JOHN 8:32

Download...

...about freedom

You wish you could feel a little more free, you say? There is a clue in the following verse, which is perhaps one of the best verses I know. I would learn it off by heart if I were you...

'You will know the truth, and the truth will set you free' (John 8:32).

Links: 10 January, 19 April, 20 November, 23 November

5 minutes more? Psalm 27

17 April

The Ten Commandments

No. 9: Envy

Do not want to take anything that belongs to someone else.
EXODUS 20:17a

And religion does make your life rich, by making you content with what you have. We didn't bring anything into this world, and we won't take anything with us when we leave. So we should be satisfied just to have food and clothes. People who want to be rich fall into all sorts of temptations and traps. They are caught by foolish and harmful desires that drag them down and destroy them. The love of money causes all kinds of trouble. Some people want money so much they have given up their faith and caused themselves a lot of pain.
1 TIMOTHY 6:6–10

Don't fall in love with money. Be satisfied with what you have. The Lord has promised that he will not leave us or desert us. That should make you feel like saying, 'The Lord helps me! Why should I be afraid of what people can do to me?'
HEBREWS 13:5–6

Refresh

God and money

God's got nothing against millionaires. God doesn't recommend that anyone be rich—he says it is difficult to be rich. He says that there are many dangers that come with being rich. He says you must take care not to let your money control you, but love God more, and so on. But he really hasn't got anything against rich people.

God advises us against dreaming about becoming rich. The Bible says that that holds obvious dangers. Those who want to be rich fall into temptations and snares and are bound by all sorts of idiotic, damaging desires that lead people down into loss and ruin.

It isn't money that's the root of all evil—it's the love of money that's the root of all kinds of evil.

Pray that you won't envy people who have nicer clothes, a more expensive bike, a better PC and so on. That's what we're talking about.

Links: 28 January, 25 June, 27 July, 4 December

5 minutes more? Psalm 32

No. 10: Covetousness

Don't want to take anyone's house, wife or husband, slaves, oxen, donkeys or anything else.
EXODUS 20:17b

Let love be your only debt! If you love others, you have done all that the Law demands. In the Law there are many commands, such as, 'Be faithful in marriage. Do not murder. Do not steal. Do not want what belongs to others.' But all these are summed up in the commandment that says, 'Love others as much as you love yourself.' No one who loves others will want to harm them. So love is all that the Law demands... So behave properly, as people do in the day. Don't go to wild parties or get drunk or be vulgar or indecent. Don't quarrel or be jealous. Let the Lord Jesus Christ be as near to you as the clothes you wear. Then you won't try to satisfy your selfish desires.
ROMANS 13:8–10, 13–14

Did you know that...

...when Martin Luther wrote his explanation of the Ten Commandments, he began each explanation, 'We must fear and love God, in such a way that we...'?

He thought that our total motivation for being good people should be that we long to glorify God with all of our heart. His explanation of the Ten Commandments is: 'We must fear and love God, in such a way that we don't tempt or compel anyone we know to depart from him, but encourage them to be faithful.'

Be faithful!

- to our friends
- to agreements
- to our families
- to God

Links: 19 April, 22 April, 25 June, 15 December

5 minutes more? Psalm 34

19 April

The Ten Commandments

The two most important commandments

'Teacher, what is the most important commandment in the Law?' Jesus answered:

Love the Lord your God with all your heart, soul, and mind. This is the first and most important commandment. The second most important commandment is like this one. And it is, 'Love others as much as you love yourself.' All the Law of Moses and the Books of the Prophets are based on these two commandments.

MATTHEW 22:36–40

Don't suppose that I came to do away with the Law and the Prophets. I did not come to do away with them, but to give them their full meaning. Heaven and earth may disappear. But I promise you that not even a full stop or a comma will ever disappear from the Law. Everything written in it must happen. If you reject even the least important command in the Law and teach others to do the same, you will be the least important person in the kingdom of heaven. But if you obey and teach others its commands, you will have an important place in the kingdom. You must obey God's commands better than the Pharisees and the teachers of the Law obey them. If you don't, I promise you that you will never get into the kingdom of heaven.

MATTHEW 5:17–20

Refresh

Jesus isn't a cool guy who relaxes all the rules

Some people hold the view that Jesus is kind and Paul is not, that Jesus is lenient and Paul is not, that Jesus is generous and Paul is not. But that's not right.

Paul is nowhere near as direct as Jesus. Jesus demands that we take the Law seriously. He says that not even a full stop or a comma will disappear from the Law. He says that he hasn't come to do away with the Law, and that our righteousness must be even greater than that of the Pharisees and the teachers of the Law.

Over the next few days we will be looking at the Sermon on the Mount and you will see that Jesus isn't easy-going, cool or laid back. He is actually quite decisive. But our hope is not based on Jesus being a cool guy who relaxes the rules—our hope is based on Jesus having the power to forgive.

Links: 26 March, 6 May, 14 November, 4 December

5 minutes more? Psalm 37

20 April

The Sermon on the Mount

Blessings

Jesus' disciples gathered around him, and he taught them:

God blesses* those people who depend only on him. They belong to the kingdom of heaven!
God blesses those people who grieve. They will find comfort!
God blesses those people who are humble. The earth will belong to them!
God blesses those people who want to obey him more than to eat or drink. They will be given what they want!
God blesses those people who are merciful. They will be treated with mercy!
God blesses those people whose hearts are pure. They will see him!
God blesses those people who make peace. They will be called his children!
God blesses those people who are treated badly for doing right. They belong to the kingdom of heaven.

God will bless you when people insult you, ill-treat you, and tell all kinds of evil lies about you because of me. Be happy and excited! You will have a great reward in heaven. People did these same things to the prophets who lived long ago.
MATTHEW 5:1–12

* 'God blesses...' (CEV) can also be read as 'Blessed are...'

Big word
Blessed

'Blessed' is one of those words that has loads of meanings, but is almost impossible to define very accurately. Some people say it means something like 'happy' or 'fortunate'. But that's not the point.

The point is that Jesus turns things on their heads. He doesn't say that it is the rich, the successful, those who have a lot of possessions or those who live it up who are 'happy' or 'fortunate'.

The really lucky people are the poor, the grieving, the patient, those who hunger for righteousness, the compassionate, those with good intentions, those who spread peace, and those who are persecuted. They have a bright future ahead of them.

Are you blessed, happy and fortunate? Now you know how you can be.

Links: 20 May, 30 November, 15 December, 16 December

5 minutes more? Psalm 42

21 April

The Sermon on the Mount

Salt and light

Jesus continued:

You are like salt for everyone on earth. But if salt no longer tastes like salt, how can it make food salty? All it is good for is to be thrown out and walked on. You are like light for the whole world. A city built on top of a hill cannot be hidden, and no one would light a lamp and put it under a clay pot. A lamp is placed on a lampstand, where it can give light to everyone in the house. Make your light shine, so that others will see the good that you do and will praise your Father in heaven.

MATTHEW 5:13–16

You used to be like people living in the dark, but now you are people of the light because you belong to the Lord. So act like people of the light and make your light shine. Be good and honest and truthful, as you try to please the Lord.

EPHESIANS 5:8–10

Di:SaipL

Are you tough enough?

Here is a song that all Christians ought to sing once, maybe twice a day. It's probably not the world's best song, I don't expect you know it—but it has meant a lot to me.

Verse:

It isn't always easy when you are at school,
Saying you love Jesus just isn't cool.
Other kids might tease you—not let you join in—
If you're tough enough to say Jesus is your friend.

Chorus:

Jesus asks if you're tough enough to show who you belong to?
Jesus asks if you're tough enough to smile whatever they do?
Stand up for Jesus, let his light shine through…
Hey, are you tough enough to say who you belong to?

BASED ON A NORWEGIAN SONG BY OLE BØRUD

Links: 1 January, 9 October, 23 November, 25 December

5 minutes more? Psalm 46

Lust

Jesus continued:

You know the commandment which says, 'Be faithful in marriage.' But I tell you that if you look at another woman and want her, you are already unfaithful in your thoughts. If your right eye causes you to sin, poke it out and throw it away. It is better to lose one part of your body, than for your whole body to end up in hell. If your right hand causes you to sin, chop it off and throw it away! It is better to lose one part of your body, than for your whole body to be thrown into hell.

MATTHEW 5:27–30

God wants you to be holy, so don't be immoral in matters of sex. Respect and honour your wife.* Don't be a slave of your desires or live like people who don't know God.

1 THESSALONIANS 4:3–5

* This can also read, 'Learn to win yourself a wife in a way that is holy and honourable.'

Refresh

How to get a boyfriend or a girlfriend

Let me stir things up a bit, not about anyone in particular, but about a certain social phenomenon—that is, boys and girls who go to parties, drink themselves half senseless and end up 'accidentally' coming on to someone or other in a dark corner or another room.

- It isn't sexy.
- It isn't healthy.
- It isn't fun, certainly not in the long run.
- It's an awful way to initiate a relationship.

But

- It's no problem dancing with someone without getting paralytic.
- It's no problem telling someone your feelings without coming on strong.

The Bible says we must win ourselves a wife or husband in holiness and honour, not in sensual desire. This is an area of life in which you can really set a good example.

Links: 2 June, 3 June, 26 November, 14 December

5 minutes more? Psalm 51

Revenge

Jesus continued:

You know that you have been taught, 'An eye for an eye and a tooth for a tooth.' But I tell you not to try to get even with a person who has done something to you. When someone slaps your right cheek, turn and let that person slap your other cheek. If someone sues you for your shirt, give up your coat as well. If a soldier forces you to carry his pack one kilometre, carry it two kilometres. When people ask you for something, give it to them. When they want to borrow money, lend it to them... You have heard people say, 'Love your neighbours and hate your enemies.' But I tell you to love your enemies and pray for anyone who ill-treats you. Then you will be acting like your Father in heaven.
MATTHEW 5:38–45a

Show love in everything you do.
1 CORINTHIANS 16:14

Did you know that...
...Jesus is stricter than the Old Testament?

Jesus says six times in the Sermon on the Mount (Matthew 5—7), 'You have heard people say...'. Then he quotes one of the laws from the Old Testament before saying, 'But I tell you...'

Each of the six times he does that, he tightens up the law—makes it stricter. He says that it isn't only what we do that's important, but the motive behind it.

Today we read that he says, among other things, 'You have heard people say, "An eye for an eye and a tooth for a tooth." But I tell you not to try to get even with a person who has done something to you. When someone slaps your right cheek, turn and let that person slap your other cheek.'

So it isn't quite true that God is strict as opposed to Jesus being soft!

Links: 2 February, 28 May, 10 November, 4 December

5 minutes more? Psalm 90

24 April

The Sermon on the Mount

Money

Jesus said:

When you do good deeds, don't try to show off. If you do, you won't get a reward from your Father in heaven. When you give to the poor, don't blow a loud horn. That's what show-offs do in the meeting places and on the street corners, because they are always looking for praise. I can assure you that they already have their reward. When you give to the poor, don't let anyone know about it. Then your gift will be given in secret. Your Father knows what is done in secret, and he will reward you... Don't store up treasures on earth! Moths and rust can destroy them, and thieves can break in and steal them. Instead, store up your treasures in heaven, where moths and rust cannot destroy them, and thieves cannot break in and steal them. Your heart will always be where your treasure is.

MATTHEW 6:1–4, 19–21

Refresh

A hand that gives never goes empty

In the Old Testament they had a rule that ten per cent of everything you earned automatically went to God (Malachi 3:10). Although Jesus doesn't say anything about this ten per cent, it's a good rule for Christians to follow. On the other hand, what Jesus says a lot about is that we should be cheerful givers who give from a thankful heart.

Many people, particularly old people, and particularly women, have understood this principle—and they give, by the bucketful. They have a heart for Christian work and so they give twenty per cent, thirty per cent—or as much as they can spare.

A lovely old lady that I knew once said, 'A hand that gives never goes empty.'

Many of these lovely old ladies are near the end of their lives, and there aren't many young people who have discovered the joy of giving. Have you?

Links: 15 April, 27 October, 4 December, 15 December

5 minutes more? Psalm 91

25 April

The Sermon on the Mount

Prayer

When you pray, don't talk on and on as people do who don't know God. They think God likes to hear long prayers. Don't be like them. Your Father knows what you need before you ask. You should pray like this:

Our Father in heaven,
help us to honour your name.
Come and set up your kingdom,
so that everyone on earth will obey you,
as you are obeyed in heaven.
Give us our food for today.
Forgive us for doing wrong,
as we forgive others.
Keep us from being tempted
and protect us from evil.

If you forgive others for the wrong things they do to you, your Father in heaven will forgive you. But if you don't forgive others, your Father will not forgive your sins.
MATTHEW 6:7–15

Hmm... just a thought...

...about prayer

You don't need to pray out loud.
You don't need to pray with fancy words and long expressions.
You don't need to go on for ages when you pray.
But you do need to pray.

Links: 21 January, 26 April, 14 June, 15 June

5 minutes more? Psalm 96

26 April
The Sermon on the Mount

Fasting

Jesus continued:

When you go without eating, don't try to look gloomy as those show-offs do when they go without eating. I can assure you that they already have their reward. Instead, comb your hair and wash your face. Then others won't know that you are going without eating. But your Father sees what is done in private, and he will reward you.

MATTHEW 6:16–18

The followers of John the Baptist and the Pharisees often went without eating. Some people came and asked Jesus, 'Why do the followers of John and those of the Pharisees often go without eating, while your disciples never do?'

Jesus answered:

The friends of a bridegroom don't go without eating while he is still with them. But the time will come when he will be taken from them. Then they will go without eating.

MARK 2:18–20

Big word
Fasting

Fasting means to stop doing something you like for a while, to make it easier to concentrate on God. In Bible times it was usual to fast by going without eating. However, here is a list of things a young person could fast from that are more relevant to modern society!

1. Sweets
2. TV
3. Videos and DVDs
4. Computer games
5. New clothes

Why don't you try it out?

Links: 7 June, 22 August, 29 August, 27 November

5 minutes more? Psalm 100

27 April

The Sermon on the Mount

Worrying

Jesus continued:

I tell you not to worry about your life. Don't worry about having something to eat, drink, or wear. Isn't life more than food or clothing? Look at the birds in the sky! They don't plant or harvest. They don't even store grain in barns. Yet your Father in heaven takes care of them. Aren't you worth more than birds? Can worry make you live longer? Why worry about clothes? Look how the wild flowers grow. They don't work hard to make their clothes. But I tell you that Solomon with all his wealth wasn't as well clothed as one of them. God gives such beauty to everything that grows in the fields, even though it is here today and thrown into a fire tomorrow. He will surely do even more for you! Why do you have such little faith?

Don't worry and ask yourselves, 'Will we have anything to eat? Will we have anything to drink? Will we have any clothes to wear?' Only people who don't know God are always worrying about such things. Your Father in heaven knows that you need all these. But more than anything else, put God's work first and do what he wants. Then the other things will be yours as well. Don't worry about tomorrow. It will take care of itself. You have enough to worry about today.

MATTHEW 6:25–34

Download

Don't worry, be happy...

'Don't worry about tomorrow. It will take care of itself. You have enough to worry about today' (Matthew 6:34).

Links: 5 January, 3 July, 28 November, 29 November

5 minutes more? Psalm 103

28 April

The Sermon on the Mount

Judging others

Jesus said:

Don't condemn others, and God won't condemn you. God will be as hard on you as you are on others! He will treat you exactly as you treat them. You can see the speck in your friend's eye, but you don't notice the log in your own eye. How can you say, 'My friend, let me take the speck out of your eye,' when you don't see the log in your own eye? You're nothing but show-offs! First, take the log out of your own eye. Then you can see how to take the speck out of your friend's eye...

Ask, and you will receive. Search, and you will find. Knock, and the door will be opened for you. Everyone who asks will receive. Everyone who searches will find. And the door will be opened for everyone who knocks. Would any of you give your hungry child a stone, if the child asked for some bread? Would you give your child a snake if the child asked for a fish? As bad as you are, you still know how to give good gifts to your children. But your heavenly Father is even more ready to give good things to people who ask. Treat others as you want them to treat you. This is what the Law and the Prophets are all about.

MATTHEW 7:1–5, 7–12

Listen to your heart and fill in...

What would you want others to do for you?

Make a list of nice things others could do for you. The longer the list, the better.

1. ______________________________
2. ______________________________
3. ______________________________
4. ______________________________
5. ______________________________
6. ______________________________
7. ______________________________
8. ______________________________

'Treat others as you want them to treat you' (Matthew 7:12a).

Links: 8 February, 10 March, 19 April, 30 December

5 minutes more? Psalm 116

29 April

The Sermon on the Mount

The two ways to live

Jesus continued:

Go in through the narrow gate. The gate to destruction is wide, and the road that leads there is easy to follow. A lot of people go through that gate. But the gate to life is very narrow. The road that leads there is so hard to follow that only a few people find it...

Anyone who hears and obeys these teachings of mine is like a wise person who built a house on solid rock. Rain poured down, rivers flooded, and winds beat against that house. But it did not fall, because it was built on solid rock. Anyone who hears my teachings and doesn't obey them is like a foolish person who built a house on sand. The rain poured down, the rivers flooded, and the winds blew and beat against that house. Finally, it fell with a crash.

When Jesus finished speaking, the crowds were surprised at his teaching. He taught them like someone with authority, and not like their teachers of the Law of Moses.

MATTHEW 7:13–14, 24–29

Di:SaipL

Some advice on building good foundations

Being wise has little to do with being intelligent. Being wise is to rejoice in Jesus' words and to do what he says. It is quite possible to be intelligent, both at school and socially, but to be foolish in God's eyes—especially if you won't listen to what Jesus says and won't try to follow his teaching.

There are two ways to live your life—God's way and the world's way. One is wise and the other is foolish. One is like building on the rock, the other is like building on sand.

What are you building your life on?

Links: 22 February, 16 August, 24 October, 19 November

5 minutes more? Psalm 118

Moses part 4 (c.1250BC)

The golden calf

After the people saw that Moses had been on the mountain for a long time, they went to Aaron and said, 'Make us an image of a god who will lead and protect us. Moses brought us out of Egypt, but nobody knows what has happened to him.' Aaron told them, 'Bring me the gold earrings that your wives and sons and daughters are wearing.' Everybody took off their earrings and brought them to Aaron, then he melted them and made an idol in the shape of a young bull. All the people said to one another, 'This is the god who brought us out of Egypt!' …

Moses went back down the mountain with the two flat stones on which God had written all his laws with his own hand, and he had used both sides of the stones… As Moses got closer to the camp, he saw the idol, and he also saw the people dancing around. This made him so angry that he threw down the stones and broke them to pieces at the foot of the mountain. He melted the idol the people had made, and he ground it into powder. He scattered it in their water and made them drink it.

EXODUS 32:1–4, 15–16, 19–20

Weird and wonderful

Gold calves and goldfish

They say that goldfish only remember things for a few seconds—stupid creatures, goldfish. But as far as God is concerned, it could seem as if people are a bit like goldfish.

Only a few days after God had led the people out of Egypt, divided the Red Sea, and given them food and drink in a miraculous way, they had forgotten everything. Moses didn't need to be away for more than a few days before they forgot God and spoilt everything.

It's easy to be a goldfish if you don't consciously try to remember the things God has done for you. Thank God for something he has done for you, and pray that you won't have a short-term memory.

Links: 7 April, 8 April, 9 April, 23 July

5 minutes more? Psalm 119:1–48 (or all of it if you feel up to it!)

1 May

Moses part 4 (c.1250BC)

The Lord renews the covenant

One day the Lord said to Moses, 'Cut two flat stones like the first ones I made, and I will write on them the same commandments that were on the two you broke...' So Moses cut two flat stones like the first ones, and early the next morning he carried them to the top of Mount Sinai, just as the Lord had commanded... Moses quickly bowed down to the ground and worshipped the Lord. He prayed, 'Lord, if you really are pleased with me, I pray that you will go with us. It is true that these people are sinful and rebellious, but forgive our sin and let us be your people.' The Lord said:

I promise to perform miracles for you that have never been seen anywhere on earth. Neighbouring nations will stand in fear and know that I was the one who did these marvellous things.

EXODUS 34:1, 4, 8–10

Big word

Covenant

A covenant is simply a deal, a contract or an agreement. Everyone who has given their life to Christ has entered into an agreement or covenant with God.

Israel's covenant was based on the Law of the Old Testament. The new covenant is based on grace and the forgiveness we can receive through Jesus' death and resurrection. The sign or seal of this new covenant is the gift of the Holy Spirit that is given to every believer (Ephesians 4:30, NIV). If you have given your life to Christ, then you've got the Holy Spirit living in you (Romans 8:16–17).

Baptism is a public statement of that agreement; when we are baptized we enter into a deal, a contract, an agreement—and promise that we will live for Jesus Christ for ever. If you aren't baptized and you love Jesus, you should think about getting baptized as soon as possible! Talk to your youth leader about it, perhaps, and take things from there?

Links: 14 January, 15 January, 7 April, 16 September

5 minutes more? Psalm 121

2 May

Moses part 4 (c.1250BC)

The spies are sent to check out the land

The Lord said to Moses, 'Choose a leader from each tribe and send them into Canaan to explore the land I am giving you.' ... After exploring the land of Canaan for forty days, the twelve men returned to Kadesh in the Paran Desert and told Moses, Aaron, and the people what they had seen. They showed him the fruit and said:

Look at this fruit! The land we explored is rich with milk and honey. But the people who live there are strong, and their cities are large and walled...

Then they started spreading rumours and saying, 'We won't be able to grow anything in that soil. And the people are like giants. In fact, we saw the Nephilim who are the ancestors of the Anakim. They were so big that we felt as small as grasshoppers.'

NUMBERS 13:1–2, 25–28a, 32–33

Check it out

Joshua and Caleb

All the spies that were sent out to spy on the land of Canaan came back scared out of their wits—all except Joshua and Caleb.

Joshua and Caleb were the only ones who had the faith to believe that the people of Israel would manage to settle in the land—but only if they would believe God. This is what they said to the people: 'If we obey the Lord, he will surely give us that land rich with milk and honey. So don't rebel. We have no reason to be afraid of the people who live there. The Lord is on our side, and they won't stand a chance against us!' (Numbers 14:8–9).

If we lose sight of God, it is easy to become weak and cowardly and duck out when it matters most. If, on the other hand, we are like Joshua and Caleb and believe God's promises, then there is no limit to what we can achieve for him.

Try to live boldly—not because you're formidably strong, but because God is!

Links: 7 May, 8 May, 9 May, 11 May

5 minutes more? Psalm 126

3 May

Moses part 4 (c.1250BC)

Forty years in the desert

After the Israelites heard the report... [they] complained to Moses and Aaron, 'We wish we had died in Egypt or somewhere out here in the desert! Is the Lord leading us into Canaan, just to have us killed and our women and children captured? We'd be better off in Egypt.' Then they said to one another, 'Let's choose our own leader and go back.' ...

Then the Lord said to Moses:

In answer to your prayer, I do forgive them. But as surely as I live and my power has no limit, I swear that not one of these Israelites will enter the land I promised to give to their ancestors. These people have seen my power in Egypt and in the desert, but they will never see Canaan. They have disobeyed and tested me too many times... Only Caleb and Joshua will go in...

I will cruelly punish you every day for the next forty years—one for each day that the land was explored. You sinful people who ganged up against me will die here in the desert.

NUMBERS 14:1a, 2–4, 20–23, 30b, 34–35

Did you know that...

...it only takes fifteen days to walk from Egypt to Israel?

But, as a punishment, the people of Israel had to walk around in the dry, hot, monotonous desert for forty years. They hadn't taken God at his word, and hadn't believed that they would have their own land some day.

People today, particularly younger people, don't talk very much about heaven—our promised land. Perhaps it's because life's too easy for us.

The Bible says that life down here on earth is like a desert compared to heaven. So it's idiotic to be so happy with the desert that we forget to dream about the promised land—I mean, to be so happy with life that we forget to dream about heaven.

Are you looking forward to heaven? You have every reason to do so.

Links: 14 March, 4 April, 4 May, 5 May

5 minutes more? Psalm 130

4 May

Moses part 4 (c.1250BC)

Don't be stubborn

It is just as the Holy Spirit says, 'If you hear God's voice today, don't be stubborn! Don't rebel* like those people who were tested in the desert. For forty years your ancestors tested God and saw the things he did. Then God got tired of them and said, "You people never show good sense, and you don't understand what I want you to do." God became angry and told the people, "You will never enter my place of rest!"' ...

The promise to enter the place of rest is still good, and we must take care that none of you miss out... We should do our best to enter that place of rest, so that none of us will disobey and miss going there, as they did.
HEBREWS 3:7–11; 4:1, 11

* or 'don't harden your hearts'.

Big word
Hardening the heart

One of the benefits of having the Holy Spirit living in us is being able to take in the information God gives us, effectively—being able to hear his voice and understand his word. Hardening the heart means not wanting to hear, not wanting to believe, not wanting to do what the Holy Spirit says.

If someone—say, a friend of yours—knows that God is calling them, but pretends not to hear him, then s/he is hardening his or her heart. The Holy Spirit is prompting their heart, but they won't listen.

If someone—say, you—think that God is trying to tell you something, but for one reason or another you pretend you can't hear it, you could be ignoring the prompting of the Holy Spirit in your heart.

Don't harden your heart, please. It's always stupid to harden your heart.

PS: Very often your conscience tells you if God's trying to tell you something. Listen to that prompting of the Spirit.

Links: 30 July, 31 October, 28 November, 29 November

5 minutes more? Psalm 150

Moses part 4 (c.1250BC)

The poisonous snakes in the desert

The Israelites had to go around the territory of Edom, so when they left Mount Hor, they headed south towards the Red Sea. But along the way, the people became so impatient that they complained against God and said to Moses, 'Did you bring us out of Egypt, just to let us die in the desert? There's no water out here, and we can't stand this awful food!' Then the Lord sent poisonous snakes that bit and killed many of them. Some of the people went to Moses and admitted, 'It was wrong of us to insult you and the Lord. Now please ask him to make these snakes go away.' Moses prayed, and the Lord answered, 'Make a snake out of bronze and place it on top of a pole. Anyone who gets bitten can look at the snake and won't die.' Moses obeyed the Lord. And all of those who looked at the bronze snake lived, even though they had been bitten by the poisonous snakes.

NUMBERS 21:4–9

Check it out

John 3:14–15

1. The people of Israel were in a sticky situation.
2. They had been disobedient and were surrounded by snakes.
3. But Moses was given instructions to make a bronze snake, hang it on a pole and lift it up.
4. Everyone who looked at the bronze snake would be saved.

The Bible says that this represents our own situation.

1. We are also in a sticky situation.
2. We are disobedient and trapped in our sin.
3. But God took his only Son and hung him on the cross.
4. Everyone who trusts in Jesus will be saved.

John 3:14–15 says that 'the Son of Man must be lifted up, just as that metal snake was lifted up by Moses in the desert. Then everyone who has faith in the Son of Man will have eternal life.'

I'm sure you know the next verse off by heart. I'm sure you do. After John 3:15 comes...

Links: 4 February, 3 May, 20 July, 4 November

5 minutes more? Proverbs 1

6 May

Moses part 4 (c.1250BC)

Moses' message to the people after forty years in the desert

Moses said to Israel:

The Lord told me to give you these laws and teachings, so you can obey them in the land he is giving you. Soon you will cross the River Jordan and take that land. And if you and your descendants want to live a long time, you must always worship the Lord and obey his laws. Pay attention, Israel! Our ancestors worshipped the Lord, and he promised to give us this land that is rich with milk and honey. Be careful to obey him, and you will become a successful and powerful nation.

Listen, Israel! The Lord our God is the only true God! So love the Lord your God with all your heart, soul, and strength. Memorize his laws and tell them to your children over and over again. Talk about them all the time, whether you're at home or walking along the road or going to bed at night, or getting up in the morning.
DEUTERONOMY 6:1–7

Download

All of your heart…

This verse is perhaps the most central one in the whole of the Old Testament. It is part of the Jewish creed. On almost every doorpost in Israel there is a very small pot. In each little pot there is a piece of paper with this verse written on it, so that the people who live there will be constantly reminded of it.

You need to learn it too.

'Love the Lord your God with all your heart, soul, and strength' (Deuteronomy 6:5).

Links: 26 March, 8 April, 19 April, 1 November

5 minutes more? Proverbs 2

7 May

Moses part 4 (c.1250BC)

Joshua takes over from Moses

Moses again spoke to the whole nation of Israel:

I am a hundred and twenty years old, and I am no longer able to be your leader. And besides that, the Lord your God has told me that he won't let me cross the River Jordan...

Then Moses called Joshua up in front of the crowd and said:

Joshua, be brave and strong as you lead these people into their land. The Lord made a promise long ago to Israel's ancestors that this land would some day belong to Israel. That time has now come, and you must divide up the land among the people. The Lord will lead you into the land. He will always be with you and help you, so don't ever be afraid of your enemies...

And so, Moses the Lord's servant died there in Moab, just as the Lord had said. The Lord buried him in a valley near the town of Beth-Peor, but even today no one knows exactly where... There has never again been a prophet in Israel like Moses. The Lord spoke face to face with him.

DEUTERONOMY 31:1–2, 7–8; 34:5–6, 10

☆ Bible personality

Joshua

Moses had led the people out of Egypt, through the Red Sea and through the desert for forty years. He was the greatest leader in the history of the people. However, to everyone's amazement, he received a clear message from the Lord that he wouldn't be the one to lead the people into the land they'd been promised. That was a job for Joshua.

Joshua had been one of the spies who had been sent out to explore the land forty years previously. They had all returned to camp and been in agreement that the land was wonderful—more than they could have wished for—but only two of the spies had thought it was realistic to conquer it. Joshua was one of them. He turned out to be one of the bravest men in the whole of the Old Testament.

The next five days' readings are about Joshua. We enter the story just before Moses dies, about 1210 years before the birth of Christ, on the eastern bank of the River Jordan.

Read on. It's interesting stuff!

Links: 2 May, 8 May, 9 May, 10 May

5 minutes more? Proverbs 3

8 May

Joshua (c.1210BC)

Joshua gets ready to occupy the land

Moses, the Lord's servant, was dead. So the Lord spoke to Joshua son of Nun, who had been the assistant of Moses. The Lord said:

My servant Moses is dead. Now you must lead Israel across the River Jordan into the land I'm giving to all of you... Long ago I promised the ancestors of Israel that I would give this land to their descendants. So be strong and brave! Be careful to do everything my servant Moses taught you. Never stop reading The Book of the Law he gave you. Day and night you must think about what it says. If you obey it completely, you and Israel will be able to take this land. I've commanded you to be strong and brave. Don't ever be afraid or discouraged! I am the Lord your God, and I will be there to help you wherever you go.

JOSHUA 1:1–2, 6–9

Listen to your heart and fill in...

Are you leadership material?

We need solid leaders. We need solid leaders like Joshua. Here is a very small and rather childish test, but try it anyway. Test yourself—are you leadership material?

Joshua trusted God's promises. Do you trust God's promises?	YES	NO
Joshua saw possibilities where others saw impossibilities. Are you like him?	YES	NO
Joshua turned neither to the left or the right. Is that you?	YES	NO
Joshua meditated on God's word night and day. Do you love God's word like that?	YES	NO

If you've circled YES more times than NO, it could be that you have leadership potential. Whatever you scored, here is a verse for your encouragement:

'I've commanded you to be strong and brave. Don't ever be afraid or discouraged! I am the Lord your God, and I will be there to help you wherever you go' (Joshua 1:9).

Links: 2 May, 9 May, 10 May, 11 May

5 minutes more? Proverbs 4

9 May

Joshua (c.1210BC)

The people cross the Jordan

Joshua spoke to the people:

Come here and listen to what the Lord our God said he will do! ... Just watch the sacred chest that belongs to the Lord, the ruler of the whole earth. As soon as the priests carrying the chest step into the Jordan, the water will stop flowing and pile up as if someone had built a dam across the river.

The Israelites packed up and left camp. The priests carrying the chest walked in front, until they came to the River Jordan. The water in the river had risen over its banks, as it often does in springtime. But as soon as the feet of the priests touched the water, the river stopped flowing, and the water started piling up... The priests stood in the middle of the dry river bed near Jericho while everyone else crossed over.

'The Lord our God dried up the River Jordan so we could walk across... because he wants everyone on earth to know how powerful he is. And he wants us to worship only him.'

JOSHUA 3:9, 11–12, 14–16a, 17; 4:23a, 24

Refresh

How to get across the Jordan?

Most people know that Moses led the people of Israel through the Red Sea when they left Egypt. But probably very few people know that Joshua did something similar forty years later.

Every once in a while in life, we meet obstacles and difficulties. God's word doesn't say that we Christians can expect a life without challenges—quite the opposite. But God has promised:

1. That he will get us through the tough times.
2. That he will be with us in the tough times.
3. That in the end, we will come out of the tough times in one piece.

What challenges or problems have you got to face in the near future? What sort of River Jordan must you cross?

Links: 2 April, 4 April, 2 May, 8 June

5 minutes more? Proverbs 8

10 May

Joshua (c.1210BC)

Seven times round Jericho

Meanwhile, the people of Jericho had been locking the gates in their town wall because they were afraid of the Israelites. No one could go out or come in. The Lord said to Joshua:

With my help, you and your army will defeat the king of Jericho and his army, and you will capture the town. Here is how to do it: march slowly around Jericho once a day for six days... But on the seventh day, march slowly around the town seven times while the priests blow their trumpets... The wall will fall down, and your soldiers can go straight in from every side.

The priests blew their trumpets again, and the soldiers shouted as loud as they could. The walls of Jericho fell flat. Then the soldiers rushed up the hill, went straight into the town, and captured it... The Lord helped Joshua in everything he did, and Joshua was famous everywhere in Canaan.

JOSHUA 6:1–3, 4b, 5b, 20, 27

Weird and wonderful

Joshua's curse

Jericho was the first town that the people of Israel captured. After the walls fell and the victory was won, Joshua cursed the town. He said that Jericho must remain deserted—even that anyone who tried to rebuild the town would lose his eldest son and eventually all his children (Joshua 6:26).

Jericho lies near an oasis with plenty of water, and it is thought that there has been a settlement there for 8,000 years. But archeological studies show that the town was deserted from the time of Joshua until 900BC (that is, for 300–400 years). Then a man called Hiel came along and had the not-so-bright idea of trying to rebuild Jericho. Listen to what happened:

'While Ahab was king, a man from Bethel named Hiel rebuilt the town of Jericho. But while Hiel was laying the foundation for the town wall, his eldest son Abiram died. And while he was finishing the gates, his youngest son Segub died. This happened just as the Lord told Joshua to say many years ago' (1 Kings 16:34).

It pays to listen to the Lord!

Links: 2 May, 8 May, 11 May, 8 June

5 minutes more? Ecclesiastes 1

11 May

Joshua (c.1210BC)

God did all the good things he had promised to do

The Lord gave the Israelites the land he had promised their ancestors, and they captured it and settled in it. There still were enemies around Israel, but the Lord kept his promise to let his people live in peace. And whenever the Israelites did have to go to war, no enemy could defeat them. The Lord always helped Israel win. The Lord promised to do many good things for Israel, and he kept his promise every time...

Joshua said:

The Lord is fearsome; he is the one true God, and I don't think you are able to worship and obey him in the ways he demands. You would have to be completely faithful, and if you sin or rebel, he won't let you get away with it. If you turn your backs on the Lord and worship the gods of other nations, the Lord will turn against you. He will make terrible things happen to you and wipe you out, even though he had been good to you before.

But the people shouted, 'We won't worship any other gods. We will worship and obey only the Lord!'

JOSHUA 21:43–45; 24:19–21

Did you know that...

...Joshua and Jesus are the same name?

The Hebrew name 'Joshua' gradually changed. As time went by, it was pronounced 'Jeshua', which in Greek is pronounced 'Jesus'.

The name means 'God is salvation'. Joshua was a saviour for the emerging nation of Israel. Jesus is our Saviour from sin and death in the emerging kingdom of God.

Links: 17 May, 8 June, 29 December, 31 December

5 minutes more? Ecclesiastes 3

12 May

The Holy Spirit

The promise of the Holy Spirit

The Lord said:

Later, I will give my Spirit to everyone. Your sons and daughters will prophesy. Your old men will have dreams, and your young men will see visions. In those days I will even give my Spirit to my servants, both men and women. I will work wonders in the sky above and on the earth below. There will blood and fire and clouds of smoke. The sun will turn dark, and the moon will be as red as blood before that great and terrible day when I appear.

Then the Lord will save everyone who faithfully worships him.
JOEL 2:28–32a

I will take away your stubborn heart and give you a new heart and a desire to be faithful. You will have only pure thoughts, because I will put my Spirit in you and make you eager to obey my laws and teachings.
EZEKIEL 36:26–27

Check it out

People in the Old Testament who had the Holy Spirit with them

Before Jesus' time, there were only a few VIP types who had the Holy Spirit with them.

- Joseph (Genesis 41:38)
- Moses (Numbers 11:25)
- Gideon (Judges 6:34)
- Saul (1 Samuel 10:6)
- David (1 Samuel 16:13)
- Micah (Micah 3:8)

But one day, said the prophet Joel, one day in the future the Holy Spirit will be given to all those who believe, not just God's VIPs. Precisely fifty days after Jesus' resurrection, ten days after his ascension to heaven, something so remarkable happened that we Christians believe the prophet's words were fulfilled (see Acts 2).

Now all of us ordinary people can live life in the Spirit. The readings over the next few days will focus on this.

Links: 1 January, 13 May, 18 May, 5 October

5 minutes more? Ecclesiastes 12

13 May

The Holy Spirit

The Holy Spirit gives things life

You created all of them by your Spirit, and you give new life to the earth.
PSALM 104:30

The Spirit of God All-Powerful gave me the breath of life... If God took back the breath that he breathed into us, we humans would die and return to the soil.
JOB 33:4; 34:14–15

Christ died once for our sins. An innocent person died for those who are guilty. Christ did this to bring you to God, when his body was put to death and his spirit was made alive.
1 PETER 3:18

Yet God raised Jesus to life! God's Spirit now lives in you, and he will raise you to life by his Spirit.
ROMANS 8:11

Did you know that...

...the Spirit gives things life?

It can be a bit difficult to get a handle on the Holy Spirit. He is quite hard to describe. The Bible does not say much about who the Holy Spirit really is, but it says an amazing amount about what the Holy Spirit does. What the Holy Spirit likes to do most is to give things life. When God created the world, the Holy Spirit was there 'moving over the water'.

Here are some things that the Holy Spirit gives life to:

- crocuses
- people
- churches
- Jesus (after he died)
- the Bible (so that it becomes the living word)
- faith
- us

You don't think he gives life to all these things? Well, it says so in the Bible. Have another look at the verses above.

Links: 1 January, 12 May, 18 May, 5 October

5 minutes more? Song of Songs 1

14 May

The Holy Spirit

God's spokesman

But now I am going back to the Father who sent me, and none of you asks me where I am going. You are very sad from hearing all this. But I tell you that I am going to do what is best for you. That is why I am going away. The Holy Spirit cannot come to help you until I leave. But after I am gone, I will send the Spirit to you. The Spirit will come and show the people of this world the truth about sin, God's justice and the judgment. The Spirit will show them that they are wrong about sin, because they didn't have faith in me…

I have much more to say to you, but right now it would be more than you could understand. The Spirit shows what is true and will come and guide you into the full truth. The Spirit doesn't speak on his own. He will tell you only what he has heard from me, and he will let you know what is going to happen. The Spirit will bring glory to me by taking my message and telling it to you.

JOHN 16:5–9, 12–14

Weird and wonderful

Jesus said it was best for the disciples that he went away

The disciples were really sad when Jesus told them he would soon have to leave them. Jesus had expected them to be upset, but he stuck to his guns—he was adamant that it was best for them that he went away. Otherwise they would never be sent… (fanfare…) the Holy Spirit, God's spokesman, who would help them get to know God better.

You can imagine how important it is to have the Holy Spirit in your life. Jesus doesn't walk around on earth in the kind of way that means we can hold his hand, or talk and chat with him—not physically, anyway. But we can get to know Jesus in a very deep and personal way through his spokesman, the Holy Spirit.

Links: 16 May, 10 October, 16 October, 3 November

5 minutes more? Song of Songs 4

15 May

The Holy Spirit

The Spirit brings us the presence of the living Christ

Jesus said to his disciples:

If you love me, you will do as I command. Then I will ask the Father to send you the Holy Spirit who will help you and always be with you. The Spirit will show you what is true. The people of this world cannot accept the Spirit, because they don't see or know him. But you know the Spirit, who is with you and will keep on living in you. I won't leave you like orphans, I will come back to you. In a little while the people of this world won't be able to see me, but you will see me. And because I live, you will live. Then you will know that I am one with the Father. You will know that you are one with me, and I am one with you...

I have told you these things while I am still with you. But the Holy Spirit will come and help you, because the Father will send the Spirit to take my place. The Spirit will teach you everything and will remind you of what I said while I was with you.

JOHN 14:15–20, 25–26

Di:SaipL

Uncertainty

We're OK about Jesus. We understand who he is and why he came.

And we're OK about God. We know enough about him to feel relatively certain in our understanding.

But the Holy Spirit...?

Well... I know that quite a few people think the whole idea of the Holy Spirit a bit spooky and incomprehensible. But he really isn't either of those things. The Spirit is there for our benefit. He helps us experience the presence of Jesus. He helps us know God's peace and blessing.

What about you? If you feel some uncertainty concerning your relationship with the Holy Spirit, it would be a good idea to talk it over with a mature Christian whom you can trust. They will be able to help you understand more about the role of the Spirit in the Christian life. They will pray with you that your uncertainties would become certainties that enable you to learn to talk with the Spirit.

Nothing makes the Christian life so full of sparkle, so exciting and meaningful, as much as knowing the fullness of the Holy Spirit in your life.

Links: 12 May, 13 May, 16 May, 3 November

5 minutes more? Song of Songs 5

16 May

The Holy Spirit

The gifts of the Spirit

My friends, you asked me about spiritual gifts... There are different kinds of spiritual gifts, but they all come from the same Spirit. There are different ways to serve the same Lord, and we can each do different things. Yet the same God works in all of us and helps us in everything we do. The Spirit has given each of us a special way of serving others. Some of us can speak with wisdom, while others can speak with knowledge, but these gifts come from the same Spirit. To others the Spirit has given great faith or the power to heal the sick or the power to perform mighty miracles. Some of us are prophets, and some of us recognize when God's Spirit is present. Others can speak different kinds of languages, and still others can tell what these languages mean. But it is the Spirit who does all this and decides which gifts to give to each of us.

1 CORINTHIANS 12:1, 4–11

Big word

Speaking in tongues

God has given us the gifts of the Spirit so that we can build one another up. 'Speaking in tongues' is one of those gifts. This happens when a person speaks out a message from God in a language they haven't learned and don't understand. (If you're not used to hearing it, it can sound quite wacky.) Then either the person themselves, or someone else, speaks out an interpretation of the message so that people can understand what God is saying. God can speak to whole churches and to individuals in this way.

PS: The gifts of the Spirit need to be used wisely and in a sensible fashion—so that they build people up rather than bringing God into disrepute (1 Corinthians 14:26; 1 Thessalonians 5:19–21).

PPS: Speaking in tongues can be used in our personal devotional time with God, not just when Christians are gathered together (1 Corinthians 14:2; Romans 8:26).

PPPS: You don't have to be able to speak in tongues to be a Spirit-led Christian (1 Corinthians 12:30).

Links: 13 May, 8 November, 12 November, 14 November

5 minutes more? Song of Songs 7

The Holy Spirit helps us in difficult situations

Jesus continued:

... Because of me, you will be dragged before rulers and kings to tell them and the Gentiles about your faith. But when someone arrests you, don't worry about what you will say or how you will say it. At that time you will be given the words to say. But you will not really be the one speaking. The Spirit from your Father will tell you what to say... Everyone will hate you because of me. But if you remain faithful until the end, you will be saved.

MATTHEW 10:18–20, 22

I am the Lord All-Powerful. So don't depend on your own power or strength, but on my Spirit.

ZECHARIAH 4:6

Christ gives me the strength to face anything.

PHILIPPIANS 4:13

Di:SaipL

It's never easy when it's difficult

Being a follower of Jesus can be tough. A lot of people are quite indifferent about Jesus, but there are some who can make life very difficult for those who openly say they belong to him. It could be a teacher, it could be a kid on your street or a group at your school or even someone you work with in the evenings or on Saturdays.

Not to worry. Jesus never said it would be easy, but he did promise to be with us and help us. When you get in a difficult situation, the best prayer is, 'Holy Spirit, help!' and you can be sure he will answer.

You can trust the Holy Spirit to give you the right words to say or show you the right thing to do in any difficult situation.

PS: Jesus said, 'I will be with you always, even until the end of the world' (Matthew 28:20).

Links: 4 March, 15 March, 21 April, 9 May

5 minutes more? Isaiah 5

The coming of the Holy Spirit

On the day of Pentecost all the Lord's followers were together in one place. Suddenly there was a noise from heaven like the sound of a mighty wind! ... Then they saw what looked like fiery tongues moving in all directions, and a tongue came and settled on each person there. The Holy Spirit took control of everyone, and they began speaking whatever languages the Spirit let them speak.

Many religious Jews from every country in the world were living in Jerusalem. And when they heard this noise, a crowd gathered. But they were surprised, because they were hearing everything in their own languages. They were excited and amazed, and said:

Don't all these who are speaking come from Galilee? Then why do we hear them speaking our very own languages? ...

Everyone was excited and confused. Some of them even kept asking each other, 'What does all this mean?' Others made fun of the Lord's followers and said, 'They are drunk.'

ACTS 2:1–8, 12–13

Weird and wonderful

Zero manipulation

Those of us who love being at powerful worship celebrations where the whole thing completely takes off...

Those of us who love it when the worship almost raises the roof... and it seems that the best times for this are late at night, or at least when it's dark...

Those of us who love a 'Spirit-charged' atmosphere...

...are those who need to remember two things about the coming of the Holy Spirit on the day of Pentecost.

1. The people who were there weren't standing with their arms raised. The original Greek says they were sitting, probably quite quietly (Acts 2:2).
2. It wasn't late at night. It was only nine o'clock in the morning! (Acts 2:15).

The Holy Spirit is the real thing. We don't need whipping up when he is there. We don't need to manipulate worship situations with the right props!

It's great when the Holy Spirit turns up, and we can feel his presence and the worship lifts the roof... and he will come whenever we welcome him—whoever is leading the worship, whatever the time of day!

Links: 5 October, 6 October, 15 October, 16 October

5 minutes more? Isaiah 6

19 May

The fruit of the Spirit

A good tree produces good fruit

People's desires make them give in to immoral ways, filthy thoughts, and shameful deeds. They worship idols, practise witchcraft, hate others, and are hard to get along with. People become jealous, angry, and selfish... They get drunk, carry on at wild parties, and do other evil things as well... No one who does these things will share in the blessings of God's kingdom. God's Spirit makes us loving, happy, peaceful, patient, kind, good, faithful, gentle, and self-controlled. There is no law against behaving in any of these ways. And because we belong to Christ Jesus, we have killed our selfish feelings and desires. God's Spirit has given us life, and so we should follow the Spirit.

GALATIANS 5:19–25

You can tell what they are by what they do. No one picks grapes or figs from thorn bushes. A good tree produces good fruit, and a bad tree produces bad fruit. A good tree cannot produce bad fruit, and a bad tree cannot produce good fruit.

MATTHEW 7:16–18

Big word

Fruit of the Spirit

You don't grow as a Christian by getting hold of yourself by the scruff of the neck and whipping yourself into shape. You grow by living in a close relationship with God, by constantly adjusting your life in line with the word of God, and by praying at all times. (That's why it's so great that you've decided to read this book!)

When you do these things, God will re-shape you in his image. He will change you for the better. The Bible says that you'll...

...have more love for the people around you
...be better at rejoicing in life
...have peace in your heart even if your circumstances are difficult
...tolerate things you don't like
...be friendly towards other people, and faithful to them
...be patient and self-controlled in situations that usually wind you up

When you allow God to nourish you, all these good things will appear in your life as naturally as apples on a well-tended apple tree.

Links: 23 February, 20 May, 21 May, 26 October

5 minutes more? Isaiah 7

20 May

The fruit of the Spirit

A good tree cannot produce bad fruit

A good tree cannot produce bad fruit, and a bad tree cannot produce good fruit.
LUKE 6:43

God blesses those people who refuse evil advice and won't follow sinners or join in sneering at God. Instead, the Law of the Lord makes them happy, and they think about it day and night. They are like trees growing beside a stream, trees that produce fruit in season and always have leaves. Those people succeed in everything they do.
PSALM 1:1–3

You used to be like people living in the dark, but now you are people of the light because you belong to the Lord. So act like people of the light and make your light shine. Be good and honest and truthful, as you try to please the Lord.
EPHESIANS 5:8–10

Check it out

How to produce a lot of fruit

Let me repeat what I said yesterday: you don't produce fruit in the Christian life by getting hold of yourself by the scruff of the neck and whipping yourself into shape.

We will only produce fruit if we (the branches) live our life in Christ (the main stem). Jesus said, 'I am the vine, and you are the branches. If you stay joined to me, and I stay joined to you, then you will produce lots of fruit. But you cannot do anything without me' (John 15:5).

If you suck up nourishment from the Bible on a regular basis, it is only a matter of time before fruit is produced. No need to strive—the fruit will grow automatically.

In the next few days' readings you'll discover that the fruit of the Spirit are actually the various attributes of God's character which are transmitted to us as we draw spiritual nourishment from him.

Links: 23 February, 19 May, 21 May, 26 October

5 minutes more? Isaiah 9

21 May

The fruit of the Spirit

God is love

Israel, I will always love you; that's why I've been so patient and kind.
JEREMIAH 31:3

God loved the people of this world so much that he gave his only Son, so that everyone who has faith in him will have eternal life and never really die.
JOHN 3:16

Real love isn't our love for God, but his love for us. God sent his Son to be the sacrifice by which our sins are forgiven. Dear friends, since God loved us this much, we must love each other. No one has ever seen God. But if we love each other, God lives in us, and his love is truly in our hearts... God stays united with everyone who openly says that Jesus is the Son of God. That's how we stay united with God and are sure that God loves us.
1 JOHN 4:10–12, 15–16

Download

The greatest love the world has ever seen!

'God loved the people of this world so much that he gave his only Son, so that everyone who has faith in him will have eternal life and never really die' (John 3:16).

Links: 30 March, 22 May, 29 July, 24 November

5 minutes more? Isaiah 11

22 May

The fruit of the Spirit

Love

Jesus answered, 'The most important [commandment] says: "People of Israel, you have only one Lord and God. You must love him with all your heart, soul, mind, and strength." The second most important commandment says: "Love others as much as you love yourself." No other commandment is more important than these.'

MARK 12:29–31

My dear friends, we must love each other. Love comes from God, and when we love each other, it shows that we have been given new life. We are now God's children, and we know him. God is love, and anyone who doesn't love others has never known him... We love because God loved us first. But if we say we love God and don't love each other, we are liars. We cannot see God. So how can we love God, if we don't love the people we can see? The commandment that God has given us is: 'Love God and love each other!'

1 JOHN 4:7–8, 19–21

Story

How the sun and the moon bet on a man's coat

Once upon a time, the sun and the moon had a bet as to who could get a man's coat off first.

'No problem,' said the wind. 'I'll win.' And he began to blow and blow. But the harder the wind howled and whined around the man, the tighter he pulled his coat around himself and wouldn't let go. Eventually the wind gave up.

'Let me try,' said the sun, and began to shine down on the man. The sun shone and shone. It got warmer. The sun made the man feel good. He straightened himself up, and was obviously very pleased with the warm weather. Eventually he unbuttoned his coat and took it off.

The only way you can change the people around you is with love...

Links: 21 May, 2 December, 3 December, 4 December

5 minutes more? Isaiah 35

23 May

The fruit of the Spirit

God rejoices over you

Our Lord, we pray that your glory will last for ever and that you will be pleased with what you have done. You look at the earth, and it trembles. You touch the mountains, and smoke goes up. As long as I live, I will sing and praise you, the Lord God. I hope my thoughts will please you, because you are the one who makes me glad.

PSALM 104:31–34

The Lord your God wins victory after victory and is always with you. He celebrates and sings because of you, and he will refresh your life with his love.

ZEPHANIAH 3:17

Download

God rejoices over you!

Learn this verse off by heart! Some people think it's the best in the Bible.

'The Lord your God wins victory after victory and is always with you. He celebrates and sings (rejoices) because of you, and he will refresh your life with his love' (Zephaniah 3:17).

PS: The Bible is not a sad book! The word 'joy' appears around 550 times!

Links: 21 May, 24 May, 31 May, 2 August

5 minutes more? Isaiah 40

24 May

The fruit of the Spirit

Joy

Fig trees may no longer bloom, or vineyards produce grapes; olive trees may be fruitless, and harvest time a failure; sheep pens may be empty, and cattle stalls vacant—but I will still celebrate (rejoice) because the Lord God saves me.
HABAKKUK 3:17–18

Always be glad because of the Lord! I will say it again: be glad.
PHILIPPIANS 4:4–5

I pray that God, who gives hope, will bless you with complete happiness and peace because of your faith. And may the power of the Holy Spirit fill you with hope.
ROMANS 15:13

Did you know that...

...joy and happiness are not the same thing?

You won't be happy all of the rest of your life. You will come up against difficulties—awful things and tough times. The joy you have in living by the Spirit is not dependent on how things are going for you, that is, on external circumstances. The Spirit's joy is a joy you have in your heart even if at times there isn't much in life to rejoice about.

The Bible encourages us to rejoice in the Lord despite our circumstances because Jesus has defeated the world (John 16:33).

Pray that God, who gives hope, will bless you with complete joy and peace because of your faith. And that the power of the Holy Spirit will fill you with hope.

Links: 23 May, 2 October, 6 October, 26 November

5 minutes more? Isaiah 49

25 May

The fruit of the Spirit

God is the God of peace

God wants everything to be done peacefully and in order.
1 CORINTHIANS 14:33

Try to get along and live peacefully with each other. Now I pray that God, who gives love and peace, will be with you.
2 CORINTHIANS 13:11b

I pray that God, who gives peace, will make you completely holy. And may your spirit, soul, and body be kept healthy and faultless until our Lord Jesus Christ returns. The one who chose you can be trusted, and he will do this.
1 THESSALONIANS 5:23–24

Refresh

The God of peace—well, sort of...?

If you think about all the wars being waged for the sake of religion, it can be difficult to imagine God being a God of peace. If you think back to the Crusades of the Middle Ages, it can be difficult to imagine God being a God of peace. If you think of the conflicts in the Middle East, it can be difficult to imagine God being a God of peace. But ask yourself who started these wars... God or men?

Pray for the innocent people caught up in religious conflicts and for peaceful resolutions to these conflicts. God is a God of peace.

If you are lying on your bed right now, it might be an idea to take Psalm 4:8 to heart—it's a little message from the God of peace to you before you fall asleep.

'I can lie down and sleep soundly (peacefully) because you, Lord, will keep me safe.'

Links: 26 May, 23 December, 27 December, 30 December

5 minutes more? Isaiah 50

26 May

The fruit of the Spirit

Peace

The Lord told Moses, 'When Aaron and his sons bless the people of Israel, they must say:

I pray that the Lord will bless and protect you, and that he will show you mercy and kindness. May the Lord be good to you and give you peace.'

Then the Lord said, 'If Aaron and his sons ask me to bless the Israelites, I will give them my blessing.'

NUMBERS 6:22–27

Don't worry about anything, but pray about everything. With thankful hearts offer up your prayers and requests to God. Then, because you belong to Christ Jesus, God will bless you with peace that no one can completely understand. And this peace will control the way you think and feel.

PHILIPPIANS 4:6–7

Big word

Peace

God's peace is huge. It says in Philippians 4:7 that it's much greater than our understanding. Here's a list of ten other things that God's peace is greater than:

1. Blunders and misunderstandings
2. A bad conscience
3. Exam nerves
4. Wandering thoughts and restlessness
5. The past
6. The future
7. Sticking-out ears
8. Boobs that are too small or too big
9. The particular mood you are in today
10. Death

PS: One more thing: 'I pray that the Lord will bless and protect you, and that he will show you mercy and kindness. May the Lord be good to you and give you peace' (Numbers 6:24–26).

Links: 19 January, 25 May, 28 May, 10 November

5 minutes more? Isaiah 53

27 May

The fruit of the Spirit

God is patient

Dear friends, don't forget that for the Lord one day is the same as a thousand years, and a thousand years is the same as one day. The Lord isn't slow about keeping his promises, as some people think he is. In fact, God is patient, because he wants everyone to turn from sin and no one to be lost... Don't forget that the Lord is patient because he wants people to be saved.

2 PETER 3:8–9, 15a

You don't think much of God's wonderful goodness or of his patience and willingness to put up with you. Don't you know that the reason God is good to you is because he wants you to turn to him?

ROMANS 2:4

Big word

Patient

If you're patient, you'll gladly wait for people for quite a long time. God is patient. God will gladly wait for people for quite a long time.

It's 2000 years since Jesus said he'd be coming back soon to set up a kingdom without grief, crying or pain. The Bible says that the reason he hasn't come back yet is so that as many people as possible will have time to understand that God wants them to have a place in heaven. It's his patience that causes the delay.

What can you do to spread the good news about heaven to your friends and family?

Links: 10 March, 28 May, 4 June, 26 December

5 minutes more? Isaiah 65

28 May

The fruit of the Spirit

Patience

But in everything and in every way we show that we truly are God's servants. We have always been patient, though we have had a lot of trouble, suffering, and hard times. We have been beaten, put in jail, and hurt in riots. We have worked hard and have gone without sleep and food. But we have kept ourselves pure and have been understanding, patient, and kind. The Holy Spirit has been with us, and our love has been real.

2 CORINTHIANS 6:4–6

Always be humble and gentle. Patiently put up with each other and love each other.

EPHESIANS 4:2

Put up with each other, and forgive anyone who does you wrong, just as Christ has forgiven you. Love is more important than anything else. It is what ties everything completely together.

COLOSSIANS 3:13–14

Di:SaipL

A disciple is patient with others

If you have older brothers and sisters…
If you have younger brothers and sisters…
If you have pushy friends…
If you have friends who can't be bothered…
If no one passes the ball to you during games…
If no one is as good as you at football…
If you prefer formal worship to charismatic worship…
If you prefer charismatic worship to any other form of worship…

… always be humble and gentle. Patiently put up with each other and love each other.

Links: 27 May, 5 June, 10 November, 20 December

5 minutes more? Jeremiah 1

29 May

The fruit of the Spirit

God is your friend

Now I tell you to love each other, as I have loved you. The greatest way to show love for friends is to die for them. And you are my friends, if you obey me. Servants don't know what their master is doing, and so I don't speak to you as my servants. I speak to you as my friends.

JOHN 15:12–15a

We used to be stupid, disobedient, and foolish, as well as slaves of all sorts of desires and pleasures. We were evil and jealous. Everyone hated us, and we hated everyone. God our Saviour showed us how good and kind he is. He saved us because of his mercy, and not because of any good things that we have done.

TITUS 3:3–5a

Did you know that...

...Jesus had a best friend?

John writes in John's Gospel that John was Jesus' best friend. What a creep!

Six times, that is 6 times (just to make that clear), John tells us that Jesus was more fond of him than the other disciples (John 13:23; 19:26; 20:2; 21:7, 20, 24). I bet the others wouldn't have agreed with that. I think that John must have had an inferiority complex or something...

John thought he was Jesus' best friend.

Well, as far as I'm concerned, I think I am.

And you—you are bound to think that you are too!

And we are all absolutely right!

Links: 7 February, 8 February, 10 February, 30 May

5 minutes more? Jeremiah 17

30 May

The fruit of the Spirit

Kindness

Always be gentle with others. The Lord will soon be here.
PHILIPPIANS 4:5

Happiness can make you smile; sorrow can crush you... Kind words are like honey—they cheer you up and make you feel strong.
PROVERBS 15:13; 16:24

Stay away from stupid and senseless arguments. These only lead to trouble, and God's servants must not be troublemakers. They must be kind to everyone, and they must be good teachers and very patient.
2 TIMOTHY 2:23–24

Hmm... just a thought...

...about kindness

The Bible says that kindness is a sure sign that someone is a follower of Christ. If you are a follower of Christ and you don't think you quite shape up to that...

...then ask Jesus to help you do something about it and be kind to everyone you meet today!

Links: 20 January, 24 May, 29 May, 4 December

5 minutes more? Jeremiah 18

31 May

The fruit of the Spirit

God is good

You are good to everyone, and you take care of all your creation.
PSALM 145:9

The Lord is kind to everyone who trusts and obeys him.
LAMENTATIONS 3:25

We will celebrate and praise you, Lord! You are good to us and your love never fails...
Shout praises to the Lord! He is good to us, and his love never fails...
Tell the Lord how thankful you are, because he is kind and always merciful...
Tell the Lord how thankful you are, because he is kind and always merciful...
Come and shout praises. Praise the name of the Lord! He is kind and good...
Praise the Lord! He is good. God's love never fails...
The Lord is good! His love and faithfulness will last for ever.
PSALM 106:1; 107:1; 118:1, 29; 135:3; 136:1; 100:5

Listen to your heart and fill in

Have you got something to thank God for?

The people of Israel knew that their God was good—they had a lot to be thankful for. The book of Psalms illustrates that very well. It's important not to forget all the good things God does for us. What have you got to rejoice and be thankful about at the moment?

1. ______________________________

2. ______________________________

3. ______________________________

Take a while to praise God—he is good and he is always kind and merciful.

Links: 1 June, 2 June, 5 June, 7 December

5 minutes more? Jeremiah 31

1 June

The fruit of the Spirit

Goodness

God planned for us to do good things and to live as he has always wanted us to live. That's why he sent Christ to make us what we are.
EPHESIANS 2:10

Instead, be kind and merciful, and forgive others, just as God forgave you because of Christ.
EPHESIANS 4:32

We should keep on encouraging each other to be thoughtful and to do helpful things.
HEBREWS 10:24

Dear friend, don't copy the evil deeds of others! Follow the example of people who do kind deeds. They are God's children.
3 JOHN 1:11a

Refresh

Encourage each other

It's difficult to be a Christian on your own. In fact, it's almost impossible. Some people are unfortunate enough not to have any Christian fellowship where they live. But unbelievably many Christians don't belong to a church or a small group because they can't be bothered or they can't bring themselves to do it for some reason or other.

If you don't belong to a Christian fellowship of some sort, then you should make an effort to do so. It is perhaps the most important thing you can do to make sure you grow as a Christian. You can't be good to each other and encourage one another if there's only one of you!

'We should keep on encouraging each other to be thoughtful and to do helpful things' (Hebrews 10:24).

Links: 31 May, 6 October, 24 November, 26 November

5 minutes more? Lamentations 1

2 June

The fruit of the Spirit

God is faithful

You know that the Lord your God is the only true God. So love him and obey his commands, and he will faithfully keep his agreement with you and your descendants for a thousand generations.
DEUTERONOMY 7:9

Even if you think you can stand up to temptation, be careful not to fall. You are tempted in the same way that everyone else is tempted. But God can be trusted (is faithful) not to let you be tempted too much, and he will show you how to escape from your temptations.
1 CORINTHIANS 10:12–13

If we are not faithful, he will still be faithful. Christ cannot deny who he is.
2 TIMOTHY 2:13

God can be trusted, and he chose you to be partners with his Son, our Lord Jesus Christ.
1 CORINTHIANS 1:9

Good news

God is faithful

God has chosen you—as his own. He's not going to run off, he's not going to give up on you and he's not going to dump you.

No one can say that they've really loved a person 100 per cent before they've done so for their whole life. 'Till death us do part…' is the promise that a couple makes when they get married.

Jesus loved you to death!
In fact, he loved you further than death.
He loved you right through death and out the other side.

When God says he is faithful, we know his words aren't empty. He isn't going to disappear before he's finished what he started, and he has shown that through what we read in the Bible.

Links: 25 May, 3 June, 29 July, 15 November

5 minutes more? Lamentations 3

3 June

The fruit of the Spirit

Faithfulness

Wisdom will protect you from the smooth talk of a sinful woman, who breaks her wedding vows and leaves the man she married when she was young…

The Law of the Lord is a lamp, and its teachings shine brightly. Correction and self-control will lead you through life. They will protect you from the flattering words of someone else's wife. Don't let yourself be attracted by the charm and lovely eyes of someone like that.

PROVERBS 2:16; 6:23–25

What I am saying is for your own good—it isn't to limit your freedom. I want to help you to live right and to love the Lord above all else.

1 CORINTHIANS 7:35

But the Lord can be trusted to make you strong and protect you from harm.

2 THESSALONIANS 3:3

Hmm... just a thought...

…about faithfulness

Most people dream about getting married some day, but no one wants a spouse who flirts and hops into bed with other people.

If you cultivate faithfulness in your relationship with God, I can guarantee you'll find it easier to be a good husband or wife later in life.

Unfaithfulness stinks.

Links: 2 June, 18 September, 26 November, 12 December

5 minutes more? Lamentations 5

4 June

The fruit of the Spirit

God is gentle

If you are tired from carrying heavy burdens, come to me and I will give you rest. Take the yoke I give you. Put it on your shoulders and learn from me. I am gentle and humble, and you will find rest. This yoke is easy to bear, and this burden is light.
MATTHEW 11:28–30

Our Lord, we belong to you. We tell you what worries us, and you won't let us fall.
PSALM 55:22

God cares for you, so turn all your worries over to him.
1 PETER 5:7

Did you know that...

...yokes are a good thing?

It sounds incredibly difficult to wear the yoke that Jesus offers, but it isn't. If you'd lived long ago and had to collect water from a well every day, you'd know that yokes are a good thing. Yokes help you to carry heavy weights more easily—they spread the load.

Perhaps you can remember the picture in the nursery rhyme book you had as a child—Jack and Jill going up the hill to fetch a pail of water, carrying a yoke and two empty buckets. The yoke was a long piece of wood shaped to fit comfortably round the neck and over the shoulders. Attached to each end was a hook on a short chain, that held the buckets by their handles.

Many people can testify that it has been easier to carry heavy loads when they have used Jesus' yoke. You should try it!

Jesus has a strong back and a lot of endurance. He can carry a lot, and he does it gently.

If you have something you need help carrying—go to Jesus!

Links: 27 May, 5 June, 7 June, 17 December

5 minutes more? Ezekiel 11

5 June

The fruit of the Spirit

Gentleness

They must always be ready to do something helpful and not say cruel things or argue. They should be gentle and kind to everyone. We used to be stupid, disobedient, and foolish, as well as slaves of all sorts of desires and pleasures. We were evil and jealous. Everyone hated us, and we hated everyone. God our Saviour showed us how good and kind he is.
TITUS 3:1b–4

Are any of you wise or sensible? Then show it by living right and by being humble and wise in everything you do. But if your heart is full of bitter jealousy and selfishness, don't boast or lie to cover up the truth... When peacemakers plant seeds of peace, they will harvest justice.
JAMES 3:13–14, 18

You belong to God, so keep away from all these evil things. Try your best to please God and to be like him. Be faithful, loving, dependable, and gentle.
1 TIMOTHY 6:11

Weird and wonderful

The better you know someone, the less you'll put up with before you explode!

It's a strange thing that the closer you are to each other, the better you know each other, and the fonder you are of each other...

...the easier it is to hurt the other
...the easier it is to be hurt by them
...the easier it is to be irritated
...the easier it is to let yourself irritate the other person
...the easier it is to argue

Let the people you live with at home notice that you are a Christian. Try hard to be kind and gentle. And if by any chance you feel hurt or you hurt someone, be the sort of person who is quick to forgive or ask for forgiveness.

Links: 4 June, 17 December, 19 December, 21 December

5 minutes more? Ezekiel 36

6 June

The fruit of the Spirit

God has self-control

When Jesus returned from the River Jordan, the power of the Holy Spirit was with him, and the Spirit led him into the desert. For forty days, Jesus was tested by the devil, and during that time he went without eating. When it was all over, he was hungry. The devil said to Jesus, 'If you are God's Son, tell this stone to turn into bread.' Jesus answered, 'The Scriptures say, "No one can live only on food."' Then the devil led Jesus up to a high place and quickly showed him all the nations on earth. The devil said, 'I will give all this power and glory to you. It has been given to me, and I can give it to anyone I want to. Just worship me, and you can have it all.' Jesus answered, 'The Scriptures say: "Worship the Lord your God and serve only him."'

LUKE 4:1–8

We have a great high priest, who has gone into heaven, and he is Jesus the Son of God. That is why we must hold on to what we have said about him. Jesus understands every weakness of ours, because he was tempted in every way that we are. But he did not sin!

HEBREWS 4:14–15

Big word

Sin

Some people think that Christianity makes too much fuss about sin.

The point about sin is not to get people stuck in a place where they can only feel that they are terrible and worthless, with no self-esteem—feeling guilty and trapped.

The point is that only when we admit that we are sinners and look beyond our failings to Jesus, do we have the chance to be set free—free to see that we need Jesus to forgive us and help us. Jesus was so self-controlled that he managed to resist all temptation. He is our hope. Without him we don't stand a chance.

If we admit to Jesus that we are sinners, and ask for forgiveness, we needn't feel weighed down and guilty any more—just forgiven and free.

Links: 7 June, 12 July, 22 August, 7 September

5 minutes more? Ezekiel 37

7 June

The fruit of the Spirit

Self-control

You can be certain that in the last days there will be some very hard times. People will love only themselves and money. They will be proud, stuck-up, rude, and disobedient to their parents. They will also be ungrateful, godless, heartless, and hateful. Their words will be cruel, and they will have no self-control or pity. These people will hate everything that is good. They will be sneaky, reckless, and puffed up with pride. Instead of loving God, they will love pleasure. Even though they will make a show of being religious, their religion won't be real. Don't have anything to do with such people.

2 TIMOTHY 3:1–5

Losing self-control leaves you as helpless as a city without a wall.

PROVERBS 25:28

Do your best to improve your faith. You can do this by adding goodness, understanding, self-control, patience, devotion to God, concern for others, and love.

2 PETER 1:5–7

Refresh

Yoga isn't necessarily the best way to attain self-control!

Perhaps you thought that only Eastern religions were into self-control and the like. Some people do use certain aspects of them to attain self-control—by practising meditation, yoga and other forms of controlled exercise.

But the Bible has another way to self-control. It says that self-control grows of its own accord when you live by the power of the Holy Spirit. It doesn't develop through various exercises, but as a fruit—the result of living your life with Jesus. Surely that makes sense, since Jesus is the only person in human history to have had complete self-control (turn back and look at yesterday).

These are the other fruit you can expect to see in yourself as a result of living for Jesus: love, joy, peace, patience, kindness, goodness, faithfulness, gentleness and, last of all, self-control.

Links: 16 April, 6 June, 22 August, 26 October

5 minutes more? Ezekiel 41

8 June

The Judges rule (c.1200–1000BC)

The time of the Judges in a nutshell

Joshua died at the age of one hundred and ten... After a while the people of Joshua's generation died, and the next generation did not know the Lord or any of the things he had done for Israel... But now the Israelites stopped worshipping the Lord and worshipped the idols of Baal and Astarte, as well as the idols of other gods from nearby nations. The Lord was so angry with the Israelites that he let other nations raid Israel and steal their crops and other possessions... The Lord had warned Israel he would do this, and now the Israelites were miserable. From time to time, the Lord would choose special leaders known as judges. These judges would lead the Israelites into battle and defeat the enemies that made raids on them... The Lord would be kind to Israel as long as that judge lived. But afterwards, the Israelites would become even more sinful than their ancestors had been.

JUDGES 2:8, 10, 12–14, 16, 18b–19a

Check it out

The people of Israel in a vicious circle

We are now in the time of the Judges, around 1200–1000BC. One thing that characterizes this period more than anything else is the vicious circle that the Israelites were trapped in:

1. Life was peaceful and prosperous for the Israelites.
2. So they forgot the Lord and turned to other gods.
3. Then things began to go badly, often incredibly badly.
4. The people were sorry and called out to the Lord...
5. ...who sent a Judge (that's why this book is called 'Judges').

1. Then the Israelites had peace and prosperity again. The circle was completed.
2. So they forgot the Lord... and so on, and so on...

This vicious circle goes round and round in the book of Judges. Check out chapters 3:8–11 and 10:1–10. Can you see the five points that were made clear above?

I wonder if you recognize yourself in all of this a tiny bit?

Links: 9 June, 10 June, 11 June, 12 June

5 minutes more? Ezekiel 47

9 June

The Judges rule (c.1200–1000BC)

Judge Deborah saves the people

After the death of Ehud, the Israelites again started disobeying the Lord. So the Lord let the Canaanite King Jabin of Hazor conquer Israel... Jabin's army had nine hundred iron chariots, and for twenty years he made life miserable for the Israelites, until finally they begged the Lord for help. Deborah the wife of Lappidoth was a prophet and a leader of Israel during those days. She would sit under Deborah's Palm Tree between Ramah and Bethel in the hill country of Ephraim, where Israelites would come and ask her to settle their legal cases. One day, Barak the son of Adinoam was in Kadesh in Naphtali, and Deborah sent word for him to come and talk with her. When he arrived, she said:

I have a message for you from the Lord God of Israel! You are to get together an army of ten thousand men from the Napthali and Zebulun tribes and lead them to Mount Tabor. The Lord will trick Sisera into coming out to fight you at the River Kishon. Sisera will be leading King Jabin's army as usual, and they will have their chariots, but the Lord has promised to help you defeat them.

JUDGES 4:1–7

Did you know that...

...there are many female leaders in the Bible?

Many people still prefer male leaders in Christian congregations and organizations. But come on, girls! There are masses of female leaders in the Bible. There ought to be more female leaders in our churches too!

Check out some of the female leaders in the Bible:

Deborah:	Army commander, leader and judge	See above
Miriam	Prophet and leader of the people	Micah 6:4
Hulda	Prophet and teacher to the high priest!	2 Chronicles 34:22
Anna	Prophet	Luke 2:36
Mary Magdalene	Evangelist	Matthew 28
Phoebe	Leader of the church in Cenchreae	Romans 16:1

Romans chapter 16 mentions other female church leaders—Tryphaena, Tryphosa, Mary, Persis, Junia and Priscilla.

Come on, girls! We desperately need you to take leadership responsibility in all sorts of areas.

Links: 10 June, 11 June, 12 June, 13 June

5 minutes more? Daniel 1

10 June

The Judges rule (c.1200–1000BC)

Judge Gideon gets a sign

Gideon prayed to God, 'I know that you promised to help me rescue Israel, but I need proof. Tonight I'll put some wool on the stone floor of that threshing-place over there. If you really will help me rescue Israel, then tomorrow morning let there be dew on the wool, but let the stone floor be dry.' And that's just what happened. Early the next morning, Gideon got up and checked the wool. He squeezed out enough water to fill a bowl. But Gideon prayed to God again. 'Don't be angry with me,' Gideon said. 'Let me try this just one more time, so I'll really be sure you'll help me. Only this time, let the wool be dry and the stone floor be wet with dew.' That night, God made the stone floor wet with dew, but he kept the wool dry.

JUDGES 6:36–40

Did you know that...

...there's a Christian organization that encourages stealing?

Gideon was the youngest brother from the poorest family in the least tribe in Israel (Judges 6:15)—and even so, God wanted it to be him who undertook the important job of being a judge! So it's probably not so strange that Gideon needed a clear sign from God before he took on the job as leader of a whole nation.

If you have time, you should read the whole story of Gideon in Judges 6–8, not just today's Bible reading. It's exciting stuff.

Did you know that Gideon is the namesake of the only Christian organization that encourages stealing? In almost every hotel room in the world you'll find a Bible. An organization called 'The Gideons' has put them there, and they say they haven't got any problem at all with hotel guests who want to swipe a Bible when they check out!

Links: 11 June, 12 June, 13 June, 14 June

5 minutes more? Daniel 2

The Judges rule (c.1200–1000BC)

Judge Samson and his hair (1)

Once again the Israelites started disobeying the Lord. So he let the Philistines take control of Israel for forty years. Manoah from the tribe of Dan lived in the town of Zorah. His wife was not able to have children, but one day an angel from Lord appeared to her and said:

You have never been able to have any children, but very soon you will be pregnant and have a son. He will belong to God from the day he is born, so his hair must never be cut... Your son will begin to set Israel free from the Philistines.

... Later, Manoah's wife did give birth to a son, and she named him Samson. As the boy grew, the Lord blessed him... The Spirit of the Lord took control of him... Samson was a leader (judge) of Israel for twenty years, but the Philistines were still rulers of Israel.

JUDGES 13:1–5, 24, 25b; 15:20

☆ Bible personality

Samson

Samson was quite a guy. He was one of the judges who were sent to the nation by God in the time before they had their own king (1200–1000BC).

In the time of the Judges, the Philistines were Israel's neighbouring nation and a constant threat. The people had turned away from the Lord and so he had given the Philistines the upper hand. (If you don't remember anything about Israel's vicious circle, turn back to page 171.) Now the Lord sent a new Judge to save them—Samson.

Samson was strong, terribly strong. His strength was proportional to the length of his hair! Strange, but true. He was so strong that it was impossible to keep him tied up. That was, until the day... (I can only tell you this much right now)... that Samson was tricked (see Judges 16:4 onwards).

If I dare draw out a moral from Samson's story, it would probably be this: 'Friends that pull you away from your friendship with God are bad friends.'

Links: 12 June, 13 June, 14 June, 15 June

5 minutes more? Daniel 3

12 June

The Judges rule (c.1200–1000BC)

Judge Samson and his hair (2)

Some time later, Samson fell in love with a woman named Delilah, who lived in Sorek Valley. The Philistine rulers went to Delilah and said, 'Trick Samson into telling you what makes him so strong and what can make him weak…' The next time Samson was at Delilah's house, she asked, 'Samson, what makes you so strong? How can I tie you up so you can't get away? Come on, tell me.' … Delilah started nagging and pestering him day after day, until he couldn't stand it any longer. Finally, Samson told her the truth. 'I have belonged to God (been a Nazirite) ever since I was born, so my hair has never been cut. If it were ever cut off, my strength would leave me, and I would be as weak as anyone else.' …

Delilah had lulled Samson to sleep with his head resting in her lap. She signalled to one of the Philistine men as she began cutting off Samson's seven braids. And by the time she had finished, Samson's strength was gone… The Philistines grabbed Samson and put out his eyes. They took him to the prison in Gaza and chained him up.

JUDGES 16:4–5a, 6, 16–17, 19, 21a

Big word

Nazirites and Nazarites

A Nazirite and a Nazarite have nothing in common, except that both have something to do with hair.

A Nazirite was someone who was separated out from other people because he was consecrated to God. 'Nazir' means 'separated'. Nazirites made a promise not to drink wine and *not to cut their hair*, among other things. The promise lasted for varying lengths of time. Samson was a Nazirite. So was the prophet Samuel (1 Samuel 1:11) and maybe John the Baptist (Luke 1:15) and Paul (Acts 18:18).

On the other hand, a Nazarite is some one who comes from Nazareth. Jesus was from Nazareth. It is thought that the fashion in Nazareth in Jesus' time was to have long hair with a centre parting—that's why Jesus is nearly always drawn with this hairstyle. No kidding!

P.S: Don't let anyone steal what God has given you. Live your life close to God and according to his will. Don't let anyone steal it from you!

Links: 8 June, 13 June, 14 June, 15 June

5 minutes more? Daniel 4

13 June

The Judges rule (c.1200–1000BC)

Judge Samson and his hair (3)

The Philistine rulers threw a big party and sacrificed lots of animals to their god Dagon... Everyone there was having a good time, and they shouted, 'Bring out Samson—he's still good for a few more laughs!' The rulers had Samson brought from the prison... They made fun of Samson for a while, then they told him to stand near the columns that supported the roof. A young man was leading Samson by the hand, and Samson said to him, 'I need to lean against something. Take me over to the columns that hold up the roof.' The Philistine rulers were celebrating in a temple packed with people and with three thousand more on the flat roof. They had all been watching Samson and making fun of him. Samson prayed, 'Please remember me, Lord God. The Philistines put out my eyes, but make me strong one last time, so I can take revenge for at least one of my eyes!' ... He pushed against the columns as hard as he could, and the temple collapsed with the Philistine rulers and everyone else still inside. Samson killed more Philistines when he died than he had killed during his entire life.

JUDGES 16:23a, 24a, 25b–28, 30b

#öfi#%/$&!!?!

An inexplicable thing that there isn't any sense in explaining

Samson was a man of God.
The Israelites were the people of God.
The Philistines had power over the Israelites.
Samson's job was to protect the Israelites from the Philistines.

But Delilah, Samson's girlfriend, tricked him and cut his hair off so that he lost his strength.
The Philistines took him prisoner and gouged out his eyes.
God gave Samson his strength back one last time.
Just to get even.
Which, you might say, was good of him.

Links: 8 June, 14 June, 15 June, 16 June

5 minutes more? Daniel 5

14 June

The Kings: Saul, David, Solomon (c.1000BC)

Hannah prays for a son

Elkanah lived in Ramah, a town in the hill country of Ephraim... Elkanah had two wives, Hannah and Peninnah. Although Peninnah had children, Hannah did not have any... Peninnah liked to make Hannah feel miserable about not having any children, especially when the family went to the house of the Lord each year... Hannah was brokenhearted and was crying as she prayed, 'Lord All-Powerful, I am your servant, but I am so miserable! Please let me have a son. I will give him to you for as long as he lives, and his hair will never be cut.'

1 SAMUEL 1:1a, 2, 6–7a, 10–11

Listen to your heart and fill in

What do you want?

Hannah wanted a son more than anything else—probably a rather impossible wish, because the Lord had 'closed her womb'. Nevertheless, she called out to the Lord. She prayed passionately, and her prayer proved to be a prayer after the Lord's heart. She had her wish fulfilled.

Be definite about what you pray for. What do you want to ask the Lord for today?

1. ______________________________

2. ______________________________

3. ______________________________

Links: 15 June, 16 June, 17 June, 18 June

5 minutes more? Daniel 6

Hannah has a son, the prophet Samuel

The Lord blessed Elkanah and Hannah with a son. She named him Samuel, because she had asked the Lord for him. The next time Elkanah and his family went to offer their yearly sacrifice, he took along a gift that he had promised to give to the Lord. But Hannah stayed at home... When it was the time of year to go to Shiloh again, Hannah and Elkanah took Samuel to the Lord's house... Hannah and Elkanah offered the bull as a sacrifice, then brought the little boy to Eli. 'Sir,' Hannah said, 'a few years ago I stood here beside you and asked the Lord to give me a child. Here he is! The Lord gave me just what I asked for. Now I am giving him to the Lord, and he will be the Lord's servant as long as he lives.' Elkanah worshipped the Lord there at Shiloh.

1 SAMUEL 1:19b–22a, 24, 25b–2:1

Listen to your heart and fill in

Prayer of thanksgiving

Hannah called her son 'Samuel' because God heard her prayer. 'El' means 'God'. 'Samu' means 'has heard'. 'Samu-el' means 'God has heard'. Logical, really.

One good thing we can learn from Hannah is to thank God when he answers our prayers. I think this is something that's incredibly easy to forget. Has God ever answered your prayers at any time? Have you got anything to thank God for?

Grab a pen and write down what you need to thank God for:

1. ______________________________

2. ______________________________

3. ______________________________

It's a good thing not to forget to thank God.

Links: 14 June, 16 June, 17 June, 18 June

5 minutes more? Daniel 7

16 June

The Kings: Saul, David, Solomon (c.1000BC)

God calls Samuel

Samuel served the Lord by helping Eli the priest, who was by that time almost blind. In those days, the Lord hardly ever spoke directly to people, and he did not appear to them in dreams very often. But one night, Eli was asleep in his room, and Samuel was sleeping on a mat near the sacred chest in the Lord's house. They had not been asleep very long when the Lord called out Samuel's name. 'Here I am!' Samuel answered. Then he ran to Eli and said, 'Here I am. What do you want?' ... When the Lord called out his name for the third time, Samuel went to Eli again and said, 'Here I am. What do you want?' Eli finally realized that it was the Lord who was speaking to Samuel. So he said, 'Go back and lie down! If someone speaks to you again, answer, "I'm listening, Lord. What do you want me to do?"' Once again Samuel went back and lay down. The Lord then stood beside Samuel and called out as he had done before, 'Samuel! Samuel!' 'I'm listening,' Samuel answered. 'What do you want me to do?' ...

As Samuel grew up, the Lord helped him and made everything Samuel said come true... Everyone in the country knew that Samuel was truly the Lord's prophet.

1 SAMUEL 3:1–5, 8–10, 19, 20b

Di:SaipL

I'm listening, Lord. What do you want me to do?

You might ask if I've heard anything from the Lord recently.

You might think it's not something that happens much these days, rather like in the reading: 'In those days, the Lord hardly ever spoke directly to people, and he did not appear to them in dreams very often.'

Perhaps we're just not listening! Samuel's story is a wonderful example to us. He was so attentive, he wanted to hear and was ready to take God seriously.

Still your heart. Welcome the Holy Spirit. Listen and be ready to be surprised by the voice of God.

Links: 14 June, 15 June, 17 June, 18 June

5 minutes more? Daniel 12

17 June

The Kings: Saul, David, Solomon (c.1000BC)

The people want a king

When Samuel was getting old, he let [his two sons] be leaders at Beersheba... One day the nation's leaders came to Samuel at Ramah and said, 'You are an old man. You set a good example for your sons, but they haven't followed it. Now we want a king to be our leader, just like all the other nations. Choose one for us!' Samuel was upset... so he prayed about it. The Lord answered:

Samuel, do everything they want you to do. I am really the one they have rejected as their king... Do everything they ask, but warn them and tell them how a king will treat them...

The people would not listen to Samuel. 'No!' they said. 'We want to be like other nations. We want a king to rule us and lead us in battle.' Samuel listened to them and then told the Lord exactly what they had said. 'Do what they want,' the Lord answered. 'Give them a king.'

1 SAMUEL 8:2, 4–7, 9, 19–22a

☆ Bible personality

Samuel

Samuel is an important person. He oversaw the transition from the time of the judges to the time of the kings. The judges had ruled the nation from the time Joshua had led the people into Canaan. All that time, the situation had been unstable and characterized by internal and external fighting. The neighbouring nations were constantly on the warpath. There was no peace. At home, the nation of Israel experienced the rollercoaster ride of the vicious circle we talked about on 8 June.

The people demanded a king. They wanted stability. Samuel was important because God gave him the job of fulfilling the people's wish—transferring leadership from judges to kings.

Samuel was the last of the fourteen Judges. He was also the first of the prophets and anointed the first king to rule over God's people.

Links: 14 June, 15 June, 16 June, 18 June

5 minutes more? Hosea 1

The people choose Saul to be king

Samuel sent messengers to tell the Israelites to come to Mizpah and meet with the Lord. When everyone had arrived, Samuel said:

The Lord God of Israel told me to remind you that he had rescued you from the Egyptians and from the other nations that abused you. God has rescued you from your troubles and hard times. But you have rejected your God and have asked for a king. Now each tribe and clan must come near the place of worship so the Lord can choose a king.

Samuel brought each tribe, one after the other, to the altar, and the Lord chose the Benjamin tribe. Next, Samuel brought each clan of Benjamin there, and the Lord chose the Matri clan. Finally, Saul the son of Kish was chosen. But when they looked for him, he was nowhere to be found... The people ran and got Saul and brought him into the middle of the crowd. He was more than a head taller than anyone else. 'Look closely at the man the Lord has chosen!' Samuel told the crowd. 'There is no one like him!' The crowd shouted, 'Long live the king!'
1 SAMUEL 10:17–21, 23–24

Weird and wonderful

Drawing lots

In the Bible, many decisions were made by drawing lots. This is the way Saul was chosen to be king. Seems a bit much, if you ask me! Here are some other things that were decided by drawing lots:

- The Israelites divided the land by drawing lots (Numbers 26:55).
- Saul, the first king, was chosen by drawing lots (see above).
- Jonathan was identified as the guilty party by drawing lots (1 Samuel 14:42).
- When the people had the temple, they drew lots to see who would lead the worship (1 Chronicles 25:7–9)...
- ... and who should be the high priest! (Luke 1:9).
- And when they needed to choose a new disciple to replace Judas, they drew lots (Acts 1:26).

This is how the people gave God the chance to determine who he wanted to choose. The only time the Bible shows drawing lots in a negative light is when the Roman soldiers who crucified Jesus threw dice for his clothes (Luke 23:34).

Links: 19 June, 20 June, 21 June, 25 June

5 minutes more? Hosea 2

The Lord rejects King Saul

One day, Samuel told Saul:

The Lord made me choose you to be king of his people, Israel. Now listen to this message from the Lord: 'When the Israelites were on their way out of Egypt, the nation of Amalek attacked them. I am the Lord All-Powerful, and now I am going to make Amalek pay! Go and attack the Amalekites! Destroy them and all their possessions. Don't have any pity…'

Saul attacked the Amalekites… Every Amalekite was killed except King Agag. Saul and his army let Agag live, and they also spared the best sheep and cattle. They didn't want to destroy anything of value, so they only killed the animals that were worthless or weak. The Lord told Samuel, 'Saul has stopped obeying me, and I'm sorry that I made him king.' Samuel was angry, and he cried out in prayer to the Lord all night…

[Samuel said to Saul,] 'Rebelling against God or disobeying him because you are proud is just as bad as worshipping idols or asking them for advice. You refused to do what God told you, so God has decided that you can't be king.'

1 SAMUEL 15:1–3a, 7a, 8–11, 23

Bible personality

King Saul

Saul was only a partial success. He reigned for twenty years and actually did what he had to do quite well. But today's reading tells us about the beginning of the end for Saul.

- Saul did what the Lord said—well, almost.
- He was obedient—to an extent.

The last years of Saul's reign were not particularly good. He was tormented by an evil spirit. To calm the king down, the king's officials summoned an awe-inspiringly talented harp player. In time, he would prove to be Saul's successor. He was a young boy called David.

Samuel's words to Saul stand as a reminder to each one of us: 'Does the Lord really want sacrifices and offerings? No! He doesn't want your sacrifices. He wants you to obey him' (1 Samuel 15:22).

Links: 20 June, 21 June, 25 June, 26 June

5 minutes more? Hosea 3

20 June

The Kings: Saul, David, Solomon (c.1000BC)

Samuel anoints David as king

One day [the Lord] said, 'Samuel, I've rejected Saul, and I refuse to let him be king any longer. Stop feeling sad about him. Put some olive oil in a small container and go and visit a man named Jesse, who lives in Bethlehem. I've chosen one of his sons to be my king.' ... When Jesse and his sons arrived, Samuel noticed Jesse's eldest son, Eliab. 'He must be the one the Lord has chosen,' Samuel said to himself. But the Lord told him, 'Samuel, don't think Eliab is the one just because he's tall and handsome. He isn't the one I have chosen. People judge others by what they look like, but I judge people by what is in their hearts.' ... Next, Jesse sent his son Shammah to him, and Samuel said, 'The Lord hasn't chosen him either.' Jesse sent all seven of his sons over to Samuel.

Finally, Samuel said, 'Jesse, the Lord hasn't chosen any of these young men. Do you have any more sons?' 'Yes,' Jesse answered. 'My youngest son David is out taking care of the sheep.' 'Send for him!' Samuel said. 'We won't start the ceremony until he gets here.' Jesse sent for David. He was a healthy, good-looking boy with a sparkle in his eyes. As soon as David came, the Lord told Samuel, 'He's the one! Get up and pour the olive oil on his head.' Samuel poured the oil on David's head while his brothers watched. At that moment, the Spirit of the Lord took control of David and stayed with him from then on.

1 SAMUEL 16:1, 6–7, 9–13a

Download

What are you looking at?

I think this is perhaps the most important verse in the Bible for a teenager to know today! You can learn it in twenty seconds, and it is good for remembering every morning when you look at yourself in the mirror:

'People judge others by what they look like, but I judge people by what is in their hearts' (1 Samuel 16:7b).

Links: 21 June, 22 June, 23 June, 28 June

5 minutes more? Hosea 11

21 June

The Kings: Saul, David, Solomon (c.1000BC)

David becomes King Saul's harp player

The Spirit of the Lord had left Saul, and an evil spirit from the Lord was terrifying him. 'It's an evil spirit from God that's frightening you,' Saul's officials told him. 'Your Majesty, let us go and look for someone who is good at playing the harp. He can play for you whenever the evil spirit from God bothers you, and you'll feel better.' ... 'A man named Jesse who lives in Bethlehem has a son who can play the harp,' one official said. 'He's a brave warrior, he's good-looking, he can speak well, and the Lord is with him.' ... David went to Saul and started working for him. Saul liked him so much that he put David in charge of carrying his weapons... Whenever the evil spirit from God bothered Saul, David would play his harp. Saul would relax and feel better, and the evil spirit would go away.

1 SAMUEL 16:14–16, 18, 21, 23

☆ Bible personality

King David

David—no one better than him; no one his equal.

David, the youngest brother.
David, the good-looking little goatherd.
David, who was secretly chosen to be king by the prophet Samuel.
David, who was 'accidentally' summoned to the king's palace.
David, who played the harp so well that he became King Saul's personal harpist.
David, who laid Goliath out cold on a hillside.
David, who won the war.
David, who ensured there was peace.
David, who wrote hundreds of psalms.
David, the greatest person in Israel in the whole of history.
David, whose star adorns the Israeli flag to this day.

David—the hero king.

Links: 18 June, 22 June, 23 June, 24 June

5 minutes more? Joel 2:28—3:21

22 June

The Kings: Saul, David, Solomon (c.1000BC)

David and Goliath (1)

The Philistine army got ready for war and brought their troops together... The Philistine army had a hero named Goliath who was from the town of Gath and was about three metres tall. He wore a bronze helmet and had bronze armour to protect his chest and legs. The chest armour alone weighed about fifty-seven kilogrammes. He carried a bronze sword strapped on his back, and his spear was so big that the iron spearhead alone weighed about seven kilogrammes. A soldier always walked in front of Goliath to carry his shield. Goliath went out and shouted to the army of Israel:

Why are you lining up for battle? I'm the best soldier in our army, and all of you are in Saul's army. Choose your best soldier to come out and fight me! ...

Saul and his men heard what Goliath said, but they were so frightened of Goliath that they couldn't do a thing.

1 SAMUEL 17:1a, 4–9, 11

Did you know that...

...Goliath was so-o-o-o-o big?

Some versions of the Bible tell us that Goliath was six cubits and one span tall.

A cubit is about 20 inches or 50cm...

A span is about 10 inches or 25cm...

... which means that Goliath was around 10 ft or 3m tall.

The same versions of the Bible say that the armour Goliath wore on his chest weighed 5000 shekels.

1 shekel is 11.4g...

5,000 shekels are 7kg...

... so the chest armour alone weighed almost 60kg—probably more than little David.

The spearhead weighed 7kg.

But nothing is too big for God.

Links: 23 June, 24 June, 25 June, 26 June

5 minutes more? Amos 5

23 June

The Kings: Saul, David, Solomon (c.1000BC)

David and Goliath (2)

'Your Majesty,' [David] said, 'this Philistine shouldn't turn us into cowards. I'll go out and fight him myself!' 'You don't have a chance against him,' Saul replied. 'You're only a boy, and he's been a soldier all his life.' But David told him:

... Sir, I have killed lions and bears... and I can kill this worthless Philistine. He shouldn't have made fun of the army of the living God! The Lord has rescued me from the claws of lions and bears, and he will keep me safe from the hands of this Philistine.

'All right,' Saul answered, 'go ahead and fight him. And I hope the Lord will help you.' ... David picked up his shepherd's stick. He went out to a stream and picked up five smooth stones and put them in his leather bag. Then with his sling in his hand, he went straight towards Goliath.

1 SAMUEL 17:32–22, 36–37, 40

Di:SaipL

Age isn't an obstacle!

Here is a list of some of the greatest men and women in the Bible. All of them were young—some were very young—when God called them. God seems to be keen on teenagers!

Joshua (Exodus 33:11)
Ruth (Ruth 2:5–6)
Samuel (1 Samuel 12:2)
Saul (1 Samuel 9:2)
David (1 Samuel 17:42)
Solomon (1 Chronicles 22:5)
Jeremiah (Jeremiah 1:6–7)
Daniel (Daniel 1:19)
Mary (Matthew 1:23)
Timothy (1 Timothy 4:12)

This is the clue: 'Don't let any one make fun of you, just because you are young. Set an example for other followers by what you say and do, as well as by your love, faith, and purity' (1 Timothy 4:12).

Links: 22 June, 24 June, 25 June, 26 June

5 minutes more? Amos 7

24 June

The Kings: Saul, David, Solomon (c.1000BC)

David kills Goliath

Goliath came towards David, walking behind the soldier who was carrying his shield... He shouted, 'Come on! When I'm finished with you, I'll feed you to the birds and wild animals!' David answered:

You've come out to fight me with a sword and a spear and a dagger. But I've come out to fight you in the name of the Lord All-Powerful. He is the God of Israel's army, and you have insulted him too! Today the Lord will help me defeat you. I'll knock you down and cut off your head, and I'll feed the bodies of the other Philistine soldiers to the birds and the wild animals. Then the whole world will know that Israel has a real God...

When Goliath started forward, David ran towards him. He put a stone in his sling and swung the sling around by its straps. When he let go of one strap, the stone flew out and hit Goliath on the forehead. It cracked his skull, and he fell face down on the ground.

1 SAMUEL 17:41, 44–46, 48–49

Hmm... just a thought...

...about size

A little boy with great faith is better equipped than a big man with no faith.

Links: 22 June, 23 June, 25 June, 26 June

5 minutes more? Amos 9

Saul becomes envious of David

David was a success in everything that Saul sent him to do, and Saul made him a high officer in his army. That pleased everyone, including Saul's other officers. David had killed Goliath, the battle was over, and the Israelite army set out for home. As the army went along, women came out of each Israelite town to welcome King Saul. They were singing happy songs and dancing to the music of tambourines and harps. They sang:

Saul has killed a thousand enemies; David has killed ten thousand enemies!

This song made Saul very angry, and he thought, 'They are saying that David has killed ten times more enemies than I ever did. Next they will want to make him king.' Saul never again trusted David.
1 SAMUEL 18:5–9

Refresh

About encouraging each other

Saul couldn't cope with anyone else but him getting the glory and the applause. The Bible says we shouldn't be like that. Rather, we ought to cheer each other on. Here's a list of things that we should do for each other:

Wait for one another.
Care for one another.
Be proud of one another.
Be good to one another.
Submit to one another.
Be patient and forgive one another.
Comfort one another.
Encourage and build one another up.
Not say bad things about one another.
Have consideration for one another.
Show hospitality to one another.
Serve one another.
Greet one another (with a kiss !?!)
Love one another.

The words 'one another' occur in the Bible 202 times. You can check some of the places yourself: 1 Corinthians 11:33; 12:25; Ephesians 4:32; 5:21; Colossians 3:13; 1 Thessalonians 4:18; 5:11; Hebrews 10:24; James 4:11; 1 Peter 4:9–10; 5:14; 1 John 4:11.

Links: 22 June, 23 June, 24 June, 26 June

5 minutes more? Jonah 1

Saul tries to kill David

One day, Saul told his son Jonathan and his officers to kill David. But Jonathan liked David a lot, and he warned David, 'My father is trying to have you killed, so be very careful. Hide in a field tomorrow morning, and I'll bring him there. Then I'll talk to him about you, and if I find out anything, I'll let you know.' The next morning, Jonathan reminded Saul about the many good things David had done for him... Saul agreed and promised, 'I swear by the living Lord that I won't have David killed!' ... One night, David was in Saul's home, playing the harp for him. Saul was sitting there, holding a spear, when an evil spirit from the Lord took control of him. Saul tried to pin David to the wall with the spear, but David dodged, and it stuck in the wall. David ran out of the house and escaped.

1 SAMUEL 19:1–4a, 6, 9–10

Listen to your heart and fill in

Good friends

Jonathan, the son of King Saul, was David's best friend. The Bible says that 'Jonathan liked David so much that they promised they would always be loyal friends' (1 Samuel 18:3).

Good friends are important—very important. What should a proper best friend be like?

1. ______________________________

2. ______________________________

3. ______________________________

Pray that you will be that kind of best friend...

Links: 22 June, 24 June, 25 June, 27 June

5 minutes more? Jonah 2

27 June

The Kings: Saul, David, Solomon (c.1000BC)

Saul dies

The Philistines fought against Israel in a battle at Mount Gilboa. Israel's soldiers ran from the Philistines, and many of them were killed. The Philistines closed in on Saul and his sons and killed three of them: Jonathan, Abinadab, and Malchishua. The fighting was fierce around Saul, and he was badly wounded by enemy arrows. Saul told the soldier who carried his weapons, 'Kill me with your sword! I don't want those godless Philistines to torture and make fun of me.' But the soldier was afraid to kill him. Then Saul stuck himself in the stomach with his own sword and fell on the blade. When the soldier realized that Saul was dead, he killed himself in the same way. Saul, three of his sons, and all of his male relatives were dead…

Saul died because he was unfaithful and disobeyed the Lord. He even asked advice from a woman who talked to spirits of the dead, instead of asking the Lord. So the Lord had Saul killed and gave his kingdom to David, the son of Jesse.
1 CHRONICLES 10:1–6, 13–14

Download

Time up, with little grace remaining…

Saul had sinned. It was the end for him. He had been unfaithful and disobeyed the Lord, and what's more, he'd asked for advice from a woman who talked to the spirits of the dead, instead of asking the Lord.

Everyone needs a little grace. Memorize this key verse about grace: 'The reward for sin is death. But God's gift is eternal life given by Jesus Christ our Lord' (Romans 6:23).

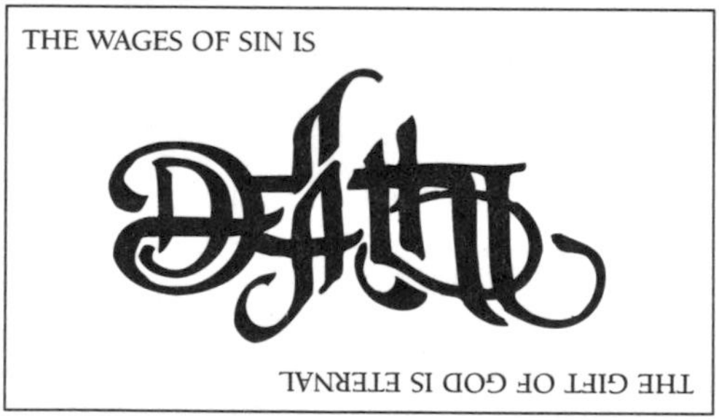

THE WAGES OF SIN IS
THE GIFT OF GOD IS ETERNAL

Links: 17 June, 18 June, 19 June, 28 June

5 minutes more? Micah 5

28 June

The Kings: Saul, David, Solomon (c.1000BC)

God's fantastic promise to David

King David moved into his new palace, and the Lord let his kingdom be at peace. Then one day, as David was talking with Nathan the prophet, David said, 'Look around! I live in a palace made of cedar, but the sacred chest has to stay in a tent.' ... That night, the Lord told Nathan to go to David and give him this message:

... David, this is what I, the Lord All-Powerful, say to you. I brought you in from the fields where you took care of sheep, and I made you the leader of my people. Wherever you went, I helped you and destroyed your enemies right in front of your eyes. I have made you one of the most famous people in the world... Now I promise that you and your descendants will be kings. I'll choose one of your sons to be king when you reach the end of your life and are buried in the tomb of your ancestors. I'll make him a strong ruler, and no one will be able to take his kingdom away from him. He will be the one to build a temple for me. I will be his father, and he will be my son.

2 SAMUEL 7:1–2, 4, 8–9, 11b–14a

Check it out

Who's God talking about?

Sit up and pay attention to this! This is one of the central chapters in the whole of the Old Testament. David says to God, 'Let me build a house (temple) for you.'

'No, no, no,' says God. 'Let me build a house (dynasty) for you.'

God promises David a successor, a son, who will build the temple. It could very well be that God has Solomon in mind when he says these things—he actually did build the temple (turn forward to page 198). But there is more to what God said than that. This son that God is talking about will also be his Son...

Hmm. Let me think. Let me think. Let me think. Who is called both David's son and God's son? Hmm. Who is it that's built a house for God's name and established a kingdom that lasts for ever? Hmm.

Get out your Bible and check Matthew 1:1 and 3:17.

Links: 1 July, 5 July, 16 July, 21 July

5 minutes more? Habakkuk 3

David mucks up big time

Late one afternoon, David got up from a nap and was walking around on the flat roof of his palace. A beautiful young woman was down below in her courtyard, bathing as her religion required. David happened to see her, and he sent one of his servants to find out who she was. The servant came back and told David, 'Her name is Bathsheba. She is the daughter of Eliam, and she is the wife of Uriah the Hittite.' David sent some messengers to bring her to his palace. She came to him, and he slept with her. Then she returned home. But later, when she found out that she was going to have a baby, she sent someone to David with this message: 'I'm pregnant!' ... Early the next morning, David wrote a letter and told Uriah to deliver it to Joab. The letter said: 'Put Uriah on the front line where the fighting is the worst. Then pull the troops back from him, so that he will be wounded and die.' ...

When the men of the city came out, they fought and killed some of David's soldiers—Uriah the Hittite was one of them... When Bathsheba heard that her husband was dead, she mourned for him. Then after the time of mourning was over, David sent someone to bring her to the palace. She became David's wife, and they had a son.

2 SAMUEL 11:2–5, 14–15, 17, 26–27

Weird and wonderful

The difference between King David and Bill Clinton!

The fact that this story is in the Bible teaches us something incredibly important.

David is the greatest king that Israel ever had. With such power, there should have been no problem hushing up this story, striking it from the records, having it edited out of the manuscripts. Many powerful men have tried precisely those tactics—Bill Clinton, for example.

The reason why David didn't try to do that can only be explained by the fact that he knew that God is a God who sees everything, knows everything—and forgives all those who bring their failings out into the light!

Links: 9 January, 1 July, 30 July, 8 September

5 minutes more? Zephaniah 3

30 June

The Kings: Saul, David, Solomon (c.1000BC)

David prays for forgiveness

A psalm by David when the prophet Nathan came to him after David had been with Bathsheba. A prayer for forgiveness

You are kind, God! Please have pity on me. You are always merciful! Please wipe away my sins. Wash me clean from all of my sin and guilt. I know about my sins, and I cannot forget my terrible guilt. You are really the one I have sinned against; I have disobeyed you and have done wrong. So it is right and fair for you to correct and punish me. I have sinned and done wrong since the day I was born. But you want complete honesty, so teach me true wisdom... Let me be happy and joyful! You crushed my bones, now let them celebrate... Make me as happy as you did when you saved me; make me want to obey! I will teach sinners your Law, and they will return to you.

PSALM 51:1–6, 8, 12–13

If we say that we have not sinned, we are fooling ourselves, and the truth isn't in our hearts. But if we confess our sins to God, he can always be trusted to forgive us and take our sins away.

1 JOHN 1:8–9

Head, shoulders, knees and toes

Sorry, sorry, sorry

1. Get yourself comfortable.
2. Shut your eyes, and in your mind go through what has happened to you over the last few days.
3. Kneel—it's a bit formal, but a good thing to do if you are in a place where you can.
4. Pray Psalm 51.
5. Sit up.
6. Read 1 John 1:8–9 out loud to yourself.
7. Thank God.

Bookmark this page and then you can use it every time you need forgiveness for something.

Links: 5 January, 7 February, 10 February, 11 February

5 minutes more? Zechariah 9

1 July

The Kings: Saul, David, Solomon (c.1000BC)

David dies—Solomon takes over

Not long before David died, he told Solomon:

My son, I will soon die, as everyone must. But I want you to be strong and brave. Do what the Lord your God commands and follow his teachings. Obey everything written in the Law of Moses. Then you will be a success, no matter what you do or where you go. You and your descendants must always faithfully obey the Lord. If you do, he will keep the solemn promise he made to me that someone from our family will always be king of Israel.

1 KINGS 2:1–4

So Solomon became king after David his father. Solomon was successful, and everyone in Israel obeyed him... The Lord made Solomon a great king, and the whole nation was amazed at how famous he was.

1 CHRONICLES 29:23, 25

Check it out

What the Bible says about success

Solomon was told by his father David that if he followed God's teachings and obeyed his commands, everything he did would succeed. There are many places in the Bible that tell us that the person who obeys God's word will know success:

'Be careful to do everything my servant Moses taught you. Never stop reading The Book of the Law he gave you... If you obey it completely, you and Israel will be able to take this land' (Joshua 1:7).

'God blesses those people... the Law of the Lord makes them happy, and they think about it day and night... Those people succeed in everything they do' (Psalm 1:1–3).

'But you must never stop looking at the perfect law that sets you free. God will bless you in everything you do, if you listen and obey, and don't just hear and forget' (James 1:25).

When we think about success, we immediately think about money, attracting the opposite sex, popularity, and so on. But that isn't what God promises us. The success God promises us is much bigger and more substantial and includes fellowship with God, peace in our hearts and eternal life!

Links: 2 July, 3 July, 4 July, 5 July

5 minutes more? Malachi 3

2 July

The Kings: Saul, David, Solomon (c.1000BC)

Solomon prays for wisdom

One night while Solomon was in Gibeon, the Lord God appeared to him in a dream and said, 'Solomon, ask for anything you want, and I will give it to you.' Solomon answered:

My father David, your servant, was honest and did what you commanded. You were always loyal to him, and you gave him a son who is now king. Lord God, I'm your servant, and you've made me king in my father's place. But I'm very young and know so little about being a leader... Please make me wise and teach me the difference between right and wrong. Then I will know how to rule your people. If you don't, there is no way I could rule this great nation of yours.

God said:

Solomon, I'm pleased that you asked for this. You could have asked to live a long time or to be rich. Or you could have asked for your enemies to be destroyed. Instead, you asked for wisdom to make right decisions. So I'll make you wiser than anyone who has ever lived or ever will live.

1 KINGS 3:5–7, 9–12

Check it out

Wisdom

I have a dream of becoming a wise old man with large, gentle eyes, completely at peace in body and soul, and always in a good mood. There are probably many ideas of what it means to be wise, but this is my image—my dream. How do you become wise? 'Respect and obey the Lord! This is the beginning of wisdom' (Proverbs 9:10). We need to realize that God is big and we are small.

'Even when God is foolish, he is wiser than everyone else, and even when God is weak, he is stronger than everyone else' (1 Corinthians 1:25).

'If any of you need wisdom, you should ask God, and it will be given to you. God is generous and won't correct you for asking' (James 1:5).

Links: 5 January, 3 July, 4 July, 8 August

5 minutes more? Malachi 4

Solomon's wisdom (1)

[Solomon] was wiser than anyone else in the world, including the wisest people of the east and of Egypt. He was even wiser than Ethan the Ezrahite, and Mahol's three sons, Heman, Calcol, and Darda. Solomon became famous in every country around Judah and Israel. Solomon wrote three thousand wise sayings and composed more than a thousand songs. He could talk about all kinds of plants, from large trees to small bushes, and he taught about animals, birds, reptiles, and fish. Kings all over the world heard about Solomon's wisdom and sent people to listen to him teach.

1 KINGS 4:30–34

Look how the wild flowers grow! They don't work hard to make their clothes. But I tell you that Solomon with all his wealth wasn't as well clothed as one of these flowers. God gives such beauty to everything that grows in the fields, even though it is here today and thrown into a fire tomorrow. Won't he do even more for you? You have such little faith!

LUKE 12:27–28

☆ Bible personality

Solomon—a good old-fashioned pop idol

Solomon, the surviving son of David and Bathsheba. He became king when he was a teenager—some sources say he was only 14. He was king for forty years.

Solomon is known for certain things in particular:

- He was a man after God's heart.
- He built the temple in Jerusalem.
- He was incredibly, incredibly wise.
- He wrote 3000 proverbs and 1005 songs.
- He had an enormous fan club.

But:

- Success went to his head.
- He became very rich.
- He had 1000 wives who eventually became his downfall.

Solomon would have been right at home in Hollywood!

Links: 5 January, 2 July, 4 July, 8 August

5 minutes more? Matthew 1

4 July

The Kings: Saul, David, Solomon (c.1000BC)

Solomon's wisdom (2)

These are the proverbs of King Solomon of Israel, the son of David. Proverbs will teach you wisdom and self-control and how to understand sayings with deep meanings. You will learn what is right and honest and fair. From these, an ordinary person can learn to be clever, and young people can gain knowledge and good sense. If you are already wise, you will become even wiser. And if you are clever, you will learn to understand proverbs and sayings, as well as words of wisdom and all kinds of riddles. Respect and obey the Lord! This is the beginning of knowledge. Only a fool rejects wisdom and good advice.

PROVERBS 1:1–7

With all your heart you must trust the Lord and not your own judgment. Always let him lead you, and he will clear the road for you to follow. Don't ever think that you are wise enough, but respect the Lord and stay away from all evil. This will make you healthy, and you will feel strong.

PROVERBS 3:5–8

Download...

...about depending on the Lord!

This is one of Solomon's greatest hits and one of my favourite verses. It's a good one to know, I think, especially if I've taken on rather too big a challenge—like writing this book, for example! It's good to know that God's got an IQ big enough for us all. Learn this verse—you're bound to need it one day.

'With all your heart you must trust in the Lord and not your own judgment' (Proverbs 3:5).

Links: 12 April, 8 December, 9 December, 10 December

5 minutes more? Matthew 2

5 July

The Kings: Saul, David, Solomon (c.1000BC)

Solomon builds the temple

Solomon ordered thirty thousand people from all over Israel to cut logs for the temple, and he put Adoniram in charge of these workers. Solomon divided them into three groups of ten thousand. Each group worked one month in Lebanon and had two months off at home. He also had eighty thousand workers to cut stone in the hill country of Israel, seventy thousand workers to carry the stones, and over three thousand assistants to keep track of the work and to supervise the workers. He ordered the workers to cut and shape large blocks of good stone for the foundation of the temple... So Solomon's workers finished building the temple... The most holy place... was lined with pure gold. There were also gold chains across the front of the most holy place. The inside of the temple, as well as the cedar altar in the most holy place, was covered with gold... Work began on the temple during Ziv, the second month of the year, four years after Solomon became king of Israel. Seven years later the workers finished building it during Bul, the eighth month of the year. It was built exactly as it had been planned.

1 KINGS 5:13–17; 6:14, 19–22, 37–38

Check it out

God's temple

It was actually David who planned to build a house for the Lord. But God didn't let him—he had spilt too much blood in all the wars he had fought (1 Chronicles 22:8). Instead, it was his son Solomon who had the honour of building the temple. It was said that the Lord had his earthly footstool in the innermost room—in the holy of holies. The temple became the focal point of the Jewish religion.

Of course it was only partially true that God lived in the temple. God doesn't allow himself to be kept captive—not in Solomon's temple nor in our church buildings. God is bigger than that. God is infinite; he is everywhere. Paul expresses this very directly: 'This God made the world and everything in it. He is Lord of heaven and earth, and he doesn't live in temples built by human hands' (Acts 17:24). Well, where does he live, then? In people. In you and me. In the hearts of everyone who welcomes him in. Don't you know that 'you are God's temple and that God's Spirit lives in you'? (1 Corinthians 3:16).

You are God's temple. You are God's dwelling place. That's quite something!

Links: 25 March, 26 March, 28 June, 15 August

5 minutes more? Matthew 3

6 July

The Kings: Saul, David, Solomon (c.1000BC)

Solomon, the end

The Lord did not want the Israelites to worship foreign gods, so he warned them not to marry anyone who was not from Israel. Solomon loved his wife, the daughter of the king of Egypt. But he also loved some women from Moab, Ammon, and Edom, and others from Sidon and the land of the Hittites. Seven hundred of his wives were daughters of kings, but he also married three hundred other women. As Solomon got older, some of his wives led him to worship their gods. He wasn't like his father David, who had worshipped only the Lord God... The Lord God of Israel had appeared to Solomon twice and warned him not to worship foreign gods. But Solomon disobeyed and did it anyway. This made the Lord very angry...

After he had ruled forty years from Jerusalem, he died and was buried there in the city of his father David. His son Rehoboam then became king.

1 KINGS 11:1–4, 9–10, 42–43

Refresh

Politically correct

The Old Testament had a distinctive law which prescribed how kings should conduct their private lives. The King's Law is found in Deuteronomy 17:14–20. Among other things, it says, 'The king must not have a lot of wives—they might tempt him to be unfaithful to the Lord.'

Solomon was wise, but not wise enough. Success went to his head. He stopped paying attention to the word of God as stated in the King's Law. He'd acquired a lot of wives in order to be politically correct, to get in favour with neighbouring kings, to show his power and gain glory. This all led to the nation of Israel's downfall.

We can learn a good deal from Solomon—a lot from his wisdom, but almost as much from his lack of it.

Links: 1 July, 2 July, 4 July, 5 July

5 minutes more? Matthew 4

Jesus is the Messiah, the promised Saviour

Then Jesus asked them, 'But who do you say I am?' Simon Peter spoke up, 'You are the Messiah, the Son of the living God.' ... Jesus told his disciples not to tell anyone that he was the Messiah.
MATTHEW 16:15–16, 20

[Paul] used the Scriptures to show them that the Messiah had to suffer, but that he would rise from death. Paul also told them that Jesus is the Messiah he was preaching about.
ACTS 17:3

[Apollos] also knew much about the Lord's Way, and he spoke about it with great excitement. What he taught about Jesus was right... After Apollos arrived in Achaia, he was a great help to everyone who had put their faith in the Lord Jesus because of God's kindness. He got into fierce arguments with the Jewish people, and in public he used the Scriptures to prove that Jesus is the Messiah.
ACTS 18:25, 27–28

Big word
Messiah

These days, to become a priest, you have to be ordained. But in those days, in Old Testament times, priests were anointed. These days, kings are crowned. But in those days, in Old Testament times, kings were anointed. These days, to be a prophet, I haven't the foggiest idea what ceremony you'd go through (it's not so usual to be a prophet any more). But in those days, in Old Testament times, to be a prophet, you were anointed.

A whole lot of oil was poured over the head of the person concerned—as a sign that he was now a priest, king or prophet. The oil was also a symbol that the person had received God's Spirit.

Messiah means 'He who has been anointed'.

We believe that Jesus is the Messiah, the Saviour who was promised in the Old Testament—the priest; the king; the prophet.

Links: 22 March, 8 July, 9 July, 23 December

5 minutes more? Matthew 5

8 July

The Messiah, God's Son...

...shall be born of a virgin

An Old Testament prophecy about the Messiah:

But the Lord will still give you proof. A virgin is pregnant; she will have a son and will name him Immanuel.
ISAIAH 7:14

This was written about Jesus:

One month later God sent the angel Gabriel to the town of Nazareth in Galilee with a message for a virgin named Mary. She was engaged to Joseph from the family of King David. The angel greeted Mary and said, 'You are truly blessed! The Lord is with you.' Mary was confused by the angel's words and wondered what they meant. Then the angel told Mary, 'Don't be afraid! God is pleased with you, and you will have a son. His name will be Jesus.'
LUKE 1:26–31

Refresh

Ready to help with nappies and wipes?

For all we know, Jesus was teased when he was little. In those days, it was frowned upon to be born outside wedlock. And Mary, poor thing, probably found things incredibly difficult—she may well have been only a teenager when Jesus was born.

As Christians, we think that sex is something that should only happen in the context of marriage, and that everyone should wait until they're married. But if you know someone who has suddenly found out that they're pregnant, even if it's the result of a moment of thoughtlessness, it's your job as a Christian to be the first to give them the encouragement they need and to support them. Carry things, look after them, be ready to help with nappies and baby wipes, and do it joyfully.

Is there someone you know who could do with some back-up?

Links: 7 July, 19 August, 23 December, 24 December

5 minutes more? Matthew 6

9 July

The Messiah, God's Son...

...shall be born in Bethlehem

An Old Testament prophecy about the Messiah:

Bethlehem Ephrath, you are one of the smallest towns in the nation of Judah. But the Lord will choose one of your people to rule the nation—someone whose family goes back to ancient times.
MICAH 5:2

This was written about Jesus:

When Jesus was born in the village of Bethlehem in Judea, Herod was king. During this time some wise men from the east came to Jerusalem and said, 'Where is the child born to be king of the Jews? We saw his star in the east and have come to worship him.' When King Herod heard about this, he was worried... Herod brought together the chief priests and the teachers of the Law of Moses and asked them, 'Where will the Messiah be born?' They told him, 'He will be born in Bethlehem, just as the prophet wrote, "Bethlehem in the land of Judea, you are very important among the towns of Judea. From your town will come a leader, who will be like a shepherd for my people Israel."'
MATTHEW 2:1–6

Weird and wonderful

Torquay 43—Man United 42

All this stuff about Messianic prophecies can seem quite amazing. A lot of what was prophesied in the Old Testament is so detailed that it can't just be a coincidence that it matches up with the facts about Jesus.

For example, imagine you got it into your head that Torquay would win the FA Cup Final against Man United 43–42 in the year 2612. Imagine you wrote that down on a scrap of paper, put the paper in a metal box and buried it. Imagine someone found the box just before the 2612 Cup Final, and Torquay really did win 43–42 against Man United. That would be amazing.

Well, that's what happens in the Bible. There are about sixty direct and hundreds of indirect prophecies in the Old Testament which were fulfilled hundreds of years after they were given—like the one about the Messiah being born in an insignificant town called Bethlehem.

Links: 7 July, 19 August, 23 December, 24 December

5 minutes more? Matthew 7

10 July

The Messiah, God's Son...

...shall ride into Jerusalem on a donkey

An Old Testament prophecy about the Messiah:

Everyone in Jerusalem, celebrate and shout! Your king has won a victory, and he is coming to you. He is humble and rides on a donkey; he comes on the colt of a donkey.
ZECHARIAH 9:9

This was written about Jesus:

As he was getting near Bethphage and Bethany on the Mount of Olives, he sent two of his disciples on ahead. He told them, 'Go into the next village, where you will find a young donkey that has never been ridden. Untie the donkey and bring it here. If anyone asks why you are doing that, just say, "The Lord needs it."' They went off and found everything just as Jesus had said. While they were untying the donkey, its owners asked, 'Why are you doing that?' They answered, 'The Lord needs it.' Then they led the donkey to Jesus. They put some of their clothes on its back and helped Jesus get on. And as he rode along, the people spread clothes on the road in front of him.
LUKE 19:29–36

Hmm... just a thought

'The Lord needs it!'

If the Lord Jesus could bring himself to say that he needed a worthless donkey, it could also be that he could use you for something special.

Nobody is better at spotting the potential in people than Jesus.

P.S. Did you know that all young donkeys have a cross-shaped mark on their backs?

Links: 24 March, 7 July, 4 November, 5 November

5 minutes more? Matthew 8

11 July

The Messiah, God's Son...

...shall be betrayed for thirty silver coins

This was written about Jesus:

Judas had betrayed Jesus, but when he learnt that Jesus had been sentenced to death, he was sorry for what he had done. He returned the thirty silver coins to the chief priests and leaders and said, 'I have sinned by betraying a man who has never done anything wrong.' ... Judas threw the money into the temple and then went out and hanged himself... The chief priests decided (to use the money) to buy a field that belonged to someone who made clay pots. They wanted to use it as a graveyard for foreigners. That is why people still call that place 'Field of Blood'. So the words of the prophet Jeremiah came true, 'They took the thirty silver coins, the price of a person among the people of Israel. They paid it for a potter's field, as the Lord had commanded me.'
MATTHEW 27:3–10

Di:SaipL

Who wants to be a millionaire?

There are two ways to live your life—God's way or the world's way. You either want to follow Jesus, or you don't want to.

In 1900, 90 per cent of the Christians in the world were rich Westerners.

In 1990, the majority of Christians in the world were poor people of Third World origin.

This shows that it is very, very difficult to be rich and follow Jesus at the same time. The Bible says we must choose. Your money or your life. God's way or the world's way.

Links: 7 July, 6 September, 7 September, 8 September

5 minutes more? Matthew 9

The Messiah, God's Son...

...shall be pierced through his hands and feet and lots shall be cast for his clothes

An Old Testament prophecy about the Messiah:

My God, my God, why have you deserted me? Why are you so far away? … I can count all my bones, and my enemies just stare and sneer at me. They took my clothes and gambled for them.

PSALM 22:1a, 17–18

This was written about Jesus:

The soldiers nailed Jesus to a cross and gambled to see who would get his clothes… People who passed by said terrible things about Jesus. They shook their heads and shouted, 'So you're the one who claimed you could tear down the temple and build it again in three days! If you are God's Son, save yourself and come down from the cross!' The chief priests, the leaders, and the teachers of the Law of Moses also made fun of Jesus. They said, 'He saved others, but he can't save himself.'

MATTHEW 27:35, 39–42a

Big word

Passion

An old-fashioned way of describing Jesus' death for us on the cross is to call it his 'passion'.

Jesus' passion. Taste the words. Jesus' passion. Jesus' passion.

Passion has two meanings: it can mean extreme suffering (a negative sense) or strength of feeling (a positive sense).

It is interesting that the word 'passion' has these two sides to it. It wasn't just nails that held Jesus to the cross and caused his passion or suffering. It was his immense love—his passion for us.

Links: 12 January, 29 March, 7 July, 12 September

5 minutes more? Matthew 10

13 July

The Messiah, God's Son...

...shall be pierced with a spear

An Old Testament prophecy about the Messiah:

I, the Lord, will make the descendants of David and the people of Jerusalem feel deep sorrow and pray when they see the one they pierced with a spear.
ZECHARIAH 12:10a

This was written about Jesus:

The soldiers first broke the legs of the other two men who were nailed there. But when they came to Jesus, they saw that he was already dead, and they did not break his legs. One of the soldiers stuck his spear into Jesus' side, and blood and water came out... All this happened so that the Scriptures would come true, which say, 'No bone of his body will be broken' and, 'They will see the one in whose side they stuck a spear.'
JOHN 19:32–34, 36–37

Did you know that...

...some people think Jesus never died?

Of course that's not what Christians think, but there are some people who say that Jesus never died. They try to explain the resurrection by saying that the disciples took him down from the cross before he was really dead.

There are three points in today's readings which prove that Jesus died. (Note that the first two are fulfilments of prophecies about the Messiah.)

1. It was normal practice to break the legs of people who were crucified. This made them die quicker. The thieves who were crucified next to Jesus had their legs broken. But not Jesus—because he was already dead.
2. To be absolutely sure that Jesus was dead, one of the soldiers stabbed Jesus in his side with a spear.
3. Not just blood but also water ran out of the wound. Dead people's blood coagulates—the blood cells clump together—and the coagulated blood cells separate from the water.

You can be assured that Jesus died. And you can be assured that he died for you!

Links: 12 January, 29 March, 7 July, 12 September

5 minutes more? Matthew 11

14 July

The Messiah, God's Son...

...will be a prophet and speak words directly from God

An Old Testament prophecy about the Messiah:

So when I want to speak to them, I will choose one of them to be a prophet like you. I will give my message to that prophet, who will tell the people exactly what I have said.
DEUTERONOMY 18:18

This was written about Jesus:

After the people had seen Jesus perform this miracle, they began saying, 'This must be the Prophet who is to come into the world!'
JOHN 6:14

When the crowd heard Jesus say this, some of them said, 'He must be the Prophet!'
JOHN 7:40

That time will come when the Lord will give you fresh strength. He will send you Jesus, his chosen Messiah... Moses said, 'The Lord your God will choose one of your own people to be a prophet, just as he chose me. Listen to everything he tells you. No one who disobeys that prophet will be one of God's people any longer.'
ACTS 3:20, 22–23

Hmm... just a thought...

...about being quick off the draw

It's so typical of me to think of what I could have said after the moment has passed. Later I think of the wittier, funnier replies I could have made, compared to the ones that came off the top of my head at the time.

It seems to me that Jesus never had this problem. It seems as though he always had the right words at the right time.

Perhaps it's because he was a prophet?

Perhaps it's because he knew what people were going to say before they said it—he heard what the Father was telling him before he replied. Get it?

Links: 7 May, 7 July, 28 July, 2 September

5 minutes more? Matthew 12

...will be a priest and have power to forgive sin

An Old Testament prophecy about the Messiah:

I have chosen someone else to be my priest, someone who will be faithful and obey me. I will always let his family serve as priests and help my chosen king.
1 SAMUEL 2:35

This was written about Jesus:

But Jesus will never die, and so he will be a priest for ever! He is for ever able to save the people he leads to God, because he always lives to speak to God for them. Jesus is the high priest we need. He is holy and innocent and faultless, and not at all like us sinners. Jesus is honoured above all beings in heaven, and he is better than any other high priest. Jesus doesn't need to offer sacrifices every day for his own sins and then for the sins of the people. He offered a sacrifice once for all, when he gave himself.
HEBREWS 7:24–27

Did you know that...

...of all the founders of religions, gurus and leaders in world history, there is only one who claims that he has power to forgive sins?

Only one: Jesus.

- If you think your biggest problem is stress, then there are lots of courses, books and people who can show you loads of ways to relax.
- If you think your biggest problem is lack of concentration, then there are lots of courses, books and people who can help you focus.
- If you think your biggest problem is failure, then there are lots of people and lots of tactics that can make you successsful.

But—if you think your biggest problem is sin, then there is only Jesus who says he can help you.

Links: 7 July, 1 September, 11 September, 18 November

5 minutes more? Matthew 13

16 July

The Messiah, God's Son...

...will be king and rule for eternity

An Old Testament prophecy about the Messiah:

'I've put my king on Zion, my sacred hill.' I will tell the promise that the Lord made to me: 'You are my son, because today I have become your father.'
PSALM 2:6–7

This was written about Jesus:

Then the angel told Mary, 'Don't be afraid! God is pleased with you, and you will have a son. His name will be Jesus. He will be great and will be called the Son of God Most High. The Lord God will make him king, as his ancestor David was. He will rule the people of Israel for ever, and his kingdom will never end.'
LUKE 1:30–33

Pilate ordered the charge against Jesus to be written on a board and put above the cross. It read, 'Jesus of Nazareth, King of the Jews.'
JOHN 19:19

'Praise the Lord! Our Lord God All-Powerful now rules as king.'
REVELATION 19:6b

Listen to your heart and fill in

Meeting the king

Apart from being the world's mightiest king, Jesus is the most generous one. What do you want to talk to him about in your audience with him today?

1. ____________________________________
2. ____________________________________

One day... our audience with him will be face to face. Won't that be great?!

'Now all we can see of God is like a cloudy picture in a mirror. Later we will see him face to face. We don't know everything, but then we will, just as God completely understands us' (1 Corinthians 13:12).

Links: 27 February, 11 March, 7 July, 5 November

5 minutes more? Matthew 14

17 July

The Messiah, God's Son...

...will carry the burden of our sins

An Old Testament prophecy about the Messiah:

He was wounded and crushed because of our sins; by taking our punishment, he made us completely well.
ISAIAH 53:5

This was written about Jesus:

After all, God chose you to suffer as you follow in the footsteps of Christ, who set an example by suffering for you. Christ did not sin or ever tell a lie. Although he was abused, he never tried to get even. And when he suffered, he made no threats. Instead, he had faith in God, who judges fairly. Christ carried the burden of our sins. He was nailed to the cross, so that we would stop sinning and start living right. By his cuts and bruises you are healed. You had wandered away like sheep. Now you have returned to the one who is your shepherd and protector.
1 PETER 2:21–25

Listen to your heart and fill in

Write your own name in these gaps in Isaiah 53:5

He was wounded and crushed because of ______________________________'s sins;

by taking ______________________________'s punishment, he made

______________________________ completely well.

Download

Now you can memorize it...

'He was wounded and crushed because of our sins; by taking our punishment, he made us completely well' (Isaiah 53:5)

Links: 22 March, 7 July, 18 July, 19 July

5 minutes more? Matthew 15

18 July

The Messiah, God's Son...

...will suffer for us

An Old Testament prophecy about the Messiah:

He was painfully abused, but he did not complain. He was silent like a lamb being led to the butcher, as quiet as a sheep having its wool cut off.
ISAIAH 53:7

This was written in the New Testament:

The Lord's angel said to Philip, 'Go south along the desert road that leads from Jerusalem to Gaza.' So Philip left. An important Ethiopian official happened to be going along that road in his chariot. He was the chief treasurer for Candace, the Queen of Ethiopia. The official had gone to Jerusalem to worship and was now on his way home. He was sitting in his chariot, reading the book of the prophet Isaiah. The Spirit told Philip to catch up with the chariot. Philip ran up close and heard the man reading aloud from the book of Isaiah. Philip asked him, 'Do you understand what you are reading?' The official answered, 'How can I understand unless someone helps me?' He then invited Philip to come up and sit beside him. The man was reading the passage that said, 'He was led like a sheep on its way to be killed. He was silent as a lamb whose wool is being cut off, and he did not say a word...' So Philip began at this place in the Scriptures and explained the good news about Jesus.
ACTS 8:26–32, 35

Di:SaipL

Someone who learns

A disciple is someone who is ready and willing to learn from Jesus. The Ethiopian official didn't really understand very much, but he was ready and willing to learn. He was a good disciple. He had realized that someone who thinks they've finished training isn't trained at all, just finished.

Right, disciple, are you ready to learn more?

Links: 7 July, 12 July, 12 September, 13 September

5 minutes more? Matthew 16

19 July

The Messiah, God's Son...

...will save us

An Old Testament prophecy about the Messiah:

The Lord will reward him with honour and power for sacrificing his life. Others thought he was a sinner, but he suffered for our sins and asked God to forgive us.

ISAIAH 53:12

This was written about Jesus:

But these words were not written only for Abraham. They were written for us, since we will also be accepted because of our faith in God, who raised our Lord Jesus to life. God gave Jesus to die for our sins, and he raised him to life, so that we would be made acceptable to God.

ROMANS 4:23–25

We die only once, and then we are judged. So Christ died only once to take away the sins of many people. But when he comes again, it will not be to take away sin. He will come to save everyone who is waiting for him.

HEBREWS 9:27–28

Good news

For ever—that's a really long time

The average person lives for just over 70 years. If you are a woman, you could live a bit longer. (Girls say that's because women are the stronger sex—and I'm just going to ignore that comment!)

Let's say you are sixteen years old. You have 70 minus 16, which is around about 54 years, left to live, if everything goes according to plan. But if you're a Christian, things are rather different.

The salvation we hope for doesn't just last for 70 – 16 = 54 years, it lasts for eternity.

'But my victory will last; my saving power will never end' (Isaiah 51:8b).

'...and now (Jesus) can save for ever all who obey him' (Hebrews 5:9).

Links: 12 January, 14 January, 15 January, 7 July

5 minutes more? Matthew 17

20 July

The Messiah, God's Son...

...will rise from the dead

This was written about Jesus:

Now, listen to what I have to say about Jesus from Nazareth. God proved that he sent Jesus to you by having him perform miracles, wonders and signs. All of you know this. God had already planned and decided that Jesus would be handed over to you. So you took him and had evil men put him to death on a cross. But God set him free from death and raised him to life. Death could not hold him in its power. What David said are really the words of Jesus, '...The Lord won't leave me in the grave. I am his holy one, and he won't let my body decay...'

My friends, it is right for me to speak to you about our ancestor David. He died and was buried, and his tomb is still here. But David was a prophet, and he knew that God had made a promise he would not break. He had told David that someone from his own family would some day be king. David knew this would happen, and so he told us that Christ would be raised to life. He said that God would not leave him in the grave or let his body decay. All of us can tell you that God has raised Jesus to life!

ACTS 2:22–25, 27, 29–32

♡ Listen to your heart and fill in

How do you use your time?

A lot of people—including teenagers—often complain that they have too much to do and not enough time to do it in. Write down some of the things that you would like to have done if you had had a bit more time.

1. ______________________________

2. ______________________________

3. ______________________________

4. ______________________________

5. ______________________________

Then look forward to heaven. There you'll have enough time for everything!

Links: 7 July, 27 September, 28 September, 29 September

5 minutes more? Matthew 18

21 July

The Messiah, God's Son...

...will come back again

An Old Testament prophecy about the Messiah:

As I continued to watch the vision that night, I saw what looked like a son of man coming with the clouds of heaven, and he was presented to the Eternal God. He was crowned king and given power and glory, so that all people of every nation and race would serve him. He will rule for ever, and his kingdom is eternal, never to be destroyed.

DANIEL 7:13–14

This was written about Jesus:

Look! He is coming with the clouds. Everyone will see him, even the ones who stuck a sword through him. All people on earth will weep because of him. Yes, it will happen! Amen. The Lord God says, 'I am Alpha and Omega, the one who is and was and is coming. I am God All-Powerful!'

REVELATION 1:7–8

Hmm... just a thought...

...about the fact that God keeps his word

As all God's promises that one day the Messiah would come have been fulfilled...

...shouldn't that give us good reason to believe that he will keep the other promises he has given us?

Links: 7 July, 29 September, 30 September

5 minutes more? Matthew 19

David's kingdom is divided in two: north and south

Rehoboam went to Shechem where everyone was waiting to crown him king. Jeroboam son of Nebat heard what was happening, and he stayed in Egypt, where he had gone to hide from Solomon. But the people from the northern tribes of Israel sent for him. Then together they went to Rehoboam and said, 'Your father Solomon forced us to work very hard. But if you make our work easier, we will serve you and do whatever you ask.' 'Give me three days to think about it,' Rehoboam replied, 'then come back for my answer.' So the people left…

Three days later, Jeroboam and the others came back. Rehoboam ignored the advice of the older advisers. He spoke bluntly and told them exactly what his own advisers had suggested: 'My father made you work hard, but I'll make you work even harder. He punished you with whips, but I'll use whips with pieces of sharp metal!' … So the people from the northern tribes of Israel went home, leaving Rehoboam to rule only the people from the towns in Judah… When the Israelites heard that Jeroboam was back, they called everyone together. Then they sent for Jeroboam and made him king of Israel. Only the people from the tribe of Judah remained loyal to David's family.

1 KINGS 12:1–5, 12–14, 17, 20

Did you know…

…about the kingdom before, during and after David's rule?

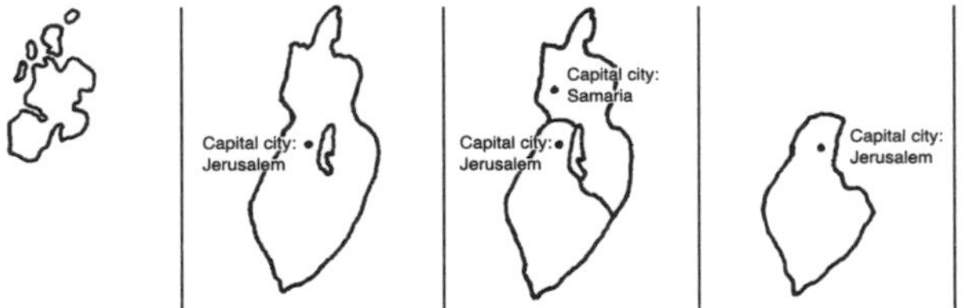

c.1210BC	c.1000–925BC	c.926BC	c.722BC	c.587BC
Joshua leads the people into the promised land.	Good times. The kings David and Solomon unite the land. Jerusalem becomes the capital city.	Solomon dies. The kingdom is divided. Samaria is the northern capital.	Samaria falls. The people are taken captive by the Assyrians.	Jerusalem falls. The people are taken into exile in Babylon.

SOURCE: DEN FULLSTENDIGE BIBELHÅNDBOKA

Links: 6 July, 23 July, 5 August, 6 August

5 minutes more? Matthew 20

King Jeroboam and the golden calves

One day, Jeroboam started thinking, 'Everyone in Israel still goes to the temple in Jerusalem to offer sacrifices to the Lord. What if they become loyal to David's family again? They will kill me and accept Rehoboam as their king.' Jeroboam asked for advice and then made two gold statues of calves. He showed them to the people and said, 'Listen everyone! You won't have to go to Jerusalem to worship any more. Here are your gods who rescued you from Egypt.' Then he put one of the gold calves in the town of Bethel. He put the other one in the town of Dan, and the crowd walked out in front as the calf was taken there. What Jeroboam did was a terrible sin. Jeroboam built small places of worship at the shrines and appointed men who were not from the tribe of Levi to serve as priests... This sinful thing led to the downfall of his kingdom.
1 KINGS 12:26–31; 13:34

Did you know that...

...the time between 1000 and 587BC is called 'the time of the kings'?

The kingdom of Israel was divided in two when Solomon died. Most of the kings of the two new kingdoms did things that were evil in the eyes of the Lord. The worship of idols flourished. People turned their hearts away from God.

But God always gave them another chance. Throughout this time, known as 'the time of the kings', God sent prophets so that the people constantly had the chance to repent. The most important prophets were Elijah, Elisha, Amos, Hosea, Isaiah, Micah, Habakkuk, Nahum, Zephaniah, Jeremiah, and Ezekiel.

We will be discovering a bit more about these prophets over the next few days. You should look forward to it—because we will be talking about men of God who lived close to God and didn't depend on earthly possessions.

Links: 30 April, 22 July, 5 August, 6 August

5 minutes more? Matthew 21

24 July

The prophets try to save the kingdom (1000–587BC)

Elijah's wager (1)

Elijah said, 'I'm a servant of the living Lord All-Powerful, and I swear in his name that I will meet with Ahab today.' ... Ahab went to meet Elijah, and when he saw him, Ahab shouted,'There you are, the biggest troublemaker in Israel!' Elijah answered:

You're the troublemaker—not me! You and your family have disobeyed the Lord's commands by worshipping Baal...

Elijah stood in front of them and said, 'How much longer will you try to have things both ways? If the Lord is God, worship him! But if Baal is God, worship him!' The people did not say a word. Then Elijah continued:

I am the Lord's only prophet, but Baal has four hundred and fifty prophets. Bring us two bulls. Baal's prophets can take one of them, kill it, and cut it into pieces. Then they can put the meat on the wood without lighting the fire. I will do the same thing with the other bull, and I won't light a fire under it either. The prophets of Baal will pray to their god, and I will pray to the Lord. The one who answers by starting the fire is God.

'That's a good idea,' everyone agreed.

1 KINGS 18:15, 16b–18, 21–24

Check it out

Different idols

Many kinds of god were worshipped by the people who lived round about Israel. The Bible calls them idols. The most popular one was Baal. He was a fertility god, so the statues of him often had exaggerated sexual organs.

There aren't many people, if any, who worship Baal today. But the Bible also talks about other idols. An unhealthy desire for money and an unhealthy preoccupation with sex are considered to be idols. And I've got a certain feeling that these are the idols that have maintained their popularity.

Check out Colossians 3:5: 'Don't be controlled by your body. Kill every desire for the wrong kind of sex. Don't be immoral or indecent or have evil thoughts. Don't be greedy, which is the same as worshipping idols.'

Links: 25 July, 26 July, 1 August, 17 September

5 minutes more? Matthew 22

Elijah's wager (2)

Elijah said to Baal's prophets, 'There are more of you, so you go first. Pick out a bull and get it ready, but don't light the fire. Then pray to your god.' They chose their bull, then they got it ready and prayed to Baal all morning, asking him to start the fire. They danced around the altar and shouted, 'Answer us, Baal!' But there was no answer. At midday, Elijah began making fun of them. 'Pray louder!' he said. 'Baal must be a god. Perhaps he's daydreaming or using the toilet or travelling somewhere. Or perhaps he's asleep, and you have to wake him up.' The prophets kept shouting louder and louder, and they cut themselves with swords and knives until they were bleeding. This was the way they worshipped, and they kept it up all afternoon. But there was no answer of any kind.
1 KINGS 18:25–29

☆ Bible personality

Elijah—a tad brave, you could say…

The prophet Elijah must have been the bravest man in the Bible. Just listen…

Once, the king accused Elijah of bringing misfortune on Israel—because it hadn't rained for three years. Elijah answered by saying that it wasn't him who had brought the misfortune, but it had been caused by all the idol-worship that was going on in the country. And he challenged the prophets of Baal to a duel (see yesterday).

There were 450 prophets of Baal in all, while Elijah was quite alone. The rest of the Lord's prophets had been killed, and if he lost the challenge, Elijah would be too.

Both sides made an altar and prepared a sacrifice. Then each side was to call on his own god. Whichever god, Baal or the Lord, set fire to the altar would be the one to win the challenge. You can read how the whole thing ended tomorrow.

But what a man! What faith! What a chance he took. But most of all: what a great God! When it comes to taking sides, you can confidently depend on him.

Links: 17 March, 10 June, 24 July, 26 July

5 minutes more? Matthew 23

26 July

The prophets try to save the kingdom (1000–587 BC)

Elijah's wager (3)

Elijah told everyone to gather around him while he repaired the Lord's altar... He placed the wood on the altar, then they cut the bull into pieces and laid the meat on the wood. He told the people, 'Fill four large jars with water and pour it over the meat and the wood.' After they did this, he told them to do it two more times. They did exactly as he said until finally, the water ran down the altar and filled the ditch. When it was time for the evening sacrifice, Elijah prayed:

Our Lord, you are the God of Abraham, Isaac, and Israel. Now, prove that you are the God of this nation, and that I, your servant, have done this at your command. Please answer me, so these people will know that you are the Lord God, and that you will turn their hearts back to you.

The Lord immediately sent fire, and it burnt up the sacrifice, the wood, and the stones. It scorched the ground everywhere around the altar and dried up every drop of water in the ditch. When the crowd saw what had happened, they all bowed down and shouted, 'The Lord is God! The Lord is God!'

1 KINGS 18:30, 33–39

Download

Please answer me, Lord!

Here is a wonderful Bible verse that you can use as a prayer. Memorize it so that you and Elijah can 'pray together' every single day!

'Please answer me, so these people will know that you are the Lord God, and that you will turn their hearts back to you' (1 Kings 18:37).

Links: 17 March, 10 June, 24 July, 25 July

5 minutes more? Matthew 24

Amos' message (1)...

Because of their double standards, the people will be taken away as captives.

You abuse the poor and demand heavy taxes from them. You have built expensive homes, but you won't enjoy them; you have planted vineyards, but you will get no wine. I am the Lord, and I know your terrible sins. You cheat honest people and take bribes; you rob the poor of justice... I, the Lord, hate and despise your religious celebrations and your times of worship. I won't accept your offerings or animal sacrifices—not even your very best. No more of your noisy songs! I won't listen when you play your harps. But let justice and fairness flow like a river that never runs dry... I will force you to march as captives beyond Damascus. I, the Lord God All-Powerful, have spoken!
AMOS 5:11–12, 21–24, 27

Hmm... just a thought...

...about double standards

Many are the words we speak,
Many are the songs we sing,
Many kinds of offerings,
But now to live the life.

Help us live the life, help us live the life
All we want to do is bring to you something real,
Bring you something true.

Now to go the extra mile, now to turn the other cheek
And to serve you with a life. Let us share your fellowship,
Even your sufferings, never let the passion die.

Help us live the life......
MATT REDMAN

Links: 15 December, 18 December, 19 December, 20 December

5 minutes more? Matthew 25

28 July

The prophets try to save the kingdom (1000–587BC)

Amos' message (2)...

But the Lord will make Israel prosper again.

My eyes have seen what a sinful nation you are, and I'll wipe you out. But I will leave a few of Jacob's descendants. I, the Lord, have spoken! ... In the future, I will rebuild David's fallen kingdom. I will build it from its ruins and set it up again, just as it used to be... I'll make Israel prosper again. You will rebuild your towns and live in them. You will drink wine from your own vineyards and eat the fruit you grow. I'll plant your roots deep in the land I have given you, and you won't ever be uprooted again. I, the Lord God, have spoken.

AMOS 9:8, 11, 14–15

Check it out

What is prophecy? How can we tell if it's from the Lord?

It is good to be clear that prophecy is much more about *forth*telling of God's word in a particular situation than a *fore*telling of the future. People still give prophecies in God's name today, so it's essential to know the 'rules of the game'. Here are some guidelines to help you:

1. Although prophecy does have a side that lays bare the secrets of our hearts for correction, it is a gift of the Holy Spirit that God has given us for comforting, encouraging and exhorting each other in the faith (1 Corinthians 14:3). It is a gift we should be eager to have (1 Corinthians 14:1).
2. If what the prophecy contains isn't in line with what we read in the Bible, it isn't from the Lord. Remember, prophecy does not have the same authority as scripture (Galatians 1:7–9).
3. Has the prophecy been offered in a humble and loving way? If prophecy is used to hurt or manipulate people, it isn't from the Lord (see Jeremiah 23:32, 1 Corinthians 14:1 and Luke 6:43). If, for example, a boy goes to a girl and says, 'The Lord has told me that we are going to get married,' then the girl shouldn't feel frightened if she doesn't want to marry that boy. The boy is being manipulative, and that's not what prophecy is for!

The Bible encourages us not to ignore prophecy, but to test it and respond (1 Thessalonians 5:20–22).

Links: 29 July, 12 August, 15 August, 16 August

5 minutes more? Matthew 26

29 July

The prophets try to save the kingdom (1000–587BC)

Hosea's message...

God's love for his people.

When Israel was a child, I loved him, and I called my son out of Egypt. But as the saying goes, 'The more they were called, the more they rebelled.' They never stopped offering incense and sacrifices to the idols of Baal. I took Israel by the arm and taught them to walk. But they would not admit that I was the one who had healed them. I led them with kndness and with love, not with ropes. I held them close to me; I bent down to feed them...

Israel, I can't let you go. I can't give you up. How could I possibly destroy you as I did the towns of Admah and Zeboiim? I just can't do it. My feelings for you are much too strong. Israel, I won't lose my temper and destroy you again. I am the Holy God—not merely a human being, and I won't stay angry.

HOSEA 11:1–4, 8–9

Weird and wonderful

Hosea and prostitutes

God told Hosea to go and get married to a prostitute! Yes, you read right—a prostitute. You can read about it for yourself—just begin in Hosea 1.

God wanted Hosea to do this to show the people how he, God, felt. God loved Israel. He'd made a covenant with them—but the people weren't faithful. They flirted shamelessly and brazenly with other gods.

Almost no one in the Bible depicts God's love better than Hosea. The first ten chapters of his book describe Israel's infidelity. In chapter 11—our chapter—God expresses the intensity of his love for his people.

'Israel, I can't let you go. I can't give you up. How could I possibly destroy you as I did the towns of Admah and Zeboiim? I just can't do it. My feelings for you are much too strong. Israel, I won't lose my temper and destroy you again. I am the Holy God—not merely a human being, and I won't stay angry' (Hosea 11:8–9).

Links: 15 February, 16 February, 14 March, 1 May

5 minutes more? Matthew 27

30 July

The prophets try to save the kingdom (1000–587BC)

Isaiah's message...

They will hear, but they won't understand.

I had a vision of the Lord. He was on his throne high above, and his robe filled the temple. Flaming creatures with six wings each were flying over him. They covered their faces with two of their wings and their bodies with two more. They used the other two wings for flying, as they shouted, 'Holy, holy, holy, Lord All-Powerful! The earth is filled with your glory.' ...

Then I cried out, 'I'm doomed! Everything I say is sinful, and so are the words of everyone around me. Yet I have seen the King, the Lord All-Powerful!' ...

After this, I heard the Lord ask, 'Is there anyone I can send? Will someone go for us?' 'I'll go,' I answered. 'Send me!' Then the Lord told me to go and speak this message to the people: 'You will listen and listen, but never understand. You will look and look, but never see.'

ISAIAH 6:1b–3, 5, 8–9

Listen to your heart and fill in

What would you have said?

Imagine you were Isaiah and experienced this completely amazing vision. You saw the Lord sitting on a throne, like a king, and all the angels were flying round on all sides while they sang, 'Holy, holy, holy!'

Then imagine you heard the same voice that Isaiah heard: 'Is there anyone I can send? Will someone go for us?' Isaiah answered, 'I'll go. Send me!'

Take a minute or so to think, and then write down what you would have said:

Links: 26 February, 18 July, 30 October, 30 December

5 minutes more? Matthew 28

Micah's message...

Humbly obey your God.

Listen, all of you! Earth and everything on it, pay close attention. The Lord God accuses you from his holy temple. And he will come down to crush underfoot every pagan altar. Mountains will melt beneath his feet like wax beside a fire. Valleys will vanish like water rushing down a ravine. This will happen because of the terrible sins of Israel, the descendants of Jacob. Samaria has led Israel to sin, and the pagan altars at Jerusalem have made Judah sin. So the Lord will leave Samaria in ruins—merely an empty field where vineyards are planted. He will scatter its stones and destroy its foundations. Samaria's idols will be smashed, and the wages of temple prostitutes will be destroyed by fire. Silver and gold from those idols will then be used by foreigners as payment for prostitutes... The Lord God has told us what is right and what he demands: 'See justice is done, let mercy be your first concern, and humbly obey your God.'
MICAH 1:2–7; 6:8

Story...
...about humility

I was perhaps about 18 years old when I really understood what humility was. I had just got my driving licence and was out driving with my best friend. I don't really know how we got talking about it, but suddenly he said, 'Knut, perhaps we both aren't really that humble, you know.' 'No, perhaps we aren't,' I said.

If I'm honest, I think he was right. We certainly didn't figure in a list of the Top 100 'most humble people in the country's history', either of us.

'We aren't that humble,' repeated my best mate. I got really irritated. Then I remember thinking, 'Perhaps not, but in any case, I'm humbler than you!'

Can you believe I thought that? Shows how humble I really was!

Links: 1 June, 3 June, 5 June, 19 December

5 minutes more? John 1

1 August

The prophets try to save the kingdom (1000–587BC)

Nahum's message...

The Lord is angry, but he will show Israel his grace.

The Lord God demands loyalty. In his anger, he takes revenge on his enemies. The Lord is powerful, yet patient; he makes sure that the guilty are always punished. He can be seen in storms and in whirlwinds; clouds are the dust from his feet... At the sight of the Lord, mountains and hills tremble and melt; the earth and its people shudder and shake. Who can stand the heat of his furious anger? It flashes out like fire and shatters stones. The Lord is good. He protects those who trust in him in times of trouble... Look towards the mountains, people of Judah! Here comes a messenger with good news of peace. Celebrate your festivals. Keep your promises to God. Your evil enemies are destroyed and will never again invade your country.

NAHUM 1:2–3, 5–7, 15

Download

The Lord is good

This is a good verse to have to hand every day. Don't just learn the words, but also the reference—then you can find it again another time you need it.

'The Lord is good. He protects those who trust him in times of trouble' (Nahum 1:7).

Links: 5 August, 6 August, 7 August, 12 August

5 minutes more? John 2

Zephaniah's message...

The Day of the Lord is near.

Be silent! I am the Lord God, and the time is near. I am preparing to sacrifice my people and to invite my guests...

If you humbly obey the Lord, then come and worship him. If you do right and are humble, perhaps you will be safe on that day when the Lord turns loose his anger...

Everyone in Jerusalem and Judah, celebrate and shout with all your heart! Zion, your punishment is over. The Lord has forced your enemies to turn and retreat. Your Lord is King of Israel and stands at your side; you don't have to worry about any more troubles. Jerusalem, the time is coming, when it will be said to you: 'Don't be discouraged or grow weak from fear! The Lord your God wins victory after victory and is always with you. He celebrates and sings because of you, and he will refresh your life with his love.'
ZEPHANIAH 1:7; 2:3; 3:14–17

Listen to your heart and fill in...

...your name

............, celebrate and shout with all your heart! ...., your punishment is over. The Lord has forced your enemies to turn and retreat. Your Lord is King of Israel and stands at your side, ...; you don't have to worry about any more troubles. ...., the time is coming, when it will be said to you: 'Don't be discouraged or grow weak from fear! The Lord your God wins victory after victory and is always with you, ... He celebrates and sings because of you, and he will refresh your life with his love, ...'

Links: 12 August, 13 August, 16 August, 27 December

5 minutes more? John 3

3 August

The prophets try to save the kingdom (1000–587BC)

Jeremiah is called to be a prophet

The Lord said: 'Jeremiah, I am your Creator, and before you were born, I chose you to speak for me to the nations.' I replied, 'I'm not a good speaker, Lord, and I'm too young.' 'Don't say you're too young,' the Lord answered. 'If I tell you to go and speak to someone, then go! And when I tell you what to say, don't leave out a word! I promise to be with you and keep you safe, so don't be afraid.' The Lord reached out his hand, then he touched my mouth and said, 'I am giving you the words to say, and I am sending you with authority to speak to the nations for me. You will tell them of doom and destruction, and of rising and rebuilding again.'

JEREMIAH 1:4–10

Good news

You are not the result of a misused condom

Today I have two bits of good news and one bit of bad news.

The first good thing:

You don't need to be full of self-confidence for God to have confidence in you. When God gave Jeremiah a challenge, Jeremiah answered, 'I'm not a good speaker, Lord, and I'm too young.' But God believed in Jeremiah. God knows all about you too. He knows how you feel. He believes in you!

The second good thing:

I once met a guy who told me he hadn't been welcomed by his parents, that his conception and birth hadn't been planned. 'I'm a condom accident,' he added flippantly. Maybe his parents hadn't planned things the way they turned out, but today's good news is that my friend, and all the others like him, were born as part of God's plan. Listen to what God said to Jeremiah, 'Jeremiah, I am your Creator, and before you were born, I chose you to speak for me to the nations.' You are just as carefully planned. God has made you just the way he wants you, and when he wants you. Yippee!

And the bad news:

There were 186,274 legal abortions carried out in England and Wales in 2001. One hundred and eighty-six thousand, two hundred and seventy-four...

Links: 15 March, 16 March, 30 July, 4 August

5 minutes more? John 4

4 August

The prophets try to save the kingdom (1000–587BC)

Jeremiah's message

Then the Lord showed me something else and asked, 'What do you see now?' I answered, 'I see a pot of boiling water in the north, and it's about to spill out towards us.' The Lord said:

I will pour out destruction all over the land. Just watch while I send for the kings of the north. They will attack and capture Jerusalem and other towns, then set up their thrones at the gates of Jerusalem. I will punish my people, because they are guilty of turning from me to worship idols. Jeremiah, get ready*! Go and tell the people what I command you to say. Don't be frightened by them, or I will make you terrified while they watch. My power will make you strong like a fortress or a column of iron or a wall of bronze. You will oppose all of Judah, including its kings and leaders, its priests and people. They will fight back, but they won't win. I, the Lord, give my word—I won't let them harm you.

JEREMIAH 1:13–19

Weird and wonderful

The Bible and saggy clothing!

In verse 17 of today's reading, the Lord tells Jeremiah, 'Be ready!' In older translations of the Bible we read that God actually tells Jeremiah to 'gird a belt around his waist'.

In Bible times, men worn a long tunic that hung right down to the ground. If they were going to do some physical work or go to war, they used to hitch the tunic up with a belt so that it wouldn't get in the way. When God tells people in the Bible to 'gird a belt around their waist', it means, 'Get ready! Be prepared!'—rather like someone telling you to 'roll up your sleeves and get on with it!'

There are other places in the Bible that give us the same message:

'Be ready and keep your lamps burning just like servants who wait up for their master' (Luke 12:35–36a).

'Be ready! Let the truth be like a belt around your waist' (Ephesians 6:14a).

'Be alert and think straight' (1 Peter 1:13a).

These days, fashions in belts come and go, but I want to ask you if you've 'girded a belt about your waist'? Are you ready to get stuck in for Jesus?

Links: 5 August, 6 August, 7 August, 28 October

5 minutes more? John 5

Remember to post
early for Christmas!
royalmail.com/greetings

Royal Mail

The Bryson Family
Loore Cottage
Kenmore Street
Aberfeldy
PH15 2BL.

Israel is invaded in 722BC: the people go into exile

Even worse, the Israelites tried to hide their sins from the Lord their God... Even though the Lord had commanded them not to worship idols, they did it anyway. So the Lord made sure that every prophet warned Israel and Judah with these words: 'I, the Lord, command you to stop doing sinful things and start obeying my laws and teachings! I gave them to your ancestors, and I told my servants the prophets to repeat them to you.' But the Israelites would not listen; they were as stubborn as their ancestors who had refused to worship the Lord their God...

During the fourth year of Hezekiah's rule, which was the seventh year of Hoshea's rule in Israel, King Shalmaneser of Assyria led his troops to Samaria, the capital city of Israel. They attacked and captured it three years later... The king of Assyria took the Israelites away as prisoners... All of that happened because the people of Israel had not obeyed the Lord their God. They rejected the solemn agreement he had made with them, and they ignored everything that the Lord's servant Moses had told them.

2 KINGS 17:9a, 12–14; 18:9–12

Big word

Stubborn

Some qualities can have both negative and positive expressions.

Being stubborn is a negative thing if you refuse to take good advice. But it is a positive thing if you are daring enough to stand up for something in a difficult situation.

Being clever is a negative thing if it causes you to look down on other people. It's a positive thing if you use that quality in a way that blesses other people.

In the Bible, the people of Israel are often described as stubborn. No other people in the course of history have had to go through more than the Jewish people. Their stubbornness has often been to their advantage and helped them. But in today's reading, being stubborn is a negative thing and everything goes pear-shaped as a result.

Make sure your particular qualities express themselves positively. Today.

Links: 22 July, 6 August, 8 August, 12 August

5 minutes more? John 6

6 August

The prophets try to save the kingdom (1000–587BC)

Judah is invaded in 587BC: the people are taken to Babylon

Zedekiah was twenty-one years old when he was appointed king of Judah, and he ruled from Jerusalem for eleven years. He disobeyed the Lord his God and refused to change his ways, even after a warning from Jeremiah, the Lord's prophet... But the Lord God felt sorry for his people, and instead of destroying the temple, he sent prophets who warned the people over and over again about their sins. But the people only laughed and insulted these prophets. They ignored what the Lord God was trying to tell them, until he finally became so angry that nothing could stop him from punishing Judah and Jerusalem. The Lord sent King Nebuchadnezzar of Babylon to attack Jerusalem... Nebuchadnezzar's troops burnt down the temple and destroyed every important building in the city. Then they broke down the city wall. The survivors were taken to Babylonia as prisoners, where they were slaves of the king and his sons, until Persia became a powerful nation... These things happened just as Jeremiah the Lord's prophet had said.

2 CHRONICLES 36:11–12, 15–17a, 19–20, 21b

Check it out

Our captivity

The people of Israel were taken to Babylon as prisoners in 587BC. But Paul says that we Christians are also prisoners!

'With my whole heart I agree with the Law of God. But in every part of me I discover something fighting against my mind, and it makes me a prisoner of sin that controls everything I do' (Romans 7:22–23).

We aren't completely free people. Although we belong to Christ, sin tries to use its power within us to control our desires and pull us away from doing the good things God wants us to do.

Like Paul, you might be thinking, 'What a miserable person I am. Who will rescue me...?' But we should come to the same conclusion as him: 'Thank God! Jesus Christ will rescue me' (Romans 7:24–25).

Jesus Christ rescues us from being prisoners of sin. By his power we can make the decisions that please God.

Links: 22 July, 7 August, 8 August, 12 August

5 minutes more? John 7

7 August

Exiled in Babylon (587–538BC)

The people are taken away to Babylon, and Daniel is one of them

In the third year that Jehoiakim was king of Judah, King Nebuchadnezzar of Babylonia attacked Jerusalem. The Lord let Nebuchadnezzar capture Jehoiakim and take away some of the things used in God's temple. And when the king returned to Babylonia, he put these things in the temple of his own god. One day the king ordered Ashpenaz, his highest palace official, to choose some young men from the royal family of Judah and from other leading Jewish families. The king said, 'They must be healthy, handsome, clever, wise, educated, and fit to serve in the royal palace. Teach them how to speak and write our language...' Four of the young Jews chosen were Daniel, Hananiah, Mishael, and Azariah, all from the tribe of Judah... God made the four young men clever and wise. They read a lot of books and became well educated. Daniel could also tell the meaning of dreams and visions.

DANIEL 1:1–4, 6, 17

☆ Bible personality

Daniel

Daniel was taken away to Babylon along with some of his people, but by some miracle he ended up working for the king. If you think the Old Testament isn't that exciting, you should read the book of Daniel. It's some book, and Daniel's some guy!

Daniel experienced some amazing things. He threw his whole heart into everything he did and had enormous faith in God. He is an amazing example to us—an extreme example.

- He was willing to learn (Daniel 1:17)
- He was brave (Daniel 6:10)
- He wasn't conceited (Daniel 2:30)
- He was trustworthy (Daniel 6:4)
- He read the Bible carefully (Daniel 9:2)
- He prayed a lot (Daniel 6:13)

But first and foremost, Daniel would not swap the true God for the small idols that the Babylonians worshipped—even though the king ordered him to (Daniel 6:13).

Links: 8 August, 9 August, 10 August, 11 August

5 minutes more? John 8

8 August

Exiled in Babylon (587–538BC)

Daniel impresses the Babylonian king

During the second year that Nebuchadnezzar was king, he had such horrible nightmares that he could not sleep. So he called in his counsellors, advisers, magicians, and wise men, and said, 'I am disturbed by a dream that I don't understand, and I want you to explain it.' ... His advisers explained, 'Your Majesty, you are demanding the impossible!' ... This made the king so angry that he gave orders for every wise man in Babylonia to be put to death, including Daniel and his three friends... In a vision one night, Daniel was shown the dream and its meaning... The king said, 'Now I know that your God is above all other gods and kings, because he gave you the power to explain this mystery.'

DANIEL 2:1–2, 10a, 12–13, 19a, 47

Check it out

Why Daniel the clever clogs was so clever

Daniel was unbelievably clever—he knew a lot about all sorts of things. But he also knew that without God on his side he was nothing. Daniel was clever enough to know that he wasn't clever enough if everything was left up to him alone.

When the king asked his magicians, advisers, counsellors and wise men to interpret the dream he'd had—without telling them what the dream was—of course they couldn't do it. But Daniel managed it. He went to God and asked him, and God explained to Daniel what the king's dream meant.

Are you facing any challenges in the days ahead? Anything you can't manage on your own? You have a big God. He will help you.

Do as Daniel did—go to God.

Do as Daniel did—use all your senses to listen out for God's voice.

Links: 31 January, 1 February, 7 August, 9 August

5 minutes more? John 9

9 August

Exiled in Babylon (587–538BC)

Daniel in the lion's den

[Daniel] did his work so much better than the other governors and officials that the king decided to let him govern the whole kingdom. The other men tried to find something wrong with the way Daniel did his work for the king... The men then told the king, 'That Jew named Daniel, who was brought here as a captive, refuses to obey you or the law that you ordered to be written. And he still prays to his god three times a day.' The king was really upset to hear about this, and for the rest of the day he tried to think how he could save Daniel...

Darius ordered Daniel to be brought out and thrown into a pit of lions. But he said to Daniel, 'You have been faithful to your God, and I pray that he will rescue you.' ... At daybreak the king got up and ran to the pit. He was anxious and shouted, 'Daniel, you were faithful and served your God. Was he able to save you from the lions?' Daniel answered, 'Your Majesty... My God knew that I was innocent, and he sent an angel to keep the lions from eating me. Your Majesty, I have never done anything to hurt you.'

DANIEL 6:3–4a, 13–14, 16, 19–22

Refresh

Prayer and bad conscience

Daniel is an example of what it means to pray. He prayed three times a day! If you're the sort of person who has a bad conscience because you don't pray often enough, here's a word of encouragement from Martin Schanche, the rally driver:

It's better to lie on a beach and think about God than sit in a church and think about the beach. God doesn't force anyone to pray! It isn't how much you pray that decides whether you are a Christian or not. God doesn't want you walking around with a bad conscience because you don't pray enough. Put all that aside—God loves you! But it's for precisely that reason that he so desperately wants to spend time with you. It's not important whether you pray once, three times or 300 times a day. But it is important that you are giving God your full attention when you do pray. Let it be God's love that drives you to prayer—not a bad conscience.

Put aside a bit of time to pray. You don't have to say much. Just be there—you and God. Right now, perhaps? Say whatever comes into your mind, and realize that it's good to be with him.

Links: 10 June, 24 July, 25 July, 26 July

5 minutes more? John 10

10 August

Exiled in Babylon (587–538BC)

The people complain about their exile

Jerusalem, once so crowded, lies deserted and lonely. This city that was known all over the world is now like a widow. The people of Judah are slaves, suffering in a foreign land, with no rest from sorrow. Their enemies captured them and were terribly cruel.

LAMENTATIONS 1:1, 3

Then I remember something that fills me with hope. The Lord's kindness never fails! If he had not been merciful, we would have been destroyed. The Lord can always be trusted to show mercy each morning. The Lord is kind to everyone who trusts and obeys him. It is good to wait patiently for the Lord to save us.

LAMENTATIONS 3:21–23, 25–26

Big word

Honesty

We can learn a lot about honesty in the Bible. On the whole, Lamentations is full of complaining about how awful things were for the people who had been taken away and forced to work in Babylon. Their proud capital city, Jerusalem, lay in ruins after the devastation inflicted by the Babylonians. The temple was a smoking, burnt-out ruin. Everything was dark and sad.

The people didn't try to gloss over things and pretend nothing had happened. *No*, the people complained. They complained to God.

When we're having a bad time, the worst thing we can do is to pretend it's not happening and say everything's fine. Lamentations teaches us that we're allowed to call out to God and complain to him when things get rough. It's best to take our anger and complaints to him.

But Lamentations also teaches us that right in the middle of hopeless situations, we can find hope. In the middle of our dark times we can find a ray of light. Look at the second set of verses in today's reading... they're so encouraging.

Links: 6 August, 11 August, 19 September, 20 September

5 minutes more? John 11

11 August

Exiled in Babylon (587–538BC)

Dry bones live again

Some time later, I felt the Lord's power take control of me, and his Spirit carried me to a valley full of bones. The Lord showed me all around, and everywhere I looked I saw bones that were dried out. He said, 'Ezekiel, son of man, can these bones come back to life?' I replied, 'Lord God, only you can answer that.' Then he told me to say:

Dry bones, listen to what the Lord is saying to you, 'I, the Lord God, will put breath into you, and once again you will live…'

As soon as I said this, the wind blew among the bodies, and they came back to life! They all stood up, and there were enough to make a large army. The Lord said:

Ezekiel, the people of Israel are like dead bones. They complain that they are dried up and that they have no hope for the future. So tell them, 'I, the Lord God, promise to open your graves and set you free. I will bring you back to Israel.'

EZEKIEL 37:1–5, 10–12

Did you know that…

…this Bible passage isn't easy to understand without a bit of explanation?

But if you know a little more about its background, that will be a help. Here are ten facts to help you understand today's text and get encouragement from it.

1. Ezekiel was a prophet.
2. He was a prophet who spoke words directly from God.
3. As well as speaking, the Old Testament prophets often did 'prophetic actions'.
4. The people of Israel were taken to Babylon as exiles.
5. Never before had they been so far down in the depths of despair.
6. Ezekiel was exiled as well.
7. The prophecy talks about the people of Israel being released from captivity and raised up again.
8. But it also speaks to us today.
9. It is a picture of how God blows his Holy Spirit into us and gives us a new and full life in Christ.
10. If you want, you can have God's Spirit breathe new life into you.

Ask God to blow his Spirit into the dry parts of your life today.

Links: 12 August, 13 August, 14 August, 15 August

5 minutes more: John 12

12 August

Exiled in Babylon (587–538BC)

King Cyrus lets the people go home

In the first year that Cyrus was king of Persia, the Lord kept his promise by telling Cyrus to send this official message to all parts of his kingdom:

I am King Cyrus of Persia. The Lord God of heaven, who is also the God of Israel, has made me the ruler of all nations on earth. And he has chosen me to build a temple for him in Jerusalem, which is in Judah. The Lord God will watch over and encourage any of his people who want to go back to Jerusalem and help build the temple. Everyone else must provide what is needed. They must give money, supplies, and animals, as well as gifts for rebuilding God's temple.
EZRA 1:1b–4

Weird and wonderful

God can use pagan kings to do his work

It has always amazed me that Cyrus, a pagan king, heard God telling him to rebuild the temple in Jerusalem. Maybe he wasn't as 'pagan' as we think if he acknowledged that the God of the Israelites was the Lord God of heaven and knew that God had given him his position of leadership.

This shows us that God can reveal himself to the most unexpected people and use them to further his plan for people on earth.

Check out what it says in Romans 13:1: 'Obey the rulers who have authority over you. Only God can give authority to anyone, and he puts these rulers in their places of power.'

Pray for those in authority over you—parents, teachers, local council officials, people in central government and the royal family. Ask God to reveal himself to them and use them for his purposes.

Links: 13 August, 14 August, 15 August, 16 August

5 minutes more? John 13

13 August

Exiled in Babylon (587–538BC)

Songs on the way home to Jerusalem (1)

I look to the hills! Where will I find help? It will come from the Lord, who created the heavens and the earth. The Lord is your protector, and he won't go to sleep or let you stumble. The protector of Israel doesn't doze or ever get drowsy. The Lord is your protector, there at your right side to shade you from the sun. You won't be harmed by the sun during the day or by the moon at night. The Lord will protect you and keep you safe from all dangers. The Lord will protect you now and always wherever you go.

PSALM 121

Download...

...about help

If the Bible you use is the Contemporary English Version, you might notice that Psalms 120—134 all have the same description above them: 'A song for worship'. Some other versions call them 'Songs of Ascent'. The people of Israel sang them on their way to worship at the temple. It's possible that they sang them on their way home from exile to build the new temple—you can imagine that they would have been pleased to be returning home after all those years of captivity, to the place where they were used to worshipping God.

There are two verses worth memorizing today:

'I look to the hills! Where will I find help? It will come from the Lord, who created the heavens and the earth' (Psalm 121:1–2).

Links: 12 August, 14 August, 15 August, 16 August

5 minutes more? John 14

14 August

Exiled in Babylon (587–538BC)

Songs on the way home to Jerusalem (2)

A song for worship:

It seemed like a dream when the Lord brought us back to the city of Zion*. We celebrated with laughter and joyful songs. In foreign nations it was said, 'The Lord has worked miracles for his people.' And so we celebrated because the Lord had indeed worked miracles for us. Our Lord, we ask you to bless our people again, and let us be like streams in the Southern Desert. We cried out as we went out to plant our seeds. Now let us celebrate as we bring in the crops. We cried on the way to plant our seeds, but we will celebrate and shout as we bring in the crops.
PSALM 126

* Zion = Jerusalem

Listen to your heart and fill in...

...what you've got to be happy about

Think: What has made you happy during the summer?

1. ______________________________
2. ______________________________
3. ______________________________

What are you looking forward to in the coming six months?

1. ______________________________
2. ______________________________
3. ______________________________

Now pray this prayer...

'Dear God, today I have thought of six things that make me happy. They are... (tell God what you wrote down in the points above). Thank you, Lord!'

Links: 12 August, 13 August, 15 August, 16 August

5 minutes more? John 15

15 August

Home from Babylon (538BC)

The temple is rebuilt

[The Lord All-Powerful said...] First, go to the hills and get wood for my temple, so I can take pride in it and be worshipped there. You expected much, but received only a little. And when you brought it home, I made that little disappear. Why have I done this? It's because you hurry off to build your own houses, while my temple is still in ruins.

HAGGAI 1:8–9

With great success the Jewish leaders continued working on the temple, while Haggai and Zechariah encouraged them by their preaching. And so, the temple was completed at the command of the God of Israel and by the orders of kings Cyrus, Darius, and Artaxerxes of Persia.

EZRA 6:14

Did you know that...

...all in all there have been three temples in Jerusalem?

Maybe you've seen pictures of the Wailing Wall in Jerusalem, where devout Jews stand, rocking backwards and forwards, as they pray. Do you know why it's called the Wailing Wall?

Here's a bit of history. In all, there have been three temples in Jerusalem.

1. The first was built by King Solomon, around 1000BC. It was massive and very beautiful. It was plundered and burnt by the Babylonians in about 600BC.
2. The second temple was the one we read about today. It was built after the people came back from Babylon, around 515BC. It was even bigger than the first one, but it was destroyed by invaders in 167BC.
3. The third temple was begun twenty years before the birth of Christ and was still not completed when Jesus visited the temple (see John 2:20). It was finished in AD64.

Only six years later, the whole town, including the temple area, was plundered by the Romans. The temple was never rebuilt. Only the foundations and the Wailing Wall remain. Today, a mosque stands where the temple once stood.

Now you can see why the only remaining bit of the temple is called the Wailing Wall and what the people there are grieving about.

Links: 28 June, 5 July, 6 August, 11 August

5 minutes more? John 16

16 August

Home from Babylon (538BC)

Ezra reads from the law

Ezra was up on the high platform, where he could be seen by everyone, and when he opened the book, they all stood up. Ezra praised the great Lord God, and the people shouted, 'Amen! Amen!' Then they bowed with their faces to the ground and worshipped the Lord. After this, the Levites... went among the people, explaining the meaning of what Ezra had read. The people started crying when God's Law was read to them. Then Nehemiah the governor, Ezra the priest and teacher, and the Levites who had been teaching the people all said, 'This is a special day for the Lord your God. So don't be sad and don't cry!' ... The Levites encouraged the people by saying, 'This is a sacred day, so don't worry or mourn!' When the people returned to their homes, they celebrated by eating and drinking and by sharing their food with those in need, because they had understood what had been read to them.

NEHEMIAH 8:5–9, 11–12

Hmm... just a thought

The Bible—yeh, baby—Hallelujah!

Now I'm going to have to stop myself getting too enthusiastic. I've just read today's text again and, you know, so often I find I feel just the same as the people we've read about today.

Nothing sets me more on fire than the Bible.

Nothing is more fulfilling for me than reading the Bible, digging into it and explaining it.

Nothing makes me happier than when I discover something new in the Bible.

What a book! What a wickedly good book!

I feel like shouting 'Hallelujah!'

Wake up, all you Bible freaks out there...

Links: 31 October, 1 November, 2 November, 3 November

5 minutes more? John 17

17 August

Home from Babylon (538BC)

The promised messenger

I, the Lord All-Powerful, will send my messenger to prepare the way for me. Then suddenly the Lord you are looking for will appear in his temple. The messenger you desire is coming with my promise, and he is on his way.

On the day the Lord comes, he will be like a furnace that purifies silver or like strong soap in a washbasin. No one will be able to stand up to him. The Lord will purify the descendants of Levi, as though they were gold or silver. Then they will bring the proper offerings to the Lord...

The day of judgment is certain to come. And it will be like a red-hot furnace with flames that burn up proud and sinful people, as though they were straw. Not a branch or a root will be left. I, the Lord All-Powerful, have spoken! But for you who honour my name, victory will shine like the sun with healing in its rays, and you will jump around like calves at play.

MALACHI 3:1–3; 4:1–2

☆ Bible personality

Malachi (Who was he, I wonder?)

Malachi is the last book in the Old Testament and was written around 500 years before Jesus was born. Take note—'Malachi' isn't the name of the person who wrote the book. Who wrote it, no one knows, but 'Malachi' is a Hebrew word meaning 'my messenger'. It is this 'messenger' that the book is all about, and hence the name of the book. The big question is, 'Who is this messenger?' I wonder... Guess!

- He will prepare the way for the Lord.
- He will come suddenly.
- He will purify the people.
- He will offer sacrifices in the right way.
- He will bring joy that can only be compared to that of calves let out in spring after a long, cold winter. (People who have seen this say it's a really cool thing to watch.)
- He will let victory shine like the sun with healing in its rays.

If you're still not sure who this is, then you can have a sneak preview of the next page.

Links: 7 July, 14 July, 19 July, 18 August

5 minutes more? John 18

18 August

The life of Jesus (c.6BC–AD27)

God has spoken through the Son

Long ago in many ways and at many times God's prophets spoke his message to our ancestors. But now at last, God sent his Son to bring his message to us. God created the universe by his Son, and everything will some day belong to the Son. God's Son has all the brightness of God's own glory and is like him in every way. By his own mighty word, he holds the universe together. After the Son had washed away our sins, he sat down at the right side of the glorious God in heaven. He had become much greater than the angels, and the name he was given is far greater than any of theirs. God never said to any of the angels, 'You are my Son, because today I have become your Father!' Neither has God said to any of them, 'I will be his Father, and he will be my Son!'

HEBREWS 1:1–5

Head, shoulders, knees and toes

What do you see?

Concentrate on the four pin-points in the middle of the picture for about 30 seconds.

Shut your eyes, lean your head back and you will see a shining circle.

Continue looking at the circle. What do you see?

'[Jesus] has the brightness of God's own glory and is like him in every way' (Hebrews 1:3a).

Links: 7 April, 5 November, 16 November, 17 November

5 minutes more? John 19

19 August

The life of Jesus (c.6BC–AD27)

The birth of Jesus

This is how Jesus Christ was born. A young woman named Mary was engaged to Joseph from King David's family. But before they were married, she learnt that she was going to have a baby by God's Holy Spirit. Joseph was a good man and did not want to embarrass Mary in front of everyone. He decided to call off the wedding quietly. While Joseph was thinking about this, an angel from the Lord came to him in a dream. The angel said, 'Joseph, the baby that Mary will have is from the Holy Spirit. Go ahead and marry her. Then after her baby is born, name him Jesus, because he will save his people from their sins.' So the Lord's promise came true, just as the prophet had said, 'A virgin will have a baby boy, and he will be called Immanuel,' which means 'God with us'.

MATTHEW 1:18–23

Check it out

Mary, Mary, Mary, Mary, Mary and Mary

There are six different Marys mentioned in the New Testament. It's easy to muddle them up and forget which one is which. They were six amazing women.

Mary 1: Jesus' mother (See Luke 2; John 2)

Mary 2: Mary Magdalene (the first to arrive at Jesus' grave on Easter Day) (See Luke 8:2; John 19:25—20:18)

Mary 3: Mother of James and John (See Matthew 27:56—28:1)

Mary 4: The one who anointed Jesus' feet (See John 11:1—12:7)

Mary 5: A church leader (See Acts 12:12)

Mary 6: A hard worker (See Romans 16:6)

The reading on 3 February was about Mary no. 4. The reading on 27 September is about Mary nos. 2 and 3. Today's reading is about Mary no. 1.

Links: 8 July, 23 December, 24 December, 25 December

5 minutes more? John 20

20 August

The life of Jesus (c.6BC–AD27)

Twelve years old

Every year Jesus' parents went to Jerusalem for Passover. And when Jesus was twelve years old, they all went there as usual for the celebration. After Passover his parents left, but they did not know that Jesus had stayed on in the city. They thought he was travelling with some other people, and they went a whole day before they started looking for him. When they could not find him with their relatives and friends, they went back to Jerusalem and started looking for him there. Three days later they found Jesus sitting in the temple, listening to the teachers and asking them questions. Everyone who heard him was surprised at how much he knew and at the answers he gave. When his parents found him, they were amazed. His mother said, 'Son, why have you done this to us? Your father and I have been very worried, and we have been searching for you!' Jesus answered, 'Why did you have to look for me? Didn't you know that I would be in my Father's house?'

LUKE 2:41–49

Good news

You're not alone

Do you feel overlooked—as if no one sees you or the things you do?

Do you think no one's bothered about your pet projects and interests?

Apart from every time you happen to do something wrong, of course!

That can be really tough.

But cheer up: you aren't alone.

You know, there isn't a single mention in the Bible about Jesus as a teenager. Not once did the world's most important person manage to get noticed as a young man. We know nothing about him from the age of 13 until he was 30. The only episode from his childhood that we hear about is when his parents thought he'd done something wrong (typical!)—the time he stayed behind in Jerusalem without telling them.

Jesus grew up just like any other Jewish boy, apart from the fact that he was 100 per cent God—waiting for the Father's perfect timing...

Links: 25 March, 26 March, 5 September, 1 December

5 minutes more? John 21

21 August

The life of Jesus (c.6BC–AD27)

Jesus is baptized by John

John wore clothes made of camel hair. He had a leather strap around his waist and ate grasshoppers and wild honey. From Jerusalem and all Judea and from the River Jordan Valley crowds of people went to John. They told how sorry they were for their sins, and he baptized them in the river... Jesus left Galilee and went to the River Jordan to be baptized by John. But John kept objecting and said, 'I ought to be baptized by you. Why have you come to me?' Jesus answered, 'For now this is how it should be, because we must do all that God wants us to do.' Then John agreed. So Jesus was baptized. And as soon as he came out of the water, the sky opened, and he saw the Spirit of God coming down on him like a dove. Then a voice from heaven said, 'This is my own dear Son, and I am pleased with him.'

MATTHEW 3:4–6, 13–17

☆ Bible personality

John the Baptist

John the Baptist was one of Jesus' relations—perhaps his cousin. A strange character—no one could totally figure him out. He lived alone by a river in the desert. He ate grasshoppers and honey that he found there. When he spoke, it was straight from the hip. But people respected him, even though they were told quite bluntly to repent of their sins. Lots of people came wanting to be baptized. One day Jesus came too.

John was the person who said, 'Here is the Lamb of God who takes away the sin of the world!' (John 1:29).

John also said, 'Jesus must become more important, while I become less important' (John 3:30).

And it was John who was the first person to understand who Jesus really was. Millions of people have understood the same thing since then. Have you?

Links: 12 May, 15 May, 28 June, 5 October

5 minutes more? Luke 2

The devil and Jesus

The Holy Spirit led Jesus into the desert, so that the devil could test him. After Jesus had gone without eating for forty days and nights, he was very hungry. Then the devil came to him and said, 'If you are God's Son, tell these stones to turn into bread.' Jesus answered, 'The Scriptures say: "No one can live only on food. People need every word that God has spoken."' … Finally, the devil took Jesus up on a very high mountain and showed him all the kingdoms on earth and their power. The devil said to him, 'I will give all this to you, if you will bow down and worship me.' Jesus answered, 'Go away Satan! The Scriptures say: "Worship the Lord your God and serve only him."' Then the devil left Jesus, and angels came to help him.

MATTHEW 4:1–4, 8–11

Download

Every word that God has spoken…

The following verse is a good one to have up your sleeve for times when you are tempted—and you will be tempted, you know. Take a couple of minutes to learn it.

'No one can live only on food. People need every word that God has spoken' (Matthew 4:4).

You could think of swapping the word 'food' for whatever it is that's tempting you…

PS: Every time the devil tempted him, Jesus countered the temptation with a Bible quotation. God's word is very powerful!

Links: 9 January, 18 September, 19 September, 20 September

5 minutes more? Luke 15

23 August

The life of Jesus (c.6BC–AD27)

The disciples

After John was arrested, Jesus went to Galilee and told the good news that comes from God. He said, 'The time has come! God's kingdom will soon be here. Turn back to God and believe the good news!' As Jesus was walking along the shore of Lake Galilee, he saw Simon and his brother Andrew. They were fishermen and were casting their nets into the lake. Jesus said to them, 'Come with me! I will teach you how to bring in people instead of fish.' At once the two brothers dropped their nets and went with him. Jesus walked on and soon saw James and John, the sons of Zebedee. They were in a boat, mending their nets. At once Jesus asked them to come with him. They left their father in the boat with the hired workers and went with him...

Once again, Jesus went to the shore of Lake Galilee. A large crowd gathered around him, and he taught them. As he walked along, he saw Levi, the son of Alphaeus. Levi was sitting at the place for paying taxes, and Jesus said to him, 'Come with me!' So he got up and went with Jesus.

MARK 1:14–20; 2:13–14

Did you know that...

...changing your name was a really popular thing to do in Jesus' time?

Simon became Peter. Saul became known as Paul. John took the middle name Mark. And Levi became Matthew.

Becoming a Christian is no small thing. Everything in your life is turned upside down. The first people who had this experience thought the change was so radical that it warranted changing their names—as a way of showing that everything was different, if you like.

If I'd become a Christian when I was grown up, rather than as a child, and if I'd dared (and if my mum wouldn't have been too upset), I would have changed my name to Christopher. Mainly because the name means 'one who carried Christ'—and that's what Christians do. They carry Christ in their hearts and by their actions out into a tough world.

What would you change your name to if you wanted to reflect what God was doing in your life?

Links: 24 August, 25 August, 26 August, 5 October

5 minutes more? Luke 24

24 August

The life of Jesus (c.6BC–AD27)

I will make you fishers of people

Jesus was standing on the shore of Lake Gennesaret, teaching the people as they crowded around him to hear God's message... Jesus got into the boat that belonged to Simon and asked him to row it out a little way from the shore. Then Jesus sat down in the boat to teach the crowd. When Jesus had finished speaking, he told Simon, 'Row the boat out into the deep water and let your nets down to catch some fish.'

'Master,' Simon answered, 'we have worked hard all night long and have not caught a thing. But if you tell me to, I will let the nets down.' They did it and caught so many fish that their nets began ripping apart. Then they signalled for their partners in the other boat to come and help them. The men came, and together they filled the boats so full that they both began to sink. When Simon Peter saw this happen, he knelt down in front of Jesus and said, 'Lord, don't come near me! I am a sinner.' Peter and everyone with him were completely surprised at the fish they had caught... Jesus told Simon, 'Don't be afraid! From now on you will bring in people instead of fish.' The men pulled their boats up on the shore. Then they left everything and went with Jesus.

LUKE 5:1, 3–11

Listen to your heart and fill in

Hey, you! Yes, you! You—you fisher of people!

What would you have done if suddenly one day Jesus had taken a walk through the area where you live and asked if you would be a fisher of people—if you would help him bring people into God's kingdom? How would you have answered?

____

____

____

Jesus is still going round asking people to be his disciples.
Are you up for it?

Links: 7 February, 9 February, 11 February, 23 August

5 minutes more? Acts 1

25 August

The life of Jesus (c.6BC–AD27)

The disciples learn to pray

When Jesus had finished praying, one of his disciples said to him, 'Lord, teach us to pray, just as John taught his followers to pray.' So Jesus told them, 'Pray in this way:

"Father, help us to honour your name. Come and set up your kingdom. Give us each day the food we need. Forgive us our sins, as we forgive everyone who has done wrong to us. And keep us from being tempted."' …

'So I tell you to ask and you will receive, search and you will find, knock and the door will be opened for you. Everyone who asks will receive, everyone who searches will find, and the door will be opened for everyone who knocks. Which one of you fathers would give your hungry child a snake if the child asked for a fish? Which one of you would give your child a scorpion if the child asked for an egg? As bad as you are, you still know how to give good gifts to your children. But your heavenly Father is even more ready to give the Holy Spirit to anyone who asks.'

LUKE 11:1–4, 9–13

Download...

...about prayer

One of the most important things a disciple can do is pray. God has promised us that he will answer us when we pray. Here is a promise from the Bible that God answers prayer. Memorize it!

'So I tell you to ask and you will receive, search and you will find, knock and the door will be opened for you' (Luke 11:9).

If you think it's difficult to know what to say when you pray, here's a suggestion for a prayer to say every morning:

Dear God, thank you for a new day. Thank you that I am yours, Jesus. Help me to be the person you want me to be. Help me to think about other people the way you think about them. I ask you, Jesus, to be with me today, and to lead me every moment, every step of the way. I pray especially for .... Help me to be a good witness for you, and let me live this day for your glory, God. Amen.

Links: 3 February, 25 April, 6 October, 3 November

5 minutes more? Acts 2

26 August

The life of Jesus (c.6BC–AD27)

How to be a great disciple

Jesus' disciples were arguing about which one of them was the greatest. Jesus knew what they were thinking, and he had a child stand there beside him. Then he said to his disciples, 'When you welcome even a child because of me, you welcome me. And when you welcome me, you welcome the one who sent me. Whichever one of you is the most humble is the greatest.'

LUKE 9:46–48

Some people brought their children to Jesus so that he could bless them by placing his hands on them. But his disciples told the people to stop bothering him. When Jesus saw this, he became angry and said, 'Let the children come to me! Don't try to stop them. People who are like these little children belong to the kingdom of God. I promise you that you cannot get into God's kingdom, unless you accept it the way a child does.' Then Jesus took the children in his arms and blessed them by placing his hands on them.

MARK 10:13–16

Download...

...about children

[Jesus said:] 'Let the children come to me! Don't try to stop them. People who are like these little children belong to the kingdom of God. I promise you that you cannot get into God's kingdom, unless you accept it the way a child does' (Mark 10:14–15).

...about grown ups

[Jesus said:] 'Let the children come to me! Don't try to stop them. People who are like these little children belong to the kingdom of God. I promise you that you cannot get into God's kingdom, unless you accept it the way a child does' (Mark 10:14–15).

Links: 5 February, 24 March, 31 July, 10 November

5 minutes more? Acts 3

27 August

The life of Jesus (c.6BC–AD27)

The first miracle: water into wine

Three days later Mary, the mother of Jesus, was at a wedding feast in the village of Cana in Galilee. Jesus and his disciples had also been invited and were there. When the wine was all gone, Mary said to Jesus, 'They don't have any more wine.' ... At the feast there were six stone water jars that were used by the people for washing themselves in the way that their religion said they must. Each jar held about a hundred litres. Jesus told the servants to fill them to the top with water. Then after the jars had been filled, he said, 'Now take some water and give it to the man in charge of the feast.' The servants did as Jesus told them, and the man in charge drank some of the water that had now turned to wine... This was Jesus' first miracle, and he did it in the village of Cana in Galilee. There Jesus showed his glory, and his disciples put their faith in him.

JOHN 2:1–3, 6–9a, 11

Di:SaipL

Jesus and feasting

One day some people asked a man called Ludvig Karlsen about this water-into-wine miracle. Ludvig Karlsen and his wife are a couple who have founded a series of centres in Norway where they try to help alcoholics and drug addicts. Over the years they have helped hundreds, maybe thousands of people find their way back to God and back to life. Ludvig Karlsen himself was an alcoholic until he had an encounter with God.

And so these people were determined to ask Ludvig Karlsen if he would consider speaking on this text! You think that's clever? Not! There were lots of people who were extremely keen to hear what he had to say and were wondering what he was possibly going to come out with. I was there. The talk was one of the most incredible I've ever heard. He turned the whole subject on its head. He didn't get stuck on whether Jesus drank wine, or how much wine Jesus had made, but he challenged us to take Jesus with us to celebrations and parties. He told us not to stop going to parties because we are Christians, but to be a witness there—to take Jesus with us. If we do that, anything can happen for the kingdom, even at a party.

Links: 28 August, 29 August, 30 August, 31 August

5 minutes more? Acts 4

Jesus calms the storm

That evening, Jesus said to his disciples, 'Let's cross to the east side.' So they left the crowd, and his disciples started across the lake with him in the boat. Some other boats followed along. Suddenly a storm struck the lake. Waves started splashing into the boat, and it was about to sink. Jesus was in the back of the boat with his head on a pillow, and he was asleep. His disciples woke him and said, 'Teacher, don't you care that we're about to drown?' Jesus got up and ordered the wind and the waves to be quiet. The wind stopped, and everything was calm. Jesus asked the disciples, 'Why were you afraid? Don't you have any faith?' Now they were more afraid than ever and said to each other, 'Who is this? Even the wind and the waves obey him!'

MARK 4:35–41

Good news

The other side

The disciples were mainly fishermen by trade. The storm must have been blowing really powerfully for these toughened fishermen to fear for their lives. Jesus woke up at last, calmed the storm and asked the disciples why they were so afraid and why they had so little faith.

- Was Jesus being critical?
- Had he got no idea of the wind's ferocity and the disciples' fear?
- Was he unreasonably hard on them?

Not at all. The clue to the whole story is found where Jesus says right at the beginning that they are going to cross over to the other side. 'Let's cross to the east side,' said Jesus. And if Jesus had said they were crossing to the other side, then they were going to cross to the other side—and get there safely.

Jesus has asked us to go with him, and we have also been promised that we'll get across to the other side—all the way across. It'll probably be a rough crossing. Sometimes Jesus will calm the storms we meet, sometimes he won't. But whatever happens, he has said that he will:

- be with us all the way
- make sure that we get safely across to the other shore

Links: 29 August, 30 August, 31 August, 1 September

5 minutes more? Acts 6

29 August

The life of Jesus (c.6BC–AD27)

Five thousand men (plus women and children)

When Jesus got out of the boat, he saw the large crowd. He felt sorry for them and healed everyone who was sick. That evening the disciples came to Jesus and said, 'This place is like a desert, and it is already late. Let the crowds leave, so they can go to the villages and buy some food.' Jesus replied, 'They don't have to leave. Why don't you give them something to eat?' But they said, We have only five small loaves of bread and two fish.' Jesus asked his disciples to bring the food to him, and he told the crowd to sit down on the grass. Jesus took the five loaves and the two fish. He looked up towards heaven and blessed the food. Then he broke the bread and handed it to his disciples, and they gave it to the people. After everyone had eaten all they wanted, Jesus' disciples picked up twelve large baskets of leftovers. There were about five thousand men who ate, not counting the women and children.

MATTHEW 14:14–21

Di:SaipL

Give and you shall get!

Think what the disciples must have felt like when they went round from family to family with the measly bit of bread they had been given to share out.

But the more they shared it out, the more they had left. Every time they broke a piece off, every time they gave it away, and every time they looked down at the bread again, it had grown back to its original size. They broke off another bit. Gave it away. Looked down. Saw it had grown back. Broke off some more. Gave it away. Looked down. Saw it was back again.

When I was a child we played a game where we threw sand in the air and chanted, 'I had so much, I gave so much away, and I had so much left,' and then showed our empty hands to each other. But it's not like that in God's kingdom. That game doesn't work there.

If you share with others the things God has given you, you will always get a refill. Be generous. Jesus said, 'If you give to others, you will be given a full amount in return. It will be packed down, shaken together, and spilling over into your lap. The way you treat others is the way you will be treated' (Luke 6:38).

Links: 30 August, 31 August, 1 September, 3 September

5 minutes more? Acts 7

30 August

The life of Jesus (c.6BC–AD27)

Peter walks on the water

By this time the boat was a long way from the shore. It was going against the wind and was being tossed around by the waves. A little while before morning, Jesus came walking on the water towards his disciples. When they saw him, they thought he was a ghost. They were terrified and started screaming...

Peter replied, 'Lord, if it is really you, tell me to come to you on the water.' 'Come on!' Jesus said. Peter then got out of the boat and started walking on the water towards him. But when Peter saw how strong the wind was, he was afraid and started sinking. 'Save me, Lord!' he shouted. Straight away, Jesus reached out his hand. He helped Peter up and said, 'You don't have much faith. Why do you doubt?' When Jesus and Peter got into the boat, the wind died down. The men in the boat worshipped Jesus and said, 'You really are the Son of God!'
MATTHEW 14:24–26, 28–33

Story
The lifeguard

This is a story—I think it is true—about a lifeguard, like the ones on *Baywatch*. It fits in well with the idea of Jesus and salvation.

One day, the lifeguard was sitting in his watchtower when he heard a frantic scream from the sea. Immediately he spotted a man who was thrashing about in the water. He grabbed his red life-preserver and raced down the ladder of the tower, along the beach and down to the water. But he stopped there.

'Run out and help the guy!' said the people who had followed him.

The lifeguard explained that he couldn't—it was too dangerous to approach the man while he was thrashing about so wildly the way he was. Quite soon the man lay completely still. He was unconscious in the water. The lifeguard swam out, dragged the man in and resuscitated him.

We don't need to be able to walk on water to be saved. But we need to call for help. And we need a Saviour to drag us out.

The verbs 'to save' and 'to rescue' mean the same thing. Will you stop thrashing about long enough for Jesus to grab hold of you and save you?

Links: 2 September, 6 September, 2 October, 5 October

5 minutes more? Acts 8

31 August

The life of Jesus (c.6BC–AD27)

Two men with demons in them

After Jesus had crossed the lake, he came to shore near the town of Gadara and started down the road. Two men with demons in them came to him from the tombs. They were so fierce that no one could travel that way. Suddenly they shouted, 'Jesus, Son of God, what do you want with us? Have you come to punish us before our time?' Not far from there a large herd of pigs was feeding. So the demons begged Jesus, 'If you force us out, please send us into those pigs!' Jesus told them to go, and they went out of the men and into the pigs. All at once the pigs rushed down the steep bank into the lake and drowned. The people taking care of the pigs ran to the town and told everything, especially what had happened to the two men. Everyone in the town came out to meet Jesus. When they saw him, they begged him to leave their part of the country.
MATTHEW 8:28–34

Bible personality
The devil

The devil is known by many different names: the tempter, the accuser, the prince of this world, Beelzebul ('prince of devils', see Matthew 12:24), Belial (meaning 'wickedness', 2 Corinthians 6:15), the snake. But Satan, or the devil, are the most common.

'Satan' is a Hebrew word and means 'adversary'. 'Devil' (*diabolos*) is Greek, and means 'accuser' or 'slanderer'. Jesus calls the devil the 'father of all lies', and says that there is nothing truthful about him (John 8:44). All the devil wants to do is cause destruction.

The Bible gives us few certain facts about the devil, but implies that...

- he was one of God's angels, but tried to be greater than God (Ezekiel 28:13–16)
- he was thrown out of heaven (2 Peter 2:4)
- he took a multitude of other rebellious angels with him (Revelation 12:8)
- he is the reason sin entered the world (Genesis 3:1)
- he still entices people away from God (2 Corinthians 11:3)
- Jesus triumphed over the devil by his death on the cross (Colossians 22:15)
- when Jesus comes back, the devil will get his final come-uppance (Revelation 20:10)

Links: 21 June, 3 September, 18 September, 20 September

5 minutes more? Acts 9

The lame man

One day some Pharisees and experts in the Law of Moses sat listening to Jesus teach. They had come from every village in Galilee and Judea and from Jerusalem. God had given Jesus the power to heal the sick, and some people came carrying a crippled man on a mat. They tried to take him inside the house and put him in front of Jesus. But because of the crowd, they could not get him to Jesus. So they went up on the roof, where they removed some tiles and let the mat down in the middle of the room. When Jesus saw how much faith they had, he said to the crippled man, 'My friend, your sins are forgiven.' The Pharisees and the experts began arguing, 'Jesus must think he is God! Only God can forgive sins.' Jesus knew what they were thinking, and he said, 'Why are you thinking that? Is it easier for me to tell this crippled man that his sins are forgiven or to tell him to get up and walk? But now you will see that the Son of Man has the right to forgive sins here on earth.' Jesus then said to the man, 'Get up! Pick up your mat and walk home.' At once the man stood up in front of everyone. He picked up his mat and went home, giving thanks to God.
LUKE 5:17–25

☆ Prime Bible personality
Jesus

Jesus is considered to be the most important person in the whole of human history. He was born in Bethlehem, ten miles from Jerusalem, between 5 and 6BC.

When Jesus was around thirty years old, he began his ministry, which lasted two to three years. He had wisdom to teach in a way nobody else has been able to do, either before or since. He also had power to do miracles and to heal people. He asked ordinary men and women to leave everything and follow him. He said he could give people eternal life.

Jesus was executed when he was 32–33 years old. After his crucifixion, he was buried in Jerusalem. But there are many stories from the days after these events which tell of people who claim that Jesus rose from the dead, that they met him in person. Even now, in our time, there are people who claim that they have met the risen Jesus.

People tend to think about Jesus of Nazareth in one of two ways:

- either he was boasting, lying through his teeth and a complete idiot
- or he was actually telling the truth and we have to admit he was God

Links: 6 February, 8 February, 3 September, 27 December

5 minutes more? Acts 10

2 September

The life of Jesus (c.6BC–AD27)

Who do you say that I am?

When Jesus and his disciples were near the town of Caesarea Philippi, he asked them, 'What do people say about the Son of Man?' The disciples answered, 'Some people say you are John the Baptist or perhaps Elijah or Jeremiah or some other prophet.' Then Jesus asked them, 'But who do you say I am?' Simon Peter spoke up, 'You are the Messiah, the Son of the living God.' Jesus told him:

Simon, son of Jonah, you are blessed! You didn't discover this on your own. It was shown to you by my Father in heaven...

From then on, Jesus began telling his disciples what would happen to him. He said, 'I must go to Jerusalem. There the nation's leaders, the chief priests, and the teachers of the Law of Moses will make me suffer terribly. I will be killed, but three days later I will rise to life.'

MATTHEW 16:13–17, 21

Listen to your heart and fill in

What's your opinion?

Who do people say Jesus is?

- A good person
- An ethical example to follow
- A person who showed a lot of love
- One of several people who received revelation from God
- Something else you've heard him described as:

____

And who do you say Jesus is?

____

____

____

Links: 7 July, 18 August, 4 November, 5 November

5 minutes more? Acts 13

Jesus heals a boy with epilepsy

Jesus and his disciples returned to the crowd. A man knelt in front of him and said, 'Lord, have pity on my son! He has a bad case of epilepsy and often falls into a fire or into water. I brought him to your disciples, but none of them could heal him.' Jesus said, 'You people are too stubborn to have any faith! How much longer must I be with you? Why do I have to put up with you? Bring the boy here.' Then Jesus spoke sternly to the demon. It went out of the boy, and at once he was healed. Later the disciples went to Jesus in private and asked him, 'Why couldn't we force out the demon?' Jesus replied:

It is because you don't have enough faith! But I can promise you this. If you had faith no larger than a mustard seed, you could tell this mountain to move from here to there. And it would. Everything would be possible for you.

MATTHEW 17:14–21

Hmm... just a thought

Even greater things

Jesus said, 'I tell you for certain that if you have faith in me, you will do the same things that I am doing. You will do even greater things, now that I am going back to the Father' (John 14:12).

Here Jesus doesn't mean greater things in the sense of things that will bring you other people's praise. He means greater things in the sense of 'seemingly more difficult' than the miracles and healing wonders that he himself did—things that will have greater consequence for the kingdom of God.

We who live in today's world have the chance to spread God's word further, and to more people, than anyone else who has lived before us. We really do have the possibility of getting God's message to the ends of the earth. There are still two billion people who have not heard about Jesus of Nazareth or experienced his power.

Are you willing to do greater things for Jesus? Have you got faith for miracles and healing? Will you take his word to the lost in the power of his Holy Spirit?

Links: 6 February, 25 April, 26 April, 1 September

5 minutes more? Acts 14

4 September

The life of Jesus (c.6BC–AD27)

The rich young man

As Jesus was walking down a road, a man ran up to him. He knelt down, and asked, 'Good teacher, what can I do to have eternal life?' Jesus replied, 'Why do you call me good? Only God is good. You know the commandments. "Do not murder. Be faithful in marriage. Do not steal. Do not tell lies about others. Do not cheat. Respect your father and mother."' The man answered, 'Teacher, I have obeyed all these commandments since I was a young man.' Jesus looked closely at the man. He liked him and said, 'There's one thing you still need to do. Go and sell everything you own. Give the money to the poor and you will have riches in heaven. Then come with me.' When the man heard Jesus say this, he went away gloomy and sad because he was very rich. Jesus looked around and said to his disciples, 'It's hard for rich people to get into God's kingdom!' The disciples were shocked to hear this.

MARK 10:17–24a

Check it out

How Jesus gave the man 'value' for money

When the disciples heard how Jesus quizzed this young, upwardly mobile man, they were shocked. Jesus thought the man had a problem. Not because he was young, and not actually because he was rich—but because he trusted in his riches more than in God. Check out the conversation between Jesus and his disciples after the man had gone:

Jesus:	It's hard for rich people to get into God's kingdom.
Jesus:	It's terribly hard to get into God's kingdom! In fact, it's easier for a camel to go through the eye of a needle than for a rich person to get into God's kingdom.
Disciples:	How can anyone ever be saved?
Jesus:	There are some things that people cannot do, but God can do anything.

P.S. Take note of the encouraging words in Mark 10:21: 'Jesus looked closely at the man. He liked him…'

Jesus is taking a close look at you… and he likes you too! If he tells you something difficult, it's because he wants the best for you.

Links: 13 January, 14 January, 15 January, 18 January

5 minutes more? Acts 15

5 September

The life of Jesus (c.6BC–AD27)

Jesus goes up to Jerusalem

Many of the people... saw the things that Jesus did, and they put their faith in him. Others went to the Pharisees and told what Jesus had done. Then the chief priests and the Pharisees called the council together and said, 'What should we do? This man is performing a lot of miracles. If we don't stop him now, everyone will put their faith in him. Then the Romans will come and destroy our temple and our nation.' One of the council members was Caiaphas, who was also high priest that year. He spoke up and said, 'You people don't have any sense at all! Don't you know it is better for one person to die for the people than for the whole nation to be destroyed?' Caiaphas did not say this on his own. As high priest that year, he was prophesying that Jesus would die for the nation. Yet Jesus would not die just for the Jewish nation. He would die to bring together all God's scattered people. From that day on, the council started making plans to put Jesus to death. Because of this plot against him, Jesus stopped going around in public. He went to the town of Ephraim, which was near the desert, and he stayed there with his disciples. It was almost time for Passover. Many of the Jewish people who lived out in the country had come to Jerusalem to get themselves ready for the festival.

JOHN 11:45–55

Weird and wonderful

How do we know Jesus' ministry lasted for three years?

It doesn't say anywhere in the Bible that Jesus' ministry lasted three years. If you read Matthew, Mark or Luke's Gospels, it even seems as if Jesus' ministry lasted only one year. But fortunately we also have John's Gospel.

In John's Gospel we read that Jesus went to Jerusalem three times (John 2:13; 5:1; and 12:12).

We know that Jesus only went to Jerusalem every Passover, that is, once a year. Thus we know that his ministry must have lasted three years.

And the third time Jesus went up to Jerusalem, the council of religious leaders plotted to kill him.

Links: 6 April, 7 April, 8 April, 9 April

5 minutes more? Acts 17

Judas takes a bribe

Judas Iscariot was one of the twelve disciples. He went to the chief priests and asked, 'How much will you give me if I help you arrest Jesus?' They paid Judas thirty silver coins, and from then on he started looking for a good chance to betray Jesus...

When Jesus was eating with his twelve disciples that evening, he said, 'One of you will hand me over to my enemies.' The disciples were very sad, and each one said to Jesus, 'Lord, you can't mean me!' He answered, 'One of you men who has eaten with me from this dish will betray me. The Son of Man will die, as the Scriptures say. But it's going to be terrible for the one who betrays me! That man would be better off if he had never been born.' Judas said, 'Teacher, surely you don't mean me!' 'That's what you say!' Jesus replied. But later, Judas did betray him.

MATTHEW 26:14–16, 20–25

Di:SaipL

Judas and Peter

Judas and Peter—you know their stories:

Judas was a disciple	Peter was a disciple
Judas promised not to betray Jesus	Peter promised not to betray Jesus
Judas betrayed Jesus	Peter deserted Jesus
Judas made a fool of himself	Peter made a fool of himself
Judas regretted what he'd done	Peter regretted what he'd done

So far, the stories are much the same. Now the differences:

Judas didn't bring his mistake to Jesus	Peter brought his mistake to Jesus
Judas felt condemned	Peter received forgiveness
Judas wasn't a disciple any more	Peter remained a disciple

A disciple is all too well aware that he or she has faults and makes mistakes. But a disciple takes those mistakes and faults to Jesus for forgiveness.

Links: 27 March, 28 March, 7 April, 11 July

5 minutes more? Acts 25

7 September

The life of Jesus (c.6BC–AD27)

Jesus prays in Gethsemane

Jesus went with his disciples to a place called Gethsemane, and he told them, 'Sit here while I pray.' Jesus took along Peter, James, and John. He was sad and troubled and told them, 'I am so sad that I feel as if I am dying. Stay here and keep awake with me.' Jesus walked on a little way. Then he knelt down on the ground and prayed, 'Father, if it is possible, don't let this happen to me! Father, you can do anything. Don't make me suffer by making me drink from this cup. But do what you want, and not what I want.' When Jesus came back and found the disciples sleeping, he said to Simon Peter, 'Are you asleep? Can't you stay awake for just one hour? Stay awake and pray that you won't be tested. You want to do what is right, but you are weak.' Jesus went back and prayed the same prayer. But when he returned to the disciples, he found them sleeping again. They simply could not keep their eyes open, and they did not know what to say. When Jesus returned to the disciples the third time, he said, 'Are you still sleeping and resting? Enough of that! The time has come for the Son of Man to be handed over to sinners. Get up! Let's go. The one who will betray me is already here.'

MARK 14:32–42

Head, shoulders, knees and toes

Be prepared!

Stand to attention. Back straight. Hands together and pray this Scout's prayer from Norway:

Dear Father in heaven up above, hear my heart's quiet prayer:
In the bustle of my daily life, let me be like Jesus there.
May I live for your glory, honour my country, my father and mother,
Obey the Scout's promise, and be helpful to others.

After this prayer, the Patrol Leader says to his patrol, 'Scouts, be prepared!'

If you have never been a Guide or a Scout, in this country or any other, then it would be good to know that after this you are supposed to raise a three-finger salute to your forehead and answer loud and clear, *Always be prepared!*

Now read the Bible passage for today again.

Links: 28 March, 8 September, 9 September, 10 September

5 minutes more? Acts 26

8 September

The life of Jesus (c.6BC–AD27)

Jesus is arrested

While Jesus was still speaking, a crowd came up. It was led by Judas, one of the twelve apostles. He went over to Jesus and greeted him with a kiss... Jesus was arrested and led away to the house of the high priest, while Peter followed at a distance. Some people built a fire in the middle of the courtyard and were sitting around it. Peter sat there with them, and a servant girl saw him. Then after she had looked at him carefully, she said, 'This man was with Jesus!' Peter said, 'Woman, I don't even know that man!' A little later someone else saw Peter and said, 'You are one of them!' 'No, I'm not!' Peter replied. About an hour later another man insisted, 'This man must have been with Jesus. They both come from Galilee.' Peter replied, 'I don't know what you are talking about!' At once, while Peter was still speaking, a cock crowed. The Lord turned and looked at Peter. And Peter remembered that the Lord had said, 'Before a cock crows tomorrow morning, you will say three times that you don't know me.' Then Peter went out and cried hard.

LUKE 22:47, 54–62

Di:SaipL

We need more people like Peter in the church

Peter is very often depicted as being impulsive and a bit thoughtless. He talked and acted before he thought. He made a fool of himself over and over again. But this is only part of the truth.

Although Peter was rather simple in regard to some things, he was the one out of all the disciples who threw himself into a project, took chances, spoke out, and got stuck into a situation courageously. True, Peter did deny Jesus, but despite that, he was the only one of the disciples who dared follow behind Jesus when he was led away as prisoner. When it came time for the disciples to choose a leader, Peter was the obvious choice. We need people like Peter, and we need them now. We have so many theorizers in the church, so many people who spend years thinking before they speak. We need a few people who will react, speak out and get on with things.

Is that you, maybe?

Links: 28 March, 11 July, 9 September, 10 September

5 minutes more? Acts 27

9 September

The life of Jesus (c.6BC–AD27)

Jesus is questioned by the council

The chief priests and the whole council tried to find someone to accuse Jesus of a crime, so they could put him to death. But they could not find anyone to accuse him. Many people did tell lies about Jesus, but they did not agree on what they said… The high priest stood up in the council and asked Jesus, 'Why don't you say something in your own defence? Don't you hear the charges they are making against you?' But Jesus kept quiet and did not say a word. The high priest asked him another question, 'Are you the Messiah, the Son of the glorious God?' 'Yes, I am!' Jesus answered. 'Soon you will see the Son of Man sitting at the right side of God All-Powerful, and coming with the clouds of heaven.' At once the high priest ripped his robe apart and shouted, 'Why do we need more witnesses? You heard him claim to be God! What is your decision?' They all agreed that he should be put to death. Some of the people started spitting on Jesus. They blindfolded him, hit him with their fists, and said, 'Tell us who hit you!' Then the guards took charge of Jesus and beat him.

MARK 14:55–56, 60–65

Check it out

Jesus' trial

It can often seem as if Jesus' trial was over before it had started. In actual fact, Jesus was dragged from one council to another before Pilate finally condemned him to death.

Thursday evening:

1. Trial before the former high priest Annas	John 18:13
2. Trial before the current high priest Caiaphas	Mark 14:55

Friday morning:

3. Trial before the whole Jewish Council	Mark 15:1
4. First trial before Pilate, the Roman governor	Matthew 27:2
5. Trial before Herod, the king of Galilee	Luke 23:7
6. Second trial before Pilate	John 18:28

All in all, Jesus was dragged through six hearings before he was found guilty. The sixth one, before Pilate, was very dubious. In your opinion—was Jesus guilty?

Links: 8 September, 10 September, 11 September, 30 December

5 minutes more? Acts 28

10 September

The life of Jesus (c.6BC–AD27)

Pilate questions Jesus

Early the next morning the chief priests, the nation's leaders, and the teachers of the Law of Moses met together with the whole Jewish council. They tied up Jesus and led him off to Pilate... During Passover, Pilate always freed one prisoner chosen by the people. And at that time there was a prisoner named Barabbas. He and some others had been arrested for murder during a riot. The crowd now came and asked Pilate to set a prisoner free, just as he usually did. Pilate asked them, 'Do you want me to free the king of the Jews?' Pilate knew that the chief priests had brought Jesus to him because they were jealous. But the chief priests told the crowd to ask Pilate to free Barabbas. Then Pilate asked the crowd, 'What do you want me to do with this man you say is the king of the Jews?' They yelled, 'Nail him to a cross!' Pilate asked, 'But what crime has he done?' 'Nail him to a cross!' they yelled even louder.

MARK 15:1, 6–14

Bible personality

Pilate

At the time Jesus lived, Israel was occupied by the Roman Empire. To avoid having to rule the whole empire from Rome in Italy, the Romans installed a governor in every single area they had occupied. The governor of Judea was called Pilate.

Usually he lived in Caesarea, but he had come to his palace in Jerusalem because it was the time of the Passover festival. Historical records from those years tell us that the Jews hated Pilate intensely. He had made himself unpopular on several occasions, including the time when he helped himself to the temple tax to build himself a palace. He had also plundered several of the Jews' holy places and taken the expensive ornaments, wall hangings and furniture.

But now the Jewish rulers were glad to have Pilate—they needed someone who would condemn Jesus. They themselves didn't have the power to condemn someone to death. But they could use the Roman governor, Pilate.

The Romans had introduced a form of execution that was new to the Jews—crucifixion.

Links: 17 July, 18 July, 19 July, 27 November

5 minutes more? Romans 1

11 September

The life of Jesus (c.6BC–AD27)

The thief on the cross

Two criminals were led out to be put to death with Jesus. When the soldiers came to the place called 'The Skull', they nailed Jesus to a cross. They also nailed the two criminals to crosses, one on each side of Jesus... One of the criminals hanging there also insulted Jesus by saying, 'Aren't you the Messiah? Save yourself and save us!' But the other criminal told the first one off, 'Don't you fear God? Aren't you getting the same punishment as this man? We got what was coming to us, but he didn't do anything wrong.' Then he said to Jesus, 'Remember me when you come into power!'

Jesus replied, 'I promise that today you will be with me in paradise.'
LUKE 23:32–33, 39–43

Did you know that...

...of all the people Jesus met, this thief is the only one he guaranteed a place in heaven?

Unjust? Not fair?
Not at all.

It's called grace.
And grace is something we all need.

Links: 13 January, 14 January, 15 January, 27 December

5 minutes more? Romans 2

12 September

The life of Jesus (c.6BC–AD27)

The death of Jesus

At midday the sky turned dark and stayed that way until three o'clock. Then about that time Jesus shouted, 'Eli, Eli, lema sabachthani?' which means, 'My God, my God, why have you deserted me?' ... Once again Jesus shouted, and then he died. At once the curtain in the temple was torn in two from top to bottom. The earth shook, and rocks split apart. Graves opened, and many of God's people were raised to life. Then after Jesus had risen to life, they came out of their graves and went into the holy city, where they were seen by many people. The officer and the soldiers guarding Jesus felt the earthquake and saw everything else that happened. They were frightened and said, ' This man really was God's Son!'

MATTHEW 27:45–46, 50–54

Weird and wonderful

Four crazy things and a stroke of genius

At the same time that Jesus died, four crazy things happened in Jerusalem.

- It went dark for three hours right in the middle of the day. But that was nothing, because...
- The earth began to shake and crack open. It frightened the soldiers who had crucified Jesus so much that they shouted, 'This man really was God's Son!' But that wasn't as crazy as it got, because...
- Dead people physically rose up and walked around the town. But even that wasn't the craziest thing.
- The craziest thing happened when the curtain that hung over the entrance to the holy of holies in the temple split in two from top to bottom. That was really crazy.

Why?

Well, people thought that God lived in the holy of holies. Only one priest could go in there, and then only once a year. It was a stroke of God's genius that the curtain tore just when Jesus died. It showed that Jesus' death opened the way into God's presence for everyone who wanted to come back to him. The fact that the curtain ripped from the top downwards shows that the way back to God was his initiative, rather than the work of human hands.

Links: 12 July, 13 July, 17 July, 18 July

5 minutes more? Romans 3

13 September

The life of Jesus (c.6BC–AD27)

Jesus is buried

Joseph from Arimathea was one of Jesus' disciples. He had kept it secret though, because he was afraid of the Jewish leaders. But now he asked Pilate to let him have Jesus' body. Pilate gave him permission, and Joseph took it down from the cross. Nicodemus also came with about thirty kilogrammes of spices made from myrrh and aloes... The two men wrapped the body in a linen cloth, together with the spices, which was how the Jewish people buried their dead. In the place where Jesus had been nailed to a cross, there was a garden with a tomb that had never been used. The tomb was nearby, and since it was the time to prepare for the Sabbath, they were in a hurry to put Jesus' body there.

JOHN 19:38–42

Check it out

Why Jesus had to die

1. Someone who is allergic to dog hair can't bear to be near dogs. In the same way, God is 'allergic' to sin and can't bear to be near sinners. Because human beings are sinful, it was impossible for God to be in a close relationship with people. But God wasn't going to stand for that. He really wanted to get back the relationship he'd had with humanity before sin entered the world. That's why Jesus had to die.
   Check out Romans 3:21–24.

2. Everybody has sinned, and God's punishment for sin is death. Humans die because humans sin. To break this cycle of sin and death, a sinless person had to be found. Of course there aren't any—only God is sinless. That's why God became human in Jesus. Jesus was 100 per cent God and 100 per cent human and 100 per cent sinless. That's why Jesus had to die.
   Check out 2 Corinthians 5:21.

3. We read in the Old Testament that the sacrifice of a perfectly healthy animal was the only offering that people could make to God for their sins, to enable them to come close to God. These offerings were only valid for a certain time. Jesus was called the Lamb of God. He was sinless and offered his life as a sacrifice for our sins so that we could come back close to God. This sacrifice is valid for ever, not just for a limited time. That's why Jesus had to die.
   Check out Romans 3:25 and Hebrews 7:26–27.

Links: 12 September, 21 October, 24 October, 4 November

5 minutes more? Romans 4

14 September

Old Testament odds 'n' ends

Noah's ark

The Lord was pleased with Noah, and this is the story about him. Noah was the only person who lived right and obeyed God. He had three sons: Shem, Ham, and Japheth. God knew that everyone was terribly cruel and violent. So he told Noah:

Cruelty and violence have spread everywhere. Now I'm going to destroy the whole earth and all its people. Get some good timber and build a boat. Put rooms in it and cover it with tar inside and out... I'm going to send a flood that will destroy everything that breathes! Nothing will be left alive. But I solemnly promise that you, your wife, your sons, and your daughters-in-law will be kept safe in the boat. Bring into the boat with you a male and a female of every kind of animal and bird, as well as a male and a female of every reptile. I don't want them to be destroyed. Store up enough food both for yourself and for them.

Noah did everything the Lord told him to do.

GENESIS 6:9–14, 17–22

Did you know...

...that Noah's ark was rather large?

An ark is actually a chest. (For those who are particularly interested: the word comes from the Latin *arca*, which means 'chest'.) Noah's 'chest' was rather large.

The Bible says that Noah's ark was 133 metres long, 22 metres wide, and 13 metres high.

That's about as long as one and a half football pitches, and as high as a four- or five-storey building.

When you think that Noah built this ark several thousand years ago, it must have been an amazing sight!

How would you react if God asked you to do something equally outrageous today?

Links: 15 September, 16 September, 25 September, 26 September

5 minutes more? Romans 5

15 September

Old Testament odds 'n' ends

Noah's ark: pouring rain and a mighty flood

Noah was six hundred years old when he went into the boat to escape the flood, and he did everything the Lord had told him to do. His wife, his sons, and his daughters-in-law all went inside with him. He obeyed God and took a male and a female of each kind of animal and bird into the boat with him… For forty days the rain poured down without stopping. And the water became deeper and deeper, until the boat started floating high above the ground. Finally, the mighty flood was so deep that even the highest mountain peaks were about seven metres below the surface of the water… The Lord destroyed everything that breathed. Nothing was left alive except Noah and the others in the boat.

GENESIS 7:5–9, 17–19, 22–23

Head, shoulders, knees and toes

To have faith = to depend upon

This is an exercise for you to do:

1. If you are sitting down, get up. (If you are lying under your duvet in a cold room, stay there and imagine you're doing this!)
2. Remain standing.
3. Find a chair.
4. Sit down on it.

You are completely and absolutely mad!

Since you last sat on it, someone could have snuck in and sawed part of the way through a leg. A screw could have come loose. How did you know the chair wouldn't collapse? That one of the legs wouldn't snap when you sat on it? Well, you can't ever be 100 per cent sure.

That is just what it means to have faith. That's what saved Noah. That's what saves us. We depend on Jesus…

'For God loved the people of this world so much that he gave his only Son, so that everyone who has faith in him will have eternal life and never really die' (John 3:16).

OK?

Links: 14 September, 16 September, 25 September, 26 September

5 minutes more? Romans 6

16 September

Old Testament odds 'n' ends

Noah's ark: the water goes down

God made a wind blow, and the water started going down... Forty days later... Noah wanted to find out if the water had gone down, and he sent out a dove. Deep water was still everywhere, and the dove could not find a place to land. So it flew back to the boat. Noah held out his hand and helped it back in. Seven days later Noah sent the dove out again. It returned in the evening, holding in its beak a green leaf from an olive tree. Noah knew that the water was finally going down... After Noah and his family had gone out of the boat, the living creatures left in groups of their own kind. Again, God said to Noah and his sons:

I am going to make a solemn promise to you and to everyone who will live after you... The rainbow that I have put in the sky will be my sign to you and to every living creature on earth. It will remind you that I will keep this promise for ever... Never again will I let flood waters destroy all life.

GENESIS 8:1b, 6–11, 18–19; 9:8–9, 12–13, 15b

Check it out

The connection between Noah's ark and baptism

After Noah was saved, God made a covenant, an agreement, with him. God promised to take care of him and sealed the agreement with the sign of a rainbow. In 1 Peter 3:20–21 we read about another agreement—a newer, better agreement with God called baptism. The sign of this agreement is the Holy Spirit, who makes life at least as colourful as a rainbow.

'Eight people went into [the ark] and were brought safely through the flood. Those flood waters were like baptism that now saves you. But baptism is more than just washing your body. It means turning to God with a clear conscience, because Jesus Christ was raised from death' (1 Peter 3:20–21).

PS: It is easy to get concerned about whether people should be baptized as infants or as adults. In these verses from 1 Peter, we find a good reason for both:

- Infant baptism marks children out for Jesus—that is, saves them—until they are old enough to be responsible for their own decisions.
- Adult baptism is a chance for grown-ups to turn to God with a clear conscience and make promises for themselves.

Links: 7 April, 1 May, 14 September, 15 September

5 minutes more? Romans 7

17 September

Old Testament odds 'n' ends

The tower of Babel

At first everyone spoke the same language, but after some of them moved from the east and settled in Babylonia, they said:

Let's build a city with a tower that reaches to the sky! We'll use hard bricks and tar instead of stone and mortar. We'll become famous, and we won't be scattered all over the world.

But when the Lord came down to look at the city and the tower, he said:

These people are working together because they all speak the same language. This is just the beginning. Soon they will be able to do anything they want. Come on! Let's go down and confuse them by making them speak different languages—then they won't be able to understand one another.

So the people had to stop building the city, because the Lord confused their language and scattered them all over the earth. That's how the city of Babel (i.e. 'confused') got its name.

GENESIS 11:1–9

Refresh

An upwardly mobile society

In the West, people are getting richer and richer. We can do more and more things. We manufacture more and more things. We consume more and more things.

At the same time, more and more people are getting worn out and sick—including young people. Not everyone can cope with climbing the career ladder, the consumer ladder and the social ladder. It costs to be upwardly mobile and make a name for yourself.

God doesn't want to climb the ladders with us and just comfort us along the way. He doesn't want any part in the rat race. God moves in the opposite direction—downwards. He shows us the sort of life we were actually made for.

Christians don't climb ladders, they follow God.

Links: 15 December, 17 December, 19 December, 21 December

5 minutes more? Romans 8

Job is put to the test (1)

Many years ago, a man named Job lived in the land of Uz. He was a truly good person, who respected God and refused to do evil. Job had seven sons and three daughters. He owned seven thousand sheep, three thousand camels, five hundred pair of oxen, five hundred donkeys, and a large number of servants. He was the richest person in the east... One day, when the angels had gathered around the Lord, and Satan was there with them, the Lord asked, 'Satan, where have you been?' Satan replied, 'I have been going all over the earth.' Then the Lord asked, 'What do you think of my servant Job? No one on earth is like him—he is a truly good person, who respects me and refuses to do evil.' 'Why shouldn't he respect you?' Satan remarked. '... Try taking away everything he owns, and he will curse you to your face.' The Lord replied, 'All right, Satan, do what you want with anything that belongs to him, but don't harm Job.' Then Satan left.

JOB 1:1–3, 6–9, 11–12

☆ Bible personality

Job

Job was rich and mighty, and he respected God—very much. No one loved God like Job did. There was no one else like Job in the whole world. But he became the victim of a bet between God and Satan.

Satan said to God, 'Why shouldn't he respect you? You are like a wall protecting not only him, but his entire family and all his property. You make him successful in whatever he does, and his flocks and herds are everywhere. Try taking away everything he owns, and he will curse you to your face.'

So Job ended up suffering—terribly. But Job wouldn't curse God.

The story of Job shows us that it is right to trust God whether things are going well or badly and to say like Job, 'If we accept blessings from God, we must accept trouble as well' (Job 1:10).

Job's most well-known saying is: 'The Lord alone gives and takes. Praise the name of the Lord!' (Job 1:21b).

Links: 9 January, 19 September, 20 September, 21 September

5 minutes more? Romans 12

19 September

Old Testament odds 'n' ends

Job is put to the test (2)

Someone rushed up to Job and said, 'While your servants were ploughing with your oxen, and your donkeys were nearby eating grass, a gang of Sabeans attacked and stole the oxen and donkeys! Your other servants were killed, and I was the only one who escaped to tell you.'

... A second one came running up and saying, 'God sent down a fire that killed your sheep and your servants. I am the only one who escaped to tell you.'

... A third one raced up and said, 'Three gangs of Chaldeans attacked and stole your camels! All your other servants were killed, and I am the only one who escaped to tell you.'

... A fourth one dashed up and said, 'Your children were having a feast and drinking wine at the home of your eldest son, when suddenly a storm from the desert blew the house down, crushing all your children. I am the only one who escaped to tell you.'

JOB 1:14–19

Good news

God is God and God is almighty

'Why is there so much evil in the world? Either God doesn't exist, or he isn't good, or he has no power...'

This is one of the oldest questions in the world. Technically speaking, it's called the 'problem of evil', and there isn't really a good answer to it. A lot of people have tried to say some very clever things about the problem of evil, but have never really got to the bottom of it. Some of the wisest things that have been said about the problem of evil are actually here in the book of Job.

But now some good news: after D-Day—the most important day in the Second World War, when the Allies landed in Normandy—King Haakon of Norway said, 'Today the Germans have lost the war.' That was in 1944, but it was to be a whole year before victory was completely assured. We have a similar situation in the spiritual realm. God is good, and he is almighty; he conquered the devil when Jesus died on the cross. However, we won't have total victory until Jesus returns. When we see evil at work in the world, we could see it as the devil's feverish death throes, and remind ourselves that we are on the winning side.

Links: 17 January, 20 September, 21 September, 13 November

5 minutes more? Romans 13

20 September

Old Testament odds 'n' ends

Job is put to the test (3)

When the angels gathered around the Lord again, Satan was there with them...

'All right!' the Lord replied. 'Make Job suffer as much as you want, but just don't kill him.' Satan left and caused painful sores to break out all over Job's body—from head to toe. Then Job sat on the ash-heap to show his sorrow. And while he was scraping his sores with a broken piece of pottery, his wife asked, 'Why do you still trust God? Why don't you curse him and die?' Job replied, 'Don't talk like a fool! If we accept blessings from God, we must accept troubles as well.' In all that happened, Job never once said anything against God... Three of Job's friends heard about his troubles. So they agreed to visit Job and comfort him. When they came near enough to see Job, they could hardly recognize him. And in their great sorrow, they tore their clothes, then sprinkled dust on their heads and cried bitterly.

JOB 2:1, 6–12

Head, shoulders, knees and toes

What you should and shouldn't do if a friend is having a rough time

Job's three friends came to him to give him some sympathy and comfort. But when they had been there a little while, they offered him some advice that was completely off the wall.

Do you know what you should do if a friend of yours is having a particularly rough time? Here are a few tips I got from a friend who is an army chaplain (and believe me, people have a tough time in the army).

1. It's usual to avoid people who are having difficulties. Don't avoid them.
2. Don't pretend as if nothing has happened to your friend.
3. The most important thing is to be there.
4. If you find it easy to talk the hind leg off a donkey, remember that it is best just to be there.
5. Don't offer loads of advice. Remember that the most important thing is just to be there.
6. Offer help with practical things—like homework, tidying up, pet care and so on.
7. Pray for your friend. People rarely say 'No' to prayer if you're brave enough to offer.

Links: 25 January, 26 January, 18 September, 21 September

5 minutes more? Romans 14

Job is put to the test (4)

Job said:

No one can oppose you, because you have the power to do what you want. You asked why I talk so much when I know so little. I have talked about things that are far beyond my understanding. You told me to listen and answer your questions. I heard about you from others; now I have seen you with my own eyes... The Lord now blessed Job more than ever; he gave him fourteen thousand sheep, six thousand camels, a thousand pair of oxen, and a thousand donkeys. In addition to seven sons, Job had three daughters... They were the most beautiful women in that part of the world, and Job gave them shares of his property, along with their brothers. Job lived for another one hundred and forty years—long enough to see his great-grandchildren have children of their own—and when he finally died, he was very old.

JOB 42:1–5, 12–13, 15–17

Hmm... just a thought...

...about strength being the result of difficult things

It is better for things to go well than to go badly.

It's better to have a lovely time than to have an awful time.

However, things go badly for us all from time to time.

I know from my own experience that when a difficult time is over, you tend to be stronger than when it started.

Perhaps the sayings are true that 'What doesn't kill you makes you grow' and 'A steep slope leads you upwards.'

Links: 25 January, 26 January, 25 February, 12 March

5 minutes more? Romans 15

22 September

Old Testament odds 'n' ends

Balaam's donkey

Balaam was riding his donkey to Moab, and two of his servants were with him. But God was angry that Balaam had gone, so one of the Lord's angels stood in the road to stop him. When Balaam's donkey saw the angel standing there with a sword, it walked off the road and into an open field. Balaam had to beat the donkey to get it back on the road... The angel moved once more and stood in a spot so narrow that there was no room for the donkey to go around. So it just lay down. Balaam lost his temper, then picked up a stick and hit the donkey. When that happened, the Lord told the donkey to speak, and it asked Balaam, 'What have I done to you that made you beat me three times?' 'You made me look stupid!' Balaam answered. 'If I had a sword, I'd kill you here and now!' ... Just then, the Lord let Balaam see the angel standing in the road, holding a sword, and Balaam bowed down.

NUMBERS 22:22–23, 26–29, 31

Refresh

Now and then, it's an advantage to have a simple faith

In discussions it is quite usual for people who don't believe in God to say things like:

- Do you really believe Jesus' mother was a virgin?
- Do you really believe that Jesus calmed the storm?
- Do you really believe Jonah was in the whale's stomach for three days?
- Do you really believe that a donkey can speak?

It's not very easy to give a sensible answer. And I agree that these things do sound rather strange if you don't believe in God. But if you believe that God created the world, then I think it's peanuts for him to make a virgin pregnant, calm a storm and make a donkey talk.

It doesn't need to be any more complicated than that.

Links: 26 February, 1 March, 24 March, 10 July

5 minutes more? 1 Corinthians 1

Ruth

'I pray that the Lord God of Israel will reward you for what you have done. And now that you have come to him for protection, I pray that he will bless you.'
RUTH 2:12

Bible personality
Ruth

Ruth's husband died. She and her mother-in-law, Naomi, left the land of Moab, where there was a famine, and travelled home to Bethlehem. Naomi tried to persuade Ruth to stay in Moab, but Ruth refused to let Naomi travel alone.

In Bethlehem, Ruth provided for herself and Naomi by gleaning in the cornfields of a man called Boaz. He was one of Naomi's relations, and a rich man. He was kind to Ruth.

At that time there was a legal system in that country by which land that had been forcibly sold could be bought back. Under the same system, the widow of a man who had died childless could marry one of the man's relations and have children who would bear her first husband's name. Anyhow, Boaz offered to buy back Naomi's land for her and to marry Ruth if none of the other relations would do so. Eventually he bought back the land and married Ruth. They had a son called Obed.

It was Boaz who said to Ruth, 'I pray that the Lord God of Israel will reward you for what you have done. And now that you have come to him for protection, I pray that he will bless you' (Ruth 2:12).

Ruth was a woman who was patient when things were difficult. She was faithful to her mother-in-law, obedient to God and coped with hostility. She is an excellent role model. It would be a good idea to read the whole of her story—go on, it's only four short chapters!

Links: 4 March, 5 March, 9 June, 24 September

5 minutes more? 1 Corinthians 2

Esther

Xerxes liked Esther more than he did any of the other young women. None of them pleased him as much as she did, and straight away he fell in love with her and crowned her queen instead of Vashti.
ESTHER 2:17

The king said, 'Esther, what brings you here? Just ask, and I will give you as much as half of my kingdom.'
ESTHER 5:3

Weird and wonderful

An Old Testament beauty contest

The king of Persia announced a competition so that he could find himself a queen—it was a sort of beauty contest. Esther was the one who ran off with all the prizes. There was just one thing, however: she was a Jew and the king didn't know!

One day, Esther's guardian, Mordecai, overheard some plans to kill the king. He managed to prevent the plot happening by telling Esther about it. The king was saved, and the guilty parties hanged.

Then the king promoted a man called Haman to a position of power in the kingdom. Haman's secret plan was to wipe out all the Jews, and to get even more power for himself. But Mordecai and Esther uncovered this plot too, and by prayer and fasting they managed to stop Haman carrying out his genocidal plan. Haman was hanged, the Jews were spared, and Mordecai was given a powerful position in the king's court.

Esther was as brave as she was beautiful. She spoke up for her people and behaved in a worthy manner. Her faithfulness caused others to have confidence in her and to love her. From that day to this she has been considered to be a prophetess.

Links: 9 June, 23 September, 7 December, 10 December

5 minutes more? 1 Corinthians 3

Jonah runs from the Lord

One day the Lord told Jonah, the son of Amittai, to go to the great city of Nineveh and say to the people, 'The Lord has seen your terrible sins. You are doomed!' Instead, Jonah ran from the Lord. He went to the seaport of Joppa and bought a ticket on a ship that was going to Spain. Then he got on the ship and sailed away to escape. But the Lord made a strong wind blow, and such a bad storm came up that the ship was about to be broken to pieces. The sailors were frightened, and they all started praying to their gods. They even threw the ship's cargo overboard to make the ship lighter. All this time, Jonah was down below deck, sound asleep... Finally, the sailors got together and said, 'Let's ask our gods to show us who caused all this trouble.' It turned out to be Jonah... The storm kept getting worse, until finally the sailors asked him, 'What should we do with you to make the sea calm down?' Jonah told them, 'Throw me into the sea, and it will calm down. I'm the cause of this terrible storm.' ... Then they threw Jonah overboard, and the sea calmed down.

JONAH 1:1–5, 7, 11–12, 15

Di:SaipL

The best place to be

If your gut feelings tell you that God wants you to do something for him, then for goodness' sake don't run away from it. There really is no better place for anyone to be than the place God has planned for you.

There are so many excuses not to do what God wants you to do with your life. In my experience I have found that the best place to be is the place God wants me.

For some people that might mean joining a discipleship program, taking a year out to serve God on a special project, or going to Bible College.

For others it might mean training for the ministry or to be a missionary.

If you are thinking about this kind of thing, then it would be good to go and talk things through with your youth pastor, cell group leader or another mature Christian.

Whatever your future might hold, every one of us needs to make sure the everyday decisions that we make—big or small—are made for God's glory.

Links: 11 January, 14 February, 3 August, 8 September

5 minutes more? 1 Corinthians 8

26 September

Old Testament odds 'n' ends

Jonah is in the fish for three days and three nights

The Lord sent a big fish to swallow Jonah, and Jonah was inside the fish for three days and three nights. From inside the fish, Jonah prayed to the Lord his God:

When I was in trouble, Lord, I prayed to you, and you listened to me. From deep in the world of the dead, I begged for your help, and you answered my prayer...

The Lord commanded the fish to vomit up Jonah on the shore. And it did.

JONAH 1:17—2:2, 10

Weird and wonderful

Jesus wasn't in the grave for more than 36 hours

Jonah is a foreshadowing—a sign—of what would happen to Jesus: it is called the 'sign of Jonah'. This is because, just as Jonah was in the fish's stomach for three days and three nights, so Jesus would be 'deep in the earth' for three days and three nights (see Matthew 12:39–40).

Hang on a minute—Jesus died on a Friday afternoon, but he rose from the dead on a Sunday morning—surely that's only one and a half days, not three whole days?!

The key to the whole thing revolves around how people counted in Bible times—in whole days. So you get Friday, Saturday and Sunday—three days.

There are other examples of this kind of counting in the Bible: from Easter to Jesus' ascension is recorded as 40 days, but is only 39 actual days. And from Easter to Pentecost is recorded as 50 days, but is really only 49 days in actual time. You could try counting it for yourself!

Links: 25 September, 27 September, 30 September, 1 October

5 minutes more? 1 Corinthians 9

27 September

Witnesses to Jesus' resurrection

The women at the grave

The Sabbath was over, and it was almost daybreak on Sunday when Mary Magdalene and the other Mary went to see the tomb. Suddenly a strong earthquake struck, and the Lord's angel came down from heaven. He rolled away the stone and sat on it. The angel looked as bright as lightning, and his clothes were white as snow... The angel said to the women, 'Don't be afraid! I know you are looking for Jesus, who was nailed to a cross. He isn't here! God has raised him to life, just as Jesus said he would. Come, see the place where his body was lying...' The women were frightened and yet very happy, as they hurried from the tomb and ran to tell his disciples.

MATTHEW 28:1–3, 5–6, 8

Did you know that...

...Christianity is in a unique position in relation to other religions?

Christianity is built on the foundation that the person who established it, Jesus, rose from the dead. If this is true, then we can draw the following mega conclusions:

- If Jesus rose from the dead, then we can be sure God exists.
- If Jesus rose from the dead, then we know there is life after death.
- If Jesus rose from the dead, then Jesus is the Way, the Truth and the Life.
- If Jesus rose from the dead, then humanity has a future and a hope.
- If Jesus rose from the dead, then we have an obligation to share this Good News!

There is strong evidence that Jesus did rise from the dead. Over the next few days we will be hearing what some of the witnesses say they experienced.

Links: 28 September, 29 September, 30 September, 1 October

5 minutes more? 1 Corinthians 10

28 September

Witnesses to Jesus' resurrection

Jesus appears to two disciples (1)

That same day two of Jesus' disciples were going to the village of Emmaus... As they were talking and thinking about what had happened, Jesus came near and started walking along beside them. But they did not know who he was. Jesus asked them, 'What were you talking about as you walked along?' The two of them stood there looking sad and gloomy. Then the one named Cleopas asked Jesus, 'Are you the only person from Jerusalem who didn't know what was happening there these last few days?' 'What do you mean?' Jesus asked. They answered:

Those things that happened to Jesus from Nazareth. By what he did and said he showed that he was a powerful prophet, who pleased God and all the people. Then the chief priests and our leaders had him arrested and sentenced to die on a cross... Some women in our group surprised us. They had gone to the tomb early in the morning, but did not find the body of Jesus. They came back, saying that they had seen a vision of angels who told them that he is alive.

LUKE 24:13–20, 22

Did you know that...

... Jesus had more than twelve disciples?

Usually we say that Jesus had twelve disciples. But that's not quite right. He had an inner circle of twelve disciples, but in addition to them, Jesus also had a group of about seventy other disciples. We read about them in Luke 10:1. Check if you like!

Today's reading is about two of this larger group of disciples.

Jesus also had some female disciples. We read about them in Luke 8:1–3: 'His twelve apostles were with him, and so were some women...'

So I'd like to announce loud and clear that being a disciple isn't a 'boy thing'.

Links: 29 September, 30 September, 1 October, 2 October

5 minutes more? 1 Corinthians 11

29 September

Witnesses to Jesus' resurrection

Jesus appears to two disciples (2)

When the two of them came near the village where they were going, Jesus seemed to be going further. They begged him, 'Stay with us! It's already late, and the sun is going down.' So Jesus went into the house to stay with them. After Jesus sat down to eat, he took some bread. He blessed it and broke it. Then he gave it to them. At once they knew who he was, but he disappeared. They said to each other, 'When he talked with us along the road and explained the Scriptures to us, didn't it warm our hearts?' So they got up at once and returned to Jerusalem. The two disciples found the eleven apostles and the others gathered together. And they learnt from the group that the Lord was really alive and had appeared to Peter. Then the disciples from Emmaus told what happened on the road and how they knew he was the Lord when he broke the bread.

LUKE 24:28–35

Weird and wonderful

So near—and yet so far!

Two of Jesus' best friends were walking along talking to each other. Jesus came and walked along with them, but they didn't recognize him.

Jesus walks right alongside you too. He isn't always very easy to recognize, not always easy to notice. But he's there.

But now and then, things just seem to click. Now and then you know he's there. Every so often when you hear God's word, you notice he's there and wants to tell you something. The disciples who were walking to Emmaus noticed it: 'When he talked with us along the road and explained the Scriptures to us, didn't it warm our hearts?'

So that's why it's good that you're making time to read the Bible. God's word strengthens our belief that Jesus walks through life alongside us.

Do you notice those times when things simply click into place? Do you notice your heart being warmed when you read God's word?

Links: 30 September, 1 October, 2 October, 3 October

5 minutes more? 1 Corinthians 12

30 September

Witnesses to Jesus' resurrection

The twelve disciples minus Thomas

The disciples were afraid of the Jewish leaders, and on the evening of that same Sunday they locked themselves in a room. Suddenly, Jesus appeared in the middle of the group. He greeted them and showed them his hands and his side. When the disciples saw the Lord, they became very happy. After Jesus had greeted them again, he said, 'I am sending you, just as the Father has sent me.' Then he breathed on them and said, 'Receive the Holy Spirit. If you forgive anyone's sins, they will be forgiven. But if you don't forgive their sins, they will not be forgiven.' Although Thomas the Twin was one of the twelve disciples, he wasn't with the others when Jesus appeared to them. So they told him, 'We have seen the Lord!' But Thomas said, 'First, I must see the nail scars in his hands and touch them with my finger. I must put my hand where the spear went into his side. I won't believe unless I do this!'

JOHN 20:19–25

Hmm... just a thought

You won't believe it before you see it!

You know what it's like to be left out! All the others saw it. All the others were there when it happened. But not you. Thomas is often criticized because he wouldn't believe. Really he was only being honest. It's good to be honest!

It was important to Jesus to meet up with Thomas. Jesus hasn't got a problem with honest people—he meets with them, sooner or later.

You know what it's like to be included! To be there when it happened. To see it for yourself. To experience something fantastic. To come racing home and tell someone—only they won't believe you! It must have been disappointing for the other disciples when Thomas wouldn't believe them—a little like when our friends won't believe in God. But you needn't give up! Jesus met up with Thomas. We can hope and pray that Jesus will meet up with our friends too.

Links: 1 October, 2 October, 3 October, 4 October

5 minutes more? 1 Corinthians 13

Witnesses to Jesus' resurrection

Doubting Thomas

A week later the disciples were together again. This time, Thomas was with them. Jesus came in while the doors were still locked and stood in the middle of the group. He greeted his disciples and said to Thomas, 'Put your finger here and look at my hands! Put your hand into my side. Stop doubting and have faith!' Thomas replied, 'You are my Lord and my God!' Jesus said, 'Thomas, do you have faith because you have seen me? The people who have faith in me without seeing me are the ones who are really blessed!' Jesus performed many other miracles for his disciples, and not all of them are written in this book. But these are written so that you will put your faith in Jesus as the Messiah and the Son of God. If you have faith in him, you will have true life.

JOHN 20:26–31

Listen to your heart and fill in

Why are you really a Christian?

Every now and then it's a good thing to remind yourself of a few good grounds for your faith. If you would describe yourself as a Christian, what are the most important reasons why for you?

1. ____

2. ____

3. ____

If you wouldn't call yourself a Christian, why not?

1. ____

2. ____

3. ____

If you are doubting, for goodness' sake don't stay away from the church youth group, youth cell group or church. Do what Thomas did: stay in contact with the other disciples. Jesus will come and meet you there with them before you know it.

Links: 22 February, 2 October, 3 October, 4 October

5 minutes more? 1 Corinthians 14

2 October

Witnesses to Jesus' resurrection

Peter

When Jesus and his disciples had finished eating, he asked, 'Simon son of John, do you love me more than the others do?' Simon Peter answered, 'Yes, Lord, you know I do!' 'Then feed my lambs,' Jesus said. Jesus asked a second time, 'Simon son of John, do you love me?' Peter answered, 'Yes, Lord, you know I love you!' 'Then take care of my sheep,' Jesus told him. Jesus asked a third time, 'Simon son of John, do you love me?' Peter was hurt because Jesus had asked him three times if he loved him. So he told Jesus, 'Lord, you know everything. You know I love you.' Jesus replied, 'Feed my sheep. I tell you for certain that when you were a young man, you dressed yourself and went wherever you wanted to go. But when you are old, you will hold out your hands. Then others will tie your belt around you and lead you where you don't want to go.' Jesus said this to tell how Peter would die and bring honour to God. Then he said to Peter, 'Follow me!'
JOHN 21:15–19

Did you know that...

...eleven of the twelve disciples died because they were Jesus' disciples?

Early traditions tell us that of the twelve disciples of Jesus, only John died a natural death—the others were all martyred. This what happened to some of them:

- James, the brother of John, was beheaded on Herod's orders in AD44 (see Acts 12:2).
- Peter was imprisoned and executed. He wouldn't be crucified the same way as Jesus, so he was hung upside down.
- Simon—some sources claim that he died a martyr's death in Persia.
- Matthew—tradition has it that he travelled to Ethiopia, Syria and Macedonia, and died a martyr's death there.
- Bartholomew preached the gospel in Armenia, among other places, where it is said he was flayed alive.
- Andrew, Peter's brother—according to tradition, he worked in Russia and Turkey before he was crucified on an X-shaped cross.

The gospel is something to live for, but also something to die for.

Links: 6 May, 3 October, 4 October, 14 November

5 minutes more? 1 Corinthians 15

3 October

Witnesses to Jesus' resurrection

You

For forty days after Jesus had suffered and died, he proved in many ways that he had been raised from death. He appeared to his apostles and spoke to them about God's kingdom. While he was still with them he said:

Don't leave Jerusalem yet. Wait here for the Father to give you the Holy Spirit, just as I told you he has promised to do. John baptized with water, but in a few days you will be baptized with the Holy Spirit... [But] the Holy Spirit will come upon you and give you power. Then you will tell everyone about me in Jerusalem, in all Judea, in Samaria, and everywhere in the world.

After Jesus had said this and while they were watching, he was taken up into a cloud. They could not see him, but as he went up, they kept looking up into the sky. Suddenly two men dressed in white clothes were standing there beside them. They said, 'Why are you men from Galilee standing here and looking up into the sky? Jesus has been taken to heaven. But he will come back in the same way that you have seen him go.'

ACTS 1:3–5, 8–11

Download

You are my witnesses

You probably know the words of 'the great commission' from Matthew's Gospel (Matthew 28:18–20): 'I have been given all authority in heaven and on earth! Go to the people of all nations and make them my disciples. Baptize them in the name of the Father, the Son, and the Holy Spirit, and teach them to do everything I have told you. I will be with you always, even until the end of the world.'

It is also worth learning the words of the great commission from Acts: '[But] the Holy Spirit will come upon you and give you power. Then you will tell everyone about me in Jerusalem, in all Judea, in Samaria, and everywhere in the world' (Acts 1:8).

You are called to be his witnesses. Be one!

Links: 9 February, 26 February, 30 July, 4 October

5 minutes more? 2 Corinthians 1

4 October

Witnesses to Jesus' resurrection

Paul

Christ died for our sins, as the Scriptures say. He was buried, and three days later he was raised to life, as the Scriptures say. Christ appeared to Peter, then to the twelve. After this, he appeared to more than five hundred other followers. Most of them are still alive, but some have died. He also appeared to James, and then to all the apostles. Finally, he appeared to me, even though I am like someone who was born at the wrong time. I am the least important of all the apostles. In fact, I caused so much trouble for God's church that I don't even deserve to be called an apostle. But God was kind! He made me what I am, and his wonderful kindness wasn't wasted.

1 CORINTHIANS 15:3b–10a

Check it out

The importance of the resurrection to Paul

For Paul, the whole of Christian belief hung on one thing: Jesus' resurrection.

Even though Paul never met Jesus in the flesh, he was persistent in his belief that Jesus had appeared to him. These are Paul's thoughts in a nutshell:

- If Jesus rose from the dead, then our Christian belief is true.
- If Jesus didn't rise from the dead, the Christian message is worthless.

Listen to what Paul writes in the bit following on from today's reading: 'If Christ wasn't raised to life, our message is worthless, and so is your faith. If the dead won't be raised to life, we have told lies about God by saying that he raised Christ to life, when he really did not… If our hope in Christ is good only for this life, we are worse off than anyone else' (1 Corinthians 15:14–15, 19).

Fortunately Paul adds: '*But Christ has been raised to life!*' (1 Corinthians 15:20).

Hello there… are you listening? *Christ has been raised to life!*

Links: 11 October, 12 October, 13 October, 14 October

5 minutes more? 2 Corinthians 2

5 October

The Church kicks off (AD27–49)

Peter's Pentecost message

On the day of Pentecost all the Lord's followers were together in one place. Suddenly there was a noise from heaven like the sound of a mighty wind! It filled the house where they were meeting... The Holy Spirit took control of everyone, and they began speaking whatever languages the Spirit let them speak. Many religious Jews from every country in the world were living in Jerusalem... Some of them kept asking each other, 'What does all this mean?' ... Peter stood with the eleven apostles and spoke in a loud and clear voice to the crowd:

Friends, and everyone else living in Jerusalem, listen carefully to what I have to say! ... This is what God led the prophet Joel to say, 'When the last days come, I will give my Spirit to everyone. Your sons and daughters will prophesy. Your young men will see visions, and your old men will have dreams. In those days I will give my Spirit to my servants... Then the Lord will save everyone who asks for his help...' Turn back to God! Be baptized in the name of Jesus Christ, so that your sins will be forgiven. Then you will be given the Holy Spirit.

ACTS 2:1–2, 4–5, 12b, 14–18, 21, 38

Download...

...about being saved

'Then the Lord will save everyone who asks for his help' (Acts 2:21).

Isn't it incredible how these terrified disciples have suddenly been changed? A month and a half earlier they gathered together because they were frightened and exhausted. And they locked the doors behind them. They had been frightened people (John 20:19).

But now—now they are standing out there, not cowering. The fear has gone. They are proud to be disciples. They preach the message: *Jesus is alive.*

Something has happened to them...

...it can happen to you too.

Jesus says that the Father will give the Holy Spirit to all those who ask him (Luke 11:13).

Links: 18 May, 6 October, 7 October, 8 October

5 minutes more? 2 Corinthians 3

The first Christians

On that day about three thousand believed his message and were baptized. They spent their time learning from the apostles, and they were like family to each other. They also broke bread and prayed together. Everyone was amazed by the many miracles and wonders that the apostles performed. All the Lord's followers often met together, and they shared everything they had. They would sell their property and possessions and give money to whoever needed it. Day after day they met together in the temple. They broke bread together in different homes and shared their food happily and freely, while praising God. Everyone liked them, and each day the Lord added to their group others who were being saved.
ACTS 2:41–47

Di:SaipL
Four essentials for growth

Long, long ago in the olden days, when I was a teenager—way back in the last century—we were taught four essentials for growth as a Christian. In just the same way that W.W.J.D. has become fashionable these days, the 'four essentials' were then. We used to say that the Christian life was like a chair with four legs:

1. Bible reading
2. Prayer
3. Breaking bread (or Communion / the Lord's Supper)
4. Fellowship (church or cell group)

The point is that you need all four things in place in your Christian life, just like a chair needs four equally balanced legs to remain upright.

Today we have been reading about the first Christians. You will find all the four essentials for Christian growth in the passage if you look carefully. Some are mentioned more than once. Ideas and illustrations do go out of fashion, you know, but these four essentials will never be out of fashion for anyone who wants to be a disciple.

How do things stand with you?

Links: 18 May, 5 October, 7 October, 8 October

5 minutes more? 2 Corinthians 4

7 October

The Church kicks off (AD27–49)

A tough day at work (1)

The time of prayer was about three o'clock in the afternoon, and Peter and John were going into the temple. A man who had been born lame was being carried to the temple door. Each day he was placed beside this door, known as the Beautiful Gate. He sat there and begged from the people who were going in. The man saw Peter and John entering the temple, and he asked them for money. But they looked straight at him and said, 'Look up at us!' The man stared at them and thought he was going to get something. But Peter said, 'I don't have any silver or gold! But I will give you what I do have. In the name of Jesus Christ from Nazareth, get up and start walking.' Peter then took him by the right hand and helped him up... Everyone saw him walking around and praising God.

ACTS 3:1–7, 9

Listen to your heart and fill in

What have you got to be thankful for?

It's no amazingly big surprise that this man got so excited. If someone's been lame all their life and is suddenly healed, it would be odd if they didn't get worked up about it. I've no idea whether you've ever been healed, but the thing is, we all have a tremendous amount to thank God for. More than enough to make you get excited too.

Write some of those things down here:

1. ________________________________

2. ________________________________

3. ________________________________

4. ________________________________

And one more thing: Christians are allowed to express their feelings, you know...

Links: 6 February, 1 September, 8 October, 9 October

5 minutes more? 2 Corinthians 5

8 October

The Church kicks off (AD27–49)

A tough day at work (2)

While the man kept holding on to Peter and John, the whole crowd ran to them in amazement at the place known as Solomon's Porch. Peter saw that a crowd had gathered, and he said:

Friends, why are you surprised at what has happened? Why are you staring at us? Do you think we have some power of our own? Do you think we were able to make this man walk because we are so religious? ... You see this man, and you know him. He has put his faith in the name of Jesus and was made strong. Faith in Jesus made this man completely well while everyone was watching.

The apostles were still talking to the people, when some priests, the captain of the temple guard, and some Sadducees arrived. These men were angry because the apostles were teaching the people that the dead would be raised from death just as Jesus had been raised from death. It was already late in the afternoon, and they arrested Peter and John and put them in jail for the night. But a lot of people who had heard the message believed it. So by now there were about five thousand followers of the Lord.

ACTS 3:11–12, 16; 4:1–4

Did you know that...

... a teacher of the Law and a teacher of the Law are not the same?

Here are ten points of cultural history for you:

1. Israel was occupied by the Romans.
2. The Romans called the area Judea, not Israel.
3. The Romans had stationed a governor in Judea—Pontius Pilate.
4. However, the Jewish did have some religious independence.
5. The Jews' highest recourse to power was the Council or the High Council.
6. The Council consisted of 70 men, called councillors.
7. All 70 of them were teachers of the Law—they had had a long education based on the Scriptures (the Old Testament).
8. The 70 men came from different parties—the Sadducees and the Pharisees.
9. The Pharisees believed in the resurrection of the dead, angels and spirits.
10. The Sadducees didn't believe in the resurrection of the dead, angels or spirits —and that's why they were angry about what Peter and John were saying.

Links: 5 October, 7 October, 9 October, 10 October

5 minutes more? 2 Corinthians 10

9 October

The Church kicks off (AD27–49)

A tough day at work (3)

The next morning the leaders, the elders, and the teachers of the Law of Moses met in Jerusalem... The officials were amazed to see how brave Peter and John were, and they knew that these two apostles were only ordinary men and not well educated. The officials were certain that these men had been with Jesus. But they could not deny what had happened. The man who had been healed was standing there with the apostles... [The officials said,] 'What can we do with these men? Everyone in Jerusalem knows about this miracle, and we cannot say it didn't happen. But to keep this thing from spreading, we will warn them never again to speak to anyone about the name of Jesus.' ... Peter and John answered, 'Do you think God wants us to obey you or to obey him? We cannot keep quiet about what we have seen and heard.' The officials could not find any reason to punish Peter and John. So they threatened them and let them go.
ACTS 4:5, 13–14, 16–17, 19–21

I am proud of the good news! It is God's powerful way of saving all people who have faith, whether they are Jews or Gentiles.
ROMANS 1:16

Di:SaipL

We cannot keep quiet about what we have seen or heard

Most people would agree that it is stupid to go around 'hitting people over the head with the Bible'—forcing Christianity on people. We are Christians, but that doesn't mean we need to behave antisocially.

Nevertheless, we all get opportunities to tell others what Jesus means to us in a completely natural way. Whether the chance is a big one or a small one, all we need to do is take it. Be courageous. Speak out.

'Yes, I believe in Jesus.' 'Yes, I am a Christian.' 'Yes, I believe that...'

Don't duck out, go for it. We've got so much to share. We simply cannot keep quiet about what we have seen and heard. So get stuck in!

Links: 7 October, 8 October, 10 October, 14 October

5 minutes more? 2 Corinthians 12

Stephen is stoned to death

God's message spread, and many more people in Jerusalem became followers. Even a large number of priests put their faith in the Lord. God gave Stephen the power to perform great miracles and wonders among the people. But some Jews from Cyrene and Alexandria were members of a group who called themselves 'Free Men'. They... talked some men into saying, 'We heard Stephen say terrible things against Moses and God!' They turned the people and their leaders and the teachers of the Law of Moses against Stephen. Then they all grabbed Stephen and dragged him in front of the council... But Stephen was filled with the Holy Spirit. He looked towards heaven where he saw our glorious God and Jesus standing at his right side. Then Stephen said, 'I see heaven open and the Son of Man standing at the right side of God!' The council members shouted and covered their ears. At once they all attacked Stephen and dragged him out of the city. Then they started throwing stones at him... As Stephen was being stoned to death, he called out, 'Lord Jesus, please welcome me!' ... Then he died.

ACTS 6:7–9a, 11–12; 7:55–58a, 59, 60b

Di:SaipL

Martyrs

A martyr is someone who dies because of their faith in Jesus. 'Martyr' is actually a Greek word that means 'witness'. Stephen was the very first martyr.

Did you know that there are more people who die for their faith nowadays than there were in the first century? About 150,000 every year. See what you can find out about the suffering church in places like China, Malaysia, Pakistan and parts of Africa. You could commit yourself to pray for these people.

Christian Solidarity Worldwide is an organization that campaigns to release people imprisoned for their faith. I recently heard some of the stories of people that CSW supports—it is quite a challenge to know what some people will endure for Jesus. When you hear these things, you realize that your own difficulties are small fry compared to what they have to put up with.

'So stop being afraid and don't worry about what people might do. Honour Christ and let him be the Lord of your life' (1 Peter 3:14b–15a).

Links: 11 October, 12 October, 13 October, 14 October

5 minutes more? 2 Corinthians 13

Saul persecutes the first Christians

The men who had brought charges against Stephen put their coats at the feet of a young man named Saul. As Stephen was being stoned to death, he called out, 'Lord Jesus, please welcome me!' He knelt down and shouted, 'Lord, don't blame them for what they have done.' Then he died. Saul approved the stoning of Stephen. Some faithful followers of the Lord buried Stephen and mourned very much for him. At that time the church in Jerusalem suffered terribly. All the Lord's followers, except the apostles, were scattered everywhere in Judea and Samaria. Saul started making a lot of trouble for the church. He went from house to house, arresting men and women and putting them in jail. The Lord's followers who had been scattered went from place to place, telling the good news.
ACTS 7:58b—8:4

☆ Bible personality
Paul

The first time we meet Saul / Paul, he is a rogue of a Pharisee who persecutes and kills Christians.

This same Paul ended his days as a Christian martyr when he was 64 years old, after having spent a long time under house arrest in Rome during the reign of the Emperor Nero.

God had big plans for Paul. Paul saw the light (literally), repented and became the first major missionary for the Christian faith.

Paul travelled round preaching in the countries north-east of the Mediterranean Sea. He founded dozens of churches, and wrote innumerable letters to them—some of which can be found in our New Testament. We can thank the apostle Paul for explaining clearly what Jesus' death and resurrection mean for our faith.

If you are looking for a role model, there are many things about Paul that are worth noting.

Links: 12 October, 13 October, 14 October, 18 October

5 minutes more? Galatians 1

12 October

The Church kicks off (AD27–49)

Saul becomes a follower of the Lord

Saul kept on threatening to kill the Lord's followers. He even went to the high priest and asked for letters to the Jewish leaders in Damascus. He did this because he wanted to arrest and take to Jerusalem any man or woman who had accepted the Lord's Way. When Saul had almost reached Damascus, a bright light from heaven suddenly flashed around him. He fell to the ground and heard a voice that said, 'Saul! Saul! Why are you so cruel to me?' 'Who are you?' Saul asked. 'I am Jesus,' the Lord answered. 'I am the one you are so cruel to. Now get up and go into the city, where you will be told what to do.' The men with Saul stood there speechless. They had heard the voice, but they had not seen anyone. Saul got up from the ground, and when he opened his eyes, he could not see a thing. Someone then led him by the hand to Damascus, and for three days he was blind and did not eat or drink.

ACTS 9:1–9

Hmm... just a thought...

...about the way Jesus identifies with those who suffer

Paul's experience on the Damascus road made him understand that when he persecuted Christians, it was the same as persecuting Jesus.

In Matthew 25:45, Jesus ends a parable by saying, 'Whenever you failed to help any of my people, no matter how unimportant they seemed, you failed to do it for me.'

By extension, this means that anyone who persecutes someone who believes in Jesus persecutes Jesus himself.

Jesus suffers with those who suffer—literally.

Links: 13 October, 14 October, 15 October, 18 October

5 minutes more? Galatians 2

Paul gets his sight back

A follower named Ananias lived in Damascus, and the Lord spoke to him in a vision. Ananias answered, 'Lord, here I am.' The Lord said to him, 'Get up and go to the house of Judas in Straight Street. When you get there, you will find a man named Saul from the city of Tarsus. Saul is praying, and he has seen a vision. He saw a man named Ananias coming to him and putting his hands on him, so that he could see again.' Ananias replied, 'Lord, a lot of people have told me about the terrible things this man has done to your followers in Jerusalem...' The Lord said to Ananias, 'Go! I have chosen him to tell foreigners, kings, and the people of Israel about me...' Ananias left and went into the house where Paul was staying. Ananias placed his hands on him and said, 'Saul, the Lord Jesus has sent me. He is the same one who appeared to you along the road. He wants you to be able to see and to be filled with the Holy Spirit.' Suddenly something like fish scales fell from Saul's eyes, and he could see. He got up and was baptized. Then he ate and felt much better. For several days Saul stayed with the Lord's followers in Damascus. Soon he went to the Jewish meeting places and started telling people that Jesus is the Son of God.
ACTS 9:10–13, 15, 17–20

Did you know that...
...God's Son is 100 per cent God?

Jehovah's Witnesses claim that Jesus isn't really God. They think something to the effect of: 'A father takes precedence over a son, and as Jesus is called God's son, then he must be something less than the father.'

You know, they have completely misunderstood the whole point. The point is that, just like...

... a cow and a calf are both cows...
... a ewe and a lamb are both sheep...
... a child and an adult are both human...
... God and the Son are both God—100 per cent God.

God can't be 90 per cent God, you know. Either he is, or he isn't; there are no half measures. Like Paul, it can sometimes take something like scales to fall off the eyes of our understanding before we completely get it. But when we do, like Paul, we are convinced that Jesus is the Son of God... and we can tell that to others.

Links: 12 October, 18 October, 19 October, 20 October

5 minutes more? Galatians 3

Paul's first missionary journey

After Barnabas and Saul had been sent by the Holy Spirit, they went to Seleucia. From there they sailed to the island of Cyprus. They arrived at Salamis and began to preach God's message in the Jewish meeting places. They also had John as a helper. Barnabas and Saul went all the way to the city of Paphos on the other end of the island... Paul and the others left Paphos and sailed to Perga in Pamphylia. But John left them and went back to Jerusalem. The rest of them went on from Perga to Antioch in Pisidia. Then on the Sabbath they went to the Jewish meeting place and sat down...

Paul and Barnabas spoke in the Jewish meeting place in Iconium, just as they had done at Antioch, and many Jews and Gentiles put their faith in the Lord. But the Jews who did not have faith in him made the other Gentiles angry and turned them against the Lord's followers... But when the two apostles found out what was happening, they escaped to the region of Lycaonia. They preached the good news there in the towns of Lystra and Derbe and in the nearby countryside... Then they went back to Lystra, Iconium, and Antioch in Pisidia... Paul and Barnabas went on through Pisidia to Pamphylia, where they preached in the town of Perga. Then they went down to Attalia and sailed to Antioch in Syria. It was there that they had been placed in God's care for the work they had now completed.

ACTS 13:4–6a, 13–14; 14:1–2, 6–7, 21b, 24–26

Listen to your heart and fill in

Paul's first missionary journey

Paul went on three journeys altogether, each lasting three years. Get a pencil and draw in the route of the first one.

Paul's first missionary journey:
Antioch in Syria—Salamis—Paphos—Perga—Antioch in Pisidia—Iconium—Lystra—Derbe—Lystra—Iconium—Antioch in Pisidia—Perga—Attalia—Antioch in Syria

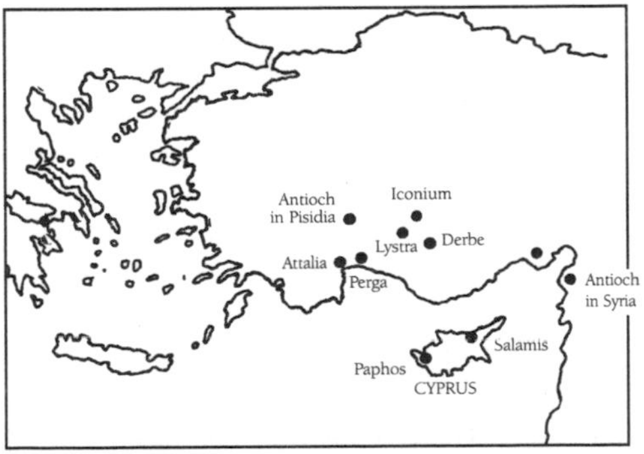

Links: 15 October, 16 October, 23 October, 13 November

5 minutes more? Galatians 4

15 October

The Church kicks off (AD27–49)

The first big church council meeting: the agenda

Some people came from Judea and started teaching the Lord's followers that they could not be saved, unless they were circumcised as Moses had taught. This caused trouble, and Paul and Barnabas argued with them about this teaching... The apostles and church leaders met to discuss this problem about Gentiles. They had talked it over for a long time, when Peter got up and said:

My friends, you know that God decided long ago to let me be the one from your group to preach the good news to the Gentiles. God... knows what is in everyone's heart. And he showed that he had chosen the Gentiles, when he gave them the Holy Spirit, just as he had given his Spirit to us. God treated them in the same way that he treated us. They put their faith in him, and he made their hearts pure. Now why are you trying to make God angry by placing a heavy burden on these followers? This burden was too heavy for us or our ancestors. But our Lord Jesus was kind to us, and we are saved by faith in him, just as the Gentiles are.

Everyone kept quiet and listened as Barnabas and Paul told how God had given them the power to perform a lot of miracles and wonders for the Gentiles.

ACTS 15:1–2, 6–12

Did you know that...

...initially the good news was the preserve of the Jews?

We take it for granted that anyone who wants to can call themselves a Christian, whatever part of the world they come from. But things only turned out that way by a cat's whisker. The heat was on at the first big church council meeting. All the disciples were there, and Paul was there. One big issue was on the agenda: should non-Jews have to be circumcised in order to be Christians? We ought to remember that this happened in AD48. Up until then, Christianity had been Jewish; all its roots were Jewish, Jesus was a Jew, and so were the disciples. Even Paul was a Jew.

Peter came up with the line of reasoning that eventually decided the matter: many non-Jews had received the Holy Spirit in a visible way; therefore God must have accepted them too. That is why people in Europe, America and other places are allowed to call themselves Christians without having to be circumcised. And that was all thanks to Peter, Paul and Barnabas, and the others. But most thanks of all go to the Holy Spirit for his leading.

Links: 26 February, 3 October, 14 October, 16 October

5 minutes more? Galatians 5

The first big church council meeting: the resolution

The apostles, the leaders, and all the church members decided to send some men to Antioch along with Paul and Barnabas. They chose Silas and Judas Barsabbas, who were two leaders of the Lord's followers. They wrote a letter that said:

We apostles and leaders send friendly greetings to all you Gentiles who are followers of the Lord in Antioch, Syria, and Cilicia. We have heard that some people from here have terribly upset you by what they said. But we did not send them! So we met together and decided to choose some men and to send them to you along with our good friends Barnabas and Paul... The Holy Spirit has shown us that we should not place any extra burden on you. But you should not eat anything offered to idols. You should not eat any meat that still has the blood in it or any meat of any animal that has been strangled. You must also not commit any terrible sexual sins. If you follow these instructions, you will do well. We send our best wishes.

The four men left Jerusalem and went to Antioch. Then they called the church members together and gave them the letter. When the letter was read, everyone was pleased and greatly encouraged.
ACTS 15:22–25, 28–31

☆ Key Bible personality
The Holy Spirit

The Holy Spirit is a person. Yes, you heard me, a person—but not in the normal understanding, of course. We call him a person to emphasize that he has his own personality. Just in the same way, Jesus has his own personality. He isn't just one of God's characteristics—he is God. He's a person.

The Holy Spirit is gentle. Many people are rather frightened of the Holy Spirit. He can seem frightening if you're not used to him. But there's really nothing to be frightened of. Most of what he does, you won't even notice at all. He does it very quietly, carefully and gently.

The Holy Spirit's most important job is to point to Jesus. He helps you believe in Jesus, get to know Jesus better, become more like Jesus. He never shows lack of consideration, but he works with considerable power in our lives if we let him.

Links: 14 May, 18 May, 5 October, 15 October

5 minutes more? Galatians 6

30: May God our Father be kind to you...

My prayer is that God our Father and the Lord Jesus Christ will be kind to you and will bless you with peace!
1 CORINTHIANS 1:3

I pray that God our Father and the Lord Jesus Christ will be kind to you and will bless you with peace!
2 CORINTHIANS 1:2

I pray that God the Father and our Lord Jesus Christ will be kind to you and will bless you with peace!
GALATIANS 1:3

I pray that God our Father and our Lord Jesus Christ will be kind to you and will bless you with peace!
EPHESIANS 1:2

I pray that God our Father and the Lord Jesus Christ will be kind to you and will bless you with peace!
PHILIPPIANS 1:2

I pray that God our Father will be kind to you and will bless you with peace!
COLOSSIANS 1:2

I pray that God will be kind to you and will bless you with peace!
1 THESSALONIANS 1:1

I pray that God our Father and the Lord Jesus Christ will be kind to you and will bless you with peace!
2 THESSALONIANS 1:2

I pray that God our Father and our Lord Christ Jesus will be kind and merciful to you and will bless you with peace!
2 TIMOTHY 1:2

I pray that God our Father and Christ Jesus our Saviour will be kind to you and will bless you with peace!
TITUS 1:4b

I pray that God our Father and our Lord Jesus Christ will be kind to you and will bless you with peace!
PHILEMON 1:3

Weird and wonderful

Almost all Paul's letters begin in the same way

Paul had a reason why he began all his letters the same way—the greetings weren't due to lack of imagination or idle chat. In fact, they were what you might be left with if you boiled the whole of Paul's message down to one sentence: 'I pray that God our Father and our Lord Jesus Christ will be kind to you and will bless you with peace!'

Another word for God being kind to us is 'grace'. In some versions of the Bible, Paul's greetings read 'Grace be to you, and peace...' Do you know what grace is? You could think of it like this:

G: God's **R:** riches **A:** at **C:** Christ's **E:** expense

Links: 13 January, 14 January, 15 January, 17 January

5 minutes more? Ephesians 1

18 October

Paul's Top 30

29: Paul, the greatest of sinners

I thank Christ Jesus our Lord. He has given me the strength for my work because he knew that he could trust me. I used to say terrible and insulting things about him, and I was cruel. But he had mercy on me because I didn't know what I was doing, and I had not yet put my faith in him. Christ Jesus our Lord was very kind to me. He has greatly blessed my life with faith and love just like his own. 'Christ Jesus came into the world to save sinners.' This saying is true, and it can be trusted. I was the worst sinner of all! But since I was worse than anyone else, God had mercy on me and let me be an example of the endless patience of Christ Jesus. He did this so that others would put their faith in Christ and have eternal life. I pray that honour and glory will always be given to the only God, who lives for ever and is the eternal and invisible King! Amen.
1 TIMOTHY 1:12–17

Hmm... just a thought

God can use even me...

If God decided to use Paul as an example of the endless patience of Christ Jesus, it wouldn't surprise me if he decided to do the same with you too!

If God can forgive and use Paul, the worst sinner of all, he can forgive and use you...

Links: 17 April, 23 October, 27 October, 2 November

5 minutes more? Ephesians 2

19 October

Paul's Top 30

28: Paul—expert on the human condition

I know that my selfish desires won't let me do anything that is good. Even when I want to do right, I cannot. Instead of doing what I know is right, I do wrong. And so, if I don't do what I know is right, I am no longer the one doing these evil things. The sin that lives in me is what does them... With my whole heart I agree with the Law of God. But in every part of me I discover something fighting against my mind, and it makes me a prisoner of sin that controls everything I do. What a miserable person I am. Who will rescue me from this body that is doomed to die? Thank God! Jesus Christ will rescue me. So with my mind I serve the Law of God, although my selfish desires make me serve the law of sin.

ROMANS 7:18–20, 22–25

Good news

God has more than a fair idea

One of the top psychiatrists in Norway, Berthold Grünfelt, once wrote an article in a Norwegian newspaper and used Romans 7 as a starting point. I quote:

Paul had deep insight into human nature. He was a realist—level headed, straight to the point—and without really being moralizing. Today's experts in psychiatry probably don't have much more to contribute to the discussion than Paul did.

It's great to hear that a recognized, contemporary psychiatrist can bring himself to say that. Does that somehow give Paul an ounce of credibility?

I should say not!

Paul has learnt what he knows from God. And God has, as we know, more than a good understanding of the human condition!

Links: 17 January, 8 November, 12 November, 13 November

5 minutes more? Ephesians 3

20 October

Paul's Top 30

27: Our salvation is completely undeserved (1)

I was circumcised when I was eight days old, and I am from the nation of Israel and the tribe of Benjamin. I am a true Hebrew. As a Pharisee, I strictly obeyed the Law of Moses. And I was so eager that I even made trouble for the church. I did everything the Law demands in order to please God. But Christ has shown me that what I once thought was valuable is worthless. Nothing is as wonderful as knowing Christ Jesus my Lord. I have given up everything else and count it all as rubbish. All I want is Christ and to know that I belong to him. I could not make myself acceptable to God by obeying the Law of Moses. God accepted me simply because of my faith in Christ. All I want is to know Christ and the power that raised him to life. I want to suffer and die as he did, so that somehow I also may be raised to life.

PHILIPPIANS 3:5–11

Big word

Righteous

Forget everything you think you know about the word 'righteous'. You need to do that in order to understand what Paul means when he uses the word. 'Cool', 'fair', and 'just' are not what Paul means here.

When Paul uses 'righteous' he means 'acquitted'. In Paul's day this word was usually used in lawsuits. If someone in the dock was found innocent, and acquitted, he was declared 'righteous'.

Paul had once been a Pharisee. That meant he believed that the only way to be called righteous—to be acceptable to God—was to keep laws and commandments. The laws were quite extreme, and it was very difficult to keep to them all.

It was quite a 'Aha!' experience for Paul when he understood that people aren't made acceptable to God due to their own effort, but by faith in Jesus.

Have you had that 'Aha!' experience yet?

Links: 20 January, 24 May, 21 October, 4 November

5 minutes more? Ephesians 4

26: Our salvation is completely undeserved (2)

By faith we have been made acceptable to God. And now, because of our Lord Jesus Christ, we live at peace with God. Christ has also introduced us to God's undeserved kindness on which we take our stand. So we are happy, as we look forward to sharing in the glory of God. But that's not all! We gladly suffer, because we know that suffering helps us to endure. And endurance builds character, which gives us a hope that will never disappoint us. All this happens because God has given us the Holy Spirit, who fills our hearts with his love. Christ died for us at a time when we were helpless and sinful. No one is really willing to die for an honest person, though someone might be willing to die for a truly good person. But God showed how much he loved us by having Christ die for us, even though we are sinful.

ROMANS 5:1–8

Did you know that...

...undeserved kindness and grace can mean the same thing?

A few years ago, when it was decided to produce an easy-to-read version of the Bible in the USA, the translators decided to cut out the word 'grace'. It may seem a little crazy to cut out such an incredibly important word, but research had shown that many young people hadn't a clue what 'grace' really meant. So it was decided to use another word.

The Contemporary English Version, which these devotional notes are based on, uses 'undeserved kindness' instead of 'grace'. So verse 2 of today's reading is: 'Christ has also introduced us to God's undeserved kindness on which we take our stand.'

It's easy to read, easy to understand.

Do you use difficult words to explain what Jesus has done for you? Cut them out! Speak plain English so your friends have a hope of understanding you!

Links: 15 January, 17 January, 19 October, 13 November

5 minutes more? Ephesians 5

22 October

Paul's Top 30

25: He who began a good work in you will complete it

Every time I think of you, I thank my God. And whenever I mention you in my prayers, it makes me happy. This is because you have taken part with me in spreading the good news from the first day you heard about it. God is the one who began this good work in you, and I am certain that he won't stop before it is complete on the day that Christ Jesus returns. You have a special place in my heart. So it is only natural for me to feel the way I do. All of you have helped in the work that God has given me, as I defend the good news and tell about it here in jail. God himself knows how much I want to see you. He knows that I care for you in the same way that Christ Jesus does. I pray that your love will keep on growing and that you will fully know and understand how to make the right choices. Then you will still be pure and innocent when Christ returns. And until that day, Jesus Christ will keep you busy doing good deeds that bring glory and praise to God.

PHILIPPIANS 1:3–11

Download...

...about finishing things in style!

Very often we are half finished with things—like the autumn term or essays or various jobs or something or other. I don't think it's particularly exciting when a job is only half finished. You're not at the beginning when everything is exciting and new. You're not nearing the end when you can breathe a little more easily. You're right in the middle of it: half way through.

Here's a verse that's worth knowing off by heart: 'God is the one who began this good work in you, and I am certain that he won't stop before it is complete on the day that Christ Jesus returns' (Philippians 1:6).

Hold on to it when you get that 'half way' feeling!

Links: 20 January, 24 May, 21 October, 4 November

5 minutes more? Ephesians 6

23 October

Paul's Top 30

24: God wants everyone to be saved

First of all, I ask you to pray for everyone. Ask God to help and bless them all, and tell God how thankful you are for each of them. Pray for kings and others in power, so that we may live quiet and peaceful lives as we worship and honour God. This kind of prayer is good, and it pleases God our Saviour. God wants everyone to be saved and to know the whole truth, which is:

There is only one God, and Christ Jesus is the only one who can bring us to God. Jesus was truly human, and he gave himself to rescue all of us. God showed us this at the right time.

1 TIMOTHY 2:1–6

Good news

Here is God's will for your life...

OK, no holding back, here is God's will for your life: 'God wants everyone to be saved and to know the whole truth.'

That probably wasn't what you'd thought! Perhaps you'd thought something more like this: A' levels or vocational training? Teacher or lawyer? University or a gap year? Australia or not Australia? And you'd probably asked God to give you a sign, and maybe you hadn't had one yet, and so you're still wondering what God's will is for your life.

Well, here is God's will for you: 'God wants everyone to be saved and to know the whole truth.'

God probably isn't going to put a mega-detailed, day-to-day plan, all tidily drawn up smack in your lap. He has got one, you know, because he is almighty. But what he really wants is for you, and everyone else, to be saved and know the whole truth.

Links: 17 April, 5 June, 27 October, 2 November

5 minutes more? Philippians 1

24 October

Paul's Top 30

23: Christ is the only foundation

Some of you say that you follow me, and others claim to follow Apollos. Isn't that how ordinary people behave? Apollos and I are merely servants who helped you to have faith. It was the Lord who made it all happen. I planted the seeds, Apollos watered them, but God made them sprout and grow. What matters isn't those who planted or watered, but God who made the plants grow. The one who plants is just as important as the one who waters. And each one will be paid for what they do. Apollos and I work together for God, and you are God's garden and God's building. God was kind and let me become an expert builder. I laid a foundation on which others have built. But we must each be careful how we build, because Christ is the only foundation.

1 CORINTHIANS 3:4–11

Refresh

The Edin Løvås fan club

The congregation in Corinth was split down the middle. Some held out for Paul. He had founded the church and had stayed there for six months before he travelled further afield. The rest of them held out for another bloke—called Apollos. We haven't a clue who he was. But he was probably the pastor or minister there.

It's important to have role models, including Christian role models—especially Christian role models. My biggest role model is Edin Løvås—the best preacher I've ever heard. He is 80 years old and totally amazing. I met him once. I was so nervous that my hands were all sweaty. The only thing I managed to say was, 'Hi, Edin Løvås. I'm your biggest fan. Bye.' He just looked at me and laughed. Somewhat embarrassing.

Even if I admire Edin Løvås, I can't build my Christian life on him. I think he and I would both agree about that. No one can lay any other foundation than the one that's already been put down for us: Jesus Christ.

Links: 14 April, 2 June, 3 June, 7 November

5 minutes more? Philippians 2

25 October

Paul's Top 30

22: All about getting confused

I am shocked that you have so quickly turned from God, who chose you because of his wonderful kindness. You have believed another message, when there is really only one true message. But some people are causing you trouble and want to make you turn away from the good news about Christ. I pray that God will punish anyone who preaches anything different from our message to you! It doesn't matter if that person is one of us or an angel from heaven. I have said it before, and I will say it again. I hope God will punish anyone who preaches anything different from what you have already believed... You stupid Galatians! I told you exactly how Jesus Christ was nailed to a cross. Has someone now put an evil spell on you?

GALATIANS 1:6–9; 3:1

Listen to your heart and fill in

Many religions

People believe so many strange things these days—everything from horoscopes to witchcraft. Take a pen and write down the things you've come across that people believe in today:

1. ______________________________
2. ______________________________
3. ______________________________
4. ______________________________
5. ______________________________
6. ______________________________
7. ______________________________
8. ______________________________
9. ______________________________
10. ______________________________

Right. Now read through today's reading again.

Links: 19 January, 19 May, 16 November, 6 December

5 minutes more? Philippians 3

26 October

Paul's Top 30

21: All about people in the last days

You can be certain that in the last days there will be some very hard times. People will love only themselves and money. They will be proud, stuck-up, rude, and disobedient to their parents. They will also be ungrateful, godless, heartless, and hateful. Their words will be cruel, and they will have no self-control or pity. These people will hate everything that is good. They will be sneaky, reckless, and puffed up with pride. Instead of loving God, they will love pleasure. Even though they will make a show of being religious, their religion won't be real. Don't have anything to do with such people. Some men fool whole families, just to get power over those women who are slaves of sin and are controlled by all sorts of desires. These women always want to learn something new, but they never can discover the truth.

2 TIMOTHY 3:1–7

Listen to your heart and fill in

Give a mark from 0–3 if the following things are characteristic of people in Britain today. 0 for not at all characteristic, 3 for totally characteristic.

Are people today…

… self-centred? ____
… greedy for money? ____
… boastful? ____
… proud? ____
… rude? ____
… disobedient to their parents? ____
… ungrateful? ____

… godless? ____
… heartless? ____
… hateful? ____
… lacking self-control? ____
… reckless (in a negative way)? ____
… indifferent to good? ____
… stuck-up? ____

TOTAL (max. 42 points) ______

We mustn't be the kind of people who make a show of being religious but whose religion isn't real (see verse 5).

Links: 14 January, 2 June, 1 November, 20 December

5 minutes more? Philippians 4

20: Treasure hunt

Promise to obey completely and fully all that you have been told until our Lord Jesus Christ returns.

The glorious God is the only Ruler, the King of kings and Lord of lords. At the time that God has already decided, he will send Jesus Christ back again. Only God lives for ever! And he lives in light that no one can come near. No human has ever seen God or ever can see him. God will be honoured, and his power will last for ever. Amen.

Warn the rich people of this world not to be proud or to trust in wealth that is easily lost. Tell them to have faith in God, who is rich and blesses us with everything we need to enjoy life. Instruct them to do as many good deeds as they can and to help everyone. Remind the rich to be generous and share what they have. This will lay a solid foundation for the future, so that they will know what true life is like.
1 TIMOTHY 6:14–19

Hmm... just a thought...
...about riches

A hand that gives is never empty.

Links: 17 April, 18 October, 23 October, 2 November

5 minutes more? Colossians 1

19: Divine protection

Finally, let the mighty strength of the Lord make you strong. Put on all the armour that God gives, so you can defend yourself against the devil's tricks. We are not fighting against humans. We are fighting against forces and authorities and against rulers of darkness and powers in the spiritual world. So put on all the armour that God gives. Then when that evil day comes, you will be able to defend yourself. And when the battle is over, you will still be standing firm. Be ready! Let the truth be like a belt around your waist, and let God's justice protect you like armour. Your desire to tell the good news about peace should be like shoes on your feet. Let your faith be like a shield, and you will be able to stop all the flaming arrows of the evil one. Let God's saving power be like a helmet, and for a sword use God's message that comes from the Spirit. Never stop praying, especially for others. Always pray by the power of the Spirit. Stay alert and keep praying for God's people. Pray that I will be given the message to speak and that I may fearlessly explain the mystery about the good news. I was sent to do this work, and that's the reason I'm in jail. So pray that I will be brave and will speak as I should.

EPHESIANS 6:10–20

Check it out

Roman armour and our armour

Paul probably wrote the letter to the Ephesians while he was a prisoner in Rome. The soldiers that guarded him were dressed like those in the picture. It was probably looking at them that gave him the inspiration to write about the armour that we as Christians can clothe ourselves with in prayer.

Links: 13 January, 14 January, 1 June, 6 November

5 minutes more? Colossians 2

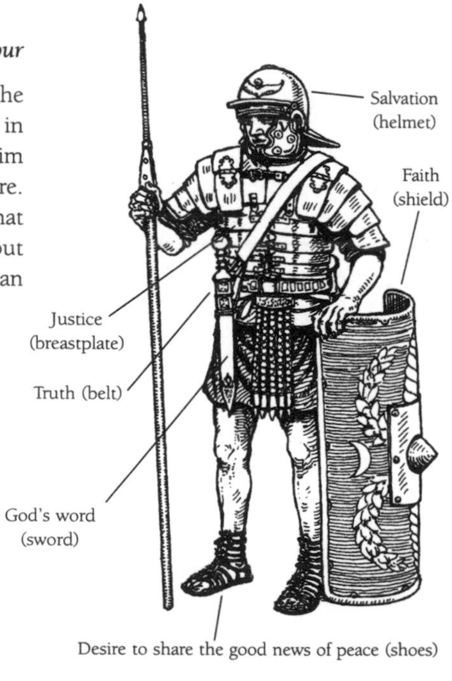

29 October

Paul's Top 30

18: Christ is God's power and wisdom

The message of the cross doesn't make any sense to lost people. But for those of us who are being saved, it is God's power at work. As God says in the Scriptures, 'I will destroy the wisdom of all who claim to be wise. I will confuse those who think they know so much.' What happened to those wise people? What happened to those experts in the Scriptures? What happened to the ones who think they have all the answers? Didn't God show that the wisdom of this world is foolish? God was wise and decided not to let the people of this world use their wisdom to learn about him. Instead, God chose to save only those who believe the foolish message we preach. Jews look for miracles, and Greeks want something that sounds wise. But we preach that Christ was nailed to a cross. Most Jews have problems with this, and most Gentiles think it is foolish. Our message is God's power and wisdom for the Jews and the Greeks that he has chosen. Even when God is foolish, he is wiser than everyone else, and even when God is weak, he is stronger than everyone else.

1 CORINTHIANS 1:18–25

Download

A verse about being wise

Some people look at Christians and think they aren't very smart—perhaps a sandwich short of a picnic, if you know what I mean.

That makes no difference.

In any case, here is a verse about someone who is smart—and that includes you, so memorize it:

'Even when God is foolish, he is wiser than everyone else, and even when God is weak, he is stronger than everyone else' (1 Corinthians 1:25).

Links: 14 April, 2 June, 24 October, 30 October

5 minutes more? Colossians 3

17: God's secret

When I talked with you or preached, I didn't try to prove anything by sounding wise. I simply let God's Spirit show his power. That way you would have faith because of God's power and not because of human wisdom. We do use wisdom when speaking to people who are mature in their faith. But it isn't the wisdom of the world or of its rulers, who will soon disappear. We speak of God's hidden and mysterious wisdom that God decided to use for our glory long before the world began. The rulers of this world didn't know anything about this wisdom. If they had known about it, they would not have nailed the glorious Lord to a cross. But it is just as the Scriptures say, 'What God has planned for people who love him is more than eyes have seen or ears have heard. It has never even entered our minds!' God's Spirit has shown you everything. His Spirit finds out everything, even what is deep in the mind of God.
1 CORINTHIANS 2:4–10

Big word
Revelation

Everything we know about God, we know because he has shown it to us. This is called revelation. Many people have a genuine experience of God by being in beautiful natural surroundings. They connect with the greatness of God by walking through a forest or across a mountain, or sailing on the ocean. They look at plants and animals and realize that there must be a God.

We can see God in creation, but there's a limit to what that can tell us about him. Only in the Bible can we find the answers to who he is, what he's like and, particularly, what he wants. Everything we know about God is found in the Bible. There we have received revelation. You can't sit in a coffee bar with your friends and imagine what God is like, you know. God's bigger than that. God is eternal. Everything we know about him, we know because he has revealed it to us.

'What God has planned for people who love him is more than eyes have seen or ears have heard. It has never even entered our minds!' (1 Corinthians 2:9). Reading the Bible is like a romp through God's secrets. That's why it is so great that you are taking time to read the Bible.

Links: 14 April, 2 June, 3 June, 24 October

5 minutes more? Colossians 4

31 October

Paul's Top 30

16: The message about Christ (1)

All who call out to the Lord will be saved. How can people have faith in the Lord and ask him to save them, if they have never heard about him? And how can they hear, unless someone tells them? And how can anyone tell them without being sent by the Lord? The Scriptures say it is a beautiful sight to see even the feet of someone coming to preach the good news. Yet not everyone has believed the message. For example, the prophet Isaiah asked, 'Lord, has anyone believed what we said?' No one can have faith without hearing the message about Christ.
ROMANS 10:13–17

Head, shoulders, knees and toes

Tips for whenever you have to speak in your small group at church or school

1. Make sure you give yourself plenty of time for preparation.
2. Think about what you want to say. You may have been given a topic, or you may need to listen to what the Lord lays on your heart.
3. Boil down what you want to say to one sentence. Keep this sentence in the back of your head while you are speaking (or even use it), so that people have a better chance of remembering your message.
4. Pray!
5. Use illustrations, Bible verses and stories to back up what you say. Your personal experience is the best story you can use.
6. Read Joshua 1:9.
7. Trust God and go for it!

It would be great if there was a whole bunch of us who liked to lead worship in small groups. Young people who do this sort of thing now tend to become the church leaders of tomorrow.

Links: 17 May, 8 November, 10 November, 21 December

5 minutes more? 1 Thessalonians 1

1 November

Paul's Top 30

15: The message about Christ (2)

Since childhood, you have known the Holy Scriptures that are able to make you wise enough to have faith in Christ Jesus and be saved. Everything in the Scriptures is God's Word. All of it is useful for teaching and helping people and for correcting them and showing them how to live. The Scriptures train God's servants to do all kinds of good deeds... When Christ comes as king, he will be the judge of everyone, whether they are living or dead. So with God and Christ as witnesses, I command you to preach God's message. Do it willingly, even if it isn't the popular thing to do. You must correct people and point out their sins. But also cheer them up, and when you instruct them, always be patient. The time is coming when people won't listen to good teaching. Instead, they will look for teachers who will please them by telling them only what they are itching to hear. They will turn from the truth and eagerly listen to senseless stories. But you must stay calm and be willing to suffer. You must work hard to tell the good news and to do your job well.

2 TIMOTHY 3:15–17; 4:1b–5

Check it out

'3:16'

It is probably a complete coincidence, but chapter 3 verse 16 seems to be the reference of several key Bible verses. You know John 3:16 already. But when you have a moment, get out a Bible and check out some other '3:16' verses:

Salvation:	John 3:16
Love	1 John 3:16
Repentance	2 Corinthians 3:16
Baptism	Luke 3:16 and Matthew 3:16
Strength	Ephesians 3:16
Worship	Colossians 3:16
The body	1 Corinthians 3:16

2 Timothy 3:16 says something very important about the Bible—that it is God's word. Some versions use the expression 'God-breathed', which means that the words of the Bible were written by men inspired by the Holy Spirit—that God has blown his Spirit into the words.

Links: 14 January, 30 May, 2 June, 20 December

5 minutes more? 1 Thessalonians 2

14: Paul's advice to Timothy

Work hard to be truly religious. As the saying goes, 'Exercise is good for your body, but religion helps you in every way. It promises life now and for ever.' These words are worthwhile and should not be forgotten. We have put our hope in the living God, who is the Saviour of everyone, but especially of those who have faith. That's why we work and struggle so hard... Don't let anyone make fun of you, just because you are young. Set an example for other followers by what you say and do, as well as by your love, faith, and purity. Until I arrive, be sure to keep on reading the Scriptures in worship, and don't stop preaching and teaching. Use the gift you were given when the prophets spoke and the group of church leaders blessed you by placing their hands on you. Remember these things and think about them, so everyone can see how well you are doing.
1 TIMOTHY 4:7b–10, 12–15

Bible personality
Timothy

Today's reading is from a personal letter from Paul to Timothy. Timothy was one of Paul's closest friends. Paul calls him 'beloved and faithful son', 'co-worker', and 'brother'. He worked with Paul for almost 17 years—right up to when Paul was executed in Rome.

There are three things that are especially important to know about Timothy:

1. He was a shy person (1 Corinthians 16:10–11).
2. He was young (1 Timothy 4:12).
3. He was one of the most important tools God used to spread the gospel.

The name 'Timothy' means 'he who honours God'. If you are the sort of person who likes to give God glory, it doesn't matter if you are a little backward in coming forward, or if you feel young. Don't let anyone make fun of you because of it. God can use you, despite what you feel about yourself!

Links: 17 April, 5 June, 18 October, 27 October

5 minutes more? 1 Thessalonians 4

3 November

Paul's Top 30

13: More about the message of Christ

You have been raised to life with Christ. Now set your heart on what is in heaven, where Christ rules at God's right side. Think about what is up there, not about what is here on earth. You died, which means that your life is hidden with Christ, who sits beside God. Christ gives meaning to your life, and when he appears, you will also appear with him in glory... Each one of you is part of the body of Christ, and you were chosen to live together in peace. So let the peace that comes from Christ control your thoughts. And be grateful. Let the message about Christ completely fill your lives, while you use all your wisdom to teach and instruct each other. With thankful hearts, sing psalms, hymns, and spiritual songs to God. Whatever you say or do should be done in the name of the Lord Jesus, as you give thanks to God the Father because of him.

COLOSSIANS 3:1–4, 15–17

Refresh

The Bible lives

Let me give the Bible a plug. It really isn't like other books. It lives. Reading the Bible can be compared to going to an IMAX cinema. As everyone knows, an IMAX cinema isn't like other cinemas—it's in 3D. The pictures 'grow' out of the screen, and it's as though the film is taking place right in the room, right before your very eyes.

Often when I read the Bible nothing happens. But now and then—on rare occasions—it's like being in an IMAX cinema. Pow! Suddenly it's like Jesus is right there in the room and is talking directly to me.

The word becomes alive, and suddenly I know that this isn't an ordinary book—this is God's book. This isn't a general book from God to humans. It's a personal letter from God to me.

It doesn't happen that often. But it does happen.

Links: 18 January, 28 May, 5 November, 14 December

5 minutes more? 1 Thessalonians 5

12: About Jesus, Name above all names

Christ encourages you, and his love comforts you. God's Spirit unites you, and you are concerned for others. Now make me completely happy! Live in harmony by showing love for each other. Be united in what you think, as if you were only one person. Don't be jealous or proud, but be humble and consider others more important than yourselves. Care about them as much as you care about yourselves and think the same way that Christ Jesus thought:

Christ was truly God. But he did not try to remain equal with God. Instead he gave up everything and became a slave, when he became like one of us. Christ was humble. He obeyed God and even died on a cross. Then God gave Christ the highest place and honoured his name above all others. So at the name of Jesus everyone will bow down, those in heaven, on earth, and under the earth. And to the glory of God the Father everyone will openly agree, 'Jesus Christ is Lord!'
PHILIPPIANS 2:1–11

Listen to your heart and fill in

What do you imagine Jesus was like?

How do you see Jesus? What was he like as a person? Write down some of the good qualities you think Jesus had.

1. ______________________________

2. ______________________________

3. ______________________________

Today's word of encouragement is 'Think the same way that Christ Jesus thought' (Philippians 2:5).

Links: 20 January, 24 May, 30 May, 20 October

5 minutes more? 2 Thessalonians 1

11: Jesus, King with a capital 'K'

Christ is exactly like God, who cannot be seen. He is the firstborn Son, superior to all creation... All things were created by God's Son, and everything was made for him. God's Son was before all else, and by him everything is held together. He is the head of his body, which is the church. He is the very beginning, the first to be raised from death, so that he would be above all others. God himself was pleased to live fully in his Son. And God was pleased for him to make peace by sacrificing his blood on the cross, so that all beings in heaven and on earth would be brought back to God. You used to be far from God. Your thoughts made you his enemies, and you did evil things. But his Son became a human and died. So God made peace* with you, and now he lets you stand in his presence as people who are holy and faultless and innocent. But you must stay deeply rooted and firm in your faith.
COLOSSIANS 1:15–23a

* or 'reconciled'

Big word
Reconciliation

When Christians talk about reconciliation, they are talking first and foremost about Jesus' death on the cross. But reconciliation isn't just a Christian word. Here are several other ways it can be used:

- If two nations have been in a bitter conflict, they need reconciliation.
- If two neighbours have argued about various things for many years, they need to be reconciled with each other—they need reconciliation.
- If two family members have fallen out with each other and aren't talking to each other any more, they need to be reconciled with each other.
- If two classmates... and so on and so on...

It was impossible for God to have anything to do with humanity because of our sin—but Jesus reconciled humanity with God by his death on the cross.

Paul says that those of us who have accepted this reconciliation with God have the best reason of all to be reconciled with others. Is there anyone you need to reconcile yourself with? Give them a call, write a letter, send an e-mail or a text message, have a chat. Don't let the opportunity pass you by.

Links: 16 January, 21 January, 28 May, 3 November

5 minutes more? 2 Thessalonians 2

6 November

Paul's Top 30

10: Being in Christ

Christ sacrificed his life's blood to set us free, which means that our sins are now forgiven. Christ did this because God was so kind to us. God has great wisdom and understanding, and by what Christ has done, God has shown us his own mysterious ways. Then when the time is right, God will do all that he has planned, and Christ will bring together everything in heaven and on earth. God always does what he plans, and that's why he appointed Christ to choose us. He did this so that we Jews would bring honour to him and be the first ones to have hope because of him. Christ also brought you the truth, which is the good news about how you can be saved. You put your faith in Christ and were given the promised Holy Spirit to show that you belong to God. The Spirit also makes us sure that we will be given what God has stored up for his people. Then we will be set free, and God will be honoured and praised.

EPHESIANS 1:7–14

Did you know that...

...Paul was in prison—a horrible prison—when he wrote this? (However, he can hardly contain himself!)

There is quite a lot of convincing evidence that Paul wrote this letter to the Ephesians while he was imprisoned in Rome between AD60 and 62. Yet he can hardly contain himself as he dictates these words, because almost the whole of Ephesians 1 is one long expression of worship of God. In the original Greek text it is a single long sentence (in English these sentences are divided up so that they are easier to read but in Greek there is no full stop and hardly a comma). It seems as if Paul is so full of enthusiasm that he can't stop praising God.

Not because he's in prison.
But because he is in Christ.

Count how many times you can see the phrases 'in him' or 'in Christ' in today's reading.

Links: 13 January, 15 January, 21 January, 1 June

5 minutes more? 2 Thessalonians 3

9: Jesus' body and blood

When we drink from the cup that we ask God to bless, isn't that sharing in the blood of Christ? When we eat the bread that we break, isn't that sharing in the body of Christ? By sharing in the same loaf of bread, we become one body, even though there are many of us... I have already told you what the Lord Jesus did on the night he was betrayed. And it came from the Lord himself.

He took some bread in his hands. Then after he had given thanks, he broke it and said, 'This is my body, which is given for you. Eat this and remember me.' After the meal, Jesus took a cup of wine in his hands and said, 'This is my blood, and with it God makes his new agreement with you. Drink this and remember me.'

The Lord meant that when you eat this bread and drink from this cup, you tell about his death until he comes.
1 CORINTHIANS 10:16–17; 11:23–26

Hmm... just a thought

Once, a Catholic nun explained something to me about Communion

What is so great, she said, is that when you go forward and receive Communion, you don't know who might come along and kneel next to you. It could be your best friend, it could be your worst enemy. But whoever it is means nothing, because when you receive the Lord's body and blood, you are one in Christ...

... said the nun.

Links: 16 May, 9 November, 14 November, 15 November

5 minutes more? 1 Timothy 1

8 November

Paul's Top 30

8: One body in Christ (1)

A body is made up of many parts, and each of them has its own use. That's how it is with us. There are many of us, but we are each part of the body of Christ, as well as part of one another. God has also given us different gifts to use. If we can prophesy, we should do it according to the amount of faith we have. If we can serve others, we should serve. If we can teach, we should teach. If we can encourage others, we should encourage them. If we can give, we should be generous. If we are leaders, we should do our best. If we are good to others, we should do it cheerfully.

ROMANS 12:4–8

Big word

Body

Paul says on several occasions that we are one body in Christ.

Ahhh—I really think that's a great expression. It says three things that are important for Christians:

1. That we are all one.
2. That we are all different.
3. That we are mutually dependent on one another—we need each other.

We are all different, but even so, we have a great deal in common. We can all do different things, but we are working towards the same goal. We all look different (thankfully), but together we make up one body.

We will look some more at the body of Christ over the next four days.

Links: 18 April, 9 November, 10 November, 11 November

5 minutes more: 1 Timothy 2

9 November

Paul's Top 30

7: One body in Christ (2)

The body of Christ has many different parts, just as any other body does... Our bodies don't have just one part. They have many parts. Suppose a foot says, 'I'm not a hand, and so I'm not part of the body.' Wouldn't the foot still belong to the body? Or suppose an ear says, 'I'm not an eye, and so I'm not part of the body.' Wouldn't the ear still belong to the body? ... A body isn't really a body, unless there is more than one part... That's why the eyes cannot say they don't need the hands. That's also why the head cannot say it doesn't need the feet. In fact, we cannot get along without the parts of the body that seem to be the weakest... If one part of our body hurts, we hurt all over. If one part of our body is honoured, the whole body will be happy. Together you are the body of Christ. Each one of you is part of his body.

1 CORINTHIANS 12:12, 14–16, 19, 21–22, 26–27

Weird and wonderful

Where is Christ's body now?

Jesus was born and lived a quiet life for thirty years. But then things took off.

He preached, helped, chatted, and healed. He came down on those who thought they were better than others. He encouraged those who had messed things up. He called people to repent and follow him. He promised people eternal life.

They killed him when he was 33 years old. They buried the body. But three days later it was gone. And forty days after that, it disappeared into heaven before the disciples' very eyes.

But where is his body now? On earth, of course!

The Bible isn't kidding when it says that we are Christ's body and each one of us is a different part of it. What is our job? The same as Jesus' body has always had: to preach, help, chat, heal. To come down on those who think they are better than others. To encourage those who have messed things up. To call people to repent and follow Jesus. To promise people eternal life.

Links: 25 May, 4 October, 14 November, 15 November

5 minutes more? 1 Timothy 3

6: One body in Christ (3)

Be sincere in your love for others. Hate everything that is evil and hold tight to everything that is good. Love each other as brothers and sisters and honour others more than you do yourself. Never give up. Eagerly follow the Holy Spirit and serve the Lord. Let your hope make you glad. Be patient in time of trouble and never stop praying. Take care of God's needy people and welcome strangers into your home. Ask God to bless everyone who ill-treats you. Ask him to bless them and not to curse them. When others are happy, be happy with them, and when they are sad, be sad. Be friendly with everyone. Don't be proud and feel that you are cleverer than others. Make friends with ordinary people. Don't ill-treat someone who has ill-treated you. But try to earn the respect of others... The Scriptures also say, 'If your enemies are hungry, give them something to eat. And if they are thirsty, give them something to drink. This will be the same as piling burning coals on their heads.'

ROMANS 12:9–17, 20–21

Did you know that...

... the Bible encourages us to heap burning coals on people's heads?!

Jesus turns a lot of things upside down. He says that instead of hating our enemies, we should love them. Instead of cursing those who curse us, we should bless them.

Heaping burning coals on someone's head was an ancient form of punishment. Instead of going to jail, you could have red-hot coals put on your head. And that's where today's reading comes into the picture. Paul's point is that if we do good to someone who's not actually expecting it, someone who doesn't deserve it, it's as if we punish them by giving them a bad conscience. They were expecting something bad, but instead got something good. Their conscience starts gnawing at them. And Paul says that that's punishment enough.

Instead of saying 'heap burning coals on someone's head', perhaps we ought to use the expression 'up-end a barbecue on someone's head'—it's approximately the same effect!

You probably know someone who has done bad things to you. Don't pay back like for like. It's better to tip the metaphorical barbecue up over their heads by doing something really nice for them!

Links: 18 April, 24 May, 9 November, 11 November

5 minutes more? 1 Timothy 4

11 November

Paul's Top 30

5: One body in Christ (4)

If our faith is strong, we should be patient with the Lord's followers whose faith is weak. We should try to please them instead of ourselves. We should think of their good and try to help them by doing what pleases them. Even Christ did not try to please himself. But as the Scriptures say, 'The people who insulted you also insulted me.' And the Scriptures were written to teach and encourage us by giving us hope. God is the one who makes us patient and cheerful. I pray that he will help you live at peace with each other, as you follow Christ. Then all of you together will praise God, the Father of our Lord Jesus Christ. Honour God by accepting each other, as Christ has accepted you.

ROMANS 15:1–7

Refresh

A challenge

I want to ask you if some time or other you've entertained the thought that maybe you are a better Christian than other people—perhaps more spiritual, more enthusiastic, more surrendered to God. If so, then take some time to read today's text carefully.

It's great to be spiritual, enthusiastic and surrendered—but when positive things are used against other people, they become negative.

Links: 24 May, 25 May, 27 May, 9 October

5 minutes more? 1 Timothy 5

12 November

Paul's Top 30

4: Love builds up

Christ chose some of us to be apostles, prophets, missionaries, pastors, and teachers, so that his people would learn to serve and his body would grow strong. This will continue until we are united by our faith and by our understanding of the Son of God. Then we will be mature, just as Christ is, and we will be completely like him. We must stop acting like children. We must not let deceitful people trick us by their false teachings, which are like winds that toss us around from place to place. Love should always make us tell the truth. Then we will grow in every way and be more like Christ, the head of the body. Christ holds it together and makes all its parts work perfectly, as it grows and becomes strong because of love.

EPHESIANS 4:11–16

Listen to your heart and fill in

What do you want to work on?

In today's reading Paul calls some people immature and others mature, and he encourages us to try to grow.

What do you think Paul thinks being a mature Christian is?

1. ______________________________

2. ______________________________

3. ______________________________

4. ______________________________

Links: 19 January, 21 April, 1 June, 13 December

5 minutes more? 1 Timothy 6

13 November

Paul's Top 30

3: Nothing can separate us from the love of God

What can we say about all this? If God is on our side, can anyone be against us? God did not keep back his own Son, but he gave him for us. If God did this, won't he freely give us everything else? If God says his chosen ones are acceptable to him, can anyone bring charges against them? Or can anyone condemn them? No indeed! Christ died and was raised to life, and now he is at God's right side, speaking to him for us. Can anything separate us from the love of Christ? Can trouble, suffering, and hard times, or hunger and nakedness, or danger and death? … I am sure that nothing can separate us from God's love—not life or death, not angels or spirits, not the present or the future, and not powers above or powers below. Nothing in all creation can separate us from God's love for us in Christ Jesus our Lord!

ROMANS 8:31–35, 38–39

Download

God's love

This passage must be, as far as I know, the strongest thing that is said about God's love. If you've got a good memory, you ought to memorize verses 38 and 39:

'I am sure that nothing can separate us from God's love—not life or death, not angels or spirits, not the present or the future, and not powers above or powers below. Nothing in all creation can separate us from God's love for us in Christ Jesus our Lord!'

If you've got a bad memory, or not much time, memorize an edited version: 'I am sure that nothing can separate us from God's love.'

Links: 17 January, 31 October, 8 November, 21 December

5 minutes more? 2 Timothy 1

14 November

Paul's Top 30

2: What if I haven't got love?

What if I could speak all languages of humans and of angels? If I did not love others, I would be nothing more than a noisy gong or a clanging cymbal. What if I could prophesy and understand all secrets and all knowledge? And what if I had faith that moved mountains? I would be nothing, unless I loved others. What if I gave away all that I owned and let myself be burnt alive? I would gain nothing, unless I loved others. Love is kind and patient, never jealous, boastful, proud, or rude. Love isn't selfish or quick-tempered. It doesn't keep a record of wrongs that others do. Love rejoices in the truth, but not in evil. Love is always supportive, loyal, hopeful, and trusting.

1 CORINTHIANS 13:1–7

Weird and wonderful

Paul in love?

These lines from 1 Corinthians have been read at every wedding I've ever been to. The fact is that they're probably read at every wedding in the world—in Christian countries, at any rate. Many people think this passage contains some of the wisest and most beautiful lines that have ever been written about love.

Just think—the person who wrote these words was probably never married!

Just think—he probably never once even had a love affair with a woman!

When he wrote this, Paul was 50 and may never have been kissed!

But no one could write such beautiful things about love without having experienced it for himself.

Paul must have felt deeply, deeply loved. Even without loving a woman, I believe he experienced the greatest love a person can experience.

From whom, you may ask?

Hint: John 3:16.

Links: 12 January, 25 May, 4 October, 15 November

5 minutes more? 2 Timothy 2

15 November

Paul's Top 30

1: Love that never fails!

Love never fails! Everyone who prophesies will stop, and unknown languages will no longer be spoken. All that we know will be forgotten. We don't know everything, and our prophecies are not complete. But what is perfect will some day appear, and what isn't perfect will then disappear. When we were children, we thought and reasoned as children do. But when we grew up, we stopped our childish ways. Now all we can see of God is like a cloudy picture in a mirror. Later we will see him face to face. We don't know everything, but then we will, just as God completely understands us. For now there are faith, hope, and love. But of these three, the greatest is love.

1 CORINTHIANS 13:8–13

Good news...

...for all those who doubt love

You fall in love. You fall head over heels in love. And if everything works out, and your feelings are returned and so on and so forth... after a lot of ifs and buts, you end up together. Yes! You're actually going out with someone! But then things begin to cool off. Your first flush of emotion is over, and then one day, one or both of you decide it's probably best to split up and call things off.

We begin to get used to love that ends. About half of the people who get married end up leaving each other. The percentage is even higher for those who live together, and higher still for people who are just going out with someone.

The good news for today is that there is a love that never ends. God has loved us with an everlasting love (see Jeremiah 31:3).

And I am so simple-minded that I believe it is easier to love another person your whole life long if you've experienced God's love first—that's an everlasting love—you know, it never ends!

Links: 12 January, 25 May, 1 April, 4 October

5 minutes more? 2 Timothy 3

16 November

Other letters in the New Testament

The letter to the Hebrews: Jesus, greater than the angels

He had become much greater than the angels, and the name he was given is far greater than any of theirs.

God has never said to any of the angels, 'You are my Son, because today I have become your Father!' Neither has God said to any of them, 'I will be his Father, and he will be my Son!'

When God brings his firstborn Son into the world, he commands all his angels to worship him... But God says about his Son, 'You are God, and you will rule as King for ever! Your royal power brings about justice. You loved justice and hated evil, and so I, your God, have chosen you. I appointed you and made you happier than any of your friends.'

The Scriptures also say, 'In the beginning, Lord, you were the one who laid the foundation of the earth and created the heavens. They will all disappear and wear out like clothes, but you will last for ever.'

HEBREWS 1:4–6, 8–11

Good news

You and Christ

The Jesus who walked the earth 2000 years ago is the same Jesus who created the world.

And the Jesus who created the world is the same Jesus you can be with as much as you like in heaven.

Have you ever wondered what Jesus is really, really, really like?

Here is the answer. Memorize it if you don't know it already.

'Jesus Christ never changes. He is the same yesterday, today, and for ever' (Hebrews 13:8).

Links: 4 May, 6 June, 15 July, 17 November

5 minutes more? Titus 1

17 November

Other letters in the New Testament

The letter to the Hebrews: Jesus is greater than Moses

My friends, God has chosen you to be his holy people. So think about Jesus, the one we call our apostle and high priest! Jesus was faithful to God, who appointed him, just as Moses was faithful in serving all God's people. But Jesus deserves more honour than Moses, just as the builder of a house deserves more honour than the house. Of course, every house is built by someone, and God is really the one who built everything. Moses was a faithful servant and told God's people what would be said in the future. But Christ is the Son in charge of God's people. And we are those people, if we keep on being brave and don't lose hope.

HEBREWS 3:1–6

Check it out

Moses and Jesus

The reason why the letter to the Hebrews is called the letter to the Hebrews is because it is a letter that was written to Hebrews. Logical, isn't it? And for clarity's sake, a Hebrew is the same as a Jew. So we could call this letter 'the letter to the Jewish Christians'.

The Old Testament is referred to throughout the whole letter, including mention of the temple, sacrifices, priests and (as in today's reading) Moses. Moses was considered to be the greatest prophet in the history of the Hebrews / Jews.

'There has never again been a prophet in Israel like Moses. The Lord spoke face to face with him' (Deuteronomy 34:10).

Can you see how incredibly much more honour Jesus deserves to get? How great he really is? Whoever you compare him with, Jesus is greater!

Links: 4 May, 6 June, 15 July, 18 November

5 minutes more? Titus 2

18 November

Other letters in the New Testament

The letter to the Hebrews: Jesus is greater than the high priests

We have a great high priest, who has gone into heaven, and he is Jesus the Son of God. That is why we must hold on to what we have said about him. Jesus understands every weakness of ours, because he was tempted in every way that we are. But he did not sin!

HEBREWS 4:14–15

...and he is better than any other high priest. Jesus doesn't need to offer sacrifices each day for his own sins and then for the sins of the people. He offered a sacrifice once for all, when he gave himself.

HEBREWS 7:27

What I mean is that we have a great high priest who sits at the right side of God's great throne in heaven. He also serves as the priest in the most holy place inside the real tent there in heaven. This tent of worship was set up by the Lord, not by humans.

HEBREWS 8:1–2

Big word

Sacrifice

As we saw yesterday, Hebrews is written to people who are well acquainted with the Old Testament. It talks about priests, the holy place, the tent of meeting—and sacrifices—as if they were the most natural things in the world.

New readers might be relieved to know that the sacrifice was not human. It was an animal—usually a lamb—that was ritually slaughtered, cut up and burnt on an altar, with the intention that God would then forgive the people's sins. The disadvantage with these sorts of sacrifice was that they had a short sell-by date; they only worked for some sins, and only for a short time.

Jesus is greater than the high priests because, unlike them, he doesn't need to make a sacrifice every day for himself and the people. The sacrifice Jesus made was a once-and-for-all offering of himself.

The sell-by date on Jesus' sacrifice? Unlimited, eternal.

Links: 1 June, 19 July, 26 November, 20 December

5 minutes more? Titus 3

19 November

Other letters in the New Testament

The letter of James

Obey God's message! Don't fool yourselves by just listening to it. If you hear the message and don't obey it, you are like people who stare at themselves in a mirror and forget what they look like as soon as they leave. But you must never stop looking at the perfect law that sets you free. God will bless you in everything you do, if you listen and obey, and don't just hear and forget.
JAMES 1:22–25

If you know someone who doesn't have any clothes or food, you shouldn't just say, 'I hope all goes well for you. I hope you will be warm and have plenty to eat.' What good is it to say this, unless you do something to help? Faith that doesn't lead to us to do good deeds is all alone and dead! ... Does some stupid person want proof that faith without deeds is useless?
JAMES 2:15–17, 20

Download...
...about freedom!

But you must ...

But you must never stop looking...

But you must never stop looking at the perfect law...

But you must never stop looking at the perfect law that sets you free...

But you must never stop looking at the perfect law that sets you free. God will bless you in everything you do...

But you must never stop looking at the perfect law that sets you free. God will bless you in everything you do, if you listen and obey...

'But you must never stop looking at the perfect law that sets you free. God will bless you in everything you do, if you listen and obey, and don't just hear and forget' (James 1:25).

Links: 20 November, 23 November, 15 December, 19 December

5 minutes more? Philemon

The letter of James: taming the tongue

By putting a bit into the mouth of a horse, we can turn the horse in different directions. It takes strong winds to move a large sailing ship, but the captain uses only a small rudder to make it go in any direction. Our tongues are small too, and yet they boast about big things. It only takes a spark to start a forest fire! The tongue is like a spark. It is an evil power that dirties the rest of the body and sets a person's entire life on fire with flames that come from hell itself. All kinds of animals, birds, reptiles, and sea creatures can be tamed and have been tamed. But our tongues get out of control. They are restless and evil, and always spreading deadly poison. My dear friends, with our tongues we speak both praises and curses. We praise our Lord and Father, and we curse people who were created to be like God, and this isn't right. Can clean water and dirty water both flow from the same spring?

JAMES 3:3–11

Di:SaipL

Keep your mouth under control!

You can tell pretty quickly whether or not a person wants to honour Jesus with their life. For example, it's not terribly impressive when people who call themselves Christians sprinkle their speech with all sorts of unpleasant words.

There are two ways to live—God's way and the world's way. What comes out of our mouth will show which way we have chosen.

- Do we boast about what others have done rather than ourselves?
- Do we let ourselves get drawn into gossip about others?
- Do we give God the glory he deserves?
- Are we quick to ask for forgiveness when something goes wrong?
- Are we quick to offer help?

I can still remember some things people said to me many, many years ago. The words we say, especially negative words, burn into a person's memory.

Try to let good things come out of your mouth when you speak.

Links: 5 June, 23 November, 26 November, 21 December

5 minutes more? Hebrews 1

21 November

Other letters in the New Testament

Peter's first letter: trials

Praise God, the Father of our Lord Jesus Christ. God is so good, and by raising Jesus from death, he has given us new life and a hope that lives on. God has something stored up for you in heaven, where it will never decay or be ruined or disappear. You have faith in God, whose power will protect you until the last day. Then he will save you, just as he has always planned to do. On that day you will be glad, even if you have to go through many hard trials for a while. Your faith will be like gold that has been tested in a fire. And these trials will prove that your faith is worth much more than gold that can be destroyed. They will show that you will be given praise and honour and glory when Jesus Christ returns.
1 PETER 1:3–7

Di:SaipL
Bullying

If you are bullied at school because you are a Christian, you ought to know that you have reason to rejoice (and you should pray for the bullies—Matthew 5:11–12).

- In the light of eternity, your difficulties are only a short phase that you must go through. And remember, Jesus is right there with you in your troubles.
- Your faith will most probably grow during this difficult time.
- Your tested faith will bring you glory and honour when Jesus returns.

If you think it is difficult to be a Christian at school, then it is more important than ever that you belong to a Christian fellowship. There may be a small fellowship of students in your school or college, or a Christian teacher. It helps to talk to other Christians about what you are going through.

You should also remember that most English schools have a 'no bullying' policy. If you are being bullied, for whatever reason, you should speak to your personal tutor or mentor, even your parents! It is against the law in Britain to bully someone because of their faith—whatever their faith.

Links: 20 February, 17 July, 13 December, 14 December

5 minutes more? Hebrews 3

Peter's second letter: the reliability of the Bible

When we told you about the power and the return of our Lord Jesus Christ, we were not telling clever stories that someone had made up. But with our own eyes we saw his true greatness. God, our great and wonderful Father, truly honoured him by saying, 'This is my own dear Son, and I am pleased with him.' We were there with Jesus on the holy mountain and heard this voice speak from heaven. All this makes us even more certain that what the prophets said is true. So you should pay close attention to their message, as you would to a lamp shining in some dark place. You must keep on paying attention until daylight comes and the morning star rises in your hearts. But you need to realize that no one alone can understand any of the prophecies in the Scriptures. The prophets did not think these things up on their own, but they were guided by the Spirit of God.
2 PETER 1:16–21

Check it out

First-hand information

The most important reason why we can believe the Bible—according to the Bible itself—is that the people who wrote it were, more often than not, there when the things happened. They themselves experienced what they later wrote about. They claimed to have first-hand information about things.

- 'We were not telling clever stories that someone had made up...'
- 'With our own eyes we saw his true greatness...'
- 'We were there with Jesus on the holy mountain...'
- 'We heard this voice speak from heaven.'

The story that Peter is referring to in today's reading can be found in Mark 9:2–13. Check it out, and compare today's reading with Mark's original account.

Links: 27 May, 7 June, 31 October, 1 November

5 minutes more? Hebrews 4

John's first letter: live in the light

The Word that gives life was from the beginning, and this is the one our message is about. Our ears have heard, our own eyes have seen, and our hands touched this Word... We are writing to tell you these things, because this makes us truly happy. Jesus told us that God is light and doesn't have any darkness in him. Now we are telling you. If we say that we share in life with God and keep on living in the dark, we are lying and are not living by the truth. But if we live in the light, as God does, we share in life with each other. And the blood of his Son Jesus washes all our sins away. If we say that we have not sinned, we are fooling ourselves, and the truth isn't in our hearts. But if we confess our sins to God, he can always be trusted to forgive us and take our sins away.

1 JOHN 1:1, 4–9

Don't be fooled, my dear friends. Every good and perfect gift comes down from the Father who created all the lights in the heavens. He is always the same and never makes dark shadows by changing.

JAMES 1:16–17

Your word is a lamp that gives light wherever I walk.

PSALM 119:105

Hmm... just a thought...

...about light

I believe in Christianity, as I believe that the sun has risen; not only because I see it, but because by it I see everything else.

C.S. LEWIS

Links: 13 April, 30 June, 24 November, 6 December

5 minutes more? Hebrews 5

24 November

Other letters in the New Testament

John's first letter: Love unites us with God and each other

We know what love is because Jesus gave his life for us... Children, you show love for others by truly helping them, and not merely by talking about it. When we love others, we know that we belong to the truth, and we feel at ease in the presence of God. But even if we don't feel at ease, God is greater than our feelings, and he knows everything. Dear friends, if we feel at ease in the presence of God, we will have the courage to come near him. He will give us whatever we ask, because we obey him and do what pleases him. God wants us to have faith in his Son Jesus Christ and to love each other. This is also what Jesus taught us to do. If we obey God's commandments, we will stay united in our hearts with him, and he will stay united with us. The Spirit that he has given us is proof that we are one with him.

1 JOHN 3:16a, 18–24

Download...

...about not feeling condemned

When we ask God to forgive us for something we have thought, said or done—he does. It's like he drops it in a deep ocean and puts a 'No Fishing' sign in the water. But we tend to dwell on things God has forgiven and forgotten—it makes our hearts uneasy and we feel condemned.

If you ever feel like that, this verse is a good one for you to remember: 'But even if we don't feel at ease, God is greater than our feelings, and he knows everything' (1 John 3:20).

Remember: when God forgives, he forgets. Ask him to help you forgive yourself! He knows how you feel—he knows everything—and he wants you to come near to him.

Links: 21 May, 22 May, 23 November, 25 November

5 minutes more? Hebrews 6

25 November

Other letters in the New Testament

God's commandments are not hard to follow

We show our love for God by obeying his commandments, and they are not hard to follow... If we have faith in God's Son, we have believed what God has said. But if we don't believe what God has said about his Son, it is the same as calling God a liar. God has also said that he gave us eternal life and that this life comes to us from his Son. And so, if we have God's Son, we have this life. But if we don't have the Son, we don't have this life. All of you have faith in the Son of God, and I have written to let you know that you have eternal life.

1 JOHN 5:3, 10–13

Love means that we do what God tells us. And from the beginning, he told you to love him.

2 JOHN 1:6

Good news

God's no.1 commandment: believe in his Son!

In the Old Testament, the only way for people to get back into relationship with God was through keeping his commandments. But when no one managed to meet these demands, God decided to make a complete change in the way people could find their way back to him.

Two chapters earlier, in 1 John 3:23, we got to find out what it now means to keep God's commandments: 'God wants us to have faith in his Son Jesus Christ and to love each other.' God's new commandment is first and foremost that we have faith in Jesus.

After the big shake-up in the way we can return to God, everybody can make it back to him if they put their faith in Jesus. And we can *know* we've made it, too. Notice the word 'know' in the last sentence of these verses from today's reading:

'And so, if we have God's Son, we have this life. But if we don't have the Son, we don't have this life. All of you have faith in the Son of God, and I have written to let you know that you have eternal life' (1 John 5:12–13).

Links: 13 April, 30 June, 23 November, 6 December

5 minutes more? Hebrews 7

Care for one another

We should keep on encouraging each other to be thoughtful and to do helpful things. Some people have got out of the habit of meeting for worship, but we must not do that. We should keep on encouraging each other, especially since you know that the day of the Lord's coming is getting closer.
HEBREWS 10:24–25

Keep being concerned about each another as the Lord's followers should. Be sure to welcome strangers into your home. By doing this, some people have welcomed angels as guests, without even knowing it.
HEBREWS 13:1–2

If you are having trouble, you should pray. And if you are feeling good, you should sing praises. If you are sick, ask the church leaders to come and pray for you. Ask them to put olive oil on you in the name of the Lord.
JAMES 5:13–14

Hmm... just a thought...

...about the church

If you don't have the church as your mother, you can't have God as your Father.
AUGUSTINE (AD400)

Links: 25 January, 14 April, 15 September, 27 November

5 minutes more? Hebrews 10

27 November

Other letters in the New Testament

Keeping eye contact

Such a large crowd of witnesses is all around us! So we must get rid of everything that slows us down, especially the sin that just won't let go. And we must be determined to run the race that is ahead of us. We must keep our eyes on Jesus, who leads us and makes our faith complete. He endured the shame of being nailed to a cross, because he knew that later on he would be glad he did. Now he is seated at the right side of God's throne! So keep your mind on Jesus, who put up with many insults from sinners. Then you won't get discouraged and give up.
HEBREWS 12:1–3

Only God can keep you from falling and make you pure and joyful in his glorious presence. Before time began and now and for evermore, God is worthy of glory, honour, power, and authority. Amen.
JUDE 1:24b–25

Weird and wonderful

Mary and Joseph had a thing about 'J'

Have you noticed how in some families all the children have names that begin with the same letter? So sweet! Mary and Joseph were just like that—well, nearly!

1. The oldest son was called Jesus. That is what the angel had commanded, so they had no choice.
2. The second was called James. He became the church's first bishop, and wrote the letter of 'James'.
3. The third was called Joses. We haven't a clue what he did.
4. The fourth was called Judas. (No, not that Judas. You're thinking about Judas Iscariot.) This Judas was the Jude who wrote the second set of verses in today's readings.
5. The youngest son broke the system—he was called Simon (Mark 6:3).

Jesus also had two or three sisters. We don't know what they were called. But if I had to guess, I'd say Judith, Jemima and Joanna!

PS: Don't let all this chat about names beginning with 'J' make you forget the fantastic verses in Hebrews 12:1–3 that you read earlier. The 'J' we need to concentrate on is *Jesus*!

Links: 14 April, 17 April, 18 August, 16 November

5 minutes more? Hebrews 11

A story about a farmer (1)

When a large crowd from several towns had gathered around Jesus, he told them this story:

A farmer went out to scatter seed in a field. While the farmer was doing it, some of the seeds fell along the road and were stepped on or eaten by birds. Other seeds fell on rocky ground and started growing. But the plants did not have enough water and soon dried up. Some other seeds fell where thorn bushes grew up and choked the plants. The rest of the seeds fell on good ground where they grew and produced a hundred times as many seeds.

When Jesus had finished speaking, he said, 'If you have ears, pay attention!'

LUKE 8:4–8

Refresh

POP

We Christians should try to be well liked by everybody. That's what the Bible says (1 Corinthians 10:31–33). We should try to please others instead of ourselves, it says.

But we should nevertheless prepare ourselves for resistance to the message about Christ. It will arouse opposition.

God's word is good, but when it is scattered around like seeds, people will receive it very differently. Some will welcome it. Others can't stand it. You've probably already noticed that—if you've tried to tell someone something of what Jesus means to you.

You'd better wise up to the fact that if your aim is to be popular, there are quicker and surer ways of getting there than by spreading the word of God.

PS: It should be the message about Christ that arouses opposition from others, not you as a person! Unfortunately, some people find it hard to tell the difference, and will oppose you!

Links: 1 November, 2 November, 3 November, 29 November

5 minutes more? Hebrews 13

29 November

Parables Jesus told

A story about a farmer (2)

Jesus' disciples asked him what the story meant. So he answered:

I have explained the secrets about God's kingdom to you, but for others I can only use stories. These people look, but they don't see, and they hear, but they don't understand.

This is what the story means: The seed is God's message, and the seeds that fell along the road are the people who hear the message. But the devil comes and snatches the message out of their hearts, so that they will not believe and be saved. The seeds that fell on rocky ground are the people who gladly hear the message and accept it. But they don't have deep roots, and they believe only for a little while. As soon as life gets hard, they give up. The seeds that fell among the thorn bushes are also people who hear the message. But they are so eager for riches and pleasures that they never produce anything. Those seeds that fell on good ground are the people who listen to the message and keep it in good and honest hearts. They last and produce a harvest.

LUKE 8:9–15

Di:SaipL

The two in the middle

I think the two sorts of people in the middle of Jesus' explanation of the parable are right on target for people in today's world.

People who are like rocky ground:

This is like when someone hears some teaching from the Bible—and they run with it for a little while—and then it's like they never heard it. They drop it, and don't think about it any more.

People who are like seedlings choked by thorn bushes:

This is like when someone hears God's message—but their hearts are crammed full with other business—good things or bad things; worries or pleasures. They have absolutely no room for God's word in their hearts—it's too full of other stuff.

On the other hand, you can recognize a disciple, because when they hear God's word, 'they keep it in good and honest hearts. They last and produce a harvest' (Luke 8:15).

Links: 19 May, 20 May, 28 November, 30 November

5 minutes more? Hebrews 13

The kingdom of heaven

Jesus told them another story:

The kingdom of heaven is like what happens when a farmer plants a mustard seed in a field. Although it is the smallest of all seeds, it grows larger than any garden plant and becomes a tree. Birds even come and nest on its branches.

Jesus also said:

The kingdom of heaven is like what happens when a woman mixes a little yeast into three big batches of flour. Finally, all the dough rises... The kingdom of heaven is like what happens when someone finds treasure hidden in a field and buries it again. A person like that is happy and goes and sells everything in order to buy that field... The kingdom of heaven is like what happens when a shop owner is looking for fine pearls. After finding a very valuable one, the owner goes and sells everything in order to buy that pearl.

MATTHEW 13:31–33, 44–46

Listen to your heart and fill in

Heaven

The kingdom of heaven appears to be small, but it...

- grows to be mega-gigantic
- has an effect on everything it comes into contact with
- creates incredible joy
- is so valuable, people will give everything they own to get it

It's not easy to say anything about heaven, but try. Write down two things you hope you won't find in heaven...

1. ____

2. ____

...and two things you hope will be there.

1. ____

2. ____

Links: 26 December, 27 December, 28 December, 30 December

5 minutes more? James 1

1 December

Parables Jesus told

96 97 98 99...

Then Jesus told them this story:

If any of you has a hundred sheep, and one of them gets lost, what will you do? Won't you leave the ninety-nine in the field and go and look for the lost sheep until you find it? And when you find it, you will be so glad that you will put it on your shoulder and carry it home. Then you will call in your friends and neighbours and say, 'Let's celebrate! I've found my lost sheep.'

Jesus said, 'In the same way there is more happiness in heaven because of one sinner who turns to God than over ninety-nine good people who don't need to.'

Jesus told the people another story:

What will a woman do if she has ten silver coins and loses one of them? Won't she light a lamp, sweep the floor, and look carefully until she finds it? Then she will call in her friends and neighbours and say, 'Let's celebrate! I've found the coin I lost.'

Jesus said, 'In the same way God's angels are happy when even one person turns to him.'

LUKE 15:3–10

Check it out

Who Jesus was talking to...

These two parables are great stories in themselves, but they get even better when you find out the reason Jesus told them: the Pharisees, those we-think-we-are-better-than-everyone-else-in-the-world types, were criticizing Jesus for hanging out with 'the wrong kind' of people and making friends with them. The beginning of Luke 15 reads: 'Tax collectors and sinners were all crowding around to listen to Jesus. So the Pharisees and the teachers of the Law of Moses started grumbling, "This man is friendly with sinners. He even eats with them." Then Jesus told them this story...'

Do you know anyone who is in need of a group of friends to join?

Links: 29 July, 30 November, 2 December, 3 December

5 minutes more? James 2

The two sons (1)

Jesus also told them another story:

Once a man had two sons. The younger son said to his father, 'Give me my share of the property.' So the father divided his property between his two sons. Not long after that, the younger son packed up everything he owned and left for a foreign country, where he wasted all his money in wild living. He had spent everything, when a bad famine spread through that whole land. Soon he had nothing to eat. He went to work for a man in that country, and the man sent him out to take care of his pigs. He would have been glad to eat what the pigs were eating, but no one gave him a thing. Finally, he came to his senses and said, 'My father's workers have plenty to eat, and here I am, starving to death! I will go to my father and say to him, "Father, I have sinned against God in heaven and against you. I am no longer good enough to be called your son. Treat me like one of your workers."' The younger son got up and started back to his father. But when he was still a long way off, his father saw him and felt sorry for him. He ran to his son and hugged and kissed him. The son said, 'Father, I have sinned against God in heaven and against you. I am no longer good enough to be called your son.'

LUKE 15:11–21

Hmm... just a thought

Never lost to God

This story is traditionally called 'the story of the prodigal son'. For a long time I thought that meant 'the story of the lost son', but it doesn't. It's more like 'the story of the son who went away and went astray'.

No one is totally lost in God's eyes, not as long as they are still alive. You may wander away and go astray, but God knows where you are and never gives up hope that one day you will come home again.

No one is lost in God's eyes, not as long as they are still alive.

Links: 11 September, 20 October, 21 October, 3 December

5 minutes more? James 3

The two sons (2)

But his father said to the servants, 'Hurry and bring the best clothes and put them on him. Give him a ring for his finger and sandals for his feet. Get the best calf and prepare it, so we can eat and celebrate. This son of mine was dead, but has now come back to life. He was lost and has now been found.' And they began to celebrate. The elder son had been out in the field. But when he came near the house, he heard the music and dancing. So he called one of the servants over and asked, 'What's going on here?' The servant answered, 'Your brother has come home safe and sound, and your father ordered us to kill the best calf.' The elder brother got so angry that he would not even go into the house. His father came out and begged him to go in. But he said to his father, 'For years I have worked for you like a slave and have always obeyed you. But you have never even given me a little goat, so that I could give a dinner for my friends. This other son of yours wasted your money on prostitutes. And now that he has come home, you ordered the best calf to be killed for a feast.' His father replied, 'My son, you are always with me, and everything I have is yours. But we should be glad and celebrate! Your brother was dead, but he is now alive. He was lost and has now been found.'

LUKE 15:22–32

Hmm... just a thought

All that matters is grace

Grace is God's undeserved love for us, and it means that...

... there is nothing you can do to make God love you more...
... and there is nothing you can do to make God love you less.

All that matters—and I mean all—is God's grace.

Links: 22 May, 24 May, 28 May, 30 May

5 minutes more? James 5

The good Samaritan

As a man was going down from Jerusalem to Jericho, robbers attacked him and grabbed everything he had. They beat him up and ran off, leaving him half dead. A priest happened to be going down the same road. But when he saw the man, he walked by on the other side. Later a temple helper came to the same place. But when he saw the man who had been beaten up, he also went by on the other side. A man from Samaria then came travelling along that road. When he saw the man, he felt sorry for him and went over to him. He treated his wounds with olive oil and wine and bandaged them. Then he put him on his own donkey and took him to an inn, where he took care of him. The next morning he gave the innkeeper two silver coins and said, 'Please take care of the man. If you spend more than this on him, I will pay you when I return.'

Then Jesus asked, 'Which one of these three people was a real neighbour to the man who was beaten up by robbers?' The teacher answered, 'The one who showed pity.' Jesus said, 'Go and do the same!'

LUKE 10:30b–37

Big word

My neighbour

Again, one of those we-think-we-are-better-than-all-the-other-people-in-the-whole-world types, a Pharisee, tried to trick Jesus with the question, 'Who is my neighbour?'... because Jews were commanded to love God, and their neighbour.

Religious Jews looked down on people from Samaria. Sometimes they even called them 'dogs' or 'mongrels'—Samaritans were considered to be the lowest of the low, so the Pharisee would have thought it wasn't very suitable for Jesus to use a Samaritan as an example of someone who had a lot of love for their neighbour!

But anyway, back to the Pharisee's question: 'Who is my neighbour?'

Well—the person who has many 'neighbours' has a lot of love for others.

The person who hasn't many 'neighbours' hasn't got much love for others.

And if you, like the Pharisee, ever look round and wonder who your neighbour is, when you are out and about on your bike or walking down to school or something, then you've got too little love in your heart for others.

Links: 30 May, 1 June, 5 June, 7 June

5 minutes more? 1 Peter 1

God creates woman

The Lord God said, 'It isn't good for the man to live alone. I need to make a suitable partner for him.' So the Lord took some soil and made animals and birds. He brought them to the man to see what names he would give each of them. Then the man named the tame animals and the birds and the wild animals. That's how they got their names. None of these was the right kind of partner for the man. So the Lord God made him fall into a deep sleep, and he took out one of the man's ribs. Then after closing the man's side, the Lord made a woman out of the rib. The Lord God brought her to the man, and the man exclaimed, 'Here is someone like me! She is part of my body, my own flesh and bones. She came from me, a man. So I will name her Woman!' That's why a man will leave his own father and mother. He marries a woman, and the two of them become like one person.

GENESIS 2:18–24

Did you know that...

... 'to be one' means the same as sleeping together—having intercourse?

When we talk about a man and a woman becoming one, it means exactly that. A man leaves his father and mother and marries a woman, and the two of them will—yes—sleep together.

In a Christian wedding service, there is usually a reading from Matthew 19, where Jesus says, 'In the beginning the Creator made a man and a woman. That's why a man leaves his father and mother and gets married. He becomes like one person with his wife. Then they are no longer two people, but one. And no one should separate a couple that God has joined together' (Matthew 19:4b–6).

God isn't a square when it comes to sex—he invented it! The same day as he created the woman, he encouraged them to become one—to have sex with one another.

But remember—he does want us to save that passionate sexual experience for the first night of our honeymoon!

Links: 6 January, 8 January, 9 January, 10 January

5 minutes more? 1 Peter 2

6 December

Mothers, fathers and children

God is our Father

But when the time was right, God sent his Son, and a woman gave birth to him. His Son obeyed the Law, so he could set us free from the Law, and we could become God's children. Now that we are his children, God has sent the Spirit of his Son into our hearts. And his Spirit tells us that God is our Father. You are no longer slaves. You are God's children, and you will be given what he has promised.

GALATIANS 4:4–7

Think how much the Father loves us. He loves us so much that he lets us be called his children, as we truly are. But since the people of this world did not know who Christ is, they don't know who we are. My dear friends, we are already God's children, though what we will be hasn't yet been seen. But we do know that when Christ returns, we will be like him, because we will see him as he truly is.

1 JOHN 3:1–2

Big word

Abba

Verse 6 of Galatians 4 says that God's Spirit tells us that God is our Father. In older translations of the Bible, this verse says that the Spirit cries, 'Abba! Father!'

'What does that mean?' you might well ask.

First of all, I need to say that 'Abba' isn't just a Swedish pop group that stayed in the charts right through the 1970s and '80s.

'Abba' is an Aramaic word. Aramaic was the dialect that Jesus spoke. The best translation of 'Abba' is probably 'Daddy'. 'Father' sounds a little bit formal and respectful, but 'Daddy' is much more intimate. The Bible says that we can call God 'Daddy'.

Pray, like it says in 1 John 3:1, that you will come to understand how much the Father loves you—so much that he lets us be called his children. Daddy's children.

And you have the strongest Daddy in the whole world. No matter what the opposition says.

Links: 28 February, 2 March, 3 March, 8 March

5 minutes more? 1 Peter 3

7 December

Mothers, fathers and children

God cares for us like a good mother

Tell the heavens and the earth to celebrate and sing; command every mountain to join in the song. The Lord's people have suffered, but he has shown mercy and given them comfort. The people of Zion said, 'The Lord has turned away and forgotten us.' The Lord answered, 'Could a mother forget a child who nurses at her breast? Could she fail to love an infant who came from her own body? Even if a mother could forget, I will never forget you. A picture of your city is drawn on my hand. You are always in my thoughts!'

ISAIAH 49:13–16

Please listen when I pray! Have pity. Answer my prayer. My heart tells me to pray. I am eager to see your face, so don't hide from me. I am your servant, and you have helped me. Don't turn from me in anger. You alone keep me safe. Don't reject or desert me. Even if my father and mother should desert me, you will take care of me.

PSALM 27:7–10

Weird and wonderful

Engorged breasts and maternal feelings

Do you know what happens if a mother forgets her breast-fed baby? Her breasts become engorged—so full of milk that the build-up of pressure causes the milk to squirt out. There are probably few things that are as painful as engorged breasts—the only relief a mother has is to feed her child. God says that just as a breast-feeding mother can't forget her child, neither can he forget his children.

God can never forget you!

Besides all that, mothers have something called maternal feelings. Maternal feelings are the strong, special, caring feelings that a mother has for her child. They are so strong and special that men don't and can't experience anything like it. Maternal feelings mean that mother and child are bonded to one another in a totally special way.

God is bonded to you in exactly the same way.

Links: 1 March, 4 March, 5 March, 8 March

5 minutes more? 1 Peter 4

A little fatherly wisdom

My child, listen closely to my teachings and learn common sense. My advice is useful, so don't turn away. When I was still very young and my mother's favourite child, my father said to me: 'If you follow my teachings and keep them in mind, you will live. Be wise and learn good sense; remember my teachings and do what I say. If you love Wisdom and don't reject her, she will watch over you. The best thing about Wisdom is Wisdom herself; good sense is more important than anything else... Hold firmly to my teaching and never let go. It will mean life for you. Don't follow the bad example of cruel and evil people. Turn aside and keep going. Stay away from them.'

PROVERBS 4:1–7, 13–15

Refresh

Have you finished learning?

Pick up all the tips, advice, wisdom and knowledge about life that you can. Be hungry to learn more.

It could be that there is even a thing or two that you could learn from your parents...

Besides that, you have the word of God. In the Bible you'll find everything that your parents might have forgotten or never said.

Remember this: the person who has finished learning hasn't learned, but is just finished.

Links: 9 March, 12 April, 3 June, 9 December

5 minutes more? 1 Peter 5

A wise son

Respect your father and mother, and you will live a long and successful life in the land I am giving you.
DEUTERONOMY 5:16

My children, if you show good sense, I will be happy, and if you are truthful, I will really be glad. Don't be jealous of sinners, but always honour the Lord. Then you will truly have hope for the future. Listen to me, my children! Be wise and have enough sense to follow the right path. Don't be a heavy drinker or stuff yourself with food. It will make you feel drowsy, and you will end up poor with only rags to wear. Pay attention to your father, and don't neglect your mother when she grows old.
PROVERBS 23:15–22

My child, obey the teachings of your parents, and wear their teachings as you would a lovely hat or a pretty necklace.
PROVERBS 1:8–9

Listen to your heart and fill in

What do you want to be when you're older?

If you're a boy, write down three things you'll do that would give your children reason to honour you:

1. ______________________________
2. ______________________________
3. ______________________________

If you are a girl, write down three qualities you hope your husband will have that will make you look up to him:

1. ______________________________
2. ______________________________
3. ______________________________

Links: 4 July, 2 December, 8 December, 14 December

5 minutes more? 2 Peter 1

The good wife

A truly good wife is the most precious treasure a man can find! Her husband depends on her, and she never lets him down. She is good to him every day of her life... She is strong and graceful, as well as cheerful about the future. Her words are sensible, and her advice is thoughtful. She takes good care of her family and is never lazy. Her children praise her, and with great pride her husband says, 'There are many good women, but you are the best!' Charm can be deceiving, and beauty fades away, but a women who honours the Lord deserves to be praised.

A man's greatest treasure is his wife—she is a gift from the Lord.
PROVERBS 31:10–12, 25–30; 18:22

Listen to your heart and fill in

Not just for girls...!

If you are a girl, using a scale from 1 to 10, mark which qualities in today's passage you would most like to have. Do you want to...

... inspire confidence
... have a good head for money
... be good to other people
... be strong and powerful
... have a cheerful nature
... be intelligent
... be good at organization
... be a good mother
... be quick to encourage others
... love the Lord

If you are a boy, use a scale from 1–10 and mark the qualities you'd value in a wife using the list above.

Boys and girls both need to remember: 'A truly good wife is the most precious treasure a man can find!' (Proverbs 31:10).

Links: 11 December, 12 December, 13 December, 14 December

5 minutes more? 2 Peter 2

11 December

Mothers, fathers and children

Song of Songs: a tribute to love (1)

He speaks: My darling, you are lovely, so very lovely—your eyes are those of a dove.

She speaks: My love, you are handsome, truly handsome—the fresh green grass will be our wedding bed...

He speaks: My darling, you are lovely, so very lovely—as you look through your veil, your eyes are those of a dove. Your hair tosses about as gracefully as goats coming down from Gilead. Your teeth are whiter than sheep freshly washed... Your breasts are perfect; they are twin deer feeding among lilies. I will hasten to those hills sprinkled with sweet perfume and stay there till sunrise. My darling, you are lovely in every way...

She speaks: His arms are branches of gold covered with jewels; his body is ivory decorated with sapphires. His legs are columns of marble on feet of gold. He stands there majestic like Mount Lebanon and its choice cedar trees. His kisses are sweet. I desire him so much! Young women of Jerusalem, he is my lover and friend.

SONG OF SONGS 1:15–16; 4:1–2a, 5–7; 5:14–16

Weird and wonderful

Songs of Songs was almost censored!

There have always been people who think that Song of Songs shouldn't have been included in the Bible. They think it doesn't fit in. Song of Songs isn't much like the other books in the Bible: it almost never mentions God and is full of sentimental, romantic themes. People have always tried to explain away what Songs of Songs is really all about. Some people think it is an allegory, a picture, of Jesus' relationship with the church. But—hello—that's pushing it a bit! Most people are now quite happy to agree that Song of Songs is about a man and a woman who are expressing how incredibly in love they are with each other. And that's it.

Song of Songs is a man and a woman's tribute to love—a fantastic tribute. Read it and enjoy! If you really want to learn something from today's reading, here it is: make up your mind now that you are going to be the sort of person who is equally proud of and in love with their spouse!

Links: 22 April, 12 December, 13 December, 14 December

5 minutes more? 2 Peter 3

12 December

Mothers, fathers and children

Song of Songs: a tribute to love (2)

He speaks: You are beautiful, so very desirable! You are tall and slender like a palm tree, and your breasts are full. I will climb that tree and cling to its branches. I will discover that your breasts are like clusters of grapes, and that your breath is the aroma of apples. Kissing you is more delicious than drinking the finest wine. How wonderful and tasty!

She speaks: My darling, I am yours, and you desire me. Let's stroll through the fields and sleep in the villages. At dawn let's slip out and see if grapevines and fruit trees are covered with blossoms. When we are there, I will give you my love.
SONG OF SONGS 7:6–12

The passion of love bursting into flame is more powerful than death, stronger than the grave. Love cannot be drowned by oceans or floods; it cannot be bought, no matter what is offered.
SONG OF SONGS 8:6b–7

Download

Love that is watertight

If you're not going out with someone: learn this Bible verse—so that you can send it as a text message on the day you may need to.

If you are going out with someone: send the verse as a text message to your loved one. And memorize it!

'Love cannot be drowned by oceans or floods' (Song of Songs 8:7).

If there's someone you really like, and you're not sure they like you… another good verse to remember is: 'Never awaken love before it is ready…' (Song of Songs 8:4b).

Links: 22 April, 11 December, 13 December, 14 December

5 minutes more? 1 John 1

13 December

Mothers, fathers and children

Some tips for the girls

It's better to stay outside on the roof of your house than to live inside with a nagging wife.

PROVERBS 21:9

A beautiful woman who acts foolishly is like a gold ring on the snout of a pig.

PROVERBS 11:22

Don't depend on things like fancy hair styles or gold jewellery or expensive clothes to make you look beautiful. Be beautiful in your heart by being gentle and quiet. This kind of beauty will last, and God considers it very special.

1 PETER 3:3–4

Honour Christ and put others first… A wife should put her husband first, as she does the Lord. Wives should always put their husbands first, as the church puts Christ first.

EPHESIANS 5:21, 24–25

Big word

Submission

'Submission' is the big word for what wives should do in putting their husbands first. There are many people (especially girls, funnily enough) who get in a huff when they hear talk of 'submission'.

When you consider that the Bible was written 2000–3000 years ago (and that's a very long time), in the Middle East (where to this day women have to wear a veil over their faces), the whole thing about submission is not as anti-women as you might think. Jesus treated women better, and took them more seriously, than probably anyone else in his time.

The Bible says that putting the other person first (submission) is an important way of getting a relationship to work. Both sides of a relationship should submit to each other. Many relationships suffer and go through rocky patches because two people begin to compete with each other—and selfishness gets a foothold. Competition is the opposite of submission. Pray that, when the day comes, your marriage relationship will be full of humility and generosity, not competitiveness—full of cooperation and not conflict. More duet and less duel.

Links: 14 December, 19 December, 20 December, 21 December

5 minutes more? 1 John 2

14 December

Mothers, fathers and children

Tips for the boys

A husband should love his wife as much as Christ loved the church and gave his life for it... In the same way, a husband should love his wife as much as he loves himself.

EPHESIANS 5:25, 28

A husband must love his wife and not abuse her... Parents, don't be hard on your children. If you are, they might give up... Do your work willingly, as though you were serving the Lord himself, and not just your earthly master. In fact, the Lord Christ is the one you are really serving, and you know that he will reward you.

COLOSSIANS 3:19, 21, 23–24

If you are a husband, you should be thoughtful of your wife. Treat her with honour, because she isn't as strong as you are, and she shares with you in the gift of life. Then nothing will stand in the way of your prayers.

1 PETER 3:7

Listen to your heart and fill in

Girls—you get a day off today!

Boys: Who would you most like to be like when you leave school or college?

1. ______________________ 2. ______________________

3. ______________________

OK. OK. OK. Forget all that, and write down three men who don't live in Hollywood or are professional footballers. Try again, a bit closer to home...

1. ______________________ 2. ______________________

3. ______________________

What is it about them that you admire so much?

1. ____

2. ____

3. ____

Links: 13 December, 19 December, 20 December, 21 December

5 minutes more? 1 John 3

15 December

God blesses...

The poor

When Jesus saw the crowds, he went up on the side of a mountain and sat down. Jesus disciples gathered around him, and he taught them:

God blesses those people who depend only on him. They belong to the kingdom of heaven!

MATTHEW 5:1–3

My friends, if you have faith in our glorious Lord Jesus Christ, you won't treat some people better than others. Suppose a rich person wearing fine clothes and a gold ring comes to one of your meetings. And suppose a poor person dressed in worn-out clothes also comes. You must not give the best seat to the one in fine clothes and tell the one who is poor to stand at the side or sit on the floor. That is the same as saying that some people are better than others, and you would be acting like a crooked judge.

JAMES 2:1–4

Refresh

Image is nothing

Right label on jeans, mobile phone and jacket: you're in.

Wrong shoes, wrong style, wrong friends: you're out.

In a healthy Christian environment there ought to be all sorts of people. There should be skaters with cut-off jeans, computer boffins with big specs and rockers with long nails. There should be pouting blondes and outdoor types in hiking boots, eccentric bookworms, extravert comedians and introspective thoughtful types... and many others besides.

God promised his kingdom to completely ordinary people—people who depend only on him. The Lord doesn't care a jot about image, he looks on the heart (1 Samuel 16:7). We should do the same.

Links: 7 February, 20 April, 24 April, 18 December

5 minutes more? 1 John 4

16 December

God blesses...

Those people who grieve

God blesses those people who grieve. They will find comfort!
MATTHEW 5:4

You have turned my sorrow into joyful dancing. No longer am I sad and wearing sackcloth. I thank you from my heart, and I will never stop singing your praises, my Lord and my God.
PSALM 30:11–12

I heard a loud voice shout from the throne:

God's home is now with his people. He will live with them, and they will be his own. Yes, God will make his home among his people. He will wipe all tears from their eyes, and there will be no more death, suffering, crying, or pain. These things of the past are gone for ever.
REVELATION 21:3–4

Refresh

Hell and damnation!

If you ever have to lead your cell group, youth meeting or student Christian Union group, quite a clever trick is to start by saying something a bit shocking—it gets people's attention. There is a story that a bishop once started his sermon by saying, 'Hell and damnation!' He then paused for a while before saying, 'Good God in heaven above!' Of course everyone thought he was swearing... it all depends on how you say these things. But you can bet your bottom dollar everyone listened to the next thing he said that Sunday!

The Sermon on the Mount is the only long sermon that Jesus gave. He started with shock tactics too. Not as bad as the bishop's, but by telling people that things are really quite the opposite of what they'd rather believe. It's not happy people who are fortunate, but those who grieve. Rich people aren't fortunate, but those who depend solely on the Lord—not those who have it easy, but those who are persecuted. Why? Because God will be with them.

The Sermon on the Mount is definitely the most quoted sermon in history.

Links: 20 April, 24 May, 27 September, 27 December

5 minutes more? 1 John 5

17 December

God blesses...

Those who are humble

God blesses those people who are humble. The earth will belong to them!
MATTHEW 5:5

Don't be annoyed with anyone who does wrong, and don't envy them. They will soon disappear like grass without rain... Be patient and trust the Lord. Don't let it bother you when all goes well for those who do sinful things. Don't be angry or furious. Anger can lead to sin. All sinners will disappear, but if you trust the Lord, the land will be yours... The poor will take the land and enjoy a big harvest.
PSALM 37:1–2, 7–9, 11

Refresh

Gimme, gimme, gimme!

We live in quite a 'gimme' culture. Perhaps you've noticed this with some of your friends. They say 'Gimme' to their parents—and hey, presto! Next time you see them they've got a new mobile or the latest PC or whatever. There are other people who say 'Gimme', but haven't got parents who can serve up the request. So sometimes kids are tempted to take things that belong to others just so that they can keep up with the in crowd. That's not right.

Nagging, cheating and stealing to get things to make you look cool is not the way Christians should behave.

Jesus says that humble people, patient people, people who trust him to supply their needs (not their wants!) are the ones who will end up with more in the long run.

PS: Remember there is a lot that money can't buy but Jesus can give—for free!

Links: 20 April, 4 June, 5 June, 30 December

5 minutes more? 2 John

18 December

God blesses...

Those who want to obey him

God blesses those people who want to obey him more than to eat or drink. They will be given what they want!

MATTHEW 5:6

As a deer gets thirsty for streams of water, I truly am thirsty for you, my God. In my heart, I am thirsty for you, the living God. When will I see your face?

PSALM 42:1–2

Jesus answered, 'Everyone who drinks this water will get thirsty again. But no one who drinks the water I give will ever be thirsty again. The water I give is like a flowing fountain that gives eternal life.'

JOHN 4:13–14

Hmm... just a thought...

...about the global village

If we thought of the world as a village with only 100 people in it, things would look like this:

- 57 Asians, 21 Europeans, 14 Americans, 8 Africans
- 52 women, 48 men
- 70 people with dark skin, 30 people with light skin
- Six people would own 59 per cent of the village's wealth
- 70 people wouldn't be able to read
- One (yes, one) person would have education beyond primary school level
- One person would own a computer

In some versions of the Bible, today's verse from the Sermon on the Mount talks about people who hunger and thirst for 'righteousness'. Righteousness is the same thing as obeying God—it's about making sure everyone gets a fair share and a fair chance—it's about loving your neighbour as much as yourself.

Think how you could ensure things are shared out more fairly in the global village.

Links: 10 March, 17 April, 20 April, 24 September

5 minutes more? 3 John

19 December

God blesses...

Those who are merciful

God blesses those people who are merciful. They will be treated with mercy!
MATTHEW 5:7

The Lord your God will have mercy—he won't destroy you or desert you. The Lord will remember his promise, and he will keep the agreement he made with your ancestors.
DEUTERONOMY 4:31

The Lord God has told us what is right and what he demands: 'See that justice is done, let mercy be your first concern, and humbly obey your God.'
MICAH 6:8

Speak and act like people who will be judged by the law that sets us free. Do this, because on the day of judgment there will be no pity for those who have not had pity on others.
JAMES 2:12–13

Big word

Mercy and compassion

Mercy and compassion are very important qualities. They mean everything. Some people think that certain churches can be rather condemning. Those kinds of churches need to show more mercy and compassion.

If you join the Salvation Army, you have to promise not to have so much as a swig of an alcoholic drink, or a single drag of a cigarette. But because their members have so much compassion for others, people don't see them as condemning types.

Mother Teresa too—she was a woman without compromise. She campaigned actively against abortion and contraception. She was never frightened to express her views; but because she was so compassionate to those who needed to be shown mercy, she was never considered to be condemning.

If we show mercy, we are shown mercy.

If we are compassionate, we are shown compassion.

Links: 20 April, 22 May, 28 May, 4 December

5 minutes more? Jude

20 December

God blesses...

Those whose hearts are pure

God blesses those people whose hearts are pure. They will see him!
MATTHEW 5:8

Who may climb the Lord's hill or stand in his holy temple? Only those who do right for the right reasons, or don't worship idols or tell lies under oath.
PSALM 24:3–4

Run from temptations that capture young people. Always do the right thing. Be faithful, loving, and easy to get along with. Worship with people whose hearts are pure.
2 TIMOTHY 2:22

Let's come near God with pure hearts and a confidence that comes from having faith. Let's keep our hearts pure, our consciences free from evil, and our bodies washed with clean water.
HEBREWS 10:22

Di:SaipL

The proverbial carpet

I believe there is a tribe in Africa who have a single rule—that anything goes. That is—as long as you're not caught, anything's permissible. They can steal, trick and swindle people as much as they like, as long as they don't get caught. An action only becomes wrong when someone else catches them doing it.

It's easy to think, 'Huh—what a stupid tribe!' But if you think about it, that's just the way we behave too. No one is criticized until they are caught. People use the train without paying—they know it's wrong. Sports personalities take drugs—they know it's wrong. Kids bunk off school—they know it's wrong. But few people will own up before they absolutely have to.

Jesus says we have to own up of our own accord. We must ask God and the people we have wronged for forgiveness as soon as we can. And it doesn't help to brush things under the carpet. To get a 'pure heart', our wrongdoing has to be brought out into the light—God's light.

If you've got something to confess to someone, go and do it as soon as you can. Then you will see God!

Links: 12 January, 5 February, 20 April, 30 June

5 minutes more? Revelation 1

Those people who make peace

God blesses those people who make peace. They will be called his children!
MATTHEW 5:9

Come, my children, listen as I teach you to respect the Lord. Do you want to live and enjoy a long life? Then don't say cruel things and don't tell lies. Do good instead of evil and try to live at peace.
PSALM 34:11–14

Do your best to live at peace with everyone.
ROMANS 12:18

But the wisdom that comes from above leads us to be pure, friendly, gentle, sensible, kind, helpful, genuine and sincere. When peacemakers plant seeds of peace, they will harvest justice.
JAMES 3:17–18

Check it out

Some important verses about creating peace (and the opposite!) around you every day

'It's no crazier to shoot sharp and flaming arrows than to cheat someone and say, "I was only fooling!"' (Proverbs 26:18–19).

'Where there is no fuel a fire goes out; where there is no gossip arguments come to an end' (Proverbs 26:20).

'It's better to take hold of a mad dog by the ears than to take part in someone else's argument' (Proverbs 26:17).

Links: 20 April, 25 May, 26 May, 23 December

5 minutes more? Revelation 2

22 December

God blesses...

Those who are treated badly

God blesses those people who are treated badly for doing right. They belong to the kingdom of heaven. God will bless you when people insult you, ill-treat you, and tell all kinds of evil lies about you because of me. Be happy and excited! You will have a great reward in heaven. People did these same things to the prophets who lived long ago.

MATTHEW 5:10–12

But you, Lord, are a mighty soldier, standing at my side. Those troublemakers will fall down and fail.

JEREMIAH 20:11a

But [the Lord] replied, 'My kindness is all you need. My power is strongest when you are weak.' So if Christ keeps giving me his power, I will gladly boast about how weak I am. Yes, I am glad to be weak or insulted or ill-treated or to have troubles and sufferings, if it is for Christ. Because when I am weak, I am strong.

2 CORINTHIANS 12:9–10

Did you know that...

...people in China are persecuted for being Christians?

Did you also know that China is the land where more people are becoming Christians than anywhere else? It's mind-blowing how many people there are becoming Christians.

For many years, people thought there weren't any Christians in China. But when people were given the freedom to practise their religion openly, Christians popped up one after another. Christianity had spread 'underground'. The authorities hadn't managed to stop God.

If you think it's difficult to be a Christian at school and in your everyday life, then straighten yourself up—you can be proud of your God. The unstoppable one is with you!

Links: 20 April, 9 October, 10 October, 11 October

5 minutes more? Revelation 3

23 December

Christmas

The Prince of Peace

Those who walked in the dark have seen a bright light. And it shines upon everyone who lives in the land of darkest shadows. Our Lord, you have made your nation stronger. Because of you, its people are glad and celebrate like workers at harvest time or like soldiers dividing up what they have taken. You have broken the power of those who abused and enslaved your people. You have rescued them just as you saved your people from Midian... A child has been born for us. We have been given a son who will be our ruler. His names will be Wonderful Adviser and Mighty God, Eternal Father and Prince of Peace. His power will never end; peace will last for ever. He will rule David's kingdom and make it grow strong. He will always rule with honesty and justice. The Lord All-Powerful will make certain that all of this is done.

ISAIAH 9:2–4, 6–7

Download

The Son

It is remarkable that Isaiah wrote this approximately 700 years before Jesus was born, and that makes it worth memorizing:

'A child has been born for us. We have been given a son who will be our ruler. His names will be Wonderful Adviser and Mighty God, Eternal Father and Prince of Peace' (Isaiah 9:6).

Links: 7 July, 9 July, 24 December, 25 December

5 minutes more? Revelation 4

24 December

Christmas

Jesus is born

About that time Emperor A____________ gave orders for the names of all the people to be listed in record books. These first records were made when Q____________ was governor of S ________. Everyone had to go to their own home town to be listed. So J ___________ had to leave N _______________ in G____________ and go to B________________ in J __________. Long ago B ______________ had been King D ______'s home town, and J __________ went there because he was from D ______'s family. M ______ was engaged to J_________ and travelled with him to B_____________. She was soon going to have a baby, and while they were there, she gave birth to her firstborn son. She dressed him in baby clothes and laid him on a bed of hay, because there was no room for them in the inn.

That night in the fields near B________________ some s ___________ were guarding their sheep. All at once an a _______ came down to them from the Lord, and the brightness of the Lord's glory flashed around them. The s___________ were frightened. But the a ______ said, 'Don't be afraid! I have good news for you, which will make everyone happy. This very day in King D______'s home town a S ___________ was born for you. He is C________ the L_____. You will know who he is, because you will find him dressed in baby clothes and lying in a bed of hay.' ...

They hurried off and found M______ and J _________, and they saw the baby lying on a bed of hay.

LUKE 2:1–12, 16

Listen to your heart and fill in

How many names from this Christmas reading can you remember off the top of your head?

Fill in the blanks. I've given you the first letter of each space to give you a hand. Check your answers in a Bible, if you've got one...

... and if you haven't got one—ask for one for Christmas! (*Word Bytes* has used the Contemporary English Version of the Bible.)

Links: 8 July, 9 July, 18 August, 19 August

5 minutes more? Revelation 5

25 December
Christmas

The Word of life

In the beginning was the one who is called the Word. The Word was with God and was truly God. From the very beginning the Word was with God. And with this Word, God created all things. Nothing was made without the Word. Everything that was created received its life from him, and his life gave light to everyone. The light keeps shining in the dark, and darkness has never put it out... The true light that shines on everyone was coming into the world. The Word was in the world, but no one knew him, though God had made the world with his Word. He came into his own world, but his own nation did not welcome him. Yet some people accepted him and put their faith in him. So he gave them the right to be the children of God. They were not God's children by nature or because of any human desires. God himself was the one who made them his children.

The Word became a human being and lived here with us. We saw his true glory, the glory of the only Son of the Father. From him all the kindness and all the truth of God have come down to us.

JOHN 1:1–5, 9–14

Big word
Incarnation

The Word—with a capital W—was there from before the beginning.

The Word—with a capital W—created the world.

The Word—with a capital W—is God.

And just now you've read that the Word became human. You've just read about 'the incarnation'. Yep! The incarnation.

What does that mean? Well, for example, 'carnival' comes from two Latin words. The 'carne' bit means 'flesh', and the 'vale' bit means 'farewell'. So a 'carnival' was originally a festival to celebrate a fast from eating meat—usually in the run-up to Easter.

'Incarnation' comes from Latin as well. The 'in' bit literally means 'in'! The 'carne' bit means 'flesh'. So 'incarnation' means 'to be in the flesh'.

The Word with a capital 'W' became incarnate, took upon himself flesh and became human.

Welcome him into your life—he will give you the right to be a child of God!

Links: 1 January, 9 February, 18 February, 21 March

5 minutes more? Revelation 6

The resurrection of the dead

My friends, we want you to understand how it will be for those followers who have already died. Then you won't grieve over them and be like people who don't have any hope. We believe that Jesus died and was raised to life. We also believe that when God brings Jesus back again, he will bring with him all who had faith in Jesus before they died. Our Lord Jesus told us that when he comes, we won't go up to meet him ahead of his followers who have already died.

With a loud command and with the shout of the chief angel and a blast of God's trumpet, the Lord will return from heaven. Then those who had faith in Christ before they died will be raised to life. Next, all of us who are still alive will be taken up into the clouds together with them to meet the Lord in the sky. From that time on we will be with the Lord for ever. Encourage each other with these words.

I don't need to write to you about the time or date when all this will happen. You know that the Lord's return will be as a thief coming at night.
1 THESSALONIANS 4:13—5:2

Refresh

No one knows when Jesus will come back

Throughout history there have been quite a few people who have claimed that they knew when Jesus would come back. They have all been wrong. However, there are still some people who think they know.

Don't listen to them!

If they bothered to open the Bible and turn to today's reading, they would see that no one knows the exact day of the Lord's return. Jesus says in Matthew 24:36 that even he doesn't know—only the Father does.

What we do know about Jesus' return is:

1. It'll be absolutely great.
2. It's nearer now than at any time in history.

Links: 31 March, 27 September, 27 December, 29 December

5 minutes more? Revelation 7

27 December

The new heaven and the new earth

No more crying

I am creating new heavens and a new earth; everything of the past will be forgotten. Celebrate and be glad for ever! I am creating a Jerusalem, full of happy people. I will celebrate with Jerusalem and all its people; there will be no more crying or sorrow in that city. No child will die in infancy; everyone will live to a ripe old age... Their work won't be wasted, and their children won't die of dreadful diseases. I will bless their children and their grandchildren. I will answer their prayers before they finish praying. Wolves and lambs will graze together; lions and oxen will feed on straw. Snakes will eat only dust! They won't bite or harm anyone on my holy mountain. I, the Lord, have spoken!

ISAIAH 65:17–20a, 23–25

Listen to your heart and fill in

Heaven

This must be the most beautiful description of heaven in the whole Bible. Isaiah uses wonderful imagery to communicate to us his understanding of heaven: the wolves and lambs will graze together! And there won't be any more cot deaths.

What do you imagine heaven will be like?

1. ______________________________

2. ______________________________

3. ______________________________

4. ______________________________

Look forward to it!

Links: 28 December, 29 December, 30 December, 31 December

5 minutes more? Revelation 15

28 December

The new heaven and the new earth

The water of life

The Lord showed me some visions in which I was carried to the top of a high mountain in Jerusalem... I saw a man who was sparkling like polished bronze... The man said, 'Ezekiel, son of man, pay close attention to everything I'm going to show you—that's why you've been brought here...' The man took me back to the temple, where I saw a stream flowing from under the entrance... I saw dozens of trees on each side. The man said:

Wherever this water flows, there will be all kinds of animals and fish, because it will bring life and fresh water to the Dead Sea... Fruit trees will grow all along this river and produce fresh fruit every month.

EZEKIEL 40:2a, 3a, 4a; 47:1a, 7–8a, 9, 12a

Refresh

Green Christianity

The prophet Isaiah is describing here how a dead environment will return to life. Quite incredible! He wrote this several thousand years before there were such things as climate-altering gases, toxic waste and acid rain.

Some Christians don't think about the environment very much because they know that one day God will make all things new—but that attitude's the biggest load of tosh possible. People who think like that ought to sort themselves out, double-quick.

Christian people are those who have the biggest reason to put used card and paper in the recycling bins, take clean aluminium foil to Oxfam, put rinsed glass jars and bottles in the right bottle bank, put washed and squashed cans in the can bank and take their carrier bags back to the supermarket.

Why?

Because God has asked us to look after the world until he comes back (Genesis 1:28).

Investigate recycling facilities in your area. Use them, and encourage others to do the same—start with your own family!

Links: 10 February, 11 February, 17 February, 21 February

5 minutes more? Revelation 19

29 December

The new heaven and the new earth

When the Son of Man comes

I am John... I was sent to Patmos Island, because I had preached God's message and had told about Jesus. On the Lord's day the Spirit took control of me, and behind me I heard a loud voice that sounded like a trumpet... When I turned to see who was speaking to me, I saw seven gold lampstands. There with the lampstands was someone who seemed to be the Son of Man. He was wearing a robe that reached down to his feet, and a gold cloth was wrapped around his chest. His head and his hair were white as wool or snow, and his eyes looked like flames of fire. His feet were glowing like bronze being heated in a furnace, and his voice sounded like the roar of a waterfall. He held seven stars in his right hand, and a sharp double-edged sword was coming from his mouth. His face was shining as bright as the sun at midday. When I saw him, I fell at his feet like a dead person. But he put his hand on me and said:

Don't be afraid! I am the first, the last, and the living one. I died, but now I am alive for evermore, and I have the keys to death and the world of the dead.

REVELATION 1:9–10, 12–18

Listen to your heart and fill in

Power and glory

The Jesus who was on the earth 2000 years ago and the Jesus who will one day come back again are the same man. But there is an important difference: when he comes next time, he will come in majesty—as the king of the universe. He will come in all the power and glory of heaven.

Use today's reading to fill in what he will look like:

Clothes: ______________________

Head and hair: ______________________

Eyes: ______________________

Feet: ______________________

Voice: ______________________

Face: ______________________

What a difference!

Links: 21 July, 17 August, 30 December, 31 December

5 minutes more? Revelation 20

30 December

The new heaven and the new earth

The final judgment

I saw a great white throne with someone sitting on it. Earth and heaven tried to run away, but there was nowhere for them to go. I also saw all the dead people standing in front of that throne. Every one of them was there, no matter who they had once been. Several books were opened, and then the book of life was opened. The dead were judged by what those books said they had done... Afterwards, death and its kingdom were thrown into the lake of fire. This is the second death. Anyone whose name wasn't written in the book of life was thrown into the lake of fire.

I saw a new heaven and a new earth. The first heaven and the first earth had disappeared, and so had the sea. Then I saw New Jerusalem, that holy city, coming down from God in heaven. It was like a bride dressed in her wedding gown and ready to meet her husband. I heard a loud voice shout from the throne:

God's home is now with his people. He will live with them, and they will be his own. Yes, God will make his home among his people. He will wipe all tears from their eyes, and there will be no more death, suffering, crying, or pain. These things of the past are gone for ever.

REVELATION 20:11–12, 14–15; 21:1–4

Download

Wiping away of tears

'He will wipe all tears from their eyes, and there will be no more death, suffering, crying, or pain. These things of the past are gone for ever' (Revelation 21:4).

Links: 13 January, 19 February, 21 February, 10 March

5 minutes more? Revelation 21

31 December

The new heaven and the new earth

Come!

I am coming soon! And when I come, I will reward everyone for what they have done. I am Alpha and Omega, the first and the last, the beginning and the end. God will bless all who have washed their robes. They will each have the right to eat fruit from the tree that gives life, and they can enter the gates of the city...

I am Jesus! And I am the one who sent my angel to tell all of you these things for the churches. I am David's Great Descendant, I am also the bright morning star.

The Spirit and the bride say, 'Come!' Everyone who hears this should say, 'Come!' If you are thirsty, come! If you want life-giving water, come and take it. It's free! ...

The one who has spoken these things says, 'I am coming soon!' So, Lord Jesus, please come soon! I pray that the Lord Jesus will be kind to all of you.
REVELATION 22:12–14, 16–17, 20–21

Hmm... just a thought...
...between kings

Hope is that Jesus will come again and judge the world.
HIS MAJESTY KING HARALD OF NORWAY

PS: Make some wise New Year's resolutions tonight!

PPS: These verses might help you:

'With all your heart you must trust the Lord and not your own judgment. Always let him lead you, and he will clear the road for you to follow' (Proverbs 3:5–6).

Links: 1 January, 17 October, 25 December, 28 December

5 minutes more? Revelation 22

Are you looking for a particular Bible passage?

Mini dictionary for the Bible

This dictionary is divided into 21 sections. The indexes below list all of the sections, and all of the entries in alphabetical order, so that you can find what you are looking for more easily.

Section Index

Alphabetical Index

Numbers refer to the sections (listed above) in which the entry is included.

1. A few basics

CEV — The Contemporary English Version of the Bible.

Old Testament — This first part of the Bible is made up of the 39 books from Genesis to Malachi. They were written mostly in Hebrew, with a few passages in Aramaic.

New Testament — This second part of the Bible is made up of the 27 books from Matthew to Revelation. They were written in Greek.

Chapter and verse numbers — These numbers were not part of the original books, but were added hundreds of years later as a way to refer to specific parts of the books of Scripture. For example, Genesis 1:3 means the book of Genesis, chapter 1, verse 3. Genesis 2:4–5 means the book of Genesis, chapter 2, verses 4 to 5. And Genesis 1—2 means the book of Genesis, chapters 1 to 2. A few books are so short that they were not divided up into chapters, and so these books only have verse numbers. In the text of the CEV, sometimes verse numbers have been combined, for example, [3-4]. One reason verse numbers might be combined is that contemporary English says things in a different order from ancient Greek and Hebrew, and so two or more verses are sometimes blended together in the CEV translation. And in lists, the verse numbers are sometimes combined into a single heading to avoid confusion. But all the meaning from the original Greek and Hebrew has been carefully included in the CEV text.

2. Scriptures, manuscripts

Ancient translations — The Old Testament was translated into Greek over the period 250–150BC. Later, the whole Bible was translated into Latin, Syriac, and some other languages. These ancient translations can sometimes show what the Hebrew or Greek text said at the time they were translated, and so the CEV notes will sometimes refer to them.

Commandments — God's rules for his people to live by. The most famous are the Ten Commandments (see Exodus 20:1–17; Deuteronomy 5:6–21).

Dead Sea Scrolls — Manuscripts found near the Dead Sea from 1947–1954. They date from about 250BC to AD68. These manuscripts include at least some parts of nearly all Old Testament books.

God's Law — God's rules for his people to live by. They are found in the Old Testament, especially the first five books.

Law and the Prophets	A term used in New Testament times to refer to the sacred writings of the Jews. The Law and the Prophets were two of the three sections of the Old Testament, but the expression sometimes refers to the entire Old Testament.
Law of Moses and Law of the Lord	Usually refers to the first five books of the Old Testament, but sometimes to the entire Old Testament.
Manuscript	In ancient times, all books were copied by hand. A copy made this way was called a manuscript.
Proverb	A wise saying that is short and easy to remember.
Psalm	A Hebrew poem. Psalms were often written in such a way that they could be prayed or sung by an individual or a group. Some of the psalms thank and praise God, while others ask God to take away sins or to give protection, comfort, vengeance, or mercy.
Samaritan Hebrew Text	The Hebrew text of Genesis to Deuteronomy used and preserved by the Samaritans (see also *Samaria*). This text uses forms of letters and many spellings that are different from the Standard Hebrew Text. It has traditionally been called the Samaritan Pentateuch.
Scriptures	Although this term now refers to the whole Bible, in the New Testament it refers to the Old Testament.
Standard Hebrew Text	The Hebrew text that is found in most Hebrew manuscripts of the Old Testament. Almost all of these manuscripts were copied after AD900 (but see also *Dead Sea Scrolls*).
Wisdom	Often refers to the common sense and practical skill needed to solve everyday problems, but sometimes involves trying to find answers to the hard questions about the meaning of life.

3. Languages

Aramaic	A language closely related to Hebrew. In New Testament times Aramaic was spoken by many Jews, including Jesus. Ezra 4:8—6:18; 7:12–26 and Daniel 2:4b—7:28 were written in Aramaic.
Greek	The language used throughout the Mediterranean world in New Testament times, and the language in which the New Testament was written.
Hebrew	The language used by most of the people of Israel until the Exile. But after the people returned, more and more people spoke Aramaic instead. Most of the Old Testament was written in Hebrew.

4. People

Aaron	The brother of Moses. Only he and his descendants were to serve as priests and offer sacrifices for the people of Israel (see Exodus 4:14–16; 28:1; Numbers 16:11—8:7).
Abel	The second son of Adam and Eve and the younger brother of Cain. Abel was killed by Cain after God accepted Abel's offering and refused to accept Cain's (see Genesis 4:1–17).
Abraham	The first of the three great ancestors of the people of Israel. Abraham was the husband of Sarah and the father of Isaac. At first Abraham's name was Abram, meaning Great Father. Then, when Abram was 99 years old, God changed Abram's name to Abraham, which means Father of a Crowd. Abraham trusted God, and so God promised that Abraham and his wife Sarah would have a son and more descendants than could be counted. God also promised that Abraham would be a blessing to everyone on earth (see Genesis 12:1–7; 17:1—18:15).
Abram	See *Abraham*.
Adam	The first man and the husband of Eve (see Genesis 1:26—3:21).
Agrippa	(1) Herod Agrippa was king of Judea AD41–44 and ill-treated Christians (see Acts 12:1–5). (2) Agrippa II was the son of Herod Agrippa and ruled parts of Palestine from AD53 to AD93 or later. He and his sister Bernice listened to Paul defend himself (see Acts 25:13–26, 32).
Antipas	(1) Herod Antipas, son of Herod the Great (see *Herod*). (2) An otherwise unknown Christian at Pergamum, who was killed because he was a follower of Christ (see Revelation 2:13).
Augustus	A title meaning 'honoured', which was given to Octavian by the Romans when he began ruling the Roman world in 27BC. He was the Roman Emperor when Jesus was born.
Cain	The first son of Adam and Eve; Cain killed his brother Abel after God accepted Abel's offering and refused to accept Cain's (see Genesis 4:1–17).
David	King of Israel from about 1010–970BC. David was the most famous king Israel ever had, and many of the people of Israel hoped that one of his descendants would always be their king (see 1 Samuel 16—30; 2 Samuel; 1 Kings 12).
Esau	The elder son of Isaac and Rebekah, and the brother of Jacob. Esau was also known as Edom and as the ancestor of the Edomites (see Genesis 25:20–34; 26:34–46; 32:1—33:16).
Eve	The first woman and the wife of Adam (see Genesis 1:26—3:21).

Felix	The Roman governor of Palestine AD52–60, who listened to Paul speak and kept him in jail (see Acts 23:24—24:27).
Festus	The Roman governor after Felix, who sent Paul to stand trial in Rome (see Acts 24:27—26:32).
Hagar	A slave of Sarah, the wife of Abraham. When Sarah could not have any children, she followed the ancient custom of letting her husband have a child by Hagar, her slave. The boy's name was Ishmael (see Genesis 16; 21:8–21).
Herod	(1) Herod the Great was the king of all Palestine 37–4BC, so he was king at the time that Jesus was born (see the note at *AD*). (2) Herod Antipas was the son of Herod the Great and was the ruler of Galilee 4BC–AD39. (3) Herod Agrippa I, the grandson of Herod the Great, ruled Palestine AD41–44.
Isaac	The second of the three great ancestors of the people of Israel. He was the son of Abraham and Sarah, and he was the father of Esau and Jacob.
Ishmael	The son of Abraham and Hagar.
Israel	See *Jacob*.
Jacob	The third great ancestor of the people of Israel. He was the son of Isaac and Rebekah, and his name was changed to Israel when he struggled with God at Peniel near the River Jabbok (see Genesis 32:22–32).
Joseph	A son of Jacob and Rachel. Joseph was sold as a slave by his brothers, but later became governor of Egypt (see Genesis 37:12–36; 41:1–57).
Lot	A nephew of Abraham and the ancestor of the Moabites and Ammonites (see Genesis 11:27; 13:1–13; 18:16—19:38).
Noah	When God destroyed the world by a flood, Noah and his family were kept safe in a big boat that God had told him to build (see Genesis 6—8).
Rebekah	The wife of Isaac, and the mother of Jacob and Esau (see Genesis 24:1–67; 25:19–28).
Sarah	The wife of Abraham and the mother of Isaac. At first her name was Sarai, but when she was old, God promised her that she would have a son, and he changed her name to Sarah. Both names mean 'princess' (see Genesis 11:29–30; 17:15–19; 18.9–15; 21:1–7).
Solomon	A son of King David and Bathsheba. After David's death, Solomon ruled Israel about 970–931BC. Solomon built the temple in Jerusalem and was widely known for his wisdom. The Hebrew text indicates that he wrote many of the proverbs and two of the psalms.

5. Prophets

Anna	A woman prophet who stayed in the temple night and day. Soon after Jesus was born, Mary and Joseph took him to the temple and presented him to the Lord, and Anna talked about the child Jesus to everyone who hoped for Jerusalem to be set free (see Luke 2:36–38).
Balaam	A foreign prophet. Balaam was hired by the king of Moab to put a curse on Israel, but instead Balaam blessed Israel (see Numbers 22—24).
Deborah	A prophet and judge who helped lead Israel to defeat King Jabin of Hazor (see Judges 4—5).
Elijah	A prophet who spoke for God in the early ninth century BC and who opposed the evil King Ahab and Queen Jezebel of the northern kingdom. Many Jews in later centuries thought Elijah would return to get everything ready for the day of judgment or for the coming of the Messiah (see 1 Kings 17—21; 2 Kings 1—2; Malachi 4:1–6; Matthew 17:10–11; Mark 9:11–12).
Elisha	A prophet who assisted Elijah and later took his place. Elisha spoke for God in the late ninth century BC, and was the prophet who healed Naaman (see 1 Kings 19:19–21; 2 Kings 2—9; 13:14–21).
Huldah	A prophet who spoke for God during the late seventh century BC. After The Book of God's Law was found in the temple, King Josiah asked her what the Lord wanted him to do (see 2 Kings 22:14–20).
Micaiah	A prophet who told King Ahab that he would die in battle against the Syrian army (see 1 Kings 22:5–38).
Moses	The prophet who led the people of Israel when God rescued them from slavery in Egypt. Moses also received laws from God and gave them to Israel (see Exodus 2—12; 19—24; Numbers 12:68).
Prophesy	To speak as a prophet (see *Prophet*).
Prophet	Someone who spoke God's message, which at times included telling what would happen in the future. Sometimes when the Spirit of God took control of prophets, they lost some or all control of their speech and actions or were not aware of what was happening around them.

6. Twelve tribes of Israel

The Bible speaks of all the people in a tribe as having descended from one of the twelve sons of Jacob. The tribes of Ephraim and Manasseh were a little different, because the people in those tribes descended from the two sons of Joseph, who was one of Jacob's sons. That would make a total of thirteen tribes, but the Bible always counts only twelve. In some passages Ephraim and Manasseh are counted as one tribe, and in other passages the Levi tribe is left out, probably because they were designated for priestly service to all the tribes, and as such, were scattered throughout the land belonging to the other tribes. People from other nations were sometimes allowed to become Israelites (see Exodus 12:38; Deuteronomy 23:1–8; and the book of Ruth), and these people would then belong to one of the tribes.

Asher	Occupied land along the Mediterranean coast from Mount Carmel to the border with the city of Tyre.
Benjamin	Occupied land between Bethel and Jerusalem. When the northern tribes of Israel broke away following the death of Solomon, only the tribes of Benjamin and Judah were left to form the southern kingdom.
Dan	First occupied land west of Judah, Benjamin, and Ephraim. But after the Philistines took control of this area, part of the tribe then moved to the northernmost area of Israel.
Ephraim	One of the largest tribes. Ephraim occupied the land north of Benjamin and south of West Manasseh.
Gad	Occupied land east of the River Jordan from the northern end of the Dead Sea north to the River Jabbok.
Issachar	Occupied land south-west of Lake Galilee.
Judah	Occupied the hill country west of the Dead Sea. When the ten northernmost tribes of Israel broke away following the death of Solomon, only the tribes of Judah and Benjamin were left to form the southern kingdom, and it was also called Judah.
Levi	The men of this tribe were to be the special servants of the Lord at the sacred tent and later at the temple, and so the people of this tribe were not given tribal land. Instead, they were given towns scattered throughout the other twelve tribes (see also *Levites*).
Manasseh	Occupied two areas of land: (1) East Manasseh lived east of the River Jordan and north of the River Jabbok in the areas of Bashan and northern Gilead. (2) West Manasseh lived west of the River Jordan and to the north of Ephraim.
Naphtali	Occupied land north and west of Lake Galilee.
Reuben	Occupied land east of the Dead Sea, from the River Arnon in the south to the northern end of the Dead Sea.
Simeon	Occupied land south-west of Judah, and was later practically absorbed into Judah.
Zebulun	Occupied land north of Manasseh from the eastern end of Mount Carmel to Mount Tabor.

7. Christ's twelve apostles

Apostle	A person chosen and sent by Christ to take his message to others. Lists of the names of Christ's twelve apostles can be found in Matthew 10:2–4; Mark 3:16–19; Luke 6:14–16; Acts 1:12–13. Later, others such as Paul and James the brother of Jesus also became known as apostles.
Simon	Also known as Peter or Cephas.
Andrew	Simon Peter's brother.
James	The son of Zebedee.
John	The son of Zebedee (James and John were also known as the 'Thunderbolts').
Philip	From Bethsaida, the home town of Simon and Andrew.
Bartholomew	Mentioned in all New Testament lists of the apostles, but nowhere else.
Thomas	Also known as The Twin.
Matthew	Also known as Levi.
James	The son of Alphaeus.
Thaddeus	Also known as Judas or Jude the son of James.
Simon	Also known as the Eager One.
Judas Iscariot	He betrayed Jesus.
Matthias	He was chosen to replace Judas Iscariot.

8. Cities, nations, and groups of people

Amalekites	A nomadic nation living mostly in the area south and east of the Dead Sea. They were enemies of Israel.
Ammon	A nation that lived east of Israel. According to Genesis 19:30–38, the people of Ammon descended from Lot, a nephew of Abraham.
Amorites	Usually a name for all the non-Israelite nations who lived in Canaan, but in some passages it may refer to one nation scattered in several areas of Canaan.
Anakim	Perhaps a group of people of great stature who lived in Palestine before the Israelites (see Numbers 13:33 and Deuteronomy 2:10–11, 20–21).
Asia	A Roman province in what is today the nation of Turkey.
Assyria	An empire of Old Testament times, whose capital city Nineveh was located in what is today northern Iraq. In 722BC Assyria conquered the kingdom of Israel and took many Israelites as captives. The Assyrians then forced people from other parts of its empire to settle on Israel's land (see 2 Kings 18:9–12).
Avvites	A nation that lived along the Mediterranean coast before the Philistines came and took their land. The Avvites who survived lived south of the Philistines.

Babylonia	A large empire of Old Testament times, whose capital city Babylon was located in south-central Mesopotamia. The Babylonians defeated the southern kingdom of Judah in 586BC and forced many of its people to live in Babylonia (see 2 Kings 25:1–12).
Canaanites	The nations who lived in Canaan before the Israelites. Many Canaanites continued to live there even after the Israelites came.
Cush	The Hebrew term for Ethiopia (see *Ethiopia* below).
Disciples	Those who were followers of Jesus and learnt from him. The term often refers to his twelve apostles.
Edomites	A nation living in Edom or Seir, an area south and south-east of the Dead Sea. According to Genesis 36:1–43, the Edomites descended from Esau, Jacob's brother.
Empire	A number of kingdoms ruled by one strong military power.
Epicureans	People who followed the teachings of a man named Epicurus, who taught that happiness should be the main goal in life.
Ethiopia	A region south of Egypt that included parts of the present countries of Ethiopia and Sudan.
Exiles	Israelites who were taken away as prisoners to Babylonia (see also *Exile*).
Gentiles	Those people who are not Jews.
Girgashites	One of the nations that lived in Canaan before the Israelites.
Hebrew	An older term for 'Israelite' or 'Jewish'.
Hittites	A nation whose capital was in what is now Turkey. The Hittites had an empire that at times controlled some kingdoms in Canaan before 1200BC, and many Hittites remained in Canaan even after the Israelites came.
Hivites	A nation that lived in Canaan before the Israelites, probably related to the Horites.
Horites	A nation that lived in Canaan before the Israelites. The Horites were also known as Hurrians.
Israel	(1) The nation made up of the twelve tribes descended from Jacob (see Section 6, *Twelve tribes of Israel*). (2) The northern kingdom, after the northern tribes broke away following the death of Solomon (see 1 Kings 12:1–20).
Jebusites	A group of Canaanite people who lived at Jebus, also known as Jerusalem (see 2 Samuel 5:6–10).
Jews	A name first used in referring to someone belonging to the tribe of Judah. Later, the term came to be used of any Israelite.
Kadesh	A town in the desert of Paran south-west of the Dead Sea, near the southern border of Israel and the western border of Edom. Israel camped at Kadesh while the twelve tribal leaders explored Canaan (see Numbers 13—14).
Levites	Those Israelites who belonged to the tribe of Levi. God chose the men of one Levite family, the descendants of Aaron, to be Israel's

priests. The other men from this tribe helped with the work in the sacred tent and later in the temple (see Numbers 3:5–10).

Medes A nation that lived in what is today north-west Iran. Their kingdom, called Media, later became one of the most important provinces of the Persian Empire, and Persian laws were referred to as the laws of the Medes and Persians (see Esther 1:19; Daniel 6:8, 12, 15).

Midianites A nomadic nation that lived mainly in the desert along the eastern shore of the Gulf of Aqaba.

Moab A nation that lived east of the Dead Sea. According to Genesis 19:30–38, the people of Moab descended from Lot, the nephew of Abraham.

Nazarenes A name that was sometimes used for the followers of Jesus, who came from the small town of Nazareth (see Acts 24:5).

Perizzites A nation that lived in the central hill country of Canaan, before the Israelites.

Persia A large empire of Old Testament times, whose capital was located in what is now southern Iran. It is sometimes called the Medo-Persian Empire, because of the importance of the province of Media.

Pharisees A group of Jews who thought they could best serve God by strictly obeying the laws of the Old Testament, as well as their own rules, traditions, and teachings.

Philistines The land along the Mediterranean coast controlled by the Philistine people was called Philistia. There were five main cities, each with its own ruler: Ashod, Ashkelon, Ekron, Gath, and Gaza. The Philistines were often at war with Israel.

Phoenicia The territory along the Mediterranean Sea controlled by the cities of Tyre, Sidon, Arvad, and Byblos. The coast of modern Lebanon covers about the same area.

Rapha Perhaps a group of people of great stature who lived in Palestine before the Israelites (see Deuteronomy 2:11, 20).

Roman Empire Controlled the area around the Mediterranean Sea in New Testament times. Its capital was Rome.

Sadducees A small and powerful group of Jews in New Testament times. They were closely connected with the high priests and accepted only the first five books of the Old Testament as their Bible. They also did not believe in life after death.

Samaria (1) The capital city of the northern kingdom of Israel beginning with the rule of King Omri (ruled 885–874BC).

(2) In New Testament times, a district between Judea and Galilee, named after the city of Samaria. The people of this district, called Samaritans, worshipped God differently from the Jews, and these two groups refused to have anything to do with one another.

Sidon	See *Phoenicia*.
Stoics	Followers of a man named Zeno, who taught that people should learn self-control and be guided by their consciences.
Tyre	See *Phoenicia*.

9. Places

Bashan	The flat highlands and wooded hills of southern Syria. Bashan was just north of the region of Gilead and was known for its fat cattle and fine grain.
Canaan	The area now covered by Israel plus Gaza, the West Bank of Jordan, Lebanon, and southern Syria (see Numbers 34:1–12). Many passages use the term to refer only to the area south of Lebanon.
Gethsemane	A garden or olive orchard on the Mount of Olives (see *Mount of Olives*).
Gilead	A region east of the River Jordan. Moab lay to the south of Gilead, and Bashan was to the north.
Hinnom Valley	A valley west and south of Jerusalem, where human sacrifice was sometimes made in Old Testament times (see *Molech*).
Mount of Olives	A mountain just east of Jerusalem, across Kidron Valley from the temple. Gethsemane, a place where Jesus and his disciples often went to pray, was on this mountain, and so were the villages of Bethany, Bethphage, and Bahurim (see Matthew 26:36; Mark 14:32; Luke 22:39; John 18:1–2).
Palestine	The area now covered by Israel, Gaza, and Jordan.
Peniel	A place near the River Jabbok where Jacob wrestled with God. Then God changed Jacob's name to Israel (see Genesis 32:22–32).
Zion	Another name for Jerusalem. Zion can also refer to the hill in Jerusalem where the temple was built.

10. Objects

Chariot	A two-wheeled cart that was open at the back and was pulled by horses.
Cistern	A hole or pit used for storing rainwater. Cisterns were sometimes dug in the ground and lined with stones and plaster, and at other times they were cut into the rock. The CEV sometimes translates 'cistern' as 'well'.
Cross	A device used by the Romans to put people to death. It was made of two pieces of timber crossed in a T, †, or X shape.
Piece of silver	In the Old Testament, this usually refers to an amount of silver weighing about 11 grammes. Coins were not invented until late Old Testament times, so when silver or gold was used to buy things, it was weighed. In traditional translations this amount is

	called a shekel. Silver and gold were worth more in biblical times than they are today.
Sackcloth	A rough, dark-coloured cloth made from goat or camel hair. Sackcloth was usually used to make grain sacks, but clothing made from it was worn in times of trouble or sorrow.
Sceptre	A decorated rod, often made of gold, that a king held in his hand as a symbol of royal power.
Scroll	A roll of paper or special thin leather used for writing on.
Sling	A weapon used to throw stones a little smaller than a tennis ball. A sling was made of a piece of leather that wrapped almost around the stone and had a leather strap at each end. The person would hold the ends of the straps and swing the sling round and round. When the person let go of one strap, the stone would fly out of the sling.
Tomb	A burial place, often made by cutting a small room out of the rock.

11. Festivals and holy days

Many of these festivals are still celebrated by Jewish people.

Festival of Purim	A festival held on the fourteenth and fifteenth of Adar, near the end of winter, when the Jews celebrated how they were saved from Haman, the evil prime minister of Persia who wanted to have them killed (see Esther 9:20–32).
Festival of Shelters	A festival in the early autumn celebrating the period of forty years when the people of Israel walked through the desert and lived in small shelters. This happy celebration began on the fifteenth day of Tishri, and for the next seven days, the people lived in small shelters made of tree branches. The name of this festival in Hebrew is Succoth.
Festival of Thin Bread	A seven-day festival straight after Passover. During this festival the Israelites ate a thin, flat bread made without yeast to remind themselves how God freed the people of Israel from slavery in Egypt and made them into a nation. The name of this festival in Hebrew is Mazzoth.
Festival of Trumpets	See *New Moon Festival*.
Great Day of Forgiveness	The tenth day of Tishri in the early autumn. On this one day of the year, the high priest was allowed to go into the most holy part of the temple and sprinkle some of the blood of a

	sacrificed bull on the sacred chest. This was done so that the people's sins would be forgiven. In English this holy day has traditionally been called the Day of Atonement, and its name in Hebrew is *Yom Kippur*.
Harvest Festival	See *Pentecost*.
New Moon Festival	A religious festival held on the day of the new moon, the day when only a thin edge of the moon can be seen. This day was always the first day of the month for the Hebrew calendar. The New Moon Festival was a time for rest from work, and a time for worship, sacrifices, celebration, and eating. The New Moon Festival in the month of Tishri in the early autumn was also called the Festival of Trumpets, and it involved even more sacrifices.
Passover	A festival held on the fourteenth day of Abib in the early spring. At Passover the Israelites celebrated the time God rescued them from slavery in Egypt. The name of this festival in Hebrew is *Pesach*.
Pentecost	A Jewish festival held in mid-spring, fifty days after Passover. At this festival Israelites celebrated the wheat harvest. Pentecost was also known as the Harvest Festival and has traditionally been called the Feast of Weeks; in Hebrew, its name is *Shavuoth*.
Sabbath	The seventh day of the week, from sunset on Friday to sunset on Saturday. Israelites worshipped on the Sabbath and rested from work.
Temple Festival	In 165BC the Jewish people recaptured the temple in Jerusalem from their enemies and made it fit for worship again. They celebrated this event each year by an eight-day festival that began on the twenty-fifth day of the month of Chislev in the late autumn. This festival is traditionally called the Festival of Dedication, or in Hebrew, *Hanukkah*.

12. Sacrifice, temple, worship

Altar	A raised structure where sacrifices and offerings were presented to God or to pagan gods. Altars could be made of rock, packed earth, metal, or pottery.
Amen	A Hebrew word used after a prayer or a blessing and meaning that what had been said was right and true.
Fire pan	A metal pan used for burning incense or carrying hot coals from the altar.
God's tent	See *Sacred tent*.
High priest	See *Priest*.

Holy place	The main room of the sacred tent and of the temple. This room contained the sacred bread, the golden incense altar, and the golden lampstand. A curtain or wall separated the holy place from the most holy place. A priest would go into the holy place once each morning and evening to burn incense on the golden altar (see also *Most holy place*).
Incense	A material that makes a sweet smell when burnt. It was used in the worship of God.
Local shrine	See *Place of worship*.
Most holy place	The inner room of the sacred tent and of the temple. In the sacred tent this room contained only the sacred chest. In Solomon's temple, the most holy place also held statues of winged creatures. Only the high priest could enter the most holy place, and even he could enter it only once a year on the Great Day of Forgiveness. The most holy place has traditionally been called the holy of holies.
Offerings	See *Sacrifices*.
Place of worship	A place to worship God or pagan gods. These places were often on a hill outside a town and have traditionally been called high places. In the CEV they are sometimes called local shrines.
Priest	A man who led the worship in the sacred tent or in the temple and who offered sacrifices. Some of the more important priests were called chief priests, and the most important priest was called the high priest.
Sacred chest	The chest or box that contained the two flat stones with the Ten Commandments written on them. The chest was covered with gold, and two golden statues of winged creatures were on the lid of the chest. These winged creatures and the chest represented God's throne on earth. Two wooden poles, one on each side, were put through rings at the corners of the chest, so that the Levites could carry the chest without touching it. The chest was kept in the most holy place (see Exodus 25:10–22).
Sacred tent	The tent where the people of Israel worshipped God before the temple was built. It has traditionally been called the tabernacle (see Exodus 26).
Sacrifices	These gifts to God included certain animals, grains, fruits, and sweet-smelling spices. Israelites offered sacrifices to give thanks to God, to ask him for his forgiveness and his blessing, and to make a payment for a wrong. Some sacrifices were completely burnt on the altar. In the case of other sacrifices, a portion was given to the Lord and burnt on the altar, then the rest was eaten by the priests or the worshippers who had offered the sacrifice.

Sacrifices to ask the Lord's blessing — Traditionally called peace offerings or offerings of well-being. A main purpose was to ask for the Lord's blessing, and so in the CEV they are sometimes called 'sacrifices to ask the Lord's blessing' (see Leviticus 3).

Sacrifices to give thanks to the Lord — Traditionally called grain offerings. A main purpose of such sacrifices was to thank the Lord with a gift of grain, and so in the CEV they are sometimes called 'sacrifices to give thanks to the Lord' (see Leviticus 2).

Sacrifices to make things right — Traditionally called guilt offerings. A main purpose was to make things right when a person had cheated someone or the Lord. These sacrifices were also made when a person had broken certain religious rules (see Leviticus 5:146:7).

Sacrifices to please the Lord — Traditionally called whole burnt offerings because the whole animal was burnt on the altar. While these sacrifices did involve forgiveness for sin, a main purpose was to please the Lord with the smell of the smoke from the sacrifice, and so in the CEV they are often called 'sacrifices to please the Lord' (see Leviticus 1).

Snuffer — A small tool used for putting out the flame of an oil lamp, or for trimming off the charred part of the wick.

Temple — A building used as a place of worship. The god who was worshipped in a particular temple was believed to be present there in a special way. The Lord's temple was in Jerusalem.

13. Customs

Ashes — People put ashes, dust, or earth on their heads, or they rolled in ash piles, dust, or earth, as a way of showing sorrow.

Circumcise — To cut off the foreskin from the male organ. This was done for Israelite boys eight days after they were born. God commanded that all newborn Israelite boys be circumcised to show that they belonged to his people (see Genesis 17:9–14).

Clean and unclean — (1) In Old Testament times, a person who was acceptable to worship God was called clean. A person who had certain kinds of diseases, who had touched a dead body, or who had broken certain laws became unclean, and was unacceptable to worship God. If a person was unclean because of disease, the disease would have to be cured before the person could be clean again. And becoming clean again involved performing certain ceremonies that sometimes included sacrifices.

(2) Animals that were acceptable as food were called clean. Those that were not acceptable were called unclean (see Leviticus 11:1–47; Deuteronomy 14:3–21).
(3) Many things including tools, dishes, houses, and land could also become unclean and unusable, especially if they were touched by something unclean. Some unclean objects had to be destroyed, but others could be made clean by being washed or placed in a fire for a short time.

Going without eating This was a way of showing sorrow, or of asking for God's help. It is also called fasting.

Tearing clothes A way of showing sorrow or anger, or of asking for God's help.

14. God, Jesus, angels

Angel A supernatural being who tells God's messages to people or protects those who belong to God.

Christ A Greek work meaning the 'Chosen One' and used to translate the Hebrew word *Messiah*. In New Testament times, many of the Jews believed that God was going to send the Messiah to set them free from the power of their enemies. The term 'Christ' is used in the New Testament both as a title and as a name for Jesus.

Eternal life Life that is the gift of God and that never ends.

Glory Something seen, heard, or felt that shows a person or thing is important, wonderful, or powerful. When God appeared to people, his glory was often seen as a bright light or as fire and smoke. Jesus' glory was seen when he performed miracles, when he was lifted up on the cross, and when he was raised from death.

God's kingdom God's rule over people, both in this life and in the next.

Holy One A name for the Saviour that God had promised to send (see *Saviour*).

Kingdom of heaven See *God's kingdom*.

LORD In the Old Testament the word LORD in capital letters stands for the Hebrew consonants YHWH, the personal name of God. Ancient Hebrew did not have vowel letters, and so anyone reading Hebrew would have to know what vowels to put with the consonants. It is not known for certain what vowel sounds were originally used with the consonants YHWH. The word LORD represents the Hebrew term Adonai, the usual word for LORD. By late Old Testament times, Jews considered God's personal name too holy to be pronounced. So they said Adonai, LORD, whenever they read YHWH.

When the Jewish scribes first translated the Hebrew Scriptures into ancient Greek, they translated the personal name of God as *Kurios*, LORD. Since that time, most translations, including the CEV, have followed their example and have avoided using the personal name of God.

Messiah	See *Christ*.
Promised One	A title for the Saviour that God promised to send (see *Saviour*).
Save	To rescue people from the power of their enemies or from the power of evil, and to give them new life and place them under God's care (see also *Saviour*).
Saviour	The one whom God has chosen to rescue or save his people (see also *Save*).
Sin	Turning away from God and disobeying the teachings or commandments of God.
Son of Man	A title often used by Jesus to refer to himself. This title is also found in the Hebrew text of Daniel 7:13 and Psalm 8:4, and God uses it numerous times in the book of Ezekiel to refer to Ezekiel.
Way	In the book of Acts the Christian life is sometimes called 'the Way' or 'the Way of the Lord' or 'God's Way'.
Winged creature	These supernatural beings represented the presence of God and supported his throne in Ezekiel 1:4–25; 10:1–22. Statues of winged creatures were on top of the sacred chest, and larger ones were in the most holy place in the temple built by Solomon. Wood carvings of winged creatures decorated the inside walls and doors of the temple, and figures of winged creatures were woven into the curtain separating the holy place from the most holy place in the sacred tent. The traditional term for winged creature is 'cherub' (or 'cherubim' for more than one).

15. Foreign gods, fortune-tellers, evil spirits

Astarte	A Canaanite goddess. Those who worshipped her believed that she gave them fertile land and many children, and that she helped their animals give birth to lots of young.
Baal	A Canaanite god. The Canaanites believed that Baal was the most powerful of all the gods.
Dagon	The chief god of the Philistines.
Demons and evil spirits	Supernatural beings that do harmful things to people and sometimes cause them to do bad things. In the New Testament they are sometimes called unclean spirits, because people under their power were thought to be unclean and unfit to worship God.

Devil	The chief of the demons and evil spirits, also known as Satan.
Evil spirits	See *Demons*.
Fortune-teller	Fortune-tellers thought they could learn secrets or learn about the future by doing such things as watching the flight of birds, looking at the livers of animals, and rolling dice.
Hermes	The Greek god of skilful speaking and the messenger of the other Greek gods.
Molech or Milcom	The national god of the Ammonites. Some Israelites offered human sacrifices to Molech in Hinnom Valley near Jerusalem.
Satan	See *Devil*.
Zeus	The chief god of the Greeks.

16. Plants, animals, and farming

Acacia	A flowering tree that produces a hard, durable wood. The sacred chest, the altars, and certain other wooden objects in the sacred tent were made of acacia wood.
Aloes	A sweet-smelling spice that was mixed with myrrh and used as a perfume.
Barley	A grain that was used to make bread.
Cedar	A tall tree once common in the Lebanon mountains and used for many of the royal building projects in Jerusalem.
Cumin	A plant with small seeds used for seasoning food.
Flax	The stalks of flax plants were harvested, soaked in water, and dried. Then their fibres were separated and spun into thread, which was woven to make linen cloth.
Hyssop	A bush with clusters of small branches. In religious ceremonies, hyssop was sometimes dipped in a liquid and then used to sprinkle people or objects.
Jackal	A wild desert animal related to wolves, but smaller.
Leviathan	A legendary sea monster representing revolt and evil, also known from Canaanite writings.
Locust	A type of grasshopper that comes in huge swarms and causes great damage to plant life.
Mint	A garden plant used for seasoning and medicine.
Mustard	A large plant with very small seeds, which were ground up and used as a spice.
Myrrh	A valuable sweet-smelling powder used in perfume.
Pomegranate	A reddish fruit with a hard rind. Figures of pomegranates were used as decorations on the high priest's robe and in the temple.
Reed	Several kinds of tall plant related to the grass family can be called reeds. Some varieties are hollow, and some grow in shallow water. The stems are strong and can be up to 5 metres long and 7 centimetres across at the base.

Rue — A garden plant used for seasoning and medicine.

Threshing — The process of separating grain from its husks. Grain was spread out at a threshing place, a flat area of stone or packed earth. People or animals walked on the grain or dragged heavy boards across it to remove the husks. Then the grain and husks were tossed into the air with a special shovel called a threshing fork. The wind would blow the light husks away, but the heavy grain would fall back to the surface of the threshing place.

Wine-pit — A hollow place cut into the rock where the juice was squeezed from grapes to make wine.

Yoke — A strong, heavy, wooden collar that fitted around the neck of an ox, so that the ox could pull a plough or a cart.

17. Society and its leaders

Citizen — A person who is given special rights and privileges by a nation or state. In return, a citizen was expected to be loyal to that nation or state.

Council — (1) A group of leaders who meet and make decisions for their people.
(2) The Old Testament refers to God's council as a group of angels who meet and talk with God in heaven.

Elders — Men whose age and wisdom made them respected leaders.

Emperor — The person who ruled an empire.

Generation — One way of describing a group of people who lived during the same period of time. In the Bible the time of one generation is often understood to be about forty years.

Judges — Leaders chosen by the Lord for the people of Israel after the time of Joshua and before the time of the kings.

Tax collectors — See *Taxes*.

Taxes — Special fees collected by the government. Taxes are usually part of the value of crops, property, or income. Taxes were collected at markets, city gates, ports, and border crossings. In New Testament times, Jews were hired by the Roman government to collect taxes from other Jews, and these tax collectors were hated by their own people.

18. Families, relatives

Ancestor — Someone born earlier in a family line, especially several generations earlier.

Clan — A group of families who were related to each other and who often lived close to each other. A group of clans made up a tribe.

Descendant	Someone born one or more generations later in a family line.
Tribe	A large group of people descended from a common ancestor (see also *Clan* and Section 6, *Twelve tribes of Israel*).

19. Events

Exile	The time in Israel's history (597–539BC) when the Babylonians took away many of the people of Jerusalem and Judah as prisoners of war and made them live in Babylonia. The northern tribes had been taken away by Assyria in 722BC.
Exodus	The people of Israel leaving Egypt, led by Moses and Aaron. This event is celebrated each year as Passover.

20. Dates

AD	*Anno Domini*, Latin for 'in the year of the Lord'. Used to date events that happened after Christ's birth. AD is often used before the number of the year. The numbering system now in use was developed about AD525. The plan was that the year of Christ's birth would be AD1, and then the years would be numbered before and after. But an error was made in assigning AD1, and by the time the error was discovered, the numbering system could not be changed. And so, the correct year of Christ's birth according to the numbering system is probably about 6BC.
BC	Before Christ. Used to date events that happened before Christ's birth. BC is used after the number of the year.
931BC	The nation of Israel split into two parts, Israel, the northern kingdom, and Judah, the southern kingdom.
722BC	Samaria, the capital of the northern kingdom, was captured by the Assyrian army.
586BC	Jerusalem, the capital of the southern kingdom, was captured by the Babylonian army.
538BC	Cyrus of Persia allowed the Jews to return to Judah.
333BC	Alexander the Great took control of Palestine.
323BC	Palestine was taken over by Ptolemy, who was one of Alexander's generals and who became the ruler of Egypt after Alexander's death.
198BC	Palestine was taken over by the Seleucids, the descendants of one of Alexander's generals. They had been the rulers of Syria since Alexander's death.
166BC	The Jews revolted, led by Judas Maccabeus and his brothers.
63BC	Rome took control of Palestine.
37BC	Herod the Great was appointed king of the Jews by the Roman government.

6BC	Jesus was born (see the note following AD above).
AD30 (or possibly AD33)	Jesus died and was raised to life.

21. The Hebrew Calendar

Nisan or Abib	First month, about mid-March to mid-April.
Iyyar or Ziv	Second month, about mid-April to mid-May.
Sivan	Third month, about mid-May to mid-June.
Tammuz	Fourth month, about mid-June to mid-July.
Ab	Fifth month, about mid-July to mid-August.
Elul	Sixth month, about mid-August to mid-September.
Tishri or Ethanim	Seventh month, about mid-September to mid-October.
Marchesvan or Bul	Eighth month, about mid-October to mid-November.
Chislev	Ninth month, about mid-November to mid-December.
Tebeth	Tenth month, about mid-December to mid-January.
Shebat	Eleventh month, about mid-January to mid-February.
Adar	Twelfth month, about mid-February to mid-March.

A Time-line of the Bible

Creation

earliest times	Humans created in God's image	

Disobedience

earliest times	Humans fall into sin (Adam and Eve), Cain and Abel, Noah and the flood, Tower of Babel	

God's People — Israel

c. 2000 BC	Abraham is called and travels into Canaan	
c. 1650 BC	The sons of Jacob move to Egypt	
c. 1250 BC	Moses leads the Israelites out of Egypt, and God calls them to be the nation who will serve him	
probably late 13th century BC	Conquering and settling in Canaan	
12th and 11th centuries BC	Israel led by military liberators called "judges"	
c. 1030–1010 BC	Israel ruled by King Saul	
c. 1010–970 BC	Israel ruled by King David	
c. 970–931 BC	Israel ruled by King Solomon	
931 BC	Israel splits into two (Israel and Judah)	*about a thousand years*
722/721 BC	The people of the north (Israel) go into exile in Assyria	
587/586 BC	The people of the south (Judah) go into exile in Babylon	
539 BC	The return from exile begins	
	The time between the Old and the New Testaments	
probably 6 BC	The coming of the king – Jesus' birth	
	When the Christian calendar was worked out in the sixth century, a mistake in working back to the date of Jesus' birth meant that it was a few years out.	
probably 30 AD	The death and resurrection of Jesus	
c. 41–65 AD	The travels and ministry of Paul	

Jesus recognized as king over everything

the future	Jesus returns to set up the new heavens and earth	

The route of the Exodus

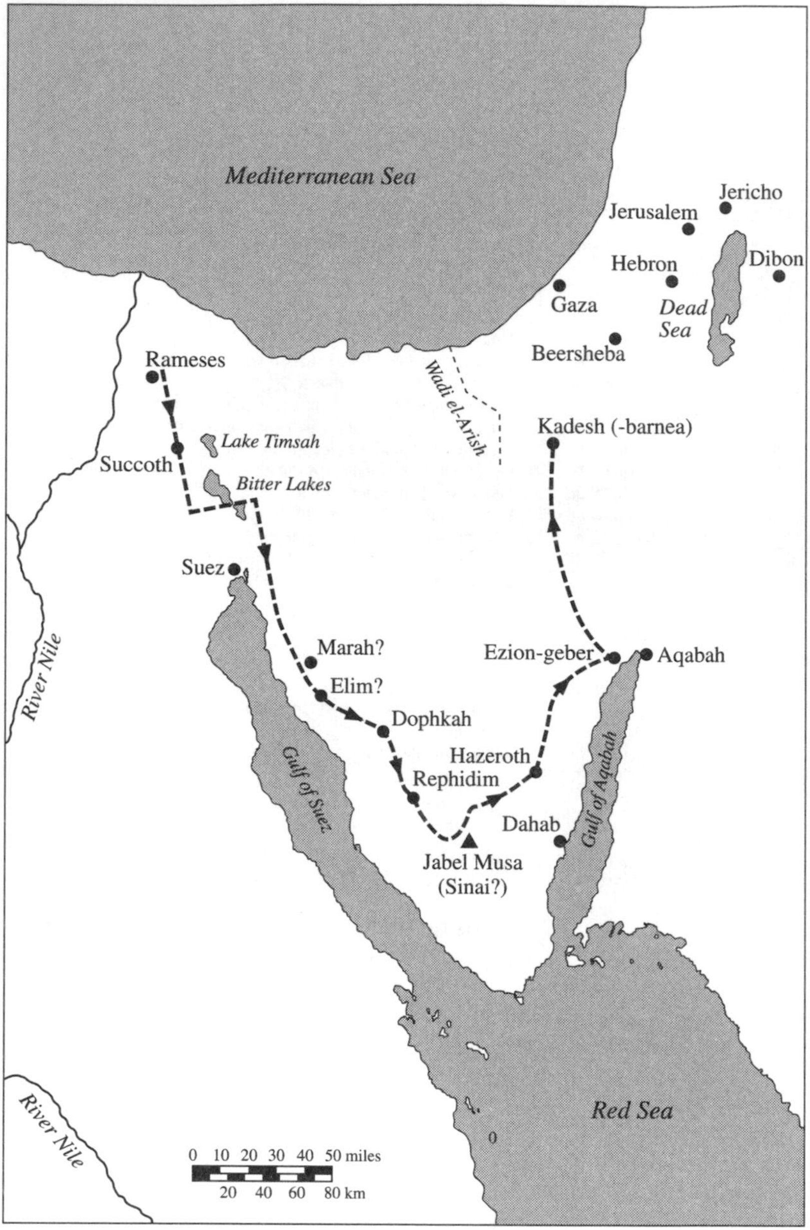

The division of Canaan

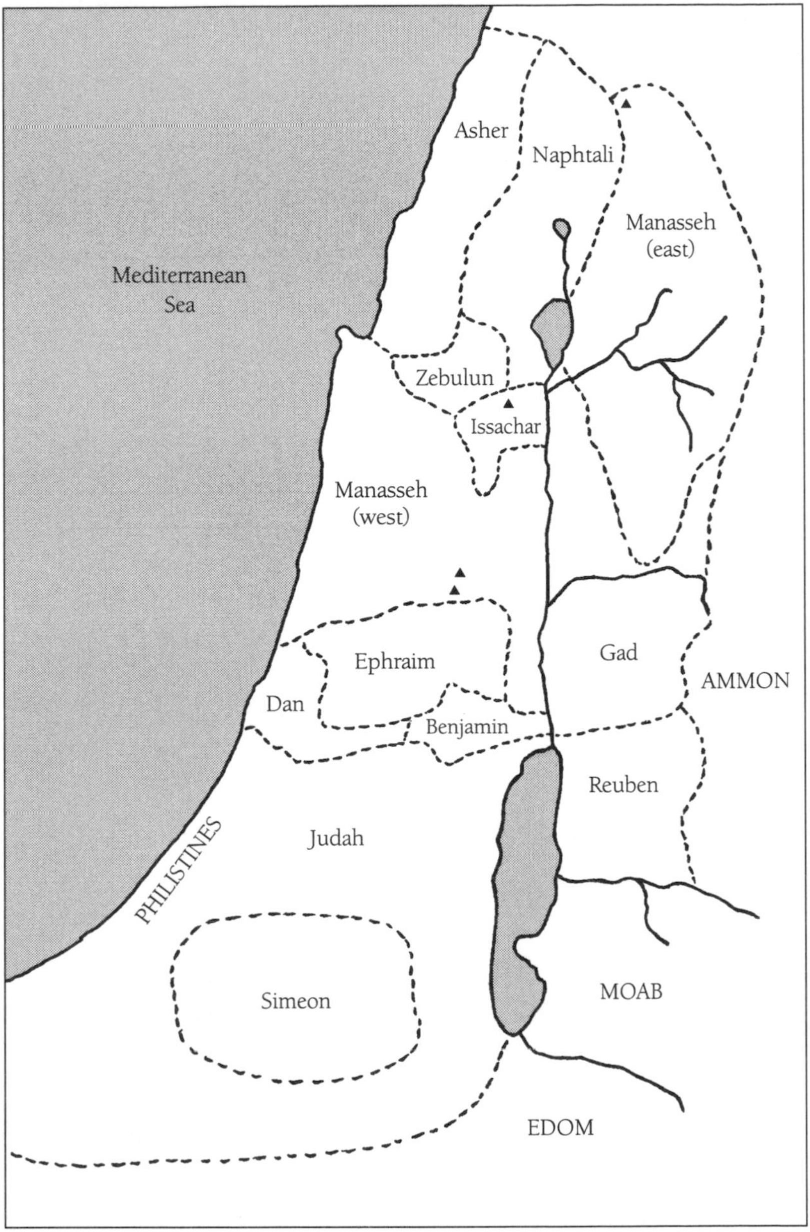

Jerusalem in the Old Testament

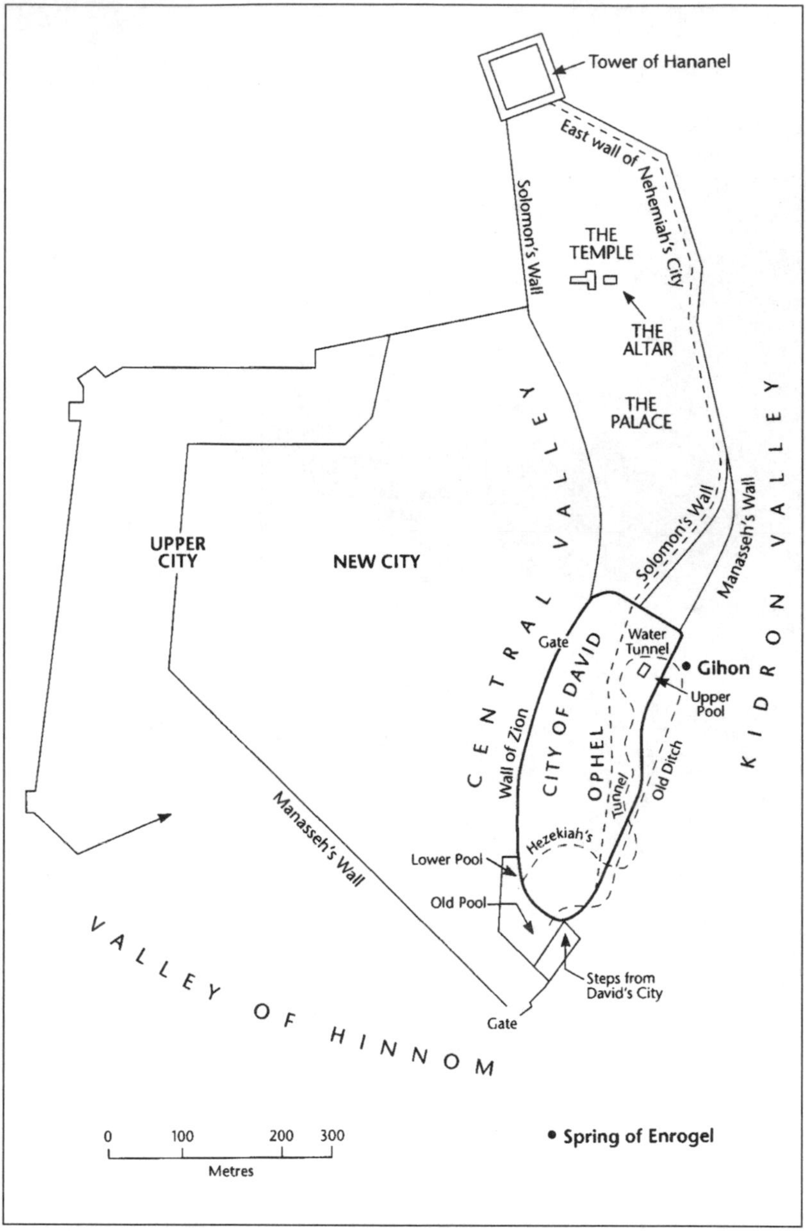

Jerusalem in the New Testament

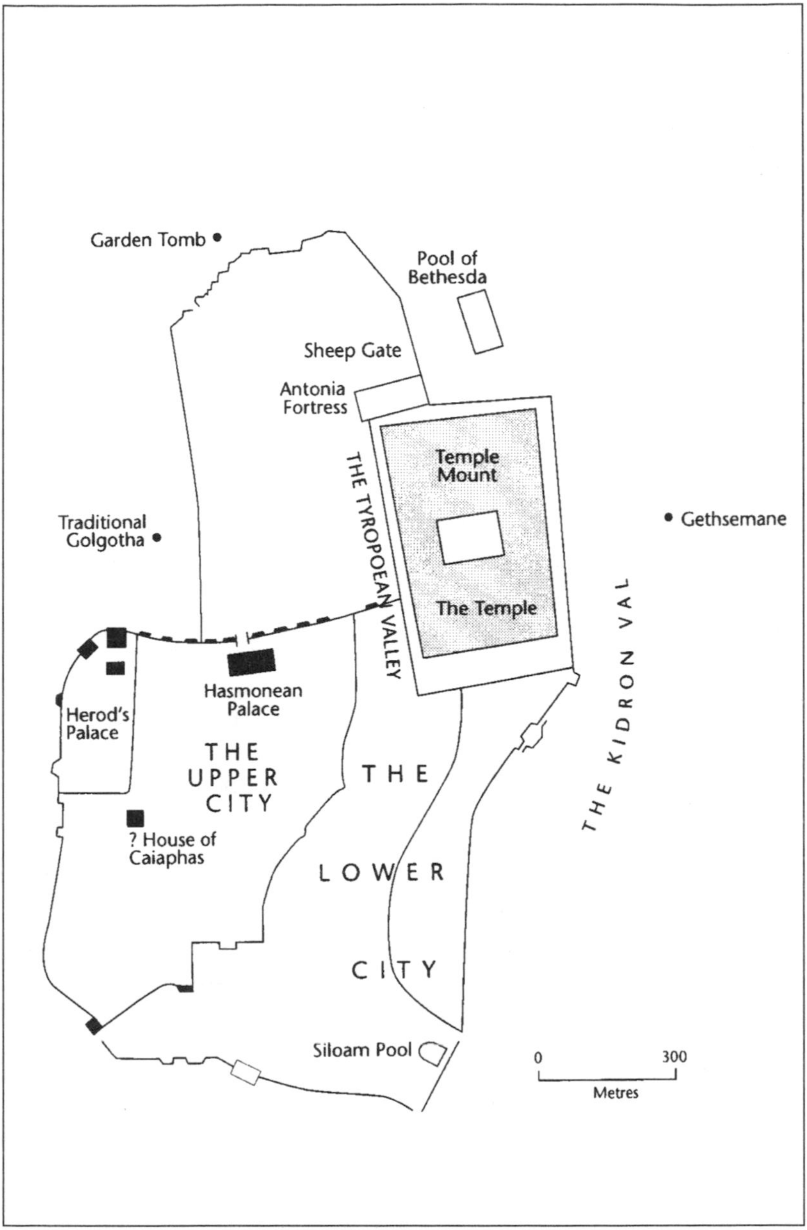

Palestine in the time of Jesus

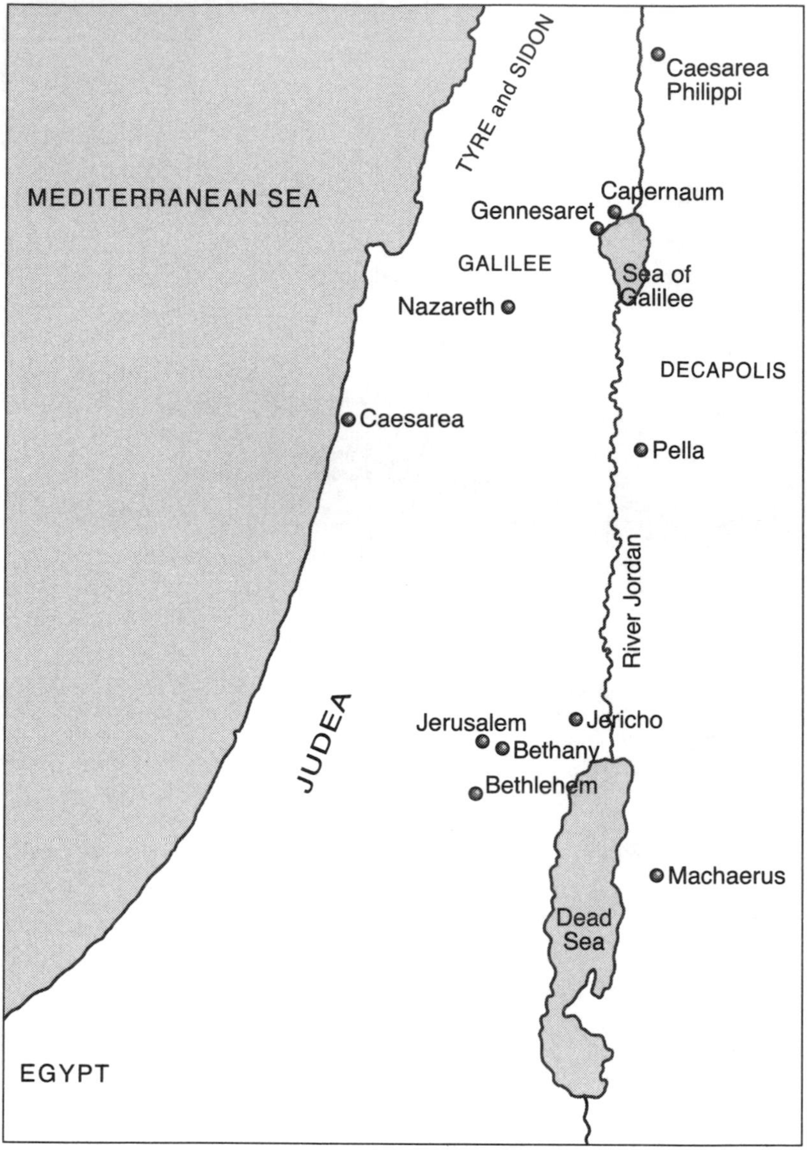

Paul's first, second and third missionary journeys

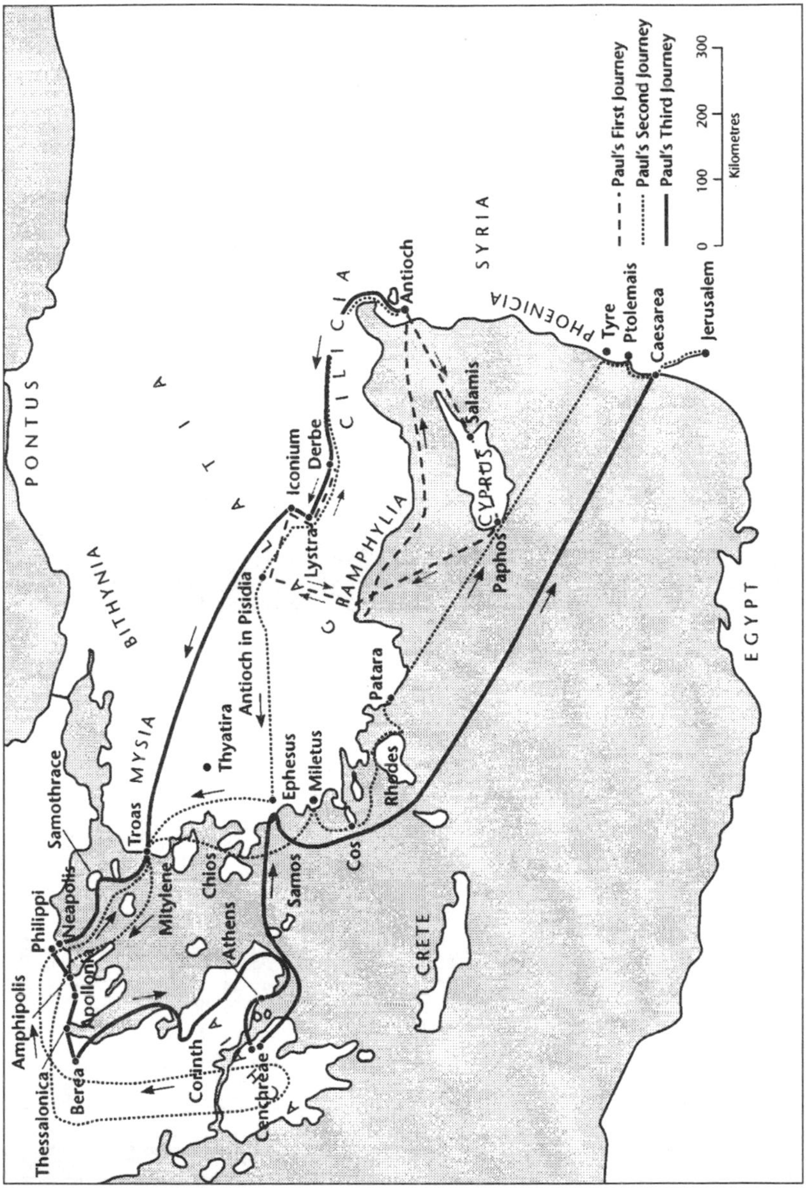

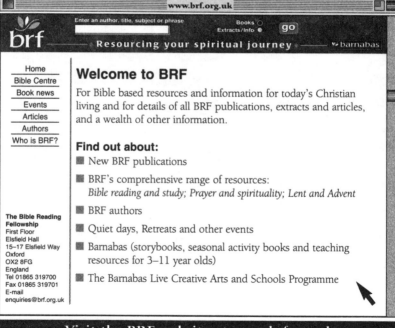